COMMUNISM
IN AFRICA

COMMUNISM
IN AFRICA

Edited by

David E. Albright

INDIANA UNIVERSITY PRESS
Bloomington & London

IN MEMORY OF MY FATHER

Manufactured in the United States of America

Library of Congress Cataloging in Publication Data
Main entry under title:

Communism in Africa.

Includes bibliographical references.
1.Africa—Foreign relations—1960- —Addresses,
essays, lectures, 2.Communism—Africa—Addresses,
essays, lectures. I.Albright, David E.
DT30.C57 327'.096 78-13813
ISBN 0-253-12814-5 1 2 3 4 5 84 83 82 81 80

Contents

Editor's Preface

THIS BOOK had its genesis in a panel on the USSR and Africa that I organized for the 1977 annual meeting of the American Association for the Advancement of Slavic Studies in Washington, D.C. The interest aroused by that panel and by the subsequent publication of three of the papers delivered there convinced me of the desirability of putting together a more comprehensive analysis of communism in Africa.

The actual preparation of the book has proved more tortuous than I initially anticipated it would be. This state of affairs has reflected not only the difficulties of assessing the evolving situation in Africa but also the heavy demands on the time and energies of the relatively few persons knowledgeable about one aspect or another of communism on the continent. Under such circumstances, the contributors to the volume deserve high praise for the patience with which they have endured my nagging and search for perfection. I can only hope that they will feel that the character of the end product in some measure justifies their indulgence.

One additional point needs to be made about the origins and development of the book. Earlier versions of chapters 1, 2, and 7 appeared in the January–February 1978 issue of *Problems of Communism*. However, all three have been revised, expanded, and updated for purposes of this volume.

My own concern with the subject of communism in Africa, it should be noted, predates work on this book by many years. That concern began with a doctoral dissertation at Columbia University on Soviet and Chinese approaches to the continent. In carrying out this study, I had the advantage of critiques from Alexander Dallin, Zbigniew Brzezinski, A. Doak Barnett, and Donald S. Zagoria—all of whom had done personal research related to the topic. Indeed, the first two had been among the pioneer analysts of communism in Africa.

Since those early days, I have benefited as well from discussions of one kind or another with several other individuals. These include not only the contributors to this volume but also Vernon Aspaturian, Gerald Bender, James Collins, Chester Crocker, Robert Legvold, William LeoGrande, James McConnell, Charles Petersen, Richard Remnek, Elizabeth Valkenier, and I. William Zartman. I am especially indebted to James Collins, Robert Legvold, Charles Petersen, Richard Remnek, and I. William Zartman—as well as to my colleagues at *Problems of Communism*—for useful comments and suggestions regarding the initial draft of my own chapter on the USSR's African policy of the 1970s.

In a more general sense, I have profited greatly from two institutional associations. During a stint as a member of the staff of the project on The United States and China in World Affairs at the Council on Foreign Relations in New York in the mid-1960s, I had the opportunity to become exposed in a personal way to the viewpoints of a number of African leaders and students of Africa and to the perspectives of many policy-makers from around the globe who were concerned in some way with African problems. Subsequently, my work at *Problems of Communism* has underscored for me the complexities of communism as an empirical phenomenon and the virtues of a broad comparative approach to Communist affairs.

Finally, I am most grateful to Kimberly Johnson-Smith for finding time in her crowded schedule to type the manuscript of the volume. As always, her husband James bore my impositions on them with utmost good humor and tolerance.

David E. Albright

COMMUNISM
IN AFRICA

INTRODUCTION

David E. Albright

THE LATTER 1970s have witnessed a revival of concern in the West about the fortunes of communism in Africa. U.S. President Jimmy Carter, for example, has expressed dismay at the enlarged military role of the USSR and Cuba on the continent in recent years.[1] Other commentators have voiced misgivings of more sweeping kinds, pointing not only to the increase in Soviet and Cuban military activities in Africa but also to the growing number of professed Marxist-Leninist regimes on the continent as well as the expansion of China's relations there.

Yet the very abruptness of the change that has occurred in the general Western mood gives many thoughtful observers pause. Does this new-found concern, they ask, reflect an accurate appraisal of the trend of events in Africa, or could it represent an overreaction to specific happenings on the continent? In short, does it flow more from emotion than from hardheaded evaluation of reality?

The annals of Western responses to African developments during the post–World War II era provide plenty of reinforcement for this uneasiness. Immediately after the war, for example, the European colonial powers firmly rejected demands for the dissolution of their empires on the continent, and they argued strongly that even the establishment of internal self-government there would in most cases require many years of preparation. Not until the last half of the 1950s, in the face of mounting African nationalist agitation, did Great Britain, France, and Belgium become convinced that the age of col-

The views expressed in this essay are those of the author and do not necessarily reflect the perspectives of the U.S. International Communication Agency or the U.S. government.

1

onialism was waning, except maybe in those territories with large immigrant populations from the metropoles. Only then did the three states decide that the best hope of retaining extensive and long-term links with their colonies on the continent lay in ushering these lands toward independence. Portugal and Spain continued to harbor illusions that they could tough things out up to the late 1960s and early 1970s, but they too eventually concluded that their causes were doomed and turned over control of their colonies to native rulers.

Perhaps a more direct parallel with the current situation stems from the 1960s. In the wake of the collapse of central authority in the Congo-Leopoldville (now Zaire) after the Belgian colony won its independence in 1960, the USSR sought to gain a foothold there by allying itself with the forces of Premier Patrice Lumumba, and the United States and its Western allies persuaded themselves that a serious Soviet threat was emerging on the continent. Although the tide of events in the Congo turned quickly against Moscow (despite sporadic resurgences of a favorable nature up through the mid-1960s), developments elsewhere kept the Western perception alive. Chief among these was the radicalization of politics and policies in African countries such as the United Arab Republic, Algeria, Ghana, and Mali— including the embrace of "scientific socialism" by their leaders. Along with this radicalization went a strengthening of ties with the USSR. By the late 1960s, however, it had become evident that verbal endorsement of "scientific socialism" did not necessarily mean a commitment to implement it on the part of the radical African leaders. Moreover, these rulers had met with great local resistance to even the modest "socialist" measures that they had sought to carry out. Indeed, some had aroused such opposition that they had brought about their own ousters. With the disappearance of a number of the radical regimes, the Western sense of a major challenge from the Soviet Union finally faded.

At the same time, circumstances on the continent have unquestionably altered in striking fashion in recent years. In the aftermath of the April 1974 revolution in Portugal, Lisbon's African empire collapsed, and avowed Marxist-Leninist regimes emerged in the former Portuguese colonies of Angola and Mozambique. Although Ethiopia went through a much more tortuous evolution after the overthrow of Emperor Haile Selassie in 1974, it too declared its adherence to Marxism-Leninism in the late 1970s under the aegis of military strongman Mengistu Haile Mariam. In 1975–76, the USSR and Cuba intervened in the Angolan civil war to help Agostinho Neto and his Popular Movement for the Liberation of Angola (*Movimento Popular de Libertação de Angola*—MPLA) assume power. Cuba deployed combat troops to bolster MPLA units, while the Soviet Union furnished the arms and logistical support for the effort. Two years later, both also became heavily involved in Ethiopia's battle to expel the invading forces of the USSR's erstwhile ally, Somalia, from the Ogaden region. Moscow not only supplied more than $1 billion in weapons and matériel for this venture but also sent the deputy commander of Soviet ground forces to direct the planning for the undertaking. Havana, for its part, provided the combat elements that spearheaded the Ethiopian drive against the Somalis.[2] These enterprises left the USSR and Cuba with quite close ties with Angola and Ethiopia. Indeed, the governments of the two African states signed treaties of friendship and cooperation with the Soviet Union,[3] and they asked Cuba not to withdraw its troops even after the passing of the crises that had originally brought these troops to their countries. As of the summer of 1979, Cuban military contingents totaling in the neighborhood of 35,000 men remained on Angolan and Ethiopian soil.[4] Finally, China in the 1970s has reentered the African arena in a determined way after having curtailed its activities during the upheavals of the Great Proletarian Cultural Revolution in the late 1960s. Chinese economic aid to African states has exceeded that of the USSR in recent years, and in June 1979 Peking demonstrated an inclination to try to inject itself into the military aid picture in a purposeful, if limited, fashion by agreeing to sell arms to Egypt's Anwar al-Sadat, who has found himself under increasingly heavy attack from fellow Arabs and their Soviet backers for signing a peace treaty with Israel.[5]

The perplexity evident on this issue strongly suggests the need for a careful, detailed examination of communism in Africa, in its various present dimensions. A survey of the available writings on the subject bolsters such a conclusion. The only substantial attempt that has been made thus far to look at the different facets of communism in Africa dates from the early 1960s.[6] Moreover, the last major study of even Soviet policy toward the continent appeared at the beginning of the 1970s.[7]

This book seeks to meet that need. As an organizing framework, it employs analysis of the dynamics of Soviet–African relations. Selection of such a framework, however, does not imply that only the

USSR has carried out activities on the continent in its own right and in accordance with its own perceived interests. Nor is the choice meant to indicate that the interests, outlooks, and policies of other Communist states and forces operating in Africa have consistently coincided with those of the USSR. It merely recognizes the utility of the specific approach in bringing about order and coherence to a far-ranging investigation. None of the Communist states and forces active on the continent, after all, has functioned in a vacuum. Even if each has pursued its own ends as it has seen them, it has interacted with fellow Communist elements to a certain degree. As a superpower, the USSR has done so with an intensity and to an extent unmatched by others. Moreover, its interactions with other Communist forces have not only varied in nature but also had diverse effects on its relations with Africa. In this sense, they have constituted at least partial determinants of those relations. Thus, there has been a concrete link between, on the one hand, the views and behavior of Communist states and elements aside from the USSR which have been at work in Africa and, on the other hand, Moscow's relations with the continent.

This framework has additional merits. In the first place, it encourages detailed attention to the perspectives and activities of the Soviet Union and to the factors that have shaped these. On the basis of superpower status alone, the USSR qualifies as the leading Communist entity that has operated on the continent. Second, the framework permits exploration of the roles that non-Communist elements have played in Communist successes and failures in Africa. Obviously, the attitudes and behavior of non-Communist African states and forces as well as those of outside powers have colored Communist outlooks on African matters and set limits to what various Communist entities have been able to do on the continent. Of all the Communist states and forces functioning in the African context, none has interacted more extensively with non-Communist elements in ways that have had an impact on its fortunes on the continent than has the Soviet Union.

In keeping with the focus of the volume, each of the individual chapters addresses itself to a particular issue bearing upon the dynamics of Soviet–African relations. Colin Legum charts the evolution of African attitudes toward the USSR, paying special heed to those features which have distinguished the 1970s from earlier periods of Soviet–African interaction. In the course of this undertaking, he looks at the differences in outlook toward the USSR among Africans and discusses the reasons for these differences. I explore the contemporary priorities, objectives, and strategy of the USSR with respect to Africa in light of changing Soviet perspectives on these matters in the post–World War II era. Edward T. Wilson appraises the effect of pre–World War II Russian and Soviet ties with Africa on Moscow's recent policy toward the continent. Jiri Valenta investigates the nature of the Soviet decision-making process in regard to the continent by focusing on a case study of the USSR's intervention in the Angolan civil war in 1975. Marina Ottaway probes the theory and practice of Marxism-Leninism in Mozambique and Ethiopia and assesses the connections between these and the behavior of the two African countries toward the Soviet Union. Edward Gonzalez analyzes the character of the relationship between Cuba and the Soviet Union in Africa in the 1970s. George T. Yu traces the history of the rivalry between the USSR and China on the continent, with particular attention to the increased Sino–Soviet competition there since the termination of the Cultural Revolution in China at the end of the 1960s. W. Scott Thompson examines the links between U.S. attitudes and behavior toward Africa and Soviet policy toward the continent, especially in the post-1970 period. In a concluding essay, I attempt to draw these various threads of analysis together and to distill their general implications for the future of communism in Africa.

These discussions, it should be noted, do not exhaust all the topics that might have been dealt with. To be precise, they do not cover the inputs of the East European countries, the smaller Communist states of Asia, or the West European powers into Soviet–African relations. However, talks with persons knowledgeable about the activities of these nations and some preliminary investigations of my own have convinced me that such inputs during the 1970s have been sufficiently minor or ancillary to the inputs of other actors that they do not warrant specific and lengthy consideration in this volume.

One further aspect of the book requires explanation. The interpretive judgments expressed in the individual chapters are not entirely consistent with one another. These inconsistencies derive from a conscious choice made when I set about assembling the volume. Since there is marked diversity of opinion among close observers of the African scene about how much influence specific factors have had on Soviet–African relations, it seemed utterly imperative for any study of the dynamics of Soviet–African relations to take account of that reality, and I recruited contributors accordingly.

My concluding essay seeks to lay out in a systematic fashion the areas of agreement and disagreement among the contributors. This summary, in turn, conditions my discussion of the prospects of communism in Africa. That is, it affords the basis for a contingency approach to the undertaking.

1

African Outlooks toward the USSR

Colin Legum

ANALYSTS OF recent Soviet policy toward Africa often tend to overlook one important fact: the continent comprises a growing number of
independent states each of which judges the policies of the major
powers by the degree to which they advance or harm its own perceived interests. Thus, while the Soviet Union may approach Africa
with a particular set of strategic objectives in mind, the tactics it employs must respond to the African context. What African leaders and
governments perceive and do about Soviet policies, in short, is an
important, perhaps crucial, determinant of Moscow's course on the
continent.

Currently, major Soviet objectives in Africa, as in the rest of the
Third World, appear to be four in number. The first is to spread the
political and economic influence of the Soviet Union in a manner consonant with its role as a world power. The second, related to the first,
is to diminish or eliminate Western influence and control. This goal, it
should be stressed, is pursued outside the general framework of
East–West détente. The third objective is to promote the USSR's
political-security interests, especially as these involve the Soviet
navy. In order to achieve effective deployment of its navy on a global
scale, for purposes of offsetting Western nuclear delivery systems
(particularly nuclear-powered missile submarines) and of projecting
Soviet political power, the USSR seeks to arrange a worldwide system of naval and air facilities similar to those obtained at an earlier
period by the Western powers.[1] Finally, the Soviet Union seeks to
counter the ideological and political challenge of the People's Republic of China (PRC).

Moscow has pursued these strategic goals in Africa through a series
of tactical moves that at first glance seem incoherent or even con-

7

tradictory. Some observers therefore tend to characterize these tactics as "opportunistic." However, such a label is valid only to the extent that the tactical maneuvers represent pragmatic, ad hoc responses to promising opportunities created by developments on the African continent. Without such opportunities, any policy course—no matter how consistent and principled—would be futile.

It is clear that through much of the half-century of Soviet–African interaction since the late 1920s the interests and attitudes of Africans did not afford the USSR many openings. Only in the post-independence period, after 1960, did certain African leaders and governments—for a variety of economic, political, and military motivations—decide to invite Soviet involvement in the affairs of the continent. The lesson of this history is important: it is essential to examine Soviet–African relations from an *African* rather than a Sovietological perspective if one is to reach valid conclusions about them.

In what follows, we shall first briefly review the reactions of Africans to the early efforts of the USSR through the Comintern and then the Cominform to win over the anticolonial movements of Africa. Then we shall examine the first decade of African independence, when the Soviets and the new post-colonial governments mutually explored the possibilities of developing expanded relations. This exploration demonstrated that African and Soviet interests tend both to converge and diverge. Analysis of the interaction permits one to identify the situations in which local interests are favorable for Soviet initiatives and those in which African governments or movements see involvement with Moscow as unwanted or even harmful.

Initial Attitudes toward the USSR

In the interwar period and especially after the 1920s, Africa's anticolonial movements explored Marxist ideas and the policies of the Soviet Union as possible sources of inspiration and support for their liberation struggle. Even a nationalist leader such as Dr. D. F. Malan, who later became the first apartheid Prime Minister of South Africa, saw "the Bolshevik victory" as having immense significance for all those engaged in the anti-imperialist struggle!

However, these explorations, despite enthusiastic encouragement and support from the Comintern and the Cominform, produced not only remarkably few positive results, but also some strongly negative ones. With few exceptions, no black leaders of any stature remained firmly attached to Moscow, and only three Communist vanguard organizations—the parties of Egypt, the Sudan, and South Africa—came into existence prior to the 1950s. At the same time, a number of black leaders once ardently pro-Soviet (such as the late George Padmore, the guiding influence for some years in the formation of Dr. Kwame Nkrumah's Pan-Africanist ideas) turned strongly against Moscow; they became either Trotskyite Fourth Internationalists or obsessive anti-Communists.[2] Moreover, several future African rulers who had sought support from Moscow or the European Communist parties (e.g., President Jomo Kenyatta of Kenya and President Félix Houphouët-Boigny of the Ivory Coast) grew highly disillusioned with Moscow even before they had won power, for they found communism incompatible with their sense of nationalism and their preference for a system of private enterprise.

It is a remarkable political phenomenon that as of the end of the 1960s the entire anticolonial struggle in Africa had failed to produce a single Marxist-minded regime, or even an important Communist party except for the three mentioned—the South African, the Egyptian, and the Sudanese—in any of the countries which had achieved their independence. The nearest thing to a Marxist regime was Ahmed Sékou Touré's government in Guinea. Significantly, Guinea had been the only British or French colony in Black Africa to completely sever its relations with the metropolitan colonial power at the point of independence. This exceptional case was the result of a personal feud between Charles de Gaulle and Sékou Touré and of the wish of other Western powers not to upset Gaullist France by supporting Guinea. As a consequence, Guinea had no option other than to turn for aid to anti-Western powers for its immediate economic survival. Even so, the "revisionist" nature of Sékou Touré's Marxist ideas put his ruling Democratic Party of Guinea (*Parti Démocratique de Guinée*—PDG) outside the framework of the international Communist movement.

The fact that international communism proved unable to exploit the situation in Africa during the anticolonial struggle is not just of historical interest, for the elements which contributed to this outcome are still at least partially relevant to the present situation. The fundamental cause of the failure was that communism and nationalism are antipathetic forces.[3] Both must rely for their success on two basic requirements: they must be mass movements, and they must produce significant numbers of vanguard cadres. The Communists had no chance of becoming mass popular movements in competition with the nationalists. At most, they could hope to produce Marxist cadres within the various nationalist movements. But because the Marxist cadres operated as cells of opposition to the predominant "bourgeois," or otherwise nonrevolutionary, elements of the nationalist leadership, they achieved, at best, only a limited influence.

One can distinguish six major characteristics of African nationalism which made it unreceptive to Soviet political and ideological overtures during the pre-independence and early post-independence periods. First, African anti-imperialism was directed against all foreign governments, not just the former colonial powers. At the historic moment when they were engaged in expelling alien rule, Africa's nationalist leaders were not about to accept the patronage of or intimate involvement with, let alone control by, even such avowedly anti-imperialist powers as the Soviet Union and its allies. Second, except in Algeria, none of the major African nationalist movements before the middle of the 1960s was truly revolutionary; instead, they were either reformist (conservative/bourgeois) or radical. Third, African nationalism was highly eclectic with regard to its political ideas. Some nationalists, especially in Francophone Africa, borrowed many of their perspectives from the Marxists but, even more, drew their basic inspiration from Western democracy and from Mahatma Gandhi and Jawaharlal Nehru. The outlooks of Nkrumah, Julius Nyerere, Kenneth Kaunda, Patrice Lumumba, and others all evidence this eclecticism. Fourth, African nationalism was strongly imbued with ideas of black consciousness, négritude, Pan-Africanism, and the "African personality," all of which tended to limit the impact of non-African concepts.[4] Even the radical socialist strand among the nationalists initially insisted on describing their ideas as "African socialism" in order to emphasize the cultural differences between themselves and the international socialists. (Although the idea of "African socialism" still persists, it has tended to be emphasized less as the independence struggle has receded into the past.) Fifth, the international aspirations of African nationalism were strongly influenced by the ideas of nonalignment and "the Third World," which ruled out close alliances with either the West or the Soviet bloc. Finally, all the nationalists— including radicals like Nkrumah, Sékou Touré, and Nyerere—denied the "historical necessity" of "class struggle," viewing it as irrelevant to the African experience.[5] Thus, Touré, who spoke Jesuitically of

Marxism in its "African dress," proclaimed: "The Marxism which served to mobilize the African populations, and in particular the working-class, has been amputated of those of its characteristics which did not correspond to the African realities."[6] His draft of Guinea's trade union manifesto declared its rejection of the class struggle "because of African social groups' identity of living conditions and lack of differentiation into antagonistic classes."[7] Nkrumah, who described himself as a "Christian Marxist," also subscribed to this view.[8]

Leeriness among African nationalists about involvement with the Soviet Union was strengthened in the early post-independence years (i.e., dating from the early or mid-1960s) by a number of experiences. First, Moscow supported Marxist and other groups that challenged the governments which came to power upon independence. Soviet backing went to such groups as the late Félix Moumié's Cameroon People's Union (*Union Populaire de Cameroun* — UPC), small Marxist intellectual groups that emerged as vestiges of the former anticolonial Democratic African Assembly (*Rassemblement Démocratique Africain* — RDA) in some of the countries of West and Equatorial Africa, and Oginga Odinga's People's Party in Kenya. Second, Moscow intervened in power struggles *within* post-independence regimes, notably in support of Patrice Lumumba in the Congo-Leopoldville — now Zaire — and of opponents of Sékou Touré in Guinea (the ostensible reason for the expulsion of the Soviet ambassador from that country in late 1961[9]). Third, Moscow tried to get the nationalists to identify themselves openly with the USSR both against the West and especially, after the Sino–Soviet rift, against China. Finally, Soviet diplomacy in general was too heavy-handed for the sensitivities of most of the leaders of the new African governments.

It should be noted that early African–Soviet encounters in the case of South Africa, Egypt, the Sudan, and Algeria differed considerably from the general pattern set out above. The first three of these countries were not typical colonial societies: each had a sophisticated urban intelligentsia, an emergent working-class proletariat, and a small Moscow-oriented Communist party. While not as advanced politically, Algeria too had a Communist party loyal to Moscow.

In South Africa, the Communist leadership was mostly white or Indian, and the local Communist party was strongly opposed by the traditional nationalist movement — the African National Congress — and later by the Pan-Africanist Congress as well. In Egypt, the local

Communists felt themselves betrayed both when the Soviets, pursuing their courtship of Gamal Abdel Nasser, remained silent about the heavy repression of the Egyptian Communist Party, and even more so when Moscow laid down the line of "national communism" as a technique to allow the Marxists to join the Nasserite regime.[10] In the Sudan, too, Moscow had the problem of advising local Communists on how to relate to the regime of General Ja'far Muhammad Numayri. Here, again, the Soviets urged a "national Communist" course, which encouraged the local Communists to support Numayri and to help him develop a new national political movement, the Sudan Socialist Union. However, this course split Sudan's Communists, and a dissident faction supported the abortive coup against Numayri in 1971,[11] an event which led to a temporary recall of ambassadors as Numayri accused the Soviets of complicity.

In the case of Algeria, Moscow likewise urged the local Communist party to merge its interests with the dominant nationalist organization, the National Liberation Front (*Front de Libération Nationale* — FLN), and this even after the less leftist-minded Houari Boumediene succeeded the radical Ahmed Ben Bella as FLN leader in 1965. Previously, at the height of the Algerian struggle for independence, Moscow had tried to steer the Algerian Communists toward a course of accommodation with France and had kept its arms shipments to the FLN at a low level in order not to upset General de Gaulle, whom the USSR was then courting.[12]

The *Realpolitik* nature of Soviet relations with Gaullist France, Nasser's Egypt, and China did not escape the African leaders, who concluded that Moscow was not nearly as pure-minded as it claimed to be in posing as the ally of the world's progressive revolutionary forces, particularly when its open support of such forces might adversely affect Soviet national interests. They came to see the Soviet Union as simply another superpower pursuing its own interests — a view which gave some substance to Peking's charges of "Soviet imperialism."

Changing Context

While these earlier African attitudes toward the Soviet Union still persist, changing interests in the continent have brought a new relationship between some of its governments and movements on the one hand and the Soviet bloc on the other. This is the consequence, in part, of two interrelated developments.

First, in the post-independence period, nationalist forces of liberation, with very few exceptions, ceased to be mass popular movements. Most of the movements came under the control of particular power groups concerned with preserving their dominant positions in highly centralized governments. Sometimes these groups have been military in nature, but the majority have consisted of civilian parties, usually centered on either a single dominant personality or a coalition of strong sectional interests, whether economic, regional, or tribal. These ruling groups always equate their interests with "the national interest," but these claims have usually been strongly challenged by competing interests who often have at least as much claim to representing the national interest as the groups in power. Thus, while it can be argued that the ruling parties of Tanzania and Somalia (which are among the few still based on mass movements) genuinely pursue national interests rather than particularist ones, this was hardly true in Idi Amin Dada's Uganda, nor is it the case in "Emperor" Bokassa I's Central African Empire or Francisco Macias Nguema's Equatorial Guinea—to name only three of the most extreme cases.

Second, some African regimes and movements, anxious to buttress their own weak power (either to ensure survival of a regime which has lost its popular base or to promote a conceived national interest), have weakened their commitment to genuine nonalignment and Pan-Africanism and have enlisted the support of major extracontinental powers, either from the West or from the East, or from both sources. Where a regime is strongly supported by one or more Western powers, the temptation is for its opposition to turn toward the Communist nations for help. This tendency is also to be found in the case of governments pursuing a national interest hostile to a neighboring state. For example, Libya, engaged in a quarrel with Egypt, turned to Moscow after President Anwar al-Sadat began to look toward the West; similarly, Somalia originally sought aid from Moscow because the U.S. and other Western powers were supporting Somalia's enemy, Ethiopia. The reverse process also occurs: governments or opposition political forces turn to Western nations when their "enemy" is buttressed by the Soviets. There is, of course, a third option, namely to look to Peking. However, this option is not as promising, because of China's inability to produce the kind of military-logistical support that either of the superpowers can provide and, especially since the end of the Cultural Revolution, because of China's perception of its primary role in the Third World as being to provide moral rather than material support to the self-reliant efforts of individual states to reject dominance by outside powers.

This trend toward externalization of African conflicts is symptomatic of the continuing weakness of the continent's own political system—in particular, of the inability of the Organization of African Unity (OAU) to resolve African disputes. In this connection, it is important to understand that the external intervention in Africa is made possible, and usually produced, by Africans themselves. Africans are not, as in the past, simply the passive victims of major foreign powers; they themselves now constitute the agents who introduce foreign powers into the continent's conflicts (whether for good or bad reasons is not immediately relevant). This aspect of foreign intervention was stressed by Nigeria's Head of State, General Olusegun Obasanjo at the Organization of African Unity's summit meeting in Khartoum in July 1978. "We African leaders," he said, "must realize that we cannot ask outside powers to leave us alone while, in most cases, it is our own actions which provide them with the excuse to interfere in our affairs." This view was endorsed by, among others, President Sékou Touré of Guinea, who struck a new note for him when he observed: "We Africans are more responsible for our misfortunes than imperialism."[13] Tanzania's President Julius Nyerere has also spoken of the role of Africans in bringing about both Communist and Western involvement in the continent's conflicts. "We regret," he remarked, "even while we recognize its occasional necessity, that an African government should ask for military assistance from a non-African country when it is faced with an external threat to its national integrity. We know that a response to such a request by any of the big powers is determined by what that big power sees as its own interest."[14]

Because economic, political, and military power are still so minimal in the majority of African states (and especially for opposition movements operating in a single-party state), the need frequently arises to enlist the support of foreign allies. Sometimes this support is solicited in conformity with the criteria set by nonalignment, but frequently this is not so.

A few key illustrations will suffice to make the point. Egypt, under Nasser, was incapable of pursuing its Pan-Arab concerns without invoking the Soviet factor to offset the U.S. factor in the Middle East;

similarly, Anwar al-Sadat cannot implement his "Egypt first" policy without U.S. support—a choice largely forced on his country by its unhappy experience with Soviet policy in Egypt and in the Middle East. Another example is Dr. Agostinho Neto's decision to seek Soviet and Cuban support to avert defeat of the forces of his Popular Movement for the Liberation of Angola (*Movimento Popular de Libertação de Angola*—MPLA) by his opponents, who enjoyed the support of both African and Western governments.[15] Typically in these cases, Africans found it necessary to involve a major foreign power in order to pursue a particular African goal.

While the changing environment in post-independence Africa has opened the way for the USSR (as indeed for Western nations and for China) to assume a new role in the continent's affairs, it has not, however, fostered the emergence of a new alliance system between foreign powers and African states. The "alliances" formed are often temporary and intended to achieve mostly short-term objectives. For example, in just over seven years (1969–77), the Sudan moved from a strong Western orientation to an even stronger Soviet orientation and back again to an essentially Western and Arab orientation.

Such rapid shifts in a nation's alliance strategy, occasioned by changing local and foreign interests, reflect the current stage of political development in many nations of the Third World; this fact in turn requires a dialectic interpretation of political relations. Those who characterize African governments or movements as being pro-Western or pro-Soviet almost always do so out of a failure to understand why certain African leaders, governments, or movements find it useful to choose a particular foreign ally at a particular point in time. These relationships are largely transient, both because most African governments are short-lived and because the central thrust of continental politics (despite some aberrations) is still toward nonalignment and the exclusion of foreign intervention in African disputes. "Hands off Africa" remains the strongest aspiration of the majority of African leaders, irrespective of the political complexion.

In striking up relationships with Moscow, Africans understand that, like themselves, the Soviets are engaged in promoting their own interests. African leaders are seldom beguiled by Soviet claims to being motivated solely by the desire to give ideological support to the world's progressive movements. A particularly fulsome example of such claims was provided by Yuriy Bernov, the Soviet ambassador to Ghana, who, in explaining his country's assistance to those "fighting for freedom,'' asserted that the USSR "does not look for advantages, does not hunt for concessions or seek political domination or military bases. In fact, we act as we are bid by our revolutionary conscience."[16]

African Reactions to Soviet Actions

We have seen how the changing African political environment has led some African leaders to consider inviting greater Soviet involvement on the continent as one means of pursuing specific African objectives. However, the decision to pursue such an option is also affected by how Africans react to previous Soviet activities on the continent. When we look at this latter dimension of the African–Soviet relationship, it is possible to discern among Africans certain broadly shared attitudes concerning Soviet behavior.

In the first place, Africans see the Soviets as engaged in a worldwide competition with the Western nations for influence, power, and trade. The "anti-imperialist" packaging of this Communist thrust finds a natural emotional response among African nationalists. Soviet readiness to support liberation movements against those in power in Rhodesia, Namibia, and South Africa—all of whom are associated in African eyes with Western economic, political, and military interests—is very much welcomed in Africa, even though Moscow's motives are clearly perceived.

On a more practical level, Africans feel that their interests are served by developing trade and aid relations with the Soviet bloc; few African governments refuse to enter into this type of relationship. At the same time, Soviet trade and aid terms are seldom felt to be exceptionally generous or advantageous.[17] Indeed, a number of African countries have in recent years registered open dissatisfaction on this subject. The terms of fishing agreements have been a particular cause of unhappiness. Both Mauritania and Guinea-Bissau, for example, have forced revisions in the fishing treaties that they initially concluded with the USSR. Another source of complaint has been the prices fixed by long-term contracts for Soviet purchases of specific commodities under barter accords. For instance, the Sudan has voiced discontent with the disadvantageous terms in its agreement to sell long-staple cotton to the USSR, and a dispute between Guinea and the Soviet Union over the price Moscow must pay for bauxite remains to be resolved.

African leaders are also frequently critical of the disproportionately small share of economic (as compared to military) assistance in the aid programs of the Soviet Union. In the years 1955–76, the USSR extended military assistance apparently totaling U.S.$5,472 million to African countries, while in the roughly comparable period of 1954–76, it offered $3,259 million in economic assistance to states on the continent. (The countries of Eastern Europe provided an additional $2,162 million in economic aid commitments in this period, but Africans tend to view Eastern Europe as distinct from the Soviet Union when it comes to questions of foreign assistance.) To be sure, Egypt received well over half of Moscow's total military aid commitments, and if one excludes both military and economic assistance to Egypt, the picture looks a little different. Other African countries obtained $1,982 million in Soviet military aid, but garnered $1,890 million in economic assistance. At the same time, one must remember that African perceptions tend to derive primarily from the recent period. During 1970–76, Soviet economic aid commitments to African countries amounted to $1,019 million, but military assistance for 1972–76 alone seems to have reached $1,000 million.[18] Of course, African complaints about the great size of Soviet military aid programs are valid only in the context of comparisons with Soviet economic aid programs; after all, if USSR military aid is great, that is only because Moscow has provided what (or, in some cases, even less than) the African states themselves have asked for.

Many African leaders complain about the selectivity of the Soviet Union's aid programs—e.g., the concentration of the 400 major Soviet projects in a relatively few countries. The majority African view likewise takes exception to the Soviet policy of channeling aid to regimes of which Moscow approves and of tying political strings to Soviet aid.

Moscow, of course, does not seek to hide the fact that its policy is to give economic aid mainly to those regimes that it regards as "progressive." At the same time, the USSR has in the past given assistance to such widely differing regimes as those of Amin's Uganda and Nigeria, neither of which qualify as "socialist countries." Nigeria is of special interest to the Soviet bloc (as it is to the Western nations) because of its enormous economic resources and its importance in Africa's political system. As a result, Moscow has offered to play a major role in developing Nigeria's iron and steel industry at Ajaokuta.[19] But after five years of studies and negotiations, the final contract has not yet been signed as of mid-1979, mainly because of difficulties over a contract price. Reflecting official views, one Nigerian newspaper commented that the country expected "a fair price from the USSR because it has proved to be a friend of nations struggling to attain economic self-sufficiency."[20]

Moreover, in dealing with the USSR, Africans feel that in certain fields Soviet technology is inferior to that of the West. Consequently, a country like Algeria elected to import American mining equipment at a time when it had no diplomatic relations with Washington, while the Marxist regime in Angola has chosen to maintain its ties with the transnational corporation Gulf Oil because of the superior American offshore oil technology and better marketing opportunities that this link offers. Despite the long period of bad relations with the West, Guinea's Sékou Touré elected to entrust development of his country's major mining resource, the bauxite deposits at Konkourie, to a consortium of French, American, and Canadian transnational corporations. Nevertheless, transnational corporations, though recognized to be highly efficient, are in general looked upon with considerable suspicion because of their economic power; therefore, Soviet antipathy to transnational operations in the Third World evokes a ready response from most Africans.

Second, Soviet policy is seen by Africans to be heavily influenced by Moscow's rivalry with Peking. Soviet diplomacy is regarded as clumsy or even downright bullying in its attempts to influence African leaders to adopt hostile attitudes toward the PRC. Such actions are a major irritant to most African countries and political movements, many of which seek to maintain a strictly neutral position vis-à-vis the two world Communist centers. By contrast, the Chinese almost everywhere on the continent are admired for the sensitivity of their diplomacy. Thus, although Tanzania has particularly friendly relations with China, Peking made no direct attempt of any kind to dissuade Tanzanian President Nyerere from endorsing the Soviet/Cuban intervention in Angola despite China's frenzied opposition to that action.[21]

Soviet diplomatic pressures in general seem to Africans to be as severe as those from any major power. During the Angolan crisis in 1975–76, Moscow pressed on Uganda's President Amin (then chairman of the Organization of African Unity) so hard to switch his stand to support for the Soviet-backed MPLA that Amin expelled the Soviet ambassador, notwithstanding Uganda's total dependence on Moscow for military aid. While expressing gratitude for that assistance, Amin declared that "the Soviet Union should not try to dictate to him what to do for the people of Uganda or Africa."[22] He complained that the Russians had withheld spare parts for his army and had insisted that Ugandan pilots get Soviet approval before being allowed to fly. Amin noted that the presidents of Sudan and Egypt and other Arab leaders had complained of similar experiences in their dealings with the Soviet Union.

Despite this exposure of his real feelings at a moment of sharp diplomatic conflict, Amin nevertheless soon resumed "normal relations" with Moscow (another telling example of how a local African interest dictates the need for a close relationship with the USSR). However, the USSR again resorted to strong-arm tactics in his hour of direst need. When Amin used his Soviet weapons to invade Tanzania in 1978, Moscow at once stopped supplying arms to Uganda and withdrew its military training team. It clearly wished to avoid involvement in another inter-African military conflict, especially one in which it might be associated with the weaker side.

President Numayri of the Sudan has also spoken of the manner in which the USSR used its military aid to pressure his regime and to intervene in the Sudan's internal affairs. In a broadcast to the nation on June 27, 1977, a month after he had expelled Soviet military advisers because of Moscow's support for Libya and Ethiopia, Numayri charged that during their seven-year stay in his country these military experts had "played a role not of development but of hindrance. The experts were here, yet 40 to 60 percent of the Soviet armaments were completely unserviceable, and we could not but ask friends to come to help with the repairing." Numayri added that, since the abortive coup against his regime in 1971, the Sudan's MIG fighters had been grounded, even though Soviet experts were on hand. He explained: "It was because the Soviet Union refused to supply us with the necessary oil. The Soviet Union set a condition for getting spare parts for Soviet airplanes and tanks, that is, they should be paid for in advance. But even after paying the money, the spare parts still failed to arrive."[23]

Africans widely perceive a racist strain in Russian dealings with colored peoples; in this respect, the "Communists" seem to behave no differently than "Western supremacists." Feelings of resentment over the situation are expressed most strongly in private conversations, but they are also reflected in the African press. The strongest antagonism, however, is reported by Africans who have studied in the USSR or in East European countries. Similar resentment over "white racism" is often strongly expressed by African military men regarding their relations with Soviet advisers—an attitude which, incidentally, does not extend to ties with Cuban advisers. In Angola, for example, diplomats found sharp distinctions in the attitudes of MPLA cadres toward Cuban and Soviet advisers.

Most African governments regard Soviet policies as opportunistic and contradictory—sometimes even cynical. This attitude has been markedly strengthened by Moscow's role in the conflicts in the Horn of Africa, where the USSR is seen to have let down its Somali ally and abandoned the Eritrean Liberation Front in the process of establishing itself as Ethiopia's patron. A number of other actions have also contributed to the widespread view that Moscow is much more concerned with promoting particular national interests than with adhering to "pure revolutionary ideology." These have included, for example, Soviet silence at the repression of the Egyptian Communist Party and the USSR's care not to offend de Gaulle during the Algerian war (both already mentioned), and Moscow's alliance with the militantly anti-Communist Libyan leader, Colonel Mu'ammar Gadhafi. Many Africans find it especially baffling that a Communist power should have lent its military support to sustain a regime like that of Amin, a man described by some prominent leaders (including President Nyerere, Kenneth Kaunda, Jomo Kenyatta, and Sir Seretse Khama) as an "African Hitler."[24] However, some African leaders (notably those with Marxist-Leninist leanings) tend to explain contradictory Soviet behavior in dialectical terms: the Soviets' positive policies require them to take account of political realities in order to exploit every opportunity to defeat "imperialism, Zionism, and the revisionists," and to strengthen the "progressive forces."

Finally, African leaders display three general views about the degree to which the USSR constitutes a threat to the continent. A number of influential leaders have come to feel that the Soviet Union poses a serious Communist threat to all non-Communist leaders and regimes. Others, perhaps fewer but no less convinced in their judgments, believe that the USSR plays a valuable role in countering the continuing domination of the West. The majority, though, take a middle position: they are uneasy about the activities of all the major powers, but they do not see the Soviet Union as either a major threat or a particularly reliable friend of African causes.

Moscow's intervention in Angola and, even more, its involvement in the conflicts in the Horn of Africa have, however, stirred debate about the true nature of Soviet ambitions and the USSR's role as a military power in Africa. Until these events, Africans had paid little attention to the writings of such Soviet military figures as Admiral of the Fleet Sergey Gorshkov, who advocates a worldwide political role for the Soviet navy.[25] This debate has sharpened the differentiation of attitudes with regard to the specifically military activities of the USSR on the continent. These attitudes therefore deserve more detailed analysis.

The Military Factor

In terms of attitudes about what military role the Soviet Union should be allowed on the continent, Africans fall into seven broad categories. First, there are pro-Moscow Marxist-Leninists who, apart from needing Soviet assistance anyway, feel friendship for the Communist world. They invariably react favorably to Soviet intervention and with hostility to any type of Western intervention. This group includes Angola's President Neto, who has termed the Soviets "Africa's true friends." It also embraces the present military regime in Ethiopia, some leading figures in Mozambique and Guinea-Bissau,[26] and individual leaders in the various liberation movements.

Even in this category, though, one finds strong elements of Afrocommunism—reflected in a desire not to be wholly dependent on Moscow, as well as in constant private complaints of irritation with Soviet diplomats and advisers. Dr. Neto, who was himself dropped by Moscow at one time, displays this ambivalence; he seems to be much happier with the Third World Cubans. Moreover, he has recently shown an interest in lessening his heavy dependence on the Soviet bloc by seeking expanded economic relations with the Western powers. Somalia manifested a similarly ambivalent attitude until its recent experience of "Soviet perfidy" when Moscow transferred its exclusive support to Ethiopia.

Second, there are pro-Peking Marxist-Leninists, who automatically suspect all forms of Soviet aid. While active among the intelligentsia and in the liberation movements, these "Maoists" have not achieved positions of power in any of the African governments.

Third, there are those governments, with either Marxist or radical leanings, who welcome Soviet help but with careful reservations. These include the governments of Algeria, Mozambique, Benin,

Guinea, Guinea-Bissau, and the People's Republic of the Congo. The last four, despite their Marxist leanings, all rely more on West European than Soviet economic aid. Perhaps most of the liberation movements in Southern Africa also fall into this category. While they rarely make public criticisms of the Soviet bloc, they engage in strenuous arguments with the Communist states in private diplomacy.

Fourth, there are governments—notably those in Libya and Uganda when it was still under Amin's rule—which are overtly anti-Communist but nevertheless find it convenient to accept military assistance from the Soviet bloc. They tend to overcompensate for their nonadherence to Marxism by sycophantic-sounding praise of the Soviet Union. At the same time, unlike those in the previous category, they are on occasion inclined to make public their differences with Moscow.

Fifth, there are governments which are genuinely nonaligned and use the Soviet bloc as only one of several sources of military supply. These include Nigeria and perhaps Algeria—although it is not easy to decide whether to place Algeria here or in category three above since that country's attitudes toward all foreign powers tend to fluctuate depending on the particular issues involved. Although those in this category, like those in the next group, tend to make pragmatic decisions about any particular Soviet policy, they are less inclined to state their objections or reservations in public.

Sixth, there is another group of nonaligned governments which, while accepting very limited Soviet military assistance, prefer, for the most part, to rely on Chinese or Western help. Those in this category—notably, Tanzania until the late 1970s and Zambia—are as suspicious of Soviet as of Western intervention elsewhere in the continent. However, they do not make *a priori* judgments based solely on the source of the intervention forces. Thus, President Nyerere of Tanzania strongly endorsed the Russian/Cuban intervention in Angola but sharply criticized the Soviet Union for supplying arms to Tanzania's neighbor Uganda;[27] by contrast, Zambia's Kaunda denounced the Russian/Cuban intervention in Angola as "the tiger and his cubs stalking in the continent," yet a few months later was ready to invite Soviet military support to help crush the Ian Smith regime in Rhodesia.[28]

Finally, there are governments and leaders who view Soviet aims in Africa with even deeper suspicion than they do Western or Chinese aims. Those in this category regard Soviet military (and economic) programs as designed to establish "control" over Africa and subvert governments of which Moscow disapproves. The bluntest warnings about the "Soviet threat in Africa" have come from two African leaders who once accepted large-scale Soviet military aid—Egypt's Sadat and the Sudan's Numayri. In a message to the peoples of Africa on May 25, 1977, President Sadat spoke—without mentioning names—about his country's experience with Soviet military ambitions.

> It is the desire of certain States to try and establish military bases in some of our States, exploiting disputes left over among us from previous regimes, and tempting us with arms on the pretext of confronting the ambitions of neighboring countries. This will involve us in the struggle among the big powers and threaten our safety and security, as well as our freedom and independence. . . . Egypt wishes to draw the attention of all African peoples and States to this plot which is aimed at returning them to superpower spheres of influence which service the economic interests and political and military considerations of those superpowers.[29]

Numayri, in a similar vein, has stated: "I would like to draw the attention of African countries which have relations with these social neocolonialists who enter Africa by flaunting the banner of supporting developing countries and liberation movements. Be careful not to fall into their trap. I sincerely advise you. My advice comes from our experience."[30] And in a June 27, 1977, Khartoum telecast, Numayri bluntly asserted, "Soviet military aid can become the basis for imposing enslavement on you."[31] Likewise, King Hassan II of Morocco is concerned about Moscow's support of Algeria in the conflict over the former Spanish Sahara and about Soviet actions in Libya, where, he claims, the USSR has built a military base supplied with some 800 tanks and 100 aircraft "of a type they [i.e., the Libyans] could not handle themselves for another twenty-five years."[32] (King Hassan's hostility toward the USSR has not, however, prevented Rabat and Moscow from entering into a long-term agreement on phosphate development.[33] This involves a U.S.$250-million Soviet loan to Morocco—the biggest single loan that the USSR has extended to any African country.)

Implacable hostility to Soviet ambitions is shared by Presidents Houphouët-Boigny of Ivory Coast, Mobuto Sese Seko of Zaire, and H. K. Banda of Malawi. Perhaps less openly hostile, but still watch-

fully suspicious regarding Soviet intentions, are the rulers of Cameroon, Kenya, Mauritania, Mauritius, Senegal, and Tunisia.

All of the countries in this seventh category prefer to get their military aid from Western sources. In fact, as demonstrated in the
conflicts in the Horn of Africa, some even invite a more extensive and
effective Western arms commitment than the Western powers themselves are willing to undertake or think prudent.

Where Interests Converge

From what has been said, it is clear that there are times when the
interests of Africans and of the Soviet Union converge and times
when they diverge. The Soviet bloc has found it expedient in pursuing
its own interests to tailor policies to the requirements of particular
African situations. However, the continent is passing through a period
of considerable instability—involving frequent changes of government, not to mention changes of policies by any given government.
Consequently, the Soviet encounter with Africa is much more likely
to continue to be marked for some time by shifts of "alliances" rather
than to produce a solid base of Soviet influence, let alone control.
Therefore, in attempting to understand current or future Soviet actions, the best one can do is delineate those situations in which African interests seem to converge with Soviet interests, and hence provide some basis for a special relationship (however temporary), and
those situations in which African interests seem to provide no opening
for the USSR.

Two major types of opportunity for Soviet action arise. The first is
in those African countries where the government finds itself in need of
substantial economic or, especially, military assistance and where it
either chooses not to, or fails to, get such aid from Western sources.
Such circumstances have occurred in states of widely differing political complexion and in all parts of the African continent. The second
type of opportunity is in countries where "liberation struggles" are
under way and African liberation movements are unable to attract
Western support and thus feel compelled to look to anti-Western
forces for military, economic, and political backing. Prior to the mid-
1970s, Portuguese Africa was the scene of most of the situations of
this nature; in the late 1970s, Southern Africa has become the major
locale for them.

Guinea offers an early example of the first kind of opportunity for Moscow. For reasons explained previously, President Sékou Touré developed close economic and military ties with the Soviet Union at the time of his break with France in the late 1950s. His need for the USSR's military assistance increased toward the latter part of the 1960s. Not only did Guinea face a threat to its security from Portugal because of Sékou Touré's active support of the Party of African Independence in Guinea-Bissau and Cape Verde (PAIGC), which was fighting to free the neighboring territory from Portuguese rule, but two of Guinea's French-connected neighbors, Senegal and Ivory Coast, gave strong backing to Sékou Touré's exiled opposition. Indeed, it is doubtful whether Sékou Touré's regime could have survived without Soviet military help. As a *quid pro quo* for this support, Guinea provided important naval and air facilities to the USSR at Conakry. After Guinea-Bissau gained its independence in 1974 and after Guinea subsequently restored friendly relations with France as well as the Ivory Coast and Senegal, however, the threats to Guinea's security diminished, and Sékou Touré began to curtail Soviet access to Conakry's facilities.

In Algeria, we have a case of a country whose main economic links are with France and Western Europe. Nevertheless, the Algerian government has responded to its troubled post-independence relationship with France by deliberately inviting Soviet military support and economic assistance, but without severing its considerable economic ties with France. Algeria's military ties with the USSR grew substantially after Algeria became involved in the Sahara conflict with its neighbors, Morocco and Mauritania, both of whom depend largely on French military aid.

Libya, after its decisive break with Egypt in 1974, entered into special military relations with Moscow since the Soviet Union was the only place where Gadhafi could obtain the arms he desired. This is a prime example of a relationship of mutual convenience—cemented by common enmity to Sadat's regime in Cairo and to Numayri's in Khartoum. Gadhafi himself espouses an Islamic revolutionary ideology which condemns "godless communism," and sharply disagrees with Moscow's policies regarding the Arab–Israeli conflict.

Somalia sought and accepted Soviet military aid in order to pursue the goal of reuniting the "five parts of Greater Somalia"—British and Italian Somaliland (which constitute the present Somalia), Djibouti, the Ogaden and other border areas of Ethiopia, and portions of the

Northern Frontier province of Kenya. This relationship was established after the civilian Somali government in the early 1960s had failed to obtain effective Western military assistance to work toward this national goal. However, after 1969, when the military, led by an avid Pan-Somali nationalist, General Siad Barre, seized power, Somalia asked for and received extensive Soviet military aid. Barre was willing, as a *quid pro quo,* to provide Moscow naval facilities in Berbera and lesser facilities in two other Somali ports.

Ethiopia had a traditional Western orientation and a heavy dependence on mainly U.S. military aid. However, when the post-imperial Addis Ababa military regime (the Dergue, as it is known) committed itself to Marxist-Leninist revolutionary policies which intensified internal opposition, especially in Eritrea and the Ogaden, Washington proved unwilling to furnish the military assistance the Dergue felt it needed to consolidate its power. Faced with widespread disintegration at home and mostly hostile neighbors (led by Somalia and the Sudan) on its frontiers, the Dergue saw an alliance with the Soviet bloc and Cuba as its only salvation.[34]

Uganda, under General Amin's dictatorial rule, found itself unable to attract the effective Western economic or military support on which the country had earlier relied, and, despite a militant pro-Palestinian stand, it failed to attract adequate Arab support. For these reasons, Amin turned to Moscow, even though he has always been strongly antagonistic to communism in any shape or form. Moscow found it expedient to enter into an arms agreement with Amin because all his neighbors were, in varying degrees, anti-Moscow and three of them (Tanzania, the Sudan, and Zaire) got military aid from, *inter alia,* China.

In the People's Republic of the Congo and Benin, the emergence some years after independence of military regimes committed, at least in theory, to Marxism-Leninism brought strains in former close relations with France. As a result, these regimes turned to Moscow as a source of military aid, even though they still depended very largely on French economic support. Mali's relations with the French also became difficult following its decision to secede from a short-lived union with Senegal; it, too, felt it necessary to find new allies, which it did in both Moscow and Peking. However, President Moussa Traore's regime in 1978 alleged that the plotters of an abortive military coup in the country had had connections with the USSR, and Mali thereafter began to phase out its military links with the Soviets.

An important factor in Mozambique's decision to establish close relations with Moscow in 1976 was an urgent need for the backing of a strong ally in light of the threats it faced along its borders. (Other considerations included Mozambique's Marxist-Leninist orientation as well as its strong brotherly ties with Angola's MPLA, which had shared its long struggle against Portugal and which finally won power mainly through the help of the USSR and Cuba.) Having emerged from its own long struggle against Portuguese colonialism, the new government founded by FRELIMO (*Frente de Libertação de Moçambique*) felt it had an inescapable commitment to help the other liberation movements in Southern Africa carry on their struggles. This commitment placed Mozambique's security in immediate jeopardy from neighboring Rhodesia and possibly, over the longer term, from its even more powerful neighbor, South Africa. It should be noted, however, that the relations of President Samora Machel's Mozambique with Moscow are not nearly as close—let alone as dependent—as those of Angola, although Mozambique's decision to strengthen its relations with Moscow did tend to alienate China, which had been FRELIMO's major non-African supporter during its liberation struggle.

The outstanding example of the second sort of opportunity for the USSR comes from Angola, where independence found three rival movements engaged in a power struggle which had assumed civil war proportions. Two of the movements, Holden Roberto's National Front for the Liberation of Angola (*Frente Nacional de Libertação de Angola*—FNLA) and Jonas Savimbi's National Union for the Total Independence of Angola (*União Nacional pro Independencia Total de Angola*—UNITA), had the support of both African and Western governments (France and the United States as well as South Africa). The third movement, Dr. Agostinho Neto's MPLA (which had a strong contingent of Marxist cadres in its leadership) appealed to Moscow and Havana for support. As a result of the effective military intervention by the Soviets and Cubans, the MPLA succeeded in gaining local ascendancy. (In order to maintain and consolidate its hold on power, the MPLA has had to rely on the continued strong support of its foreign allies.)

Other liberation movements in Southern Africa have similarly looked to the Communist nations for backing in their struggle against regimes in Rhodesia, Namibia, and South Africa, which they see as Western in origin. Moscow's terms for support are that the movements refuse China's aid and appear on international platforms to denounce Peking's stand in the quarrel between the two world Communist centers. Reactions to this demand have differed. When the African National Congress (ANC) of South Africa, despite its long tradition of nationalist opposition to communism at home, failed to attract any Western military support for its liberation struggle, it accepted the only other option, which was to seek aid from the Communist countries. The Soviets, supported by the majority pro-Moscow cadres in the ANC, succeeded in getting the ANC to come out strongly against China. In the case of the divided Zimbabwe (Rhodesian) liberation movement, the dominant military cadres of the Zimbabwe African National Union (ZANU) chose not to forfeit the assistance they had long received from China. Moscow therefore gave its support to Joshua Nkomo's Zimbabwe African People's Union (ZAPU), despite the fact that its leadership is known to have strong links with important Western interests and to have what Marxists describe as "bourgeois tendencies." The other major liberation movement in Southern Africa, the South-West African People's Organization (SWAPO) of Namibia, has to date insisted on maintaining a nonaligned posture as between Moscow and Peking, although a cadre of pro-Soviet Marxists has recently begun to play a more prominent role inside the organization.

Perhaps a majority of African leaders endorse the view that only the Communist powers (the Soviet bloc, China, and Cuba) can be counted upon to provide military support to the liberation movements in Rhodesia, Namibia, and South Africa. They therefore give their approval to Communist military involvement in the "liberation struggle" (especially in Southern Africa) subject to the qualifications made by Nigeria's Head of State, General Olusegun Obasanjo, in his speech to the Khartoum summit of the Organization of African Unity in July 1978. He declared:

> To the Soviets and their friends I should like to say that, having been invited to Africa in order to assist in the liberation struggle and the consolidation of national independence, they should not overstay their welcome. Africa is not about to throw off one colonial yoke for another. Rather, they should hasten the political, economic and military capability of their African friends to stand on their own. . . . [35]

Divergent Interests

Just as the course of events in Africa produces local interests that facilitate Soviet efforts to establish special relationships on the continent, so other situations create serious obstacles to Soviet ambitions. These situations arise not just because of African nationalism, with its preference for nonalignment and for noninterference by foreign powers in the continent's internal conflicts, but also because of particular circumstances.

First of all, some African governments have had unhappy experiences as a result of a deep involvement with the Soviet bloc. The outstanding examples are, of course, Egypt, the Sudan, and Somalia. Egypt placed considerable reliance on Soviet support in the effort to recoup the losses of the 1967 war in the Middle East. However, Cairo grew increasingly perturbed by what it perceived as insufficient help from the USSR, and in 1972 Sadat expelled Soviet military advisers as a prerequisite to turning for support to the West. Although Soviet arms shipments to Egypt appear to have taken a temporary turn upward again as Cairo prepared for the war of October 1973, Sadat's disillusionment with Moscow continued to grow. Finally in March 1976, the Egyptian president abrogated the Treaty of Friendship and Cooperation and ordered the end of Soviet access to naval facilities in Alexandria. In the Sudan's case, President Numayri's regime, upon winning power in a military coup in 1970, proclaimed itself oriented toward the "progressive forces in the world." Its leadership was originally made up of a coalition of radical nationalists, Arab socialists, Marxists, and Baathists. When the radical nationalists, headed by Numayri, resisted the policies of the Communists and Baathists, the two latter groups attempted a coup. This failed, and Numayri reacted strongly against Moscow, building his own regime on support from China, Arab countries (especially Egypt and Saudi Arabia), and, more recently, the Western nations. Somalia, too, became hostile to the Soviet Union when the latter decided in 1976 to replace the United States as Ethiopia's source of military aid. In November 1977, President Barre tore up his friendship treaty with the USSR, expelled the Soviet military advisers in his country, and terminated Soviet use of Somali sea and air facilities.[36]

As a consequence of their experiences, Egypt, the Sudan, and Somalia have emerged as leaders of a coalition of anti-Soviet forces on the continent. These three states view Soviet policy in the Horn as designed to gain "control" of the Red Sea and to use the Horn as a base of operations to destabilize the Sudan, Egypt, and Kenya. They see an even larger Soviet strategy aimed at extending influence over the entire northeastern portion of Africa—from Kenya along the Indian Ocean and Red Sea littoral to Egypt in the Mediterranean, inland to the Sahara frontier of Chad and then down the Nile valley to link up with Uganda, and finally back to the coast via Kenya.[37]

The Egyptian-Sudanese-Somali perspective would doubtless enjoy even greater support in Africa if the black African states did not regard it as being too closely linked with Arab interests in the area. This impression may have been strengthened by the Egyptian-Sudanese-Somali initiative, backed by Saudi Arabia, to organize a summit of Red Sea states—all of which, except for Ethiopia, belong to the Arab League.[38] The black African states are also hesitant to join the Sudan and Egypt in supporting Somalia against Ethiopia because black Africans remain opposed to Somalia's support of secessionism in Eritrea and to Mogadiscio's use of force as a means to change the border between Somalia and Ethiopia and help "liberate" the Somali population in the Ogaden.

Morocco, despite its considerable economic relations with the Soviet Union (especially in connection with phosphates), has increasingly turned against Moscow because of the latter's support for Libya in its conflict with Egypt and particularly because of Soviet backing for Algeria's stand in the Western Sahara conflict. Moscow initially attempted to maintain a neutral position on the Western Sahara imbroglio. It faced a dilemma in the fact that Ali Yatta, leader of the Moroccan Communists and a loyal Soviet-line Marxist, ardently supported King Hassan's annexation of large portions of the territory, whereas Algeria, a major Third World friend of the USSR, vigorously championed the cause of the Polisario Front, which sought independence for the territory. Moscow showed that its major interest was not to upset Algeria when it finally indicated in June 1977 that it backed "the inalienable right of the population of Western Sahara to self-determination."[39] The decision to take this step predictably angered King Hassan, and also severely strained the loyalty of the Moroccan Communist Party to Moscow.

In addition to one-time "allies" who have grown disillusioned with Soviet policies, there are some African leaders who have never had close dealings with Moscow and who view the Soviet presence in Africa as anathema. President Houphouët-Boigny of the Ivory Coast affords a good example. A vigorous champion of capitalism at home and of close ties with France in his foreign relations, he has come into conflict with various radical African governments—e.g., those of the late Dr. Kwame Nkrumah in Ghana and of Sékou Touré in Guinea, both of which he has charged with being under "Communist influence." Moscow, for its part, has made no attempt to hide its hostility toward Houphouët-Boigny's government. In part, this open enmity arises from the fact that in 1969 Houphouët-Boigny ordered the Soviet diplomatic mission to leave after accusing its personnel of involvement in student strikes against his regime. Diplomatic relations have never been restored. Moreover, the Ivorian leader has put himself at the head of a campaign to warn Africa against the dangers of Soviet "penetration." His campaign parallels that led by Egypt, the Sudan, and Somalia, but the two centers of opposition to Moscow have not yet merged.

The only other prominent black African leaders who adopt a hostile attitude toward Moscow are Malawi's president, Dr. H. K. Banda, and Zaire's president, Mobutu Sese Seko. Banda basically shares Houphouët-Boigny's political outlook. As for Mobutu, his quarrels with the Soviets originated in the early post-independence struggles of Zaire—when it was still known as the Congo—over the USSR's attempts to intervene to assist the first prime minister, Patrice Lumumba, to stay in power. Subsequently, in 1967, the Soviets gave military backing to a rebellion against Mobutu, and when this failed, they gave sanctuary and extended support to one of the defeated leaders of that insurrection, Antoine Gizenga. But the bitterest issue between Moscow and Kinshasha has been over Angola. Mobutu was the principal supporter of the opponents of the MPLA, and he sees the Soviet role in the MPLA-dominated Angola as a direct threat to himself and his regime.

Prospects

Afro–Soviet relations have undergone numerous changes in the last 20 years and still remain in a state of considerable flux. Some Soviet successes in fostering special relationships on the continent have not lived up to their promise so far. Governments in each of the three areas which earlier seemed to offer the greatest potential for

Moscow—Egypt, the Sudan, and Somalia—have dealt the Soviet Union heavy setbacks. Angola can be counted among Soviet achievements—but thanks largely to the important Cuban role. Furthermore, it is too early to speculate intelligently about whether the Angolan-Soviet relationship will prove more durable than Moscow's relationships with Egypt, the Sudan, and Somalia. It is likewise impossible at present to predict the outcome of the risky Soviet enterprise in the Horn of Africa.

This last venture, it is worth underscoring, exceeds in scale and commitment anything that the Soviet bloc has attempted in Africa or the Middle East since Nikita Khrushchev fashioned military ties with Gamal Abdel Nasser's Egypt in the late 1950s. In terms of military input, the Soviet-Cuban undertaking in the Horn dwarfs the Angolan enterprise of 1975–76, with the contribution of matériel in the Horn case approaching $2 billion as of mid-1979. The combined air- and sealifts of arms and manpower that the USSR staged in late 1977 to save the Ethiopian army from defeat in the Ogaden constituted by far the largest operation of its kind that the Soviet Union had ever essayed.

The enterprise also represents perhaps the most hazardous venture in which the Soviet bloc has ever become engaged in the Third World—hazardous in the sense that when the Soviets first decided to shift their military support from Somalia to Ethiopia in 1977, the chances of their succeeding in buttressing the nascent Marxist revolutionary regime of Lt. Col. Mengistu Haile Mariam were highly uncertain. The risks that Moscow took and the size of its military commitment are indications of the importance that it attaches to expanding its influence in the Red Sea area of Africa.[40]

African reactions to the Soviet-Cuban military intervention in the Horn have been fairly mild to date. The Soviets have justified their move on three separate grounds: (1) it was a legitimate response to a request for military aid from a sovereign African government; (2) it met an international responsibility to assist an independent African country to resist aggression by an invading army (from Somalia); and (3) it fulfilled an "international duty" to "a progressive revolutionary movement" resisting reactionary forces determined to prevent its victory. Apropos of the last justification, it should be noted that Soviet commentators and theoreticians have described the struggle in Ethiopia as "one of the greatest revolutions of the second half of the 20th century, and surely the biggest and most profound social revolution on the African continent."[41] A substantial number of African states have endorsed the first two of these stated Soviet rationales. While the third has overtones of "exportation of revolution," it has drawn little criticism—perhaps because African countries assign overriding importance to defending the principle of the inviolability of established borders.

But if Soviet and Cuban military intervention made it possible for the Ethiopian army to drive the Somalis' regular forces out of the Ogaden by March 1978, the task of defeating the Eritrean liberation forces has proved more difficult—possibly as a result of the fact that Cuba has refused to allow its combat forces to be used against the Eritreans. As of the summer of 1979, the Eritrean resistance remains unbroken, although it has been weakened militarily. Meanwhile, the "great Ethiopian revolution" has bogged down because of the resistance in Eritrea and the Mengistu regime's failure to consolidate its control in several other provinces, notably in the Ogaden as well as in Bale, Sidamo, and Tigre. The promise of a "Marxist-Leninist revolutionary government," to replace the present military regime, still continues to be merely a promise—mainly as a consequence of the lack of sufficient "vanguard cadres" to take over the institutions required to run a full-fledged revolutionary system, and of Mengistu's own suspicions of Ethiopian Marxists. With regard to the latter impediment, it should be emphasized that Marxists trained earlier have been among the most militant opponents of Mengistu's regime. In addition, the country's disastrous economic conditions have proved to be as intractable as the security problems facing the military government. Thus, while Soviet-Cuban intervention has contributed in an important way to sustaining the Mengistu regime, it has not yet succeeded in helping the regime to consolidate the revolution to which it remains wed.

Although the commitment in the Horn of Africa continues to be the USSR's top priority in Africa, the Soviet Union and Cuba have also begun to devote greater attention to Southern Africa. Their military support for the liberation movements of Rhodesia, Namibia, and South Africa has increased considerably in the last few years, and as already indicated, the great majority of African states endorse Soviet-Cuban, as well as Chinese, military aid for the liberation struggle in Southern Africa. However, the USSR's interest in the area clearly goes far beyond just giving military assistance to the particular liberation organizations of its choice. Soviet longer-term strategy has been set forth in a "Manifesto for the Freedom, Independence, National Revival and Social Progress of the Peoples of Tropical and Southern Africa," which was first published in Moscow in the late summer of 1978.[42] This manifesto claims to be "the synthesis of the collective thought of a number of communist and workers' parties of Africa" (not specifically named) meeting sometime in 1978 at an undisclosed venue, and it depicts the initial gathering of the assembled parties as of "great historical significance both for the world communist movement and for the struggle of national and social liberation of our continent." The essential strategy that the manifesto advocates is the creation of a united front between Communists and progressive nationalists and working-class parties. As a model, the document cites the alliance established between the African National Congress of South Africa (ANC) and the South African Communist Party. Moreover, it goes on to describe the Soviet Union as the "sincere friend" of the liberation movements and condemns China and "Maoists" as enemies along with imperialist and other reactionary forces. How viable this strategy will turn out to be in Southern Africa will probably depend on the pace at which the national liberation movements there achieve results. The longer the individual struggles persist, the greater the pressures for radicalization of the movements.

Judged in terms of overall Soviet strategic objectives, Africa has not afforded the USSR any conspicuous successes thus far. Nevertheless, Moscow in recent years would appear to have committed increased resources there and, in fact, to have accorded the continent a much higher priority than have Western powers. But, as the analysis above emphasizes, success or failure in the Soviet case (as in the case of Western policy toward Africa) is likely to depend less on the capacity of the Soviet Union to provide aid than on the degree to which the economic and military assistance offered by Moscow is perceived by Africans to be relevant to their aspirations and interests.

2

Moscow's African Policy of the 1970s

David E. Albright

SINCE 1975, Soviet activity in Africa has increased markedly. One need cite only a few facts to illustrate the point. During the course of 1975, Moscow, persuaded that the Portuguese at last intended to turn Angola over to local rule, threw the full weight of its support behind the Popular Movement for the Liberation of Angola (*Movimento Popular de Libertação de Angola*—MPLA), one of three rival claimants to power in the colony; and after the Portuguese withdrew in November of that year, the combination of a massive influx of Soviet arms and significant numbers of Cuban combat forces helped install an MPLA government in Luanda. This chain of events ultimately led to the signing of a treaty of friendship and cooperation between the USSR and the new People's Republic of Angola in October 1976.[1] In March and April 1977, Nikolay Podgornyy, then President of the USSR Supreme Soviet, made the first major trip through the continent by a top Soviet leader. He and a retinue of 120 persons stopped in Tanzania, Zambia, Mozambique, and Somalia. During his stay in Mozambique, the USSR and the newly independent People's Republic of Mozambique concluded a treaty of friendship and cooperation.[2] Shortly before Podgornyy's trip—in December 1976—Soviet authorities had signed a secret military assistance agreement with Ethiopia's Provisional Military Administrative Council (PMAC), and after Lieutenant Colonel Mengistu Haile Mariam, the PMAC's Chairman, expelled most U.S. officials and caused Washington to cease providing military aid to Addis Ababa in April 1977, the USSR became Ethiopia's sole arms supplier. Subsequently, when the Mengistu

The views expressed in this chapter are those of the author and do not necessarily reflect the perspectives of the U.S. International Communication Agency or the U.S. government.

35

regime found its survival threatened by domestic rebellions and a Somalian attempt to take control of the Ogaden area, the Soviet Union and Cuba collaborated in mounting an enormous military operation to help Addis Ababa reassert its writ over the territories it claimed, with Moscow alone committing an estimated $1 billion in weapons and matériel plus about 1,000 military advisers. By late 1978, the Soviet and Cuban assistance had largely accomplished its purpose, and in November 1978 the USSR and Ethiopia signed a formal treaty of friendship and cooperation.[3]

Such a trend raises some obvious questions. For example, what place does Africa now occupy in Soviet calculations? Has there been some shift in Soviet global priorities? If so, what might the nature of that change be? If not, what accounts for the increased activity? What kinds of perspectives inform Soviet behavior? Does Moscow have some grand design for Africa that it is seeking to implement? If so, what is the character of that broad vision? Or does Soviet policy flow from less grandiose considerations? If so, what sorts of factors govern Soviet outlook and actions with regard to the continent?

These questions have intrinsic importance, for the general capacity of the USSR to make its weight felt around the globe has been growing during the last decade or so—at least in military terms.[4] Beyond this consideration, the substantial controversy that has marked recent discussion of Soviet intentions toward Africa—with assessments ranging from the basic irrelevance of these intentions to the dynamics of events on the continent, to the imminence of Armageddon there[5]—suggests the need for an effort to explore the questions in systematic fashion.

In trying to assess where Africa fits into broad Soviet thinking about the outside world today, it is essential to bear in mind that Moscow does not approach the continent in a tabula rasa fashion, free of prior impressions. The USSR has now had more than two decades of direct experience with Africa and Africans, and while that experience probably does not determine present Soviet outlook in any mechanistic way, it does appear to color current Soviet attitudes to some extent. At the very least, it affords a framework within which Moscow evaluates changing realities on the continent and judges the significance of new developments. For this reason, it deserves a brief review here.

The Historical Backdrop

Significant Soviet involvement in Africa dates back only to the mid-1950s, and it developed initially in quite a specific context.[6] In the wake of the 1955 Bandung Conference of African and Asian States, Moscow became convinced that it had erred in regarding the passage of lands from colonial status to political independence in the post–World War II era as formalistic and essentially meaningless. Indeed, it now perceived that a major restructuring of the world political scene was under way. As Nikita Khrushchev observed at the 20th Congress of the Communist Party of the Soviet Union (CPSU) in February 1956, "the present disintegration of the imperialist colonial system is a postwar development of world-historical significance."[7] Within such a context, events in Africa took on a new importance. While the USSR initially focused on the Arab North, its interest soon expanded to the continent as a whole.[8]

The assessment that the demise of colonialism loomed on the horizon in no way altered Moscow's fundamental preoccupation with the United States and Western Europe, but it did generate some significant expectations on Moscow's part. According to Leninist doctrine, imperialism constituted "the highest stage of capitalism," and the breakup of the colonial system would deal a major, if not lethal, blow to world imperialist forces. Thus, in Soviet eyes the disappearance of colonialism would inevitably redound to the advantage of the USSR and its socialist allies. Moreover, while Soviet observers had few illusions about the outlooks of contemporary leaders in many newly independent countries,[9] there was a sense of a rising revolutionary tide that would submerge these leaders and launch their states onto a "genuinely socialist" course. In fact, one finds certain parallels in the optimism of Soviet commentary about events in former colonial lands in the mid- and late 1950s and that which pervaded Bolshevik outpourings on world revolution in the years immediately after the October Revolution of 1917.

From the Soviet standpoint, then, the critical question was how to capitalize on this favorable trend in the colonial and newly independent areas. Until late 1957, Moscow pursued what might best be termed a "defensive" option. Perceiving the correlation of global forces to favor the United States and its Western allies, Soviet leaders sought cooperation with former colonial lands in Asia and Africa as a means of buttressing the USSR's position against any possible Western onslaught. This approach was formalized in Khrushchev's enunciation at the 20th Party Congress of the concept of a "zone of peace" embracing the socialist countries and those states which "proclaimed nonparticipation in blocs as a principle of their foreign policy."[10]

After the USSR successfully launched both an intercontinental ballistic missile and an artificial earth satellite toward the end of 1957, however, Moscow adopted a more "forward" strategy based on the premise that a situation of mutual deterrence now prevailed between East and West in military terms. That is, it attempted to encourage the newly independent states, whose ranks were growing rapidly, to "consolidate" their political independence by embarking on the "socialist path of development." It cited the USSR's achievements as evidence that socialism constituted the wave of the future, and it held out the inducement of concrete economic aid to those that chose such a course.[11]

In practice, the USSR found many ex-colonial states far less tractable than it had anticipated. Perhaps the most notable case—and certainly the most grievous to Moscow—occurred during the Congo-Leopoldville imbroglio of 1960–61.[12] The Afro-Asian nations unanimously approved the dispatch of U.N. troops to the Congo in July 1960 in the wake of the mutiny of the Congolese *Force Publique,* the intervention of Belgian troops, and the secession of Katanga Province; but differences quickly developed among them regarding the U.N. operation. These eventually led to a major split in Afro-Asian ranks after Congolese President Joseph Kasavubu dismissed the country's Soviet-backed premier, Patrice Lumumba. To Soviet dismay, the U.N. General Assembly, with major African support, recognized a Kasavubu delegation as the legal representative of the Republic of the Congo and spurned a Lumumba delegation.[13]

As a consequence of such experiences, Moscow during 1959–61 reappraised its view of the newly emergent states in Asia and Africa, and it decided that it had been too facile in assuming that the crumbling of the colonial system heralded an imminent swing of these states toward the Communist orbit or that a revolutionary tide was flowing high throughout the Afro-Asian area. It now tried to distinguish between countries where genuine revolutionary potential existed and countries where it did not. Having made that determination, it began to devote the vast preponderance of its energies to the former.

In general, African states dominated the favored group. With the establishment of the so-called Casablanca bloc in January 1961, this African contingent took concrete organizational shape. The bloc included Guinea. Ghana, Mali, Morocco, and the United Arab Republic.

Over the next two years, the Casablanca bloc gradually lost cohesiveness as a grouping and finally became submerged in the larger Organization of African Unity. Morocco distinguished itself from the other countries by giving vent to its basic conservatism, and Guinea had a falling out with the USSR over what Ahmed Sékou Touré apparently regarded as Soviet efforts to push his regime toward extremist policies. But the radical states of Ghana, Mali, and the United Arab Republic—plus Algeria after it gained independence in 1962—remained at the heart of the Soviet approach to the Third World for a number of years thereafter. More important, the behavior of these states seemed to confirm the Soviet judgment that genuine revolutionary opportunities existed in their domains. Not only did they show increasing willingness to collaborate with the USSR on matters of foreign policy, but they also indicated at least a desire to move in the direction of radical domestic reforms.[14]

For Moscow, the thorny issue during these years was how to nurture such "progressive" trends so that perceived revolutionary potential might ultimately be realized. Contrary to earlier Soviet assumptions, the "deepening" of the revolution had not swept away the existing leaderships of these states and brought new rulers to the fore; rather, the old leaders had themselves been responsible for the adoption of more radical postures. Equally important, few steeled Marxist-Leninists yet existed in any of the countries involved, and as the Guinean episode clearly underscored, current rulers displayed great sensitivity to anything which smacked of either internal or external challenges to their own authority.

Hence, despite considerable misgivings on the part of some Soviet analysts and political figures,[15] the USSR wound up endorsing the credentials of "revolutionary democrats"—statesmen "who sincerely advocate noncapitalist methods for the solution of national problems and declare their determination to build socialism."[16] Underlying this endorsement was a twofold calculation. First, Moscow believed that by encouraging local Marxist-Leninists to work together with the "revolutionary democrats," it could "educate" the latter to embrace "scientific socialism" wholeheartedly and reshape their societies and policies accordingly. In line with this belief, the USSR even pressed the formal Communist parties in the United Arab Republic and Algeria to disband and join the official government parties in the two countries. Second, Moscow deemed that the USSR could reinforce such local "educational" efforts by selective measures of its own, especially by providing political training and by extending economic assistance to enterprises in the state sector.[17]

Life again administered disappointments, however. By 1965, Soviet commentators were acknowledging that the "revolutionary democratic" states faced many severe problems, especially in the economic realm.[18] These analysts soon began to suggest that the revolutionary process there would probably turn out to be more protracted than originally forecast.[19] The overthrow of President Ahmed Ben Bella of Algeria by Colonel Houari Boumediene in June 1965 produced yet another shock. While Boumediene's perspectives and the nature of his policies greatly reduced the specific damage to Soviet interests, the coup pointed up the possibility that the "revolutionary democrats" did not have the requisite skill and resources to forestall, or at least to thwart, internal challenges and that "reactionary" takeovers in their constituencies were not wholly inconceivable. The ouster of President Kwame Nkrumah in Ghana in February 1966 transformed this possibility into reality.

In the aftermath of Nkrumah's overthrow, Moscow undertook a fundamental reexamination of its outlook toward the Third World in general, and it reached two key conclusions: (1) The "revolutionary democratic" leaders in the Third World suffered from such monumental faults that they would probably never effect a transition to "genuine" socialism.[20] (2) The Third World offered no promise of great revolutionary advances in the discernible future, for "reactionary" forces still retained the upper hand over "progressive" forces everywhere. As one Soviet writer put it with respect to Africa, "the effective achievements of the national liberation movement on the continent, the establishment, in a few years, of dozens of new national states tended to create the erroneous impression that the struggle was almost at an end, that the way to liberation was easy and the forces of imperialism were played out"; but now "as the African revolution gains in depth, the internal weaknesses and objective difficulties in the liberation movement on the continent become increasingly evident."[21] At the heart of the problem, according to Soviet commentators, lay the prevailing conservatism of African society.[22]

Out of this reassessment, in turn, gradually emerged a new Soviet approach to the Third World. This approach, aptly characterized by one Western observer as a "strategy of counterimperialism,"[23] had several components. On the political plane, it entailed emphasis on states and political groups of some inherent importance rather than on those which happened to qualify as "progressive" by Soviet standards. No longer, in short, would the USSR pursue revolutionary will-o'-the-wisps; instead, it would select countries for courtship on the basis of their intrinsic significance. Tied in with this new political pragmatism was a geographic—or, to be more precise, a geopolitical—feature. Henceforth, Moscow would concentrate its attention on the countries in a broad arc to the south of Soviet borders, from North Africa around to South Asia. These countries included not only "progressive" Arab states such as Algeria and the United Arab Republic, but also states formally aligned with the West such as Turkey and Iran. Finally, economic relations would take place in a different context. Instead of trying to use economic aid to win political influence, the USSR would exploit its own political and economic strength to gain privileged economic positions for itself. In effect, it would seek to produce an "international division of labor" with Third World countries.[24] After this new approach had gradually been implemented over a period of several years, Premier Aleksey Kosygin finally accorded it formal sanction in early 1971 in his report to the 24th CPSU Congress.[25] .

The Third World has, of course, never surpassed the United States (with its superpower capacities), Western Europe (with its imposing combination of military and industrial might), and East Asia (with its increasingly hostile People's Republic of China and its economically dynamic Japan) on the list of Soviet priorities. But Moscow's revised approach to the Third World did amount to a downgrading of its general position on that list. Thus, the approach virtually guaranteed a major reduction of Soviet interest in Africa as a whole, and especially in sub-Saharan Africa.

To be sure, Moscow still valued correct and businesslike relations with all African countries willing to deal with it, and Soviet officials behaved accordingly in their contacts throughout the continent. Moreover, the USSR showed itself quite capable of wooing African states that it judged to be intrinsically important. Nigeria afforded the classic example. Although the process was somewhat tortuous and Soviet analysts displayed many qualms along the way, Moscow came to support the central government headed by Colonel (later General)

Yakuba Gowon against the Ibo secessionist forces of Biafra under Lieutenant Colonel Odumegwu Ojukwu, and the USSR eventually extended military assistance to Gowon to help quell the rebellion.[26] Thus, the Soviet Union emerged from the civil war years of the late 1960s with enhanced stature and substantial goodwill in this most populous and potentially wealthy African country.

Nonetheless, the level of Moscow's concern with Africa in toto dropped significantly. Aid figures provide a good index. From 1954 to 1964, Soviet economic aid extended to the Third World totaled U.S. $3,794 million. Of that, $1,766 million went to African countries, with sub-Saharan African states getting $477 million. Over the ensuing decade—i.e., 1965–74—Soviet aid extended to the Third World climbed to $5,634 million. Of that figure, African countries received $715 million, with sub-Saharan Africa garnering only $194 million. If one compares the two periods, Africa's share of overall aid fell from 47 to 13 percent; North Africa's, from 34 to 9 percent; and sub-Saharan Africa's, from 13 to 4 percent.[27]

The Picture since the Mid-1970s

Recent years, clearly, have brought some major changes on the international political scene, and these have in turn stimulated rethinking in the USSR on a number of issues. For example, the energy crisis, the world economic recession, the victories of Communist armies in Indochina, and other developments of the first half of the 1970s seem to have provoked debate about whether the global balance of forces has shifted irreversibly in favor of the socialist world.[28] Similarly, the rising fortunes of some Communist parties in Western Europe appear to have stirred disagreements about the proper course to be followed in this important region.[29] Yet thus far one searches in vain for hints of a basic reexamination of either the assumptions underlying the approach that Moscow adopted toward the Third World in the late 1960s or the fundamentals of that approach.

While Soviet commentators have continued to proclaim that socialism will ultimately triumph in Third World lands, they have evinced great reserve about the prospects for the arrival of such a millennium in Africa in the foreseeable future. To be sure, they have distinguished between states with a "capitalist orientation" and states with a "socialist orientation," but they have defined the latter cate-

gory in modest terms. Two African experts, for example, have
written:

> The socialist orientation is not a special social formation, but a stage of
> transition from precapitalist or early capitalist phases to socialism via
> intermediate stages; it is the highest stage of the national-democratic
> revolution. The movement along that way is headed by the revolution-
> ary democrats, who rely on the awakening sections of the peasantry,
> the working class, the petty bourgeoisie, and the patriotically-minded
> national intelligentsia, including the military.[30]

Pravda has been more expansive on the precise features of a
"socialist orientation." These include:

> . . . the strengthening of political independence on the basis of an
> uncompromising struggle against imperialist exploitation; the establish-
> ment of people's state power; development of the economy; improve-
> ment of the working population's social, material and cultural stan-
> dards; the elimination of feudal exploitation; the restriction of rapacious
> tendencies on the part of local capitalists; a growth in employment;
> strengthening the public sector in industry and the cooperative move-
> ment in agriculture; the application of scientific principles in the sphere
> of economic planning; an alliance with the socialist community; and *the
> gradual creation of the political, material, social and cultural precon-
> ditions for the transition to building socialism.*[31]

Moreover, Soviet analysts have eschewed any suggestion that opt-
ing for the "socialist orientation" automatically removes a state from
the capitalist sphere. Indeed, according to V. Solodovnikov, Director
of the African Institute of the USSR Academy of Sciences in the late
1960s and early 1970s and subsequently Soviet ambassador to Zambia, "a specific feature of the development of the socialist-oriented
countries in Africa is that even after their choice of the non-capitalist
way they are still in the orbit of the world capitalist economic
system."[32]

Since the late 1970s, it is true, Soviet observers have perceived not
only a widening of the circle of countries with a socialist orientation
but also the emergence of "revolutionary democratic parties of a new
type" within some countries in this circle; however, they have carefully distinguished such parties from Communist parties. To describe
these bodies, they have adopted the label "vanguard party" or "a
vanguard revolutionary contingent of workers and peasants." Furthermore, while they have acknowledged the claims of the "van-

guard" parties to be Marxist-Leninist organizations, they have at the same time maintained that only "some points from the theory of scientific socialism have been introduced into the theories of rebuilding African society along socialist lines."[33] *Pravda* in the late summer of 1978 made the Soviet attitude toward these "vanguard" parties abundantly clear by publishing an account of what purported to be a document drawn up at a recent conference of Communist and Workers' Parties of Tropical and Southern Africa. This document called for cooperation between Communists and revolutionary democrats but left no doubt that "detachments of the broad national liberation movements" with "progressive aspirations" in countries like Angola, Mozambique, Ethiopia, Benin, and Madagascar belonged in the latter category.[34]

Equally trenchant, Soviet commentators have argued that "the progress of socialist-oriented countries is obstructed by serious obstacles of an objective and sometimes subjective nature."[35] In expanding upon impediments of the former type, they note, for instance, that "the socialist-oriented countries have found it very difficult to carry out agrarian transformations against the odds of the extremely backward countryside, the shortage of material and financial resources and specialists, the resistance put up by the reactionaries, and the conservative attitudes of the bulk of the peasants."[36] With respect to difficulties of the latter sort, Soviet analysts have contended that "forces that occupy an intermediate position in the socio-class structure" frequently "support progressive initiatives, objectively help to promote the national-democratic revolution and oppose the capitalist way of development, but at the same time are often inconsistent and irresolute and are sometimes unable to take a clear-cut stand on various fundamental problems relating to their country's social development."[37]

Even Ethiopia, the African state for whose revolutionary zeal the Kremlin leadership has appeared to have the greatest respect,[38] confronts major obstacles in Soviet eyes. Despite the fact that "the program of the national democratic revolution has not remained on paper" there, "the country is experiencing great problems." Not only is it "short of personnel" and "funds," but it also "lacks experience." Moreover, "shots fired from around the corner and shooting on the borders follow in close succession."[39]

As a consequence of such impediments, Soviet writers have maintained, "present-day development of individual countries cannot rule out the possibility of departure from or breaches in the non-capitalist way of development."[40] A typical elaboration of this judgment pointed out that while states such as Ghana, Guinea, Mali, Egypt, Algeria, Tanzania, the People's Republic of the Congo, Somalia, the People's Republic of Benin, and Ethiopia have at one time or another declared their commitment to a "socialist orientation," not all have steadfastly upheld this commitment. "Some of them," the article declared, "have either deviated from the progressive line or slowed their advance." In certain cases, this situation has resulted from the ouster of "progressive" leaders because of overestimations and excesses on their parts; in others, it has stemmed from the "betrayal" of "the cause of socialist orientation" by particular leaders or from "interference" in local domestic affairs by "some outside imperialist forces."[41]

For all these reasons, Soviet commentators depict "the shaping of independent Africa" as a "long and complicated process." "Apparently," they say, "an appreciable period of time may pass before all African nations ultimately find the road which accords with their interests." In the meantime, "every year, serious political shake-ups, changes and conflicts occur in one spot on the continent or another," and "imperialist circles carry on their subversive activities, using the services of local reaction opposed to progressive socio-economic changes."[42] Of course, they add, "Africa's revolutionary democratic forces" are displaying increased ability "to learn from their mistakes and setbacks and to adjust their policies to the concrete situation,"[43] and there has been a "growth of the vigilance of the peoples, who are coming to better comprehend the unseemly role that the local bourgeoisie and feudal reaction, in concert with imperialism, are playing at the current stage."[44] Nevertheless, they conclude, it is to be expected that "reactionary forces" will "launch recurrent attacks against the gains of the working people in African countries."[45]

The evidence also indicates that Moscow has persisted in trying to apply standards of intrinsic merit—skewed though these may be by Soviet interests—in its dealings with Third World countries. As the foregoing capsulization of the present Soviet image of Africa implies, embrace of the "socialist orientation" represents a positive step in Soviet eyes, but it does not confer exalted status upon a country.[46] Certainly, it does not trigger any specific commitments on the part of the USSR. By the same token, classification as a country of "capitalist orientation" has no great stigma attached to it. These generalizations are borne out by data on Soviet economic aid extended to the Third World in 1975–77. Known credits totaled $2,566 million. Of these, $459 million were earmarked for African countries. While Algeria ($290 million) and Somalia ($63 million) accounted for the bulk of that figure, Tunisia, categorized as a state of "capitalist orientation" by Soviet writers, received $55 million, and Ghana, another capitalist-oriented country from Moscow's standpoint, got $1 million. Even more telling, the USSR's offerings to Afghanistan, Turkey, and India, none of which qualified as a state of "socialist orientation" (although Afghanistan subsequently earned that label after a military coup in April 1978 led to the installation of a leftist regime there), came to a total of $1,415 million, more than triple its commitments to all of Africa.[47]

As for the geographic focus of Soviet attention in the Third World, there have been many signs that concentration on states in an arc around the USSR's southern borders still prevails. For example, Leonid Brezhnev in his report to the 25th CPSU Congress in February 1976 described the Soviet-Indian treaty of friendship and cooperation as of "enormous importance," and he pledged that "close political and economic cooperation with the Republic of India is our steady course."[48] The electoral defeat of Indira Gandhi's Congress party in the spring of 1977 and the accession to power of rulers less inclined toward cooperation with Moscow by no means caused the USSR to pack its bags and go home; rather, the Soviet Union has taken great pains to persuade the new leaders of India of the mutual interests served by maintaining bilateral relations at a reasonably intimate level. In May 1977, for instance, Moscow extended an additional $340 million of economic aid to New Delhi—despite the fact that India still had $460 million in old Soviet credits that it had not drawn upon. Moreover, the terms that the USSR laid down for the new credits were the most favorable that it had ever offered India.[49]

Similarly, Moscow has evinced no disposition to allow its setbacks in portions of the Arab world in the 1970s to deter it from attempting to exert major influence in the affairs of the Middle East. Not only did the USSR go ahead with economic aid projects in Egypt as a means of preserving a role there even in the face of escalating conflict with President Anwar al-Sadat,[50] but on October 1, 1977, it issued a joint statement with the United States looking toward a Geneva peace conference on the Middle East in which the USSR would function as a cochairman.[51] Later, after the launching of Sadat's peace initiative toward Israel in November 1977 and especially after the Egyptian-

Israeli summit talks under American auspices in the summer of 1978, Moscow sought to prevent itself from being shut out of the peace-making process by encouraging Arab opposition to Sadat's efforts.[52]

As mentioned previously, Moscow provided both Turkey and Afghanistan with whopping new economic credits in 1975–77. In June 1978, during a visit to the USSR by Turkey's Prime Minister Bulent Ecevit, Kremlin officials endeavored to strengthen Soviet-Turkish ties further. The two countries signed a "political document on the principles of good-neighborly and friendly cooperation" and agreed to conclude a three-year trade accord calling for an annual trade turn-over of $1 billion.[53] After the coup that brought a radical government to power in Kabul in April 1978, the USSR moved quickly to effect closer relations with Afghanistan as well. Not only did the two states sign four new economic aid pacts (worth about $16 million) and a new trade agreement, but Moscow also consented to increase the number of its advisers in Afghanistan. By November 1978, the total of Soviet advisers in the country had reached an estimated 3,000–4,000 with as many as half assigned to the armed forces. On December 5, 1978, the USSR capped its undertakings by entering into a treaty of friendship, good neighborliness, and cooperation with the leftist Afghan regime. This provided, among other things, for continued development of cooperation between the two parties "in the military field on the basis of appropriate agreements between them."[54]

Prior to the onset of major political turmoil in Iran during 1978, the Soviet Union pushed hard to expand its commercial links with the Shah's government. By the end of 1977, Iran had become the largest purchaser of Soviet equipment in the Third World, and discussions were under way for Soviet participation in a variety of new Iranian development projects whose value ran to several billion dollars.[55] A contract covering one of the most important of these, the construction of a second trans-Iranian gas pipeline, was subsequently signed in April 1978.[56]

Such links caused Moscow to maintain a public neutrality toward the Shah throughout much of 1978 despite the growing indications of opposition to his rule. However, when it became apparent that the days of his reign were numbered, the USSR mounted a massive prop-aganda campaign to place the blame for Iran's troubles on the United States, to associate itself with the emergent forces of the opposition, and thereby to try to ensure a significant role for itself in the post-Shah era.[57]

As pointed out earlier, the great bulk of the economic assistance that the Soviet Union offered to Africa during 1975–77 went to Algeria and Tunisia. Both of these countries fall within the areas upon which the USSR began to focus in the late 1960s.

Finally, dediction to creating an international division of labor between the developing countries and the USSR has continued to pervade all Soviet discussions of international economic relations. A survey of Soviet-African trade, for instance, depicts the USSR's logical role as a supplier of machinery, equipment, and other producer goods to Africa, and a purchaser of finished and semi-finished goods from African countries. To assist the African nations to expand their exports of the latter types of commodities, according to the article, the Soviet Union has granted "nonreciprocal preferences on the import of such goods," has accepted "goods turned out by industrial enterprises built with Soviet assistance in repayment of credits," has included "special clauses in long-term agreements on the priority expansion of the export of manufactured goods to the Soviet Union," has considered "the potentialities for purchases" in Africa when drawing up plans for the Soviet economy, and so on.[58]

To be sure, a growing number of Soviet analysts have exhibited a sense that the USSR lacks the capabilities to achieve such an ambitious goal in quick order. They have placed mounting stress on the need for a long-term approach to the industrial backwardness of the developing countries. The author of a 1978 article, for example, pointed out that "in order to cut their lag [behind the principal capitalist states] in mean per capita industrial output by even two-thirds, the developing countries of South and Southeast Asia would have to increase their industrial per capita output 16-fold, those of Africa 12-fold, and those of Latin America 3-fold." He went on to say that "estimates have shown that, given the real growth rate of industry from 1960 to 1976, it would take the first group of states over 60 years to achieve even this intermediate goal, while the second group would require at least 40 years and the third—about 30 years." "Even then," he emphasized, "the per capita output of industrial goods would be only an eighth, a sixth and two-thirds of the level attained by the developed capitalist states in the mid-1970s."[59] Implicit in such discussions is a conviction that for years to come the major items of economic utility to the USSR that large portions of the Third World will have to sell will be foodstuffs and raw materials— items for which there is by and large only a limited Soviet demand. Equally telling, these Soviet observers have highlighted the substantial progress toward industrialization that at least a portion of the developing countries have made despite the fact that they remain within the world capitalist system. Thus, one writer noted that the gap in industrial output per capita between "the most economically backward regions" and the "main industrial capitalist centres" declined appreciably between 1960 and 1976—from 1:32 to 1:23 for South and Southeast Asia, from 1:28 to 1:18 for Africa, and from 1:5 to 1:4.5 for Latin America.[60] Behind such discourses seems to lie a fear that the economic progress of these countries will render them less inclined to establish an international division of labor with the USSR than they would have been if, in accordance with the earlier predictions of Soviet analysts, they had found themselves unable to achieve industrial development while staying within the world capitalist system.

Nevertheless, even these Soviet commentators have persistently contended that the only way for Third World states genuinely to overcome their "age-old industrial backwardness" is through association with "world socialism." That is, "the struggle for a cardinal solution" to the problem of the industrial backwardness of the developing countries "demands that . . . a strictly scientific approach be worked out to the global prospects for the industrialization of the former colonies and semi-colonies according to fundamentally different principles of social and international relations than those inherent in capitalism."[61]

What emerges from this analysis, then, is a picture of basic continuity since the late 1960s in Moscow's broad outlook and approach toward Africa. This, in turn, suggests continuity in the level of priority that the USSR has attached to the continent. In other words, Africa in general has remained well down on a rank ordering of Soviet concerns, with sub-Saharan Africa falling considerably below North Africa on the list.

In light of this consideration, it would appear that the step-up of Soviet activities on the continent since 1975 probably reflects an increase in opportunities rather than any change in approach. Even a cursory examination reveals that throughout most of the 1970s Africa has afforded Moscow more openings to expand its influence than has any other area of the Third World.

A Grand Design?

The preceding analysis of the overall Soviet view of Africa raises serious questions about the existence of any grand design for the continent as a whole in Moscow's policy, for it indicates that the USSR places the countries of the Arab North and the sub-Saharan South in separate categories. A survey of Soviet undertakings in Africa leads to the conclusion that in fact no grand design exists.[62] This is not to say that the USSR lacks objectives in Africa. On the contrary, one can identify four discrete goals that the Soviet Union has pursued with some consistency. It is essential to understand the nature of these in order to appreciate why one can find no broad scheme underlying Soviet activities. Therefore, let us look at each of them briefly.

First, the USSR has sought forms of local support that would ease the logistical problems of maintaining its naval forces in waters surrounding Africa. In this connection, it is important to recall that in the early 1960s Moscow opted for a "blue-water" navy rather than one designed simply for coastal defense.[63] By 1964, the Soviet Union had deployed surface combat ships for the first time in the Mediterranean Sea—i.e., in the North African area.[64] Since then, it has extended regular naval activities to the waters along both the east and west coasts of Africa.

That the USSR has wanted to work out arrangements with local governments that would facilitate these operations is beyond doubt. For example, it has requested and received permission for its vessels to make calls at a variety of ports in littoral states.[65] During the 1970s, it gained regular access to port facilities in Conakry, Guinea, for its West African Patrol and to air facilities elsewhere in the country from which its naval aircraft could carry out aerial reconnaissance of Atlantic sea lanes and U.S. carrier transits along them. But when Guinean President Sékou Touré in the late 1970s decided to abandon his decade-old policy of hostility toward his immediate neighbors and heavy dependence on Moscow, he cut off Soviet use of the air facilities.[66] In the early 1970s, the Soviet Union acquired more or less exclusive use of seven airfields in Egypt from which it appears to have conducted, among other things, reconnaissance of the Mediterranean, and it obtained the right to various kinds of services at four harbors on Egypt's Mediterranean coast—Port Said, Alexandria, Mersa Matruh, and Sollum—and at Berenice on the Red Sea. At Alexandria, the USSR enjoyed first call on a shipyard for heavy repair and maintenance; at Mersa Matruh, it even had construction under way of some facilities designed solely for its use. As a result of the gradual deterioration of Soviet-Egyptian relations which began in 1971, however, Moscow by early 1976 had lost all these forms of support.[67]

Also in the early 1970s, the USSR persuaded Somalia to let it set up a naval complex at Berbera on the Gulf of Aden and to give Soviet planes access to airfields in locations from which they could reconnoiter the Indian Ocean. By the mid-1970s, the Berbera complex comprised a deep-water port, housing for about 1,500 persons, a communications facility, storage facilities for an estimated 175,000 barrels of fuel, an airfield eventually to have 13,000 to 15,000 feet of surfaced runway, and a facility for handling and storage of tactical missiles.[68] Somalia's expulsion of all Soviet advisers in November 1977 over Moscow's supply of arms to Addis Ababa, however, ended all the privileges that the USSR has acquired in Somalia.[69]

The treaty of friendship and cooperation that the USSR signed with Angola in October 1976 called for "cooperation in the military sphere" on the basis of unpublished "agreements which are being concluded between them." This "cooperation" has included Soviet access to Luanda airfields for purposes of conducting reconnaissance flights over the sea lanes of the Atlantic Ocean and visits of Soviet military vessels to Angolan ports.[70]

Finally, according to the treaty of friendship and cooperation that the Soviet Union concluded with Ethiopia in November 1978, the two states "shall continue to cooperate in the military field" in "the interests of ensuring the defense capability" of both. Prior to the initialing of this treaty, there had been reports that the Soviets had at least temporarily set up a "floating base" at one of the Dahlak islands off Massawa to provide upkeep for their units operating in the Red Sea.[71]

What general import all these efforts have, on the other hand, is a matter of controversy, for the longer-range motives behind them remain murky. As many observers have pointed out, the Soviet navy over the last two decades has developed substantial new capabilities to contribute to strategic deterrence, to deny an adversary the use of the sea by disrupting sea lanes, and to establish a naval presence abroad to back up Soviet foreign policy.[72] Furthermore, as other commentators have underscored, broad Soviet statements of military doctrine have contemplated the employment of all these types of capabilities.[73] Yet no one can say with assurance how Moscow weights these missions in the specific context of Africa and its surrounding waters—most critically, what importance it attaches to strictly military concerns as opposed to politico-military concerns. Consequently, speculations on the subject can and do differ.[74]

Any attempt to resolve the controversy definitively here would plainly be fruitless. Nevertheless, it is worth noting one consideration that may bear indirectly on the issue. Thus far, the Soviet Union has not managed to acquire in Africa bases in the traditional sense (i.e., territory and/or facilities over which it exercises treaty-based rights of sovereignty), and this state of affairs inherently tends to impose constraints on the balance that Moscow strikes with respect to naval missions. To be sure, it makes little difference in terms of support for the deployment of Soviet naval forces whose flag flies over an installation as long as those forces have access to it;[75] but in calculations regarding the priority of missions, Moscow cannot with impunity ignore the absence of nominal sovereignty and the need to retain the goodwill of the countries furnishing support. The Egyptian and Somalian cases aptly demonstrate that support for Soviet naval forces may evaporate if a local government perceives Soviet actions to be contradictory to its own interests—and that such a development can seriously complicate Soviet deployments.[76] This consideration suggests that the USSR may well elect to concentrate on the sorts of undertakings which are mutually acceptable to it and to local governments as long as it continues to lack wholly satisfactory means to project power into the region independently and thus to require the logistical support of local governments. These for the most part are likely to fall into the "naval presence" category.

Second, the Soviet Union has endeavored to gain a voice in African affairs. To some extent, this goal has manifested itself in terms of military activity. From 1970 through 1977, for example, the USSR has maintained an average of 51 ships a day in the Mediterranean.[77] Concentrated in the eastern portions of the sea, these forces have served, among other things, to register continuing Soviet concern with the Arab–Israeli conflict—a matter of importance to all the states of North Africa and especially to Egypt. Indeed, the Soviet Union has on occasion employed these forces to affect the course of the conflict.[78] While the USSR's use and improvement of the naval facilities at Berbera, Somalia, probably had more to do with Soviet activities in the Indian Ocean than with anything else,[79] it should not be forgotten that Berbera lies close to the strategic Strait of Bab el Mandeb. To exit from the Red Sea, all vessels must pass through this narrow passageway. Thus, a state that militarily dominated the seas near the Strait would possess a great deal of potential influence in the countries of the Red Sea littoral. In other words, it would be in a position to affect developments in the Horn of Africa, as well as in a number of key Middle Eastern states. Although a number of considerations entered into the Soviet Union's decision in late 1977 to help Ethiopia expel the invading forces of Somalia from the Ogaden, significant among them was a desire to solidify its standing among African countries generally. Because the borders that African states have inherited from the colonial powers typically defy ethnic, economic, and geopolitical rationality, the Organization of African Unity has sought to avoid chaos by establishing the cardinal principle that these borders should not be altered by force, and Somalia's actions violated that principle in the eyes of most African governments.[80] Last but not least, one purpose behind Moscow's extension of massive military aid to the MPLA in Angola during 1975–76 seems to have been to stake out a role for the USSR in Southern Africa. Moscow recognized that the collapse of the Portuguese empire in Africa had fundamentally altered the situation in the region. As a result of the disintegration of what had been a fairly solid phalanx of white redoubts, it was now conceivable that all the states in the region might come under black rule in the not too distant future. Consequently, Soviet leaders sought to win the respect of national forces still waging guerrilla struggles in Southern Africa by demonstrating that the USSR had both the capacity and the will to provide effective military assistance to friends there.[81]

But hints of a Soviet desire to have a say in the continent's affairs have by no means been confined to military action. Moscow has gone to some lengths to court the larger and more significant African states, regardless of their particular political orientations. For instance, it has promised to help Nigeria build what, when completed, will constitute the largest iron and steel complex in Africa. Since the selection of a site for the complex in July 1975 and the signing of an agreement the following month that committed the USSR to provide a detailed design for it, however, negotiations on the precise terms of Soviet participation have proved difficult.[82] As of the summer of 1979, the issue remains unresolved. In 1975, Soviet officials began to conduct negotiations with Morocco concerning an agreement on development of phosphate deposits at Meskala. This proposed agreement called for Soviet construction of extraction and processing facilities in return for a guaranteed supply of phosphate rock for a specified number of years. The negotiations hit a temporary snag in late 1975–early 1976 after the USSR decided to support the undertakings of the Polisario Front, a guerrilla group seeking independence for the Spanish Sahara, which Morocco and Mauritania had carved up between them in 1975.

But Moscow succeeded in reviving the project in 1977, evidently by providing private assurances to the Moroccans that it recognized their territorial claims in the Spanish Sahara. The two countries formally consummated the deal in March 1979. Their agreement covers a 30-year period, and according to Rabat, the combined credit and trade transactions contemplated under it will total $10 billion by the end of the 20th century, thus making Morocco the USSR's chief African trading partner.[83] Finally, Moscow in 1975–76 wooed the new military regime in Ethiopia despite the USSR's existing treaty of friendship and cooperation with Somalia, Ethiopia's much smaller and less populous neighbor which regarded Ethiopia as its archenemy. This courtship led in December 1976 to the signing of a secret accord which provided for Soviet arms shipments to Addis Ababa valued, according to Western estimates, at somewhere between $100 million and $200 million. Within little more than a year, Soviet arms deliveries to the Ethiopian military government had passed the $1 billion mark.[84]

Furthermore, Moscow has since 1978 gone to great pains to discourage formation of what it calls "miniblocs" in Africa. In the wake of the Soviet-Cuban intervention in the Horn in 1977–78 and especially since the invasion of Zaire's Shaba Province in the spring of 1978 by former Katangese gendarmes based in Angola and operating with weapons supplied by the Soviet bloc, moderate African states have sharply criticized the behavior of both the USSR and Cuba on the continent, and some have proposed the creation, with the assistance of Western powers, of pan-African military forces to deal with local conflict situations. The USSR has campaigned strongly against such schemes, denouncing them as "neocolonialist" efforts to split the Organization of African Unity (OAU) and turn it away from nonalignment. Soviet commentaries on the subject have fairly explicitly acknowledged that forces of this kind would inevitably limit Moscow's influence on African events.[85]

Third, the USSR has tried to undermine Western influence in Africa. This objective has long figured in Soviet behavior on the continent, but the signs of its existence have altered substantially in recent years. Up to the mid-1960s, offers of economic aid, in the form of both credits and technical assistance, had been the key indicator of Soviet desire to reduce Western influence in Africa. With Moscow's decision to focus its attention on those countries in an arc around the USSR's southern borders, however, the volume of such offers to African states had inevitably declined.[86] Moreover, Soviet leaders have apparently felt less need to challenge Western economic positions on the continent,[87] for they have viewed these as weakening because of essentially natural economic processes. Certainly, Soviet analysts have interpreted the proportional drop of Western investments in the Third World since the mid-1960s—and the proportional rise of Western investments in advanced industrial countries—as a trend of some consequence.[88]

At the same time, the USSR has clearly maneuvered to establish itself as sole military supplier and/or political patron of a number of African states which formerly looked fundamentally to the West for support.[89] In the early 1970s, for instance, Moscow began to extend military aid to the repressive and erratic regime of Idi Amin in Uganda. By June 1975, the USSR had provided an estimated 12 MIG fighters and bombers, 60 light tanks, 100 armored personnel carriers, 50 antiaircraft guns, 200 antitank weapons, and 850 bombs and missiles, and the weapons were still flowing. After the Israeli raid at Entebbe Airport in July 1976, Moscow even replaced the MIG aircraft that the Israelis had damaged or destroyed. Not until late 1978, when it became apparent that Amin's days in power might be numbered, did the USSR cease to meet his military requests, and even then it did not end its diplomatic support until after he had retreated from Kampala in the face of a military drive by invading Tanzanian and Ugandan exile forces in April 1979.[90] In 1974, the USSR also concluded a $1 billion military agreement with Libya. Deliveries under this agreement have included MIG-23 fighters, TU-22 medium bombers, various types of missile systems, and an array of modern ground equipment. Since the weaponry that Libya has received exceeds what the Libyan armed forces can absorb, the USSR has in effect provided Libya with the means to function as an arsenal for local African and Middle Eastern forces that enjoy Tripoli's favor.[91] As mentioned earlier, the Soviet Union in late 1976 committed itself to furnish major amounts of arms to Ethiopia, and Moscow became Addis Ababa's only source of supplies after the Ethiopian Military Council expelled most American personnel from the country in April 1977. By the spring of 1978, the USSR had furnished more than $1 billion in military aid to the Addis Ababa government.[92] Even Soviet support for the MPLA in Angola in 1975–76 seems in part to have reflected a wish to erode Western influence. Moscow obviously did not want to see the Portuguese colonial regime there give way to a government composed of forces backed by the West in general and by the United States in particular.[93]

Fourth, the Soviet Union has striven to keep the People's Republic of China (PRC) from expanding its role in Africa and to reduce that role in every way possible. Rivalry between the two Communist powers for influence on the continent dates from the late 1950s and the early stages of the Sino–Soviet dispute. During the last half of the 1960s, Peking's preoccupation with domestic conflict arising from the Great Proletarian Cultural Revolution and China's stridently militant line in foreign policy combined to lessen greatly the challenge that the PRC posed to the USSR in Africa, but since the end of the Cultural Revolution in 1969 Peking has revived its efforts to expand its influence in the area. In the process, it has carefully nurtured traditional ties and branched out in new directions as well. During the early 1970s, it forged particularly strong links with many of the African liberation movements.[94]

Several Soviet actions in Africa in recent years appear to have been direct responses to Chinese ventures. For instance, although Tanzania had long maintained warm relations with China and displayed a general coolness toward the USSR, Soviet President Podgornyy stopped first in Dar es Salaam on his trek around Africa in early 1977, and he took that occasion to announce a new $19.2 million Soviet loan to Tanzania.[95] In addition, Moscow has commenced to provide military aid to the guerrillas from Southern Africa training in Tanzania and Mozambique, thereby ending what was once a Chinese monopoly.[96] Elsewhere, the USSR in 1976 countered a 1975 Chinese loan of $17 million for economic development to Guinea-Bissau, which had gained independence in September 1974 after a protracted guerrilla war against the Portuguese, by offering the fledgling state credits of $13 million. The latter figure, it is worth noting, exceeds the economic aid that Moscow has extended to Angola, a close ally and a country with nearly 10 times the population of Guinea-Bissau.[97] Perhaps most striking, the main factor behind the USSR's initial decision to back the MPLA in Angola in early 1975 seems to have been a desire to prevent the Chinese from becoming the dominant outside power in Southern Africa. China had been providing military advisers and arms for Holden Roberto's National Front for the Liberation of Angola at camps in Zaire since late 1973/early 1974, and the Chinese had also worked more harmoniously than the Soviets with the Front for the Liberation of Mozambique (*Frente de Libertação de*

Moçambique—FRELIMO), the Zimbabwe African National Union (ZANU) of Rhodesia (the Rhodesian group with the most effective guerrilla forces), and the South-West African People's Organization of Namibia. Thus, China was in a good position to have considerable sway with any black governments that might emerge in the region as the result of the new strategic situation produced by the demise of the Portuguese empire. Moscow apparently deemed some action necessary to ward off this threat, and it commited itself to assisting the MPLA.[98]

These, then, constitute the discernible Soviet goals in Africa. They hardly indicate the existence of a grand design. To begin with, the bearing any individual objective has had on Soviet behavior has varied widely from place to place. To some extent, of course, this variation has reflected the relevance of that objective in specific contexts, but relevance alone does not account for it. There have been cases where, on the surface of things, a particular goal would appear to be relevant yet has had no perceptible impact on Soviet actions. The search for local support for Soviet naval forces, for example, has not visibly affected Soviet activities vis-à-vis Ivory Coast. Nor has the wish to curtail Chinese influence seemed to have much relationship to what the USSR has been doing in most of North Africa or in the Horn. By the same token, the wish to have a voice in African affairs has had no obvious effect on Soviet courtship of Guinea-Bissau or Tunisia. Finally, the intent to undermine Western influence has played no identifiable role in Soviet dealings with Chad, Senegal, or Mauritania.

More significant, there has been no evident hierarchy of objectives. In some situations, to be sure, the USSR has managed to pursue a number of the goals simultaneously because they have been essentially complementary. For example, the Soviet Angolan operation served both to check the growth of Chinese influence and to diminish Western influence. In other situations, however, Soviet objectives have conflicted, and Moscow has not always resolved the resultant policy dilemmas in the same way. For instance, it initially opted to furnish arms to Ethiopia to reduce Western influence in that country, even though it risked loss of naval facilities in Somalia by doing so. Then, after Somalia threw its regular military forces behind the Somali guerrillas fighting to wrest the Ogaden region from Ethiopia, Soviet desire to win a major voice in African affairs appears to have figured prominently in Moscow's decision to continue to supply arms to Ethiopia, for the USSR found that most African countries opposed Somalia's effort to alter borders by means of force. In this particular case, these two goals seem to have taken precedence over that of garnering local African support for the deployment of Soviet naval forces. By electing to endorse the Algerian-backed, anti-Moroccan Polisario Front in the former Spanish Sahara in 1975–76, on the other hand, Moscow plainly subordinated the same two goals to other considerations. This endorsement antagonized Morocco and caused it to back away from the phosphate deal with the USSR that it was weighing—a deal which would create substantial "division of labor" between Morocco and the Soviet Union and thereby reduce Western economic influence in the North African country. Soviet backing of the Polisario Front also complicated Moscow's attempts to gain a significant say in continental affairs, for Algeria subsequently failed to carry the day on the Saharan issue in either the OAU or the Arab League. While the precise reasons for the USSR's actions in this instance are by no means clear, a wish to retain Algeria's goodwill in order to ensure that the port of Algiers remained open to calls by Soviet ships may well have entered into Soviet calculations. That Algeria's general capacity to provide support for the projection of Soviet power into Africa and its environs figured heavily in Soviet thinking seems likely in view of the timing of the decision. Moscow apparently decided to support the Polisario Front in late 1975 during the same period in which the Boumediene government made the Algiers airport available to the USSR for use in connection with the Angolan crisis.[99] The absence of any consistent ordering of Soviet objectives is further attested by developments in Soviet-Moroccan relations during 1977–78. As mentioned earlier, the USSR evidently reversed itself on the Saharan question and thus persuaded Rabat to go ahead with the phosphate deal.

Policy in Sum

In light of the foregoing discussion, one can best characterize recent Soviet policy in Africa as reactive and opportunistic. It has been reactive in the sense that key Soviet initiatives have come in response to developments and trends in the African countries themselves and to the behavior of other major outside powers. On balance, local African conditions have been of greater importance in triggering Soviet actions. Had not elements of the Ethiopian military overthrown Haile Selassie and subsequently embarked on a "socialist" revolution, for example, it is debatable whether Moscow would have had the chance to enhance its position in Ethiopia. Certainly, the opportunity to do so would not have been as great. Similarly, the inability of the MPLA, FNLA, and UNITA to form some type of coalition government in Angola and the MPLA's determination to install itself in office by whatever means required gave the USSR the essential opening that led to its Angolan operation. Even the Soviet Union's arms agreements with Libya and Uganda resulted from local requests, not from prodding on Moscow's part. The behavior of outside powers has served primarily to set the limits of Soviet actions.

Soviet policy has been opportunistic in the sense that the USSR has sought to take advantage of virtually every opening that has presented itself in Africa, whatever Moscow's prevailing political line or existing commitments. The situation in the Horn affords a classic illustration. During the early 1970s, the Soviet Union provided Somalia with sufficient arms to transform itself into a significant military power, despite the fact that Moscow knew full well that the Somalis claimed territory—including the Ogaden region of Ethiopia—which officially belonged to Somalia's neighbors. At the same time, the USSR rendered support to Eritrean nationalists fighting the Addis Ababa government for independence from Ethiopia.[100] Yet in the wake of the 1974 military takeover in Ethiopia, the Soviet Union began to woo the new rulers in Addis Ababa. Moreover, when the growing internal chaos stemming from attempts at far-reaching social reforms and from the challenge of secessionist movements in Eritrea and the Ogaden compelled the Ethiopian military government to turn to Moscow for the additional arms that the country's traditional supplier, the United States, was reluctant to furnish, Soviet leaders responded favorably. As noted previously, the USSR soon became Addis Ababa's sole source of weapons. To try to reconcile Somalia and the Eritrean liberation forces to this state of affairs, Moscow promoted a plan for a federation of Marxist countries that would encompass Ethiopia, Somalia, Eritrea, and even Djibouti (the small French colony on the Red Sea that Mogadiscio regards as Somali patrimony but that became independent in June 1977). However, both Somalia and the Eritreans rejected the plan.[101] For a time, Moscow continued to supply weapons to Somalia as well as to Ethiopia, but after Siad Barre committed regular Somali troops to the struggle in the Ogaden in July

1977, the Soviet Union cut off the flow of arms to Mogadiscio. It was this action that ultimately prompted Somalia to expel all Soviet advisers.

The opportunistic aspect of Soviet policy has had drawbacks for the USSR that all too frequently get overlooked in recitations of the advances that the Soviet Union has registered in Africa during the 1970s. Specifically, the USSR's position in several areas where it has become deeply involved rests on something less than the solidest of foundations. The Horn and Angola provide the prime examples.

In the Horn, Soviet leaders have now in all likelihood alienated Siad Barre sufficiently to make it impossible for the USSR to recoup its losses in Somalia so long as he remains in power.[102] In addition, Moscow's backing of Ethiopia has poured new coals on the already hot fires of ire that Egypt and Sudan manifest toward the Soviet Union, for these two African countries, both Red Sea powers themselves, have supported the causes of the Eritreans and Somalia. Thus, Soviet fortunes in the region have come to depend essentially on Ethiopia, and particularly on the Mengistu regime.

Yet there have been telling signs of a lack of total harmony between Mengistu and Moscow. Despite—or, perhaps more accurately, because of—Addis Ababa's heavy dependence on the USSR and its Cuban ally for military aid, Mengistu showed reluctance throughout 1977 to dispense with the services of a small team of Israeli military advisers that had been working in Ethiopia since the first part of the year, and he did not in fact order the advisers to leave until Soviet officials became so incensed by Israeli Foreign Minister Moshe Dayan's open acknowledgment of Israeli military cooperation with Ethiopia that he had no choice in the matter. Even then, he did not entirely sever military ties with Jerusalem.[103] It would also appear that Mengistu has wanted more direct Soviet and Cuban assistance in the fighting in Eritrea than he has been able to get.[104] Although he has managed to make headway in his efforts to crush the Eritrean rebels anyway,[105] Moscow's unwillingness to back him to the hilt has clearly vexed him. Most important, Mengistu has not proved receptive to Moscow's proddings to set up a vanguard party as quickly as possible. While he has paid lip service to the idea of creating such a party, he has dragged his feet on the matter. Indeed, he has gone to some lengths to underscore the vanguard role of the Military Council, and he has been most sensitive to any incipient challenges to his authority from civilians of traditional Marxist-Leninist persuasion.[106] Just how deep his personal ideological convictions run is hard to say, but one cannot help observing in this regard that prior to late 1977 his Marxist-Leninist rhetoric escalated in accord with his growing need of Soviet assistance to stay in power.

Were Mengistu to disappear from the political scene, however— and Addis Ababa has disclosed that there were nine attempts to assassinate him between September 1977 and June 1978 alone[107]—the friction between the USSR and Ethiopia might well increase. His departure could conceivably bring to the fore a currently quiescent "moderate" faction within the Ethiopian armed forces which would probably not be as favorably disposed toward the Soviets as he is.[108]

The situation in Angola has features even more disquieting from the viewpoint of the USSR than that in the Horn. In the first place, the denouement of the civil war turned out to be far less decisive than it looked in 1976. During 1977–78, the MPLA government headed by Agostinho Neto encountered some continuing resistance from secessionists in the Cabinda enclave and from FNLA elements in the north and northwest, and it faced a major insurgency problem in the center and southeast, where a large segment of UNITA forces had survived their earlier battles with Cuban and MPLA units and were now exploiting UNITA's roots among the Ovimbundu, Angola's largest tribe, to wage an effective guerrilla war against the largely Kimbundu-based Neto regime.[109] Indeed, Cuba in late 1977 apparently had to expand its military forces in Angola by about 20 percent to help the MPLA forces try to cope with the situation.[110] Furthermore, Jonas Savimbi, the leader of UNITA, ruled out any compromise with Neto and the MPLA unless Cuban and Soviet personnel left the country.[111]

In mid-1978, the Luanda regime decided to reinforce its efforts to pacify the countryside by attempting to deprive the rebels of support from at least neighboring outside powers, and by early 1979 it had made some progress toward this goal. For instance, the Neto government in the wake of the invasion of Zaire's Shaba Province in March 1978 by former Katangese gendarmes based in Angola, moved to reduce the long-standing hostility of Zaire's President Mobutu Sese Seko and to normalize Angolan-Zairian relations. Subsequently, Neto paid a state visit to Kinshasa, and Mobutu traveled to Luanda on a similar mission. During the latter's stay in Angola, the two countries agreed to reopen the Benguela railroad—the chief route by which Zaire's copper had reached the sea prior to the Angolan civil war of 1975–76—and concluded other accords on trade and communications. As a result of these developments, the guerrilla forces in the

Cabinda enclave and the north and northwest of Angola appear to
have lost their prime backer, and their activity has greatly diminished.[112] However, the rapprochement's impact in Ovimbundu
territory has been quite limited. Luanda has also put great pressure on
the South-West African People's Organization (SWAPO), which oper-
ates in South African-controlled Namibia from Angolan sanctuaries,
to work with the United Nations to bring about a cease-fire in
Namibia and the territory's transition to independence through
U.N.-supervised elections. The government hopes that SWAPO will
win such elections and set up a government friendly to it in Wind-
hoek. This chain of events would cut UNITA off geographically from
its main supplier of arms, South Africa, and ease the problem of handling the UNITA insurgency. The pressure from Luanda has in fact
caused SWAPO to accept, if reluctantly, the U.N. scheme for effecting
Namibian independence.[113]

Nevertheless, it is by no means clear that the Neto government's
various undertakings will resolve its security problems. As of mid-
1979, for example, there is considerable uncertainty as to whether the
South African government and SWAPO will ultimately adhere to the
terms of the U.N. plan for ensuring Namibian independence and, if
so, whether SWAPO will succeed in dominating the government that
emerges from U.N.-supervised elections. Meanwhile, UNITA continues to cause substantial disruption in the central and southeastern
portions of Angola, even though there seems to be some decrease
since mid-1978 in its capacity to pose difficulties there.[114] Thus, the
USSR could conceivably find itself drawn deeper and deeper into a
political quagmire in seeking to prop up the MPLA regime, or if there is
some move toward reconciliation of the country's diverse nationalist
elements on the basis of Savimbi's conditions, Moscow might be
asked to withdraw its personnel. Unconfirmed reports emanating from
Dar es Salaam suggest that the Soviets are aware of these possibilities
and have been attempting to prevent them from becoming reality. According to the reports, Soviet representatives have contacted UNITA
with a proposal for a cease-fire and for incorporation of UNITA into the
Luanda government as a kind of junior partner—a proposal which
Savimbi has rejected.[115]

Perhaps more troubling from the Soviet perspective than UNITA's
determination to pursue an insurgent course until Soviet and Cuban
advisers leave the country is Neto's unmistakable resolve since mid-
1978 to lessen his dependence on the USSR. The Angolan govern-

ment has renewed ties with Portugal. It has entertained the foreign minister of Belgium and stressed to him the importance it attaches to broadening and diversifying its international links. It has turned to Western companies for assistance in expanding its oil production. And it has avidly sought recognition from and the improvement of relations with the United States, although it has made plain that it will not order the departure of Cuban troops merely to achieve those goals.[116] Moreover, Neto in a speech in early December 1978 underscored the significance of these moves by laying great emphasis on the need to defend "the independence of the party."[117]

These initiatives on Neto's part appear to flow from two considerations. To begin with, Soviet and Cuban assistance in the economic realm has not proved as beneficial as expected. Despite the presence of Soviet and Cuban personnel in virtually every phase of Angola's economic life, the economy remains pretty much a shambles even in mid-1979, three years after the winding down of the civil war.[118] Second, the Angolan president and his supporters are convinced that the USSR encouraged the plotters of an abortive coup against the Neto regime in May 1977. This coup—led by Nito Alves, Minister of the Interior prior to November 1976, and José van Dunem, the political commissar of the army in southern Angola, and involving a group of Portuguese Communists who had come to Angola in late 1975 to escape reprisals for their role in the attempted leftist takeover in Lisbon in November 1975—nearly toppled Neto, and it took a heavy toll of the leadership in Angola. Seven of the 33 members of the MPLA Central Committee and many other party officials perished at the hands of the insurrectionists.[119]

The foregoing analysis, it should be stressed, is not meant to suggest that the Soviet position in either Ethiopia or Angola will inevitably crumble. To the contrary, the needs of both countries for military and other forms of support from the USSR and Cuba may well dictate close ties with Moscow for years to come.[120] Nevertheless, opportunism breeds opportunism, and if the rulers in Ethiopia or Angola perceive ways to enhance their own interests through attenuation of their links with the Soviet Union, Moscow could experience some jolting reversals.

Prospects

While past policy imposes certain constraints on what the Soviet Union can do in Africa in the coming years, it does not necessarily predetermine future policy. Therefore, a few final words on the broad outlook for the years immediately ahead are in order.

Soviet policy toward the continent will depend fundamentally on two sets of variables: (1) Moscow's perspectives on Africa, including the relative priority that it attaches to the continent and the general way in which it approaches the continent, and (2) the opportunities that Africa presents. In trying to speculate about the first set, perhaps the most fruitful tack is to consider what factors might produce changes in current Soviet perspectives and to assess the likelihood of such factors arising.

If Moscow perceived growing chances for what it deemed to be "genuine" Marxist-Leninist breakthroughs in Africa, it might conclude that its stake in developments on the continent had escalated. That conclusion, in turn, could lead to revisions in its approach toward Africa. At the end of the 1970s, Ethiopia probably offers the greatest possibilities for such a breakthrough. Yet Soviet analysts do not hold out great hope for a "real" revolutionary turn of events even there.[121]

A revamping of existing Soviet strategy toward the Third World might also alter Moscow's outlook toward Africa. In view of the fact that the present strategy has not yielded monumental gains for the USSR, such a development is not totally inconceivable, but it does appear unlikely. The current strategy has had some positive results, and Soviet leaders clearly recognize these.[122] Furthermore, events during 1978–79 in Iran, Afghanistan, and a number of other countries around the USSR's southern borders have provided Moscow with major new openings to try to exploit. Hence, the incentives for a modification of approach currently do not seem very strong.

Lastly, a Soviet determination that Africa had become a decisive battleground for great-power competition would obviously bring about a shift in Moscow's perspectives vis-à-vis the continent. In this connection, it should be noted that Soviet observers do assert that "this continent holds an increasingly important place in the policy of the Western powers."[123] Such assertions, however, fall far short of recognizing Africa as the key arena of great-power rivalry. Indeed, one has a hard time imagining how the continent as a whole could ever take on this character in Moscow's eyes. Only specific portions of it—e.g., the eastern parts of North Africa, the Horn, and perhaps Southern Africa—appear at all likely to acquire that degree of significance in Soviet thinking. From a geopolitical standpoint, moreover, it seems highly doubtful that these areas would supersede Europe or East Asia in the USSR's priorities. Moscow's visible preoccupation in early 1979 with the Chinese invasion of Vietnam, a Soviet ally, served to underline the point.

All things considered, then, it appears probable that the USSR will continue to endorse the basic policy framework to which it has adhered since the late 1960s and that the overall parameters of Soviet policy toward Africa will not change. Such prospects mean that Soviet goals on the continent will in all likelihood remain the same, too.

But Soviet policy could still undergo some modification in line with the nature of the opportunities available to the USSR in Africa. One cannot, of course, predict with any certainty what openings the Soviet Union may enjoy in any specific area of the world in the years immediately ahead, but it does seem reasonably safe to say that those in Africa will probably be at least as extensive as those anywhere else in the Third World, and greater than those in most places. Africa at the end of the 1970s is the scene of some of the most intense international and domestic conflicts in the Third World, and this state of affairs will quite likely persist. Such a probability suggests that Soviet activity on the continent will at minimum stay at about the level of the late 1970s and could even mount.

Whether the USSR will continue to operate in as reactive and opportunistic a fashion as it has in the 1970s, however, is a moot point. Repeated Soviet successes in Africa and elsewhere in the Third World, for example, could induce Moscow to cease merely reacting to openings on the continent and to function in an expansionist manner there. Yet it is far from obvious that the USSR will be able to score a long string of triumphs in Africa. Much will depend on the behavior of both African states and outside powers,[124] and Moscow already seems to sense a hardening of attitudes toward the USSR from each of these quarters that limits its actions on the continent. Such, at least, was the implication of Soviet responses to the dispatch of troops by France and Belgium—with logistical support from the United States—to restore order in Zaire's Shaba Province in the spring of 1978, to accusations of Soviet and Cuban involvement in the invasion that had produced the chaos, and to ensuing agitation by a number of African countries for the creation of pan-African forces to deal with similar challenges.[125] As long as Moscow feels inhibitory influences of this sort, the probability of the USSR's embarking on an expansionist path in Africa appears fairly low.

As for Soviet opportunism, it may be significant that during 1978 a few Soviet analysts began to hint that the complexities of intra-African conflicts dictated increased caution about involvement in them.[126] But old habits do not die easily, and Moscow may have to encounter concrete setbacks—noticeably absent to date—before it alters this aspect of its political style. Developments on the continent, especially in those states with which the USSR has forged strong links in the 1970s, and/or the actions of outside powers could administer such setbacks in the future, yet reverses are by no means inevitable. If they do not materialize, one should in all likelihood expect persisting Soviet efforts to take advantage of whatever openings arise—even though exploiting them may require boldness and entail a substantial degree of risk.

3

Russia's Historic Stake in Black Africa

Edward T. Wilson

IN LATE 1976 and early 1977, as Moscow forged far-reaching military ties with Ethiopia, few outsiders knew that a similar alignment was contemplated by Russia nearly three centuries earlier as a means of undermining the Ottoman Empire.[1] Indeed, some of the most astute observers of the Kremlin's current foreign policy are unaware of the historical background to recent Soviet activity in Black Africa. Yet knowledge of Russia's long-standing interests in the continent—not to mention the decades of on-the-spot experience of Russian explorers, military advisers, and political activists—guided Soviet negotiators on that occasion, as it had in the Kremlin's numerous African initiatives since the mid-1950s. These initiatives did not arise from a sudden awareness of the importance of Black African nationalism, as described in the world press; rather, they came in the context of long and patient cultivation of early African political leaders, the production of a substantial body of specialized Russian literature on Africa, and even specific policy precedents.

When, in the 19th century, officers of the Russian Imperial Guard were successful in drawing the present borders of the Ethiopian state, the rationale behind their efforts was not altogether different from that underlying recent Soviet ventures in support of Ethiopian territorial integrity. In fact, most of the basic motivations that guide Soviet involvement in Africa today were discernible in much earlier Russian activity. Then, as now, there was a strong desire to take advantage of local unrest to steer African political development in directions deemed compatible with Russia's global interests. Perhaps even more powerful was the ambition to thwart the designs and curtail the influence of Western nations on the continent. And finally, there was an important strategic incentive to find facilities on African shores which

67

would support Russia's emergence as a world maritime power and minimize the handicap of distance in communications between Russia's Baltic and Far Eastern ports.

In an era when competition for territorial acquisition was a dominant aspect of international politics, Russia's pre–World War II initiatives in Black Africa were not crowned by dramatic success. Attempts to establish colonies in Madagascar and on the Red Sea coast failed; projects to secure protectorates over Ethiopia and part of contemporary Eritrea collapsed; and a bid for a port in Djibouti came to naught. But in the process of playing an active role in the great imperial contests over African real estate, Russia did acquire some key leverage over the activities of Britain, France, and Italy. Moreover, in the 1920s and 1930s, individuals serving the foreign policy interests of Moscow managed to threaten the imperial status quo in British and French colonial Africa. At the same time, they made important contributions to the development of Black African trade unions and nationalist organizations, thereby accelerating the independence process.

Thus, the century of active Russian involvement in the affairs of sub-Saharan Africa was not without distinct ideological and practical benefit for the practitioners of post–World War II Soviet African policy. The legacies of this involvement were to become significant during the efflorescence of African independence in the early 1960s and the era of renewed Russian concern for the region after the mid-1970s.

The Tsarist Period

By the latter part of the 19th century, Russia had established as the cardinal ingredient of its African policy support of indigenous nationalism as a means of undermining the strength of rival European powers. Specifically, its prerevolutionary African efforts were based on the search for allies and local causes through which to develop a pattern of influence. During the last decades of the century, this was evidenced in a firm operating concert with France against Britain. The two powers each consistently supported the other's African initiatives, rarely embarking on new ventures without mutual consultation. As it became clear at the turn of the century that France was losing its bid to thwart British designs in the Nile Basin, Russia characteristically withdrew to a more cautious posture. This probing and opportunist course, typical of early Russian behavior, was to have many subsequent and current parallels.

The first practical attempt to establish Russia on sub-Saharan African shores was made by Peter the Great, whose naval ambitions included the creation of a maritime route to India. In 1723, he dispatched two vessels to inaugurate contact with the "highly esteemed king and owner of the glorious island of Magaskar [sic]."[2] Although the project to set up a Madagascar colony was aborted when one of the vessels proved unseaworthy, the desire for a strategic Indian Ocean way station was not abandoned and indeed became an important item on the list of Russia's subsequent African ambitions.

Catherine the Great (1762–96) brought the Mediterranean and North African area into the Russian ken when, hoping to secure an anti-Turkish ally, she sent Count Alexis Orlov and a Russian fleet to the Aegean in 1770 to help Greece liberate itself from the Turks. Orlov, although he failed to achieve this primary aim, did successfully engage the Turkish fleet, giving Russia a new self-image as a Mediterranean power.[3] Russian naval officers began to explore the Mahgreb littoral, returning with useful geographic and political information. For example, M. G. Kokovstov, as a "Russian noble in search of curiosities," took soundings of the Tunis harbor. In the course of this undertaking he met the Bey, who he reported desired a peace treaty with Russia.[4] Not only were Kokovstov's assessments of local power configurations a good example of the impressive genealogy of Russian political reporting on Africa; his nautical measurements were a fascinating harbinger of contemporary Russian naval interests in this part of the world.

In the Mameluk rebellion in Egypt, Catherine saw a further chance to gain an ally by encouraging local separatism. To support the Egyptian Bey's uprising against the Turks in 1772, Count Orlov sent Russian officers, disguised as Englishmen, with arms and ammunition to Ali Bey, the Mameluk leader. Later in the year, Catherine dispatched a Russian naval squadron to help the Mameluks beseige the Turks at Jaffa. In 1783–84, Russia's first consul in Alexandria, Baron de Thonus, negotiated an agreement whereby Russia would officially recognize the independence of the Beys in exchange for the right to quarter troops in Egypt. As a result, by 1786, one-fourth of the Egyptian militia was composed of Tsarist soldiers, thus allowing Catherine to keep close tabs on Egyptian military positions.[5] Despite the fact that the angered Turks declared war on Russia and crushed the Mameluks in 1788, Catherine did achieve a significant presence and some influence in Egypt.

But it was Ethiopia that ultimately became the focal point of early

Russian involvement in Africa. The apostle of that involvement was a Kievan monk, Porfiriy Uspenskiy (1804–85), who set forth on paper a powerful rationale for Russian religious and political penetration of the area. Heading a Russian spiritual mission to Jerusalem on the eve of the Crimean War (1854–56), he wrote a detailed political history of Ethiopia, stressing its growing political power, its potential for leadership in northeast Africa, and its ideal location for the dissemination of Christianity southward into Black Africa. Were Russia to protect Ethiopian territorial integrity and encourage expansion of the country's borders to the Red Sea coast, Uspenskiy saw an opportunity for the Tsars to reunite the churches of the two states and invite Ethiopia to fuse its apostolic succession with that of Russia. Hence, the head of the Holy Synod would be in charge of Ethiopia's religious and perhaps political affairs.[6]

Later, as plans proceeded for the construction of the Suez Canal, Uspenskiy's arguments for a Russian move into Ethiopia became more compelling. Possibly out of fear of the British reaction to this "religious" scheme, however, the Tsarist government did not immediately act upon Uspenskiy's advice. But his writings did provide a solid body of reference on the political and religious background of the area, and as a result of his theses, the Holy Synod strongly backed Russian involvement in Ethiopia. In short, Uspenskiy's conviction that a strong Ethiopia would be an asset to Russia developed into a cornerstone of Imperial Russia's perspective on Africa.

An economic dimension to Russia's interest in northeast Africa was added by a scientific mission headed by Colonel E. P. Kovalevskiy which arrived in the Upper Nile area of the Sudan in 1847 to explore a gold deposit for the Egyptians.[7] Kovalevskiy, under the auspices of the government-subsidized Imperial Russian Geographical Society, was able to gain important first-hand knowledge of the region and to provide St. Petersburg with valuable intelligence on the relative military capabilities of Ethiopia and Egypt. He also involved Russia in the search for the Nile's sources, an endeavor which had intrigued Europeans since the days of the Emperor Nero. Although Kovalevskiy did not succeed in all his undertakings, he did produce a useful collection of strategic information for Russia and promote interest in African exploration.

Kovalevskiy's activities came at a critical time for the Tsars. After the Crimean War, Britain, to the dismay of St. Petersburg, managed to establish itself in northeastern Africa. Tsarist concern over the

Court of St. James' stake in Africa heightened with the victory over the Ethiopians at the Battle of Magdala in 1868 and with the opening of the Suez Canal in 1869. London's purchase of a controlling share in the Canal Company in 1875 caused the Russians particular anxiety about maintaining free access to the Canal, and the closing of the Canal to their ships during the Russo–Turkish war of 1877 confirmed their worst fears. While St. Petersburg recognized the importance of free access to the Canal to Russia's national security, the British military occupation of Egypt in 1882 doomed Russian and French efforts to prevent Britain from gaining undisputed authority over Suez.

It was primarily this issue that led Tsar Alexander III (1881–94) to plunge his country into the anti-British game in Africa. Russia's world view in the latter part of the 19th century put Britain on the opposite side of a chessboard that included India, Afghanistan, Turkey, Egypt, Ethiopia, the Nile, and Suez. Whatever its failures in the Canal area, there was a persistent and lively prospect that Russia might gain a permanent foothold in Africa—an objective that resulted in repeated efforts to obtain a protectorate over the Danakil region (now Eritrea). A firmly established Russian presence on the shores of the Red Sea could simultaneously afford St. Petersburg an opportunity to thwart Britain's ambition to control a swath of imperial territory from the Cape of Good Hope to Cairo and maintain a secure Suez lifeline to India. In addition, Russian domination of the sources of the Nile might permit St. Petersburg to accomplish the scheme that Egypt's rulers, including now the British, had traditionally feared—namely, the turning of Egypt into a desert through manipulation of the Nile's sources. With all these factors in mind, Alexander III came up with a comprehensive plan to solve Russia's strategic dilemma vis-à-vis Britain by simultaneously blockading the Suez Canal, diverting fresh water from Egypt, unleashing 100,000 Sudanese tribesmen against the British, and inciting India and Afghanistan.[8]

Although this ambitious grand design did not materialize, some of its elements were high on the agenda of a Cossack, N. I. Ashinov, who made a concerted effort to establish a "New Moscow" colony on Tajura Bay at the mouth of the Red Sea in 1888–89.[9] Following a characteristic pattern after the Russian defeat in the Crimean War, Ashinov's expedition was financed and encouraged by the Slavophiles and accompanied by a priest appointed by the Holy Synod. While Ashinov and his 175 Russian settlers set sail for Africa without official recognition, their venture provoked open opposition from the Italians and the British, who were particularly concerned about the arms that Ashinov was delivering to the Ethiopians. In keeping with growing Franco-Ethiopian cooperation, the French, who had a protectorate in nearby Obok, initially welcomed the party. When Ashinov refused to raise the French flag or to acknowledge French sovereignty in the area, however, the French conducted punitive maneuvers, bombarding the settlement and killing some of the settlers. Curiously, the moderate manner in which Tsar Alexander used the Russian navy merely to pull out the survivors tended to solidify ties between Russia and France, which soon afterward entered into a formal military alliance.[10] Although the Tsar thus managed to disassociate himself from the colonization attempt, the head of the Holy Synod and the most prominent Slavophile of his day, Constantine Pobedonostsev, did not fare so well. Because of his prior identification with the effort, he experienced considerable embarrassment at its outcome.

As Ashinov's adventures proved, outright seizure of real estate on the Red Sea coast by Russia would not have been tolerated by Britain, France, or Italy. Nevertheless, the Russians did maintain a steady interest in Tajura Bay and the adjacent Raheita Sultanate, taking every possible opportunity to explore the region and to flirt with local leaders of the adjoining Danakil area. The abortive "New Moscow" initiative also served to stimulate the first significant Russian public interest in the faraway continent. With the spilling of Russian blood on African soil, a new bond had been sealed.

Even before Ashinov's ignominious return in 1889, the Minister of War, General Vannovskiy, had sent a reconnaissance officer to the region. Given the Anglo-Russian relationship in the area, it made particularly good sense for him to choose Lieutenant V. F. Mashkov, a veteran of Russia's Central Asian campaigns who was well versed in his government's African and global strategic priorities. Diplomatic moves on the eve of Mashkov's departure included a request to the French to assure safe passage for this "scientific" emissary of the Imperial Russian Geographical Society and a declaration to the Italians that the Russian government firmly supported Ethiopian independence. The British, for their part, were not misled about the real nature of Mashkov's mission. As *The Times* of London caustically intoned: ". . . the astronomic, geological, meteorological, botanical and zoological observations which the Geographic Society can reasonably anticipate from Mr. Mashkov . . . will prove about as valuable to science . . . as were the startling archeological discoveries of . . . Mr. Pickwick."[11]

Having used Italian arms in his successful bid for the throne, Ethiopian Emperor Menelik II had been obliged to sign the 1889 Treaty of Ucciali, which the Italians had interpreted as legal grounds for declaring a protectorate over the country. However, Menelik was determined to keep the conduct of his foreign affairs independent of the Italians. He gave Mashkov a hero's welcome and asked for further help from the Russians. During this and a subsequent visit in 1891, Mashkov offered military advice to the Ethiopians and made overtures with respect to economic, military, and religious "protection."[12] Mashkov thus had the distinction of becoming the first Russian to hold official talks with an African chief of state. In so doing, he provided assurances of support that were important to the evolution of Menelik's nationalist strategy.

The new Tsar, Nicholas II (1894–1917), proved as interested in Africa as Alexander III. A year after his coronation, he formally received a full-fledged embassy from Menelik II, who was approaching a direct military confrontation with the Italians. Made up largely of military men, this mission was entertained and briefed by all official and Slavophile segments of Russian society. Moreover, it returned to Addis Ababa with modern weapons and the promise of diplomatic and military cooperation.[13]

Without the assurance of political support in Europe—not to mention the modern weapons that were forthcoming from the Russian government—Menelik probably would not have gone so far as to assert his independence and take on the Italians at Adowa. This decision resulted in total victory for his African army in March 1896. (As the first major defeat of a modern European army by a non-European power, Adowa has constituted a source of pride for subsequent generations of African nationalists.) While Russian as well as French arms were helpful in achieving this victory, the strategic advice of Captain N. S. Leontiev, who had come to Ethiopia in 1895 as part of an expedition headed by Captain A. N. Eliseyev, was equally critical. Menelik, in effect, followed the historical example set by Russia in its combat with Napoleon, allowing enemy forces to penetrate well into the interior of the country and then cutting off their sources of supply.[14]

Adowa produced a new high point in Russo–Ethiopian relations: Leontiev was accorded an Ethiopian title and asked to represent Menelik in negotiations with the Italians. Shortly after the battle, a Russian Red Cross mission arrived in Addis Ababa to establish the first numerically significant Russian presence in the area. Its outgrowth, the Russian Hospital, continued to function even into the post–World War II period.

Adowa had other effects as well. In Italy, it caused the fall of the Crispi government, and in Africa, by temporarily eliminating the Italians from the game, it brought about a fundamental realignment of the power balance.

The British, distressed by the losses of their Italian ally, immediately authorized Lord Cromer to undertake a reconquest of the Sudan. For their part, the French seized the moment to proceed with their transcontinental plan to thwart British efforts to forge a north–south Axis, and to gain territory for France. Captain Jean B. Marchand was to cross Africa west to east via the French equatorial regions, secure French claims to the Bahr-el-Ghazal area, and thus establish French power on the West Bank of the Nile southwest of Khartoum. Meanwhile, M. Lagarde would cross Ethiopia from Obok and join Marchand at Fashoda, thus sealing off both banks of the White Nile to the British. Simultaneously, the French encouraged Menelik to occupy the area between his western boundaries and the White Nile.[15]

Following Adowa, Russia as well as France maintained a fully accredited diplomatic mission at Menelik's court, and Tsar Nicholas II specifically and personally instructed M. Vlassov, head of the Russian mission, to cooperate with the French in halting Britain's "Cape to Cairo" dream.[16] Thus, Russia participated in the great rush for the Nile as an active ally of the French and the Ethiopians. By the end of 1897, Menelik had mobilized a quarter of a million Ethiopian troops for the Nile campaign, and, delighted to diversify his dependence on outsiders, he invited both French and Russian officers to accompany his forces.

In fact, officers from the Russian Imperial Guards had prominent commands in Menelik's army, acting simultaneously on instructions from both the Russian and the Ethiopian governments. They provided the Ethiopian columns with invaluable strategic and technical assistance. In the process of exploring the Nile area and supplying the Ethiopian army with modern topographic data, Russian officers also helped to fix many of the current borders of Ethiopia.[17] Over about four months, roughly 20,000 square miles were added to Ethiopian territory with the help of these Russians, and the country was extended southward to the shores of Lake Rudolph.[18]

Of all the Russian adventures in these years, the most interesting in many ways were those of a certain Colonel L. K. Artamonov, who was attached to the troops of Ras Tsesema heading west toward the Nile. Artamonov led Tsesema and his sizable forces to the Sobat River on the White Nile, where they arrived in July 1898. There, sighting no other contingents, they raised the Ethiopian flag to signify Ethiopia's fulfillment of its commitments under the Franco-Ethiopian Nile Convention. Since there were no French troops on the west bank, Artamonov and two Cossacks swam the crocodile-infested river to raise the French flag on the other side.[19]

This success, however, marked the beginning of the end of the Nile campaign for the French and the Ethiopians. A few weeks later, Marchand's beleaguered forces arrived at the Sobat and faced Kitchener's Anglo-Egyptian forces alone at Fashoda. Although the Russians threatened for some months after this diplomatic crisis to throw their support behind the French—to the point of massing Russian troops in the Caucasus—they backed down when it became clear that the French were not going to enter into large-scale conflict with the British. While the Russians maintained their mission in Addis Ababa until World War I, and even contemplated a revival of political and church ties plus new commercial projects,[20] Ethiopia no longer held much promise for anti-British intrigue.

But other parts of the African continent continued to attract attention in St. Petersburg for much the same reasons. The Boer rebellion in South Africa seemed to offer admirable opportunities, if not for gains in Africa, then at least for moves in other portions of the international chessboard. In fact, the initial British reverses in 1899 prompted the Tsar to think aloud to his sister: ". . . it is pleasant for me to know that the ultimate means of deciding the war in South Africa lies entirely in my hands . . . just a telegraphic order to all the troops in Turkestan to mobilize and to advance toward the frontier [of India]."[21] Military maneuvers were actually undertaken in Turkestan, and thought was again given to a possible occupation of the Bosphorus.

In a more direct sense, the Boers themselves received much Russian sympathy and even more practical support. As a popular St. Petersburg newspaper described it, "many thousands of people who have never previously heard of the Boers and who cannot even pronounce their names wish them success, if only because they are standing up for their independence."[22] A volunteer corps of 30 Imperial Guard reservists saw service with the Boers at Bloemfontein, and in 1900 a 26-man Russian medical detachment opened a hospital in New Castle. The Tsar's intense personal interest in the Boer War also prompted the Russian General Staff to assign a liaison officer, Colonel V. I. Romeiko-Gurko, to the Boer front. There he was able to advise the Afrikaner military command and, at the same time, collect valuable intelligence for the Tsar on the contemporary military tactics of the British as well as on the local political situation.

Thus, in the early 20th century a guiding objective of the Kremlin in Africa was to threaten the position of Russia's principal world rivals. Even after the Boer cause seemed lost, Tsar Nicholas clung to the idea of using this powerful indigenous anti-British group against the British. Foreign Minister V. N. Lamsdorff and Minister of War V. V. Sakharov corresponded about possible ways to exploit Boer activism, and even seriously considered an incredible scheme advanced by former Boer General Pinaar-Joubert in 1905. Joubert proposed to incite sufficient black unrest in South Africa and elsewhere in Black Africa to divert British attention during a Boer renaissance. Russia was to obtain a protectorate over the geographical entity that would result from a Boer victory in return for military and financial support. In a moment of weak judgment, Lamsdorff expressed interest in the plan; however, he was later dissuaded from participation by the Russian ambassador to France, who had personally interviewed Joubert.[23]

As the anti-British impetus in Russia's African policy abated in the wake of European diplomatic realignments and the Russian defeat in the 1905 Russo–Japanese War, so too did active Russian interest in Africa. But the results of the long history of Tsarist involvement were not unimpressive. A sizable body of information on Africa had been accumulated which would later provide a useful resource for Communist decision-makers. British and Italian aims had been frustrated, at least temporarily, and Ethiopia's territorial integrity had been maintained. Indeed, its borders had even been expanded. Russia's African initiatives had paid off in terms of leverage against Britain in other parts of the world, as in 1898 when Whitehall adopted a conciliatory attitude toward Russian designs in the Far East in order to temper the Kremlin's involvement in the Nile basin. With comparatively few resources and minimal commitments, the Tsars succeeded in establishing a presence on the African stage at a time when the continent first emerged as an important theater for European political contests.

The Soviet Period: The First Decade

The 1917 turning point for Russia was dramatic. In its wake, the country had to confront not only the consequences of World War I but also civil war, revolution, and Allied intervention. At the same time, there was overwhelming pressure for radical change both in domestic political institutions and social structures and in the very concept of Russia's self-image in the international arena.

The magnitude of their internal and European problems afforded the Bolsheviks every reason to abandon the African intrigues of the Tsars, who despite their noble sense of adventure had failed to make any permanent strategic gains on the continent. But the Bolsheviks did not altogether discard the African concerns of their predecessors. Faced with the prospect of armed invasion by Britain and France, the Communists were determined to undermine both of these powers by mounting rearguard actions in their colonies. Sizable military contingents from the French colonies, for example, had seen action on the western front in World War I, and the Bolsheviks felt that fomenting unrest in these territories might prevent use of such troops against Russia. At the same time, the Communists thought that by sabotaging the colonial rear of Britain and France, they would be striking a blow for revolution in Europe. According to this thesis, they would thereby deprive the capitalist empires of the raw materials and cheap labor that were their lifeblood.

Vladimir Lenin also believed that Africa might become a breeding ground for further wars. In his view, imperialist territorial rivalries in Africa had contributed to the outbreak of World War I. Since the competition could no longer be satisfied by the acquisition of un-claimed African lands, the expansionist drives of imperialist states had to be resolved through the redistribution of existing territory. Therefore, Africa might continue to be a focal point of imperialist conflict.[24]

In the subsequent years of the first decade of Bolshevik rule, a re-markable quantity of literature was produced which reiterated these themes. Much of it was a direct outgrowth of Imperial Russian schol-arship, and many of the authors were holdovers from that earlier era. The dean of the corps was Mikhail Pavlovich (alias Weltman), a men-tor of Lenin. He had begun to write about African affairs during the Boer War, and by the early 1920s he had succeeded in focusing the attention of the new regime on problems of the colonial world, or the "East," as it was known in Communist parlance. An activist like Lenin, he organized study circles in the Russian army; published a monthly journal, *Novyy Vostok;* established an Institute of Eastern Studies; and taught at the Communist University for the Toilers of the East, KUTVU.[25] These undertakings provided solid background for later Black African studies units at Moscow's Lumumba University and at the Soviet Academy of Sciences.

Unhampered by any colonial responsibilities of either an economic or administrative nature and blessed with a rich prerevolutionary data base, Russian scholars devoted considerable sympathetic attention to African social and cultural institutions. In the process they developed remarkably accurate insights into incipient political developments. Pavlovich, for instance, made a concerted effort to analyze the psychological effects of the war and colonial rule on Africans, predicting the emergence of a new and radical world view that could be exploited to the advantage of Soviet foreign policy.[26]

Signs that the Wilsonian principles of self-determination were taking root in Africa first appeared in the coastal areas of British West Africa. Contributors to the *Gold Coast Independent,* for example, asked: "Shall we develop as a free people under the 'Union Jack' or be made hewers of wood and drawers of water?"[27]

Soon afterward, Madagascans took the lead in French Africa, demanding, "Why, if everyone was equal when it came to dying for France, should not everyone have a say in the political future of the empire?"[28] Prince Touvalou Houénou of Dahomey became a prominent exponent of this nationalist viewpoint, wondering whether French Africans had died so "the chains of the survivors could be riveted more securely."[29] To further their cause, Houénou, the Martiniquais René Maran, and other black intellectuals in Paris set up the Ligue Universelle de Défense de la Race Nègre (LDRN) in 1924, an organization inspired in part by the pan-Africanist movement led by Marcus Garvey in the United States.

As the new Communist leadership in Russia saw it, there were good reasons to try to exploit the growing self-awareness among blacks and the anticolonial sentiments that this awareness was breeding in Africa. But such an effort faced enormous obstacles. Aside from the great distances involved, the Bolsheviks had no territorial base or governmental establishment in Africa which might serve as a staging ground for major ventures. Moreover, Africa lacked a proletarian class and a sufficiently high rate of literacy to allow their usual printed propaganda campaigns. Of no less importance, the mammoth domestic problems and limited resources of the Soviet Union imposed severe practical limitations on what could be done in an area of demonstrably secondary priority. In the light of such deterrents, it was a token of the Bolsheviks' energy and missionary zeal that they persisted with their African enterprises.

Official policy emerged within the forum of the Communist International (Comintern), which came into being in 1919 as an alliance of Communist parties to universalize the revolution but by 1922 had devolved into a functional foreign policy arm of the Soviet government. At the Second Comintern Congress in 1920, Lenin elaborated the rationale for Soviet involvement in the colonial world. Departing from Leon Trotsky's contention that colonial revolution would be a by-product of the revolution in Europe, Lenin theorized that a Communist victory in Europe hinged on the prior success of the revolution in the colonies. Given the urgency of colonial revolution, he offered the colonial territories a shortcut to communism, explaining that they could avoid the stage of capitalist transformation by reliance on the Russian proletariat.[30]

Early strategies used by the Bolsheviks to encourage African nationalism included reliance on non-Russian activists to foster revolutionary and anticolonial goals. Black Americans were among the first to be considered for this role, and evidence suggests that during the 1920s the Communists tried to infiltrate the Garvey movement. While they did not accomplish their basic objective, they did manage to persuade a number of black American youths, including Garveyites, to leave America and study in Moscow at KUTVU.[31]

In addition to attempting to enlist American blacks for the revolutionary cause in Africa, the Comintern put great emphasis on the role of the European Communists, particularly the Communist Party of Great Britain (CPGB) and the French Communist Party (PCF). The European Communists did have easier access to the colonies than their Soviet counterparts, and they made some progress toward fulfilling the Comintern's directives. For example, the PCF formed an overseas branch in Tunis and published its message in the local Arabic press. The CPGB, however, proved reluctant to subscribe actively to the dissolution of the Empire. This reluctance illustrates one of the main dilemmas the Comintern confronted in its reliance on European "comrades" as African agents. Their higher loyalties were too often to the metropole—a fact frequently obvious to Africans.

By the Fifth Comintern Congress in 1924, members of the organization recognized that neither American blacks nor European Communists had made any appreciable impact in Africa, and the Comintern determined to involve itself more directly in the undertaking. Subsequently, it tried working through individual African leaders. Whether or not Houénou and his LDRN received financial support from Moscow is uncertain, but it is clear that Lamine Senghor, who revived the LDRN in 1926 and renamed it Le Comité de Défense de la Race Nègre, was an avowed Communist working for Moscow's foreign policy interests. Senghor's Comité established branches in France's main ports and attracted several hundred African members. It also made concerted efforts to gain wide distribution in Africa for its monthly journal, *La Voix des Nègres,* whose editorial stance included warnings that blacks would no longer tolerate being used as "strike breakers, stool pigeons . . . or counterrevolutionary soldiers" and would "turn upon the only author of universal misery: international imperialism."[32]

Another approach the Comintern used was strong support for the Third World movement launched at the Anticolonial Conference in Brussels in 1927. This conference, attended by key nationalist leaders such as Ho Chi Minh, was a forerunner of the later Afro-Asian People's Solidarity Conferences. Representing the French African territories, Lamine Senghor delivered a violent denunciation of imperialism, for which he was rewarded with incarceration by the French government. The concluding manifesto of the gathering cited Russia as "an historical example of a free union of nations and races constructed on the ruins of imperialism" and as the "guiding star" of the liberation movements. Following the Comintern's example, the conference adopted a resolution focusing specifically on the economic plight of the blacks in Africa.[33] A lasting legacy of Brussels was the organization of the League Against Imperialism and for Colonial Independence (LAI). Based in Germany, where it issued a quarterly journal, *The Anti-Imperialist Review,* the LAI maintained European offices in London and Paris, while it had national branches in India, Latin America, and North Africa. For a decade after 1927, the LAI's European offices and its Executive Office in Germany played an active part in the development of the Comintern's relationship with Black Africa.

The Later Soviet Period

The policy changes which emanated from the Sixth Comintern Congress in 1928 were so comprehensive that many observers have been tempted to conclude that the Soviets abandoned the colonial world at this juncture.[34] On the contrary, the years 1927–33 marked a high point in Comintern concern for this area, including Africa. Specifically, the organization sought to exploit the impetus that the world depression gave to indigenous African forces working for independence.

Evidence that interest in the colonies was not waning was provided by the emphasis on colonial issues during the discussion at the Congress and particularly by its adoption of a new revolutionary strategy, the "united front from below." This strategy involved a shift away from reliance on "bourgeois" nationalists and toward dependence on a "fighting front" led by the "proletariat"—a reflection in part of Soviet fears of an imperialist invasion of the USSR in the aftermath of the 1927 rupture in Anglo-Soviet relations. In line with the break with bourgeois nationalists, the Comintern rejected Garvey's movement. However, it still prodded European Communists to increase their activities on behalf of colonial revolution by organizing local parties and trade unions in the colonies, penetrating mass peasant organizations, and making special efforts with women and youth. In this way, it was held, the proletarian class struggle could be carried to less developed societies.

The Sixth Comintern Congress also issued specific directives making Black Africa a priority target among the colonies. Significant evidence of implementation was forthcoming in 1930 with the formation of an International Trade Union Committee of Negro Workers (ITUC-NW). The ITUC-NW became a lively organization largely through the efforts of James Ford, an American Communist, and George Padmore, a Trinidadian who was to figure prominently in Comintern work and later in the African nationalist movement during the early independence era.

By establishing contact through the ITUC-NW with African activists such as E. F. Small of Gambia, I.T.A. Wallace-Johnson of Sierra Leone, and Jomo Kenyatta of Kenya, the Comintern began an important and close association with the nationalist leadership in Britain's Black African colonies. Small and two other West Africans, Garan

Kouyaté of Senegal and Herbert Macauley of Nigeria, were elected to the ITUC-NW, and all three were immediately invited to Moscow. George Padmore, as the ITUC-NW's secretary, opened an office in the Kremlin.[35]

This institutional landmark was followed by a strong emphasis on the employment of trusted African revolutionaries. Men like Small, Wallace-Johnson, and Kouyaté became staunch supporters of the USSR. In the course of their subsequent organizational work among Africans in London, Paris, and West Africa, they transmitted the Communist message through the ITUC-NW mouthpiece, *The Negro Worker,* and provided practical advice to African nationalists. Moreover, as a result of their obvious entrée into the African milieu, and their frequent journeys between Moscow and Africa, they kept the Russians up to date on developments in the African colonies.

A further consequence of the Sixth Comintern Congress was the establishment in the USSR of a program of African studies. It was based on guidelines set forth by the Soviet scholar A. A. Shiik and conducted under the auspices of the Scientific Research Association for the Study of National and Colonial Problems (NIANKP). This new program was sufficiently broad to lay the groundwork for all later Soviet African studies. It covered not only general subjects such as African military conscription and immigration problems but also the situations of individual countries.[36] Moreover, scholars associated with NIANKP's African Bureau—such as I. I. Potekhin—subsequently presided over the renaissance of Soviet African studies in the 1950s.

From the Soviet standpoint, the Depression represented a sign of capitalist weakness and a signal of African unrest, and it ushered in a new era of optimism in Soviet thinking about Africa's revolutionary potential—a point often missed by contemporary European and American observers. In Soviet eyes, the Depression was a clear demonstration to colonial peoples of the relative fragility of the capitalist economic system as well as a threat to the well-being of Black Africans. As suppliers of raw materials, they were suffering from the decline in world market demand; and as colonial subjects, they were enduring a threefold burden of intensified taxation, forced-labor recruitment, and land expropriation. Because of these factors, Soviet observers maintained, discontent had begun to spread throughout sub-Saharan Africa. Examples offered by Comintern writers were the general strike resulting from the protests of market women against a head tax in Nigeria in 1929, attacks on British tax collectors in Kenya, and an uprising against French forced-labor policies during the construction of the Congo–Ocean railroad.[37] Land expropriation, the Communists were convinced, was especially inflammatory in a continent where most of the people were farmers.

Equally promising as a revolutionary sign to Soviet analysts was the first evidence that a modern industrial work force was emerging in Africa. What could provide a better basis for the development of a revolutionary proletariat there? South Africa clearly led other territories in terms of class formation, but the extractive industries of the Congo and West Africa were also accelerating "sociological development" in these areas. Moreover, the maritime industry was aiding the expansion of the black working population and was contributing to labor unrest among many newly urbanized Africans who found themselves unemployed in European ports.[38]

At this point, Russia seemed ready to move into the social and economic vacuum with its own formula for revolution. As Alexander Lozovskiy, Chairman of the Profintern, the Comintern's trade union arm, stated at his organization's Fifth Congress in 1930, "our job is to make use of this huge amount of combustible material, to make allies for ourselves of these vast masses seething with hatred. . . ."[39] The Profintern congress reiterated the importance of organizing Black African workers and pointed to embryonic trade union movements in Sierra Leone, the Congo, and Mozambique as foundations for future Communist activity in Africa. Subgroups singled out for special attention were the urban African workers and the expanding numbers of African sailors and port workers.[40]

It is well to remember here that the Depression encouraged a "two-camp" interpretation of the global economic system and, correspondingly, a revival of long-standing Soviet concerns about a potential military attack on the USSR by the capitalist European powers. At this point, Comintern pronouncements once again betrayed a fear of French mobilization. This was apparently sparked by maneuvers of the African colonial forces in France and by government-sponsored development of railroads in French West and French Equatorial Africa. It was in this context that the Fifth Congress of the Profintern opted to initiate a widespread propaganda campaign in Africa.

By 1931, the Comintern was calling upon the faithful to form new Communist cells within the colonies in Africa and to convert existing factory cells into secret, illegal parties. The ITUC-NW was to be the leading agent of the new strategy, conducting propaganda through *The Negro Worker* and other periodicals and treatises published by George Padmore. In these publications, the USSR was constantly singled out as the economic, social, and political model for Africa. But the message was often more practical and specific: Africans were advised to abandon legal channels as the means for change and attack the entire system rather than merely its representatives, such as individual governors or administrators. Complete revolutionary scenarios were laid out for various African countries. While *The Negro Worker* was confiscated by colonial authorities, it boasted a readership of several thousands in Europe and Africa, thanks to the efforts of its West African correspondents, Wallace-Johnson and Small, and its East African correspondent, Jomo Kenyatta.[41]

Other Comintern offshoots were involved in the effort to realize the African revolution. A case in point was the International of Seamen and Harbor Workers, founded in 1931. This body opened Seamen's Clubs in Africa, encouraged action committees in the port cities, and started trade unions for black maritime workers. During the 1920s, the International Labor Defense, created to give legal assistance to workers in "capitalist" countries, also extended its activities into Africa, establishing branches in South Africa, Kenya, Nigeria, Sierra Leone, and Senegal. Its organs berated the "crimes" of colonial officials and championed the cause of African political prisoners, giving continuous assistance to Lamine Senghor's successor, Garan Kouyaté, and his followers in the LDRN.

Throughout the 1930s, the LAI also operated as an instrument to harass colonial governments and support the nationalists. Its secretariat published both the *Anti-Imperialist Review* and an *Information Bulletin,* and it persuaded the editors of African newspapers to subscribe to the Comintern news service, *Inprecorr.* Even more irritating to the British government was the LAI's role as a pro-African pressure group within Britain. Reginald Bridgeman, the head of the British LAI and a member of the CPGB, constantly badgered the Secretary of State for the Colonies about the civil rights of Black Africans. His remonstrations were echoed by sympathizers in the British press and parliament. In addition, Bridgeman subsidized such African nationalist efforts as the African Service Bureau, a body that Wallace-Johnson, Padmore, and other leaders established in London in 1937 as a central anticolonial directorate.

There were subtle differences in the methods that the Comintern used to transmit its teachings to Africans in French and British territories. In both cases, it conducted work in the metropoles with the help of associated international bodies such as the ITUC-NW, the ILD, and the LAI. Organizations of a regional character such as the LDRN of French West Africa and the Negro Welfare Association of British West Africa were its arms in the colonies. It also used both the British and the French Communist parties concurrently with these groups. But the organizational links were stronger in the French colonies than in the British territories.

In French West Africa, the LDRN played a substantial role in fostering revolutionary perspectives. During the late 1920s, the LDRN expanded its activities in France under the leadership of Garan Kouyaté. After 1927, it set out to broaden the distribution of its journal, *La Race Nègre*. It also sought to establish branches, trade union committees, and study circles in French Africa, and it had a hand in the 1929 Congo uprisings and in revolts in Upper Sangha Province of Ubangui-Chari (now the Central African Empire) the same year. When the PCF in 1929 offered Kouyaté a subsidy in order to tighten its hold over the organization, Kouyaté initially accepted. But after the PCF tried to dictate his editorial policies, he turned to the Comintern directly for financial help. As a result of the positive impressions he derived from his two visits to Russia, his organization and journal followed Moscow's positions, causing the more moderate elements within the LDRN to break away in 1931.[42]

Meanwhile, the PCF itself intensified its campaign to encourage revolutionary activities and establish contacts with Black Africans. Various methods were explored: the PCF Colonial Commission under Jacques Doriot published a monthly *Bulletin Colonial* with an activist message; the party conducted a drive to recruit Africans as members; and French Communists in 1929 led an anticolonial demonstration of Madagascans in Tananarive and afterward published a local paper, *Le Reveil Malgache*, to expose Madagascans to Communist thought.

With respect to British Africa, Communist bodies such as the LAI, the ILD, and the CPGB were useful, but they were less significant than the work of individual Africans such as E. F. Small, the editor of *Gambia Outlook* and a founding member of the National Congress of British West Africa. In 1929, Small organized one of the first important African trade unions, the Bathurst Trade Union. In the same year, he led a general strike which crippled the Gambian economy for more than two weeks. That venture, at a time when unionism was outlawed in the British colonies, earned him the attention of the colonial authorities.

Another individual, I.T.A. Wallace-Johnson, stood out during the 1930s as an even more important agitator. After his graduation from KUTVU, the Comintern in 1937 sent him to Nigeria, where he organized the African Workers' Union of Nigeria and made plans for a monthly publication as well as a training school for trade unionists. Despite the stringent repressive measures of British authorities, the Nigerian union succeeded in attracting several hundred members in Lagos and in forming two provincial branches. Later, Wallace-Johnson also became involved in efforts to raise the political consciousness of Nigerian women.

When British authorities forced him to leave Nigeria in 1933, Wallace-Johnson went to the Gold Coast, where there was a restless intelligentsia and a rapidly growing local press. Having triggered Britain's enactment of the 1934 Sedition Law, Wallace-Johnson led a protest against it in Accra and carried the nationalist message into remote areas of the Gold Coast interior. To awaken political consciousness among Gold Coast youth, he in early 1934 founded the West African Youth League (WAYL), which soon became an important radical nationalist organization. In the 1935 Gold Coast elections, the League greatly contributed to the defeat of the pro-government candidate, Dr. Nanka Bruce.

Wallace-Johnson was assisted in these Gold Coast enterprises by a fellow graduate of KUTVU, Bankole Awooner-Renner. Awooner-Renner was the founder of the Ashanti Freedom Society and a self-declared Bolshevik; he was subsequently to conceive a plan to establish a West African "Soviet Union" and to cooperate with Kwame Nkrumah in setting up the West African National Secretariat in London.[43] Another important source of support was the local Gold Coast press. Early in 1935, for example, Wallace-Johnson collaborated with the Nigerian nationalist, Nnamdi Azikiwe, to bring out a new organ, the influential *African Morning Post*.

Eventually, Wallace-Johnson's efforts in the Gold Coast were rewarded with a sedition charge and arrest. The conviction doubled his popularity, as well as the membership of the West African Youth League. Subsequently, he turned his attention to his native Sierra Leone, where he organized a section of the WAYL in 1938. This effort attracted a mass following and spearheaded widespread anti-British agitation. The colonial authorities took a variety of steps to curb him, and he was incarcerated in Sierra Leone during World War II.

Wallace-Johnson's unsung importance to the West African independence movement deserves underscoring. He helped to initiate the
process of party organization in three colonies. He devised various
schemes for uncompromising struggle against British authority, con-
centrating on organizing women and youth. He facilitated and expanded the circulation of *The Negro Worker* and other instruments of
propaganda. And through his work with the ITUC-NW, he helped to
encourage communication among the various elements of the African
independence movement.

The rise of Adolf Hitler to power in Germany in 1933 as well as the
growing prominence of fascism in the 1930s set in train developments
that eventually caused a decline in Soviet African concerns during the
latter part of the decade. In Germany, Hitler's rise had disastrous
consequences for the Communists almost overnight. The offices of
the German Communist Party were sacked, Comintern headquarters
in Berlin were raided, and the ITUC-NW offices in Hamburg were
closed. Moreover, Padmore was imprisoned for several weeks. In the
face of this assault, the ITUC-NW, along with other Comintern operations, moved its headquarters to Copenhagen. Alarmed by these
events, Moscow soon began to alter its world view and to realign its
policies toward France and Britain. By 1935, the Comintern had
abandoned its "united front from below" strategy and had decided
instead to promote broad antifascist coalitions. (The USSR, to be
sure, did make strenuous efforts to interest the Western democracies
in Ethiopia's plight in 1935, but these can be interpreted as much in
antifascist as in anticolonial terms.)

This new policy was dramatically illustrated when the Comintern
withheld subsidies for *The Negro Worker,* despite Padmore's urgent
pleas for support. Informed in August 1933 of the Comintern's decision to disband the ITUC-NW, Padmore issued a violent denunciation
of the Kremlin for abandoning the cause of African liberation. The
Comintern responded with a series of attacks against him, and he
found himself expelled from the party in 1934. His rejoinder to Moscow was a classic statement of African nationalist self-reliance: "It is
high time for the Negroes to stop depending on other people to fight
their battles."[44]

While James Ford and Wallace-Johnson remained affiliated with the
Comintern after 1934, many Africans followed Padmore in breaking
with it. They had suddenly come face-to-face with the long-standing
reality that Russia's own national security interests constituted the
prime determinant of its policy toward Africa.

Despite his quarrel with Moscow, however, Padmore continued to adhere to the tenets of Marxism-Leninism and in his later career as an "elder statesman" of the African independence movement, he influenced no small number of African policy-makers in that direction—notably, Kwame Nkrumah, who asked Padmore to become his chief foreign policy adviser after Ghana won its independence in 1957. Padmore worked consistently with nationalist leaders to help them build political parties and interterritorial bodies. For example, the ad hoc committee that he formed with Azikiwe and Wallace-Johnson to support nationalists in the Gold Coast and later Ethiopia was eventually transformed into the International African Service Bureau, a functional replacement for the ITUC-NW after World War II. Although this body was not officially aligned with the Comintern, the ties between the two were strong: Wallace-Johnson was its general secretary, and a part of its funding came from the LAI.

Padmore was typical of many African nationalist leaders. While they displayed disillusionment with Moscow's policy gyrations, they retained a basic loyalty to the Marxist creed and capitalized substantially on the tactical and organizational training that they had received from the Comintern.

The South African Experience

The situation in South Africa differed economically, racially, and historically from that in the rest of colonial Africa. Thus, it merits separate consideration—particularly since the South African Communist Party (SACP) is the oldest Communist party in Africa and was the largest on the continent prior to World War II. A forerunner of the SACP emerged during World War I as a result of schisms within the indigenous white labor movement in South Africa's industrial and urban areas. At that time, a splinter group led by Sidney Bunting and David Ivon Jones formed the International Socialist League. This body emphasized the need to build bridges with non-white labor and help the latter to organize, and it was instrumental in the formation in 1917 of the Industrial and Commercial Workers Union of Africa (ICU), which became the largest black African movement in South Africa during the 1920s.

In 1921, the International Socialist League and other white leftist elements joined to form the SACP and immediately affiliated with the

Comintern. Despite its dominance by whites, however, the SACP recognized the revolutionary potential among blacks—especially in light of the founding in 1912 of the African National Congress, the first black nationalist political organization in South Africa. Consequently, the party sought to establish firm ties with blacks. Individual African labor and political leaders such as J. B. Marks and Moses Kotane held top posts in a variety of Communist and Communist-front groups while playing key roles in strictly nationalist and African organizations, including the ANC. Clements Kadalie, the ICU leader, sometimes took Communist positions as well. But by 1926, the issue of Communist control had split the ICU leadership, and a purge of Communist officers took place. Though such leadership splits, as well as official repression, caused a rapid decline in the black labor movement as a whole, some elements remained affiliated with the Paris-based League Against Imperialism.

In the eyes of the SACP leadership, Moscow was a source of pride and inspiration, and its doctrinal advice and financial support were eagerly accepted. Following the Comintern line, the SACP in the early and mid-1920s endeavored to develop a multi-racial leadership and to forge links with non-Communist groups, and it registered significant gains in both regards.[45] It convinced Africans from an early date that white Communists were among the few Europeans who actively welcomed African political participation and supported their struggle for equal rights and social justice. Similarly, it was the first among non-black groups to protest against such government measures as the poll tax and the pass system for influx control.[46]

But the SACP was weakened in its effort to spread the Marxist-Leninist message by Moscow's abrupt and frequently heavy-handed intervention in its operations. The Comintern's adoption of the "united front from below" strategy at its Sixth Congress in 1928 caused the SACP not only to renounce the substantial achievements that Bunting and his colleagues had made in building ties with a broad range of African nationalists and labor leaders, but also to urge the creation of a "native republic" and thus to alienate much white support.[47] By 1931, the Comintern had even brought about the expulsion from the party of Bunting and the white leaders of two major South African labor organizations and the installation of more malleable leaders. In 1935, when Moscow rediscovered the virtues of a broad-based antifascist front, another group of prominent SACP members, both black and white, was purged from the party, further reinforcing the local image that the SACP was a tool of Soviet foreign policy. This image seemed to receive undeniable confirmation when the Soviet-German pact of 1939 brought an end to the party's popular front doctrines of the mid-1930s.

In sum, Soviet involvement in South Africa during the interwar years can be viewed essentially in terms of wasted opportunities rather than achievements, although distance—as Tsarist Russia had found earlier with respect to support for the Boers—may have precluded decisive effort in any case. Nonetheless, Moscow did expose a significant number of key South Africans to its philosophy on race and social relations as well as to its techniques of political organization.

Conclusion

Although Africa did not predominate in Russia's international concerns during the years preceding World War II, Russia did enter the postwar era with the foundations for a meaningful relationship with the continent. By that time, it had amassed a large body of relevant information about Africa. As a result of repeated enterprises—from the early explorations of Kovalevskiy and Eliseyev to the later clandestine operations of the Comintern—it had accumulated valuable strategic data about African geography, society, and political life. Even more important, Moscow through both overt and covert means had kept close tabs on indigenous nationalist sentiment—first in Ethiopia and South Africa, then in the increasingly restless colonies of British and French West Africa. This intelligence enabled the USSR to recognize at a remarkably early date the emergence of one of the most important 20th-century trends in the Third World.

The effective flow of information to Russia during its long years of contact with Africa had also permitted the development of a trained corps of Soviet African experts after 1929. Pursuing the work begun by Pavlovich and profiting from generations of Russian experience and scholarship, these specialists led the striking postwar renaissance of Soviet academic interest in Black Africa. Not only did this group provide practical advice on African affairs to the post-Stalin leadership in the Kremlin, but its members were among the first foreign scholars invited to visit Black Africa after independence because of their long-standing ties with African leaders.

Perhaps most significant, the Soviets, by identifying themselves with African nationalist ambitions, had promoted the development of a political atmosphere in Black Africa conducive to further involvement in the region. In this connection, it should be stressed that, for Africans, exposure to Russia had both a modernizing and politicizing effect. Key national leaders came under the influence of Communist thought and consequently sought to apply Marxist-Leninist solutions to their social and political problems. On a practical level, Africans learned from Communists the importance of propaganda and the utility of establishing newspapers and organizing international conferences to further their political ends. Similarly, contacts with Communists convinced Africans of the wisdom of giving high priority to the creation of trade union, youth, and women's organizations and to the formation of study groups. Such bodies provided the nuclei for Africa's political parties.

Africans found encouragement in Comintern literature, Comintern-sponsored gatherings, and organizations like the ITUC-NW to transfer allegiance to larger political entities and to rise above family, tribe, and religious affiliations. Through its many channels, the Comintern not only provided them with a forum in which to meet and exchange ideas but also strengthened their nationalist sentiments by persuading them that their struggle was continental in scope and had the support of a major world power. In this sense, the Comintern contributed valuable psychological conditioning for the independence movement. Indeed, Africa's rapid political evolution after World War II owed much to Moscow's efforts during the interwar period to foster the conviction among Africans that they were the masters of their own destiny.

As a consequence of this effort, a pronounced inclination toward radical political solutions developed in key segments of the independence movement. Trade union, youth, and women's organizations resembling those in the USSR emerged in a number of places, and with the transition of African countries to independence, they soon gained official status as national institutions. Thus, they constituted an ideal infrastructure for fraternal ties with the USSR. Furthermore, many of those who assumed the reins of power in the new nations had either received training in the Soviet Union during the interwar period or worked with Comintern activists in Europe and Africa. Distrusting the Western powers, these leaders were prone to sympathize with the Communist message and to welcome Soviet counsel. Even those least attracted to the Communist faith tended to give Moscow, whatever its own selfish motivations, credit for bestowing a cloak of legitimacy on their struggle at a time when friends were few. With the wholesale granting of sovereignty to British and French African colonies in the late 1950s and early 1960s, Moscow had the opportunity to capitalize fully on these assets.

By the mid-1960s, it is true, Moscow had become disillusioned with the "revolutionary democrats" as a result of the failure of independent Africa to transform itself according to Marxist-Leninist precepts. But by then the USSR had foreign policy options in Africa other than exclusive reliance on these "revolutionary democrats," and it modified its approach to the continent accordingly. Transcending the ideological confusion that many Western observers ascribed to Soviet actions in the Third World in this thermidorean era was the traditional *Realpolitik* of Russian statecraft, with its time-honored concerns for security and economic benefit. Just as Tsarist focus on Turkey, Afghanistan, and Iran was resurrected, so too were the maritime and other preoccupations of Imperial Russia restitched into the quilt of Soviet-African relationships of the 1970s.

Nowhere is this return to historic objectives more readily apparent than in the Horn of Africa, a region whose strategic importance has been enhanced by the Arab–Israeli conflict and by geographic proximity to Indian Ocean sea lanes. The Russians, frustrated in Somalia, have reverted to promoting Ethiopia's territorial integrity with as much as U.S.$1 billion in arms[48]—a policy which could one day bring access rights to Red Sea ports and the very opportunities to interdict maritime traffic that so fascinated Tsarist planners. Likewise, the military advice of Soviet General V. I. Petrov on the recent Ethiopian offensive in the Ogaden was more than a shadow of an earlier era. While it can hardly be said that such initiatives would never have been undertaken without the precedents of Imperial Russian *Realpolitik,* it can reasonably be concluded that Russia's long years of exploration and cultivation served as a vital preconditioner for contemporary Soviet behavior.

4

Soviet Decision-Making on the Intervention in Angola

Jiri Valenta

THE SOVIET-CUBAN intervention in Angola in 1975 represented a major departure in Soviet foreign policy. Here for the first time the USSR underwrote the deployment of allied combat units at long distance, outside its sphere of influence. That fact had profound effects on U.S. policy-makers. It caused considerable doubt about Soviet intentions and about Soviet interpretations of détente, and it was an important contributing factor in the temporary freeze in Soviet-American relations in 1976.

Despite the significance of the Soviet-Cuban intervention in Angola, however, little attention has thus far been paid to the complexities of Soviet decision-making regarding this intervention. Interpretations that have been put forward with respect to the Soviet venture have for the most part tended to emphasize only one or two isolated factors that influenced the USSR. One school of thought—subscribed to by, among others, former Secretary of State Henry Kissinger—views the intervention largely in the context of USSR–U.S. rivalry, seeing the Soviet-Cuban involvement as the main factor in the escalation of the

This study is based primarily on a content analysis of open Soviet, East European, Cuban, African, and Portuguese sources. In addition, I have drawn on interviews with several Portuguese officers who served in Angola in 1975, and with officials of a number of African governments. I am also indebted to Professor John A. Marcum for his suggestions and his willingness to let me consult the draft of the second volume of his study of the Angolan revolution. Finally, I wish to acknowledge the financial support of the Research Foundation of the Naval Postgraduate School in Monterey in the preparation of this study and the intellectual stimulation provided by the students who participated in my seminar on the Great Powers in Africa at the Naval Postgraduate School—particularly Captain Gary McGraw, U.S. Army; Captain Richard Mahlum, U.S. Army; and Lieutenant Richard Shields, U.S. Navy.

Angolan civil war and the U.S. role as an attempt to counterbalance Soviet and Cuban activities.[1] Another line of thinking, represented by persons such as John Stockwell, former chief of the U.S. Central Intelligence Agency's Angolan Task Force, likewise sees the Soviet-Cuban intervention in terms of the rivalry between the superpowers, but it interprets the intervention as a response to early U.S. escalation of the Angolan civil war.[2] A third school of thought regards the intervention essentially as an outgrowth of the Sino–Soviet conflict.[3] Most of the commentators, moreover, assume that the Cubans acted in Angola as "Gurkhas of the Russian Empire" (to borrow an expression from Senator Patrick Moynihan) or as "Russian mercenaries" (in the words of the Chinese).[4]

This chapter, in contrast, will argue that the Angolan intervention resulted from a highly complex Soviet decision-making process. To sustain this point, it will look in detail at the process during a number of specific stages: the period prior to January 1975, January–August 1975, August–September 1975, October–November 1975, and December 1975–January 1976.

The Pre–January 1975 Period

In late 1974, when it became obvious that Angola was going to attain independence in the near future, the national liberation movement there, unlike those in the other Portuguese African territories, consisted of three rival sub-movements: the *Frente Nacional de Libertação de Angola* (National Front for the Liberation of Angola or FNLA), *União Nacional pro Independencia Total de Angola* (National Union for the Total Liberation of Angola or UNITA), and *Movimento Popular de Libertação de Angola* (Popular Movement for the Liberation of Angola or MPLA). Why did the USSR decide to support only the MPLA? The answer probably lies in the Marxist orientation of that movement, in the Soviet Union's long-standing ties with the organization, and in Moscow's suspicions of the MPLA's rivals. A close look at the history of the prior relationship between the USSR and the MPLA tends to sustain such a judgment.

Soviet political and material backing of the MPLA predated the era of U.S.-Soviet détente as well as the so-called "second scramble" for Africa, as Tanzanian President Julius Nyerere described Sino–Soviet rivalry on the continent in the late 1960s. Significant Soviet backing for the MPLA first became manifest in the early 1960s. Moscow's decision to extend such support appears to have reflected two basic considerations. To begin with, this was the period when Nikita Khrushchev turned toward Africa with high expectations that Soviet aid would induce the national liberation movements to embark upon a direct transition to socialism, and Soviet sources at the time noted suggestively that the genesis of the MPLA could be traced back to the emergence of Angolan Marxist groups and especially to the foundation of the Angolan Communist Party in October 1955.[5] The actions of Agostinho Neto, leader of the MPLA, bolstered Soviet hopes about the organization's potential for carrying out revolutionary transformations. During the early 1960s, he inititated contacts not only with Fidel Castro in Cuba but also with the clandestine Portuguese Communist Party, particularly its secretary-general, Alvaro Cunhal. Indeed, Neto became a personal friend of Cunhal, and it was through Cunhal's assistance that Neto made his first trip to Moscow in 1964.[6]

Second, the MPLA constituted the most satisfactory vehicle through which the USSR might pursue its own ends in Angola. By the early 1960s, the Soviets had concluded that Holden Roberto and his FNLA, the MPLA's only rival at that juncture, was pro-Western, with "close ties with American public and semi-official organizations."[7] To some extent, this judgment had a basis in fact. After Roberto had visited the United States in 1959, the FNLA had established a wide range of links with Americans (including sporadic contact with the Central Intelligence Agency). Moreover, for a while in the early 1960s the Kennedy administration seemingly contemplated a fundamental revision of U.S. policy with regard to Portuguese Africa. In April 1961, for instance, the United States endorsed the self-determination of Portuguese African colonies in supporting a resolution of the United Nations General Assembly calling for reforms in Angola.[8] By 1962, however, Portuguese pressures and threats to withdraw from NATO had caused Washington to back away from this position and to withhold strong support from the FNLA. The Berlin crisis of 1961, in particular, had demonstrated to U.S. officials the strategic value of American refueling facilities in the Portuguese-owned Azores.

The MPLA, by contrast, looked likely to be receptive to Soviet support and perhaps even susceptible to Soviet manipulation. It lacked other sponsors, and it gave clear signs of being weaker than the FNLA. The rank-and-file backers of the MPLA came from a variety of quarters—primarily from mixed-blood *mulatos assimilados* in

Luanda and other big cities and from the Kimbundu people in north-central Angola—while the FNLA had a concentrated base in the Bakongo tribe of northern Angola, which is one of the largest in the country and whose branches even spill over into Zaire. Furthermore, the MPLA leadership had always suffered from internal dissension.[9] Last but not least, the prominent role of the FNLA in the bloody revolt of 1961 had left most observers with the impression that the FNLA was the major military force in Angola's struggle for independence.

In any event, the MPLA's military efforts evoked public praise in 1961 from Khrushchev, who expressed confidence in an ultimate MPLA victory.[10] Subsequently, Soviet intelligence operatives became active in Angola, and the USSR initiated its sporadic channeling of funds to the MPLA. Except for a brief pause in 1964, exclusive Soviet backing of this group continued uninterrupted well into the late 1960s.[11]

During the late 1960s, however, after military coups in a number of "progressive" African countries—notably Ghana in 1966 and Mali in 1968—Moscow revised its outlook toward Africa's revolutionary regimes and national liberation movements. No longer did the Soviet leadership anticipate that such regimes and movements would effect a rapid transition to socialism. Soviet analysts, for example, ceased to refer to Neto's (and the MPLA's) Marxist orientation and to his close connections with the Communist Party of Angola. Instead, they emphasized the MPLA's "progressive" (read pro-Soviet) foreign policy orientation. This they contrasted with the subservience of Roberto's FNLA to "American imperialism."[12]

Although not a major factor in the USSR's support for the MPLA at the outset, Sino–Soviet rivalry assumed increasing importance in this regard as the 1960s progressed. In 1964, the Chinese, in an effort to cultivate relations with the FNLA, invited Roberto and other officials of the organization to Peking. Although Roberto did not go at that time, the Chinese later in the year entertained Roberto's former foreign minister, Jonas Savimbi, who had broken with the FNLA in 1963–64 because of conflicts with Roberto and other FNLA leaders over ethnic matters, and offered Savimbi some financial assistance and military training.[13] Subsequently, in March 1966, Savimbi established UNITA, comprised mainly of members of his own Ovimbundu tribe. (The Ovimbundu constitute one of the largest ethnic groups in Angola.) Since its inception in 1966, Moscow has regarded UNITA as a body under Maoist control.[14] In view of these Chinese flirtations with the MPLA's rivals, it became essential from Moscow's standpoint to have links with the MPLA so as not to be shut out of the influence game in Angola.

Relations with the MPLA took on even greater significance in the Sino–Soviet context in the wake of the Warsaw Pact invasion of Czechoslovakia in 1968. This event proved temporarily detrimental to Soviet interests in both the independent African states and the national liberation movements on the continent. Most of the regimes and movements denounced the invasion, and the prestige and influence of China, slowly emerging from the cloud of the Great Proletarian Cultural Revolution, began to rise. Indeed, China for the time being acquired an ascendant position in many parts of the continent. Among the few defenders and apologists of the Soviet Union, however, was the MPLA.[15]

The early 1970s brought fresh reasons for the USSR to back the MPLA. By this time, as John Marcum has noted, there were already indications that the days of the Portuguese dictatorship were numbered, for it was beset by demoralization and defection within its African forces and by terrorism and economic dislocation at home.[16] As a consequence, the Soviets viewed the situation in Angola as explosive and pregnant with opportunities. For example, V. Solodovnikov, the director of the African Institute of the USSR Academy of Sciences (the Soviet "think tank" dealing with African affairs), in 1970 predicted the speedy defeat of Portuguese colonialism in Africa, and he acknowledged publicly that the USSR was providing the MPLA with "military equipment, various armaments, ammunitions, means of transportation and communications equipment" and that MPLA "military personnel and political cadres" were being trained in the Soviet Union.[17]

This general assessment of the situation was not unique to Moscow, and that fact provided additional incentive for Soviet support of the MPLA. True, the United States, after a major review of American policy toward Southern Africa in 1969 (NSSM 39—the so-called "tar baby" report), discounted the vulnerability of the Portuguese regime at home and in its African colonies. Moreover, the strategic importance of the Azores base, demonstrated anew during the 1973 Arab–Israeli war, convinced American policy-makers of the necessity of maintaining good relations with the Portuguese dictatorship. But China was quite another matter. In fact, Peking stepped up its aid to the FNLA and UNITA in the early 1970s. For example, the Chinese invited Zaire's President Mobuto Sese Seko, the FNLA's principal African champion, to Peking in January 1973, and then Roberto himself in December 1973. During the latter's visit, the Chinese entered into a military assistance agreement providing for future Chinese training of the FNLA at bases in Zaire. In June 1974, not long after the coup in Portugal in April, 120 Chinese advisers (guerrilla warfare specialists) arrived in Zaire to work with the FNLA forces. Furthermore, the Chinese began to ship arms to the FNLA.[18]

The fall of Marcello Caetano's regime in Lisbon, of course, profoundly altered the situation in Angola, for it opened up the possibility of Angola's gaining independence in the foreseeable future. But not until the fall of 1974, with the ouster of General António de Spínola as head of the revolutionary military government in Portugal, did it become certain that independence loomed on the near horizon and that a provisional government embracing all existing national liberation movements in Angola would be formed. During the interim period, it should be noted, the USSR behaved hesitantly and did not immediately increase its military aid to the MPLA. Thus, some observers such as John Stockwell have attributed the escalation of Soviet military involvement in Angola during 1975 to a reaction to the Chinese activities cited above and to the CIA's extension of covert funding to the FNLA in July 1974.[19] This conclusion rests on the assumption that the USSR had no interest in thwarting the transfer of power to a government which would include the FNLA and UNITA, but that assumption is difficult to credit in light of past Soviet attitudes toward these two groups as well as Moscow's record of encouragement of the MPLA. A much more likely explanation of Soviet circumspectness would be Moscow's uncertainty about the political and military prospects of the MPLA.

Indeed, there were plenty of grounds for uncertainty. Despite Soviet military aid in the early 1970s, the MPLA found itself in the throes of a crisis toward the end of 1973. On the military front, a Portuguese offensive late in the year had left it almost defeated and for the moment virtually incapable of retaliating.[20] In the political sphere, the leadership had fragmented into three competing factions (similar to those in existence in the early 1960s). One was headed by Neto, the chairman of the organization. The so-called "eastern faction" was led by Daniel Chipenda, a vice-chairman of the MPLA, the military commander on the Zambian front, a former Portuguese professional soccer player, and (like Jonas Savimbi) an Ovimbundu. A final group was composed of Brazzaville-based *mestizo* intellectuals under the direction of another MPLA vice-chairman, Father Joaquim Pinto de Andrade.[21] In response to this situation, Moscow had in early 1974 suspended its aid to Neto and had begun to supply a small amount of material help to his chief opponent, Chipenda.[22]

Not until the late summer or early fall of 1974 did the USSR opt to resume assistance to Neto's faction, via the Congo-Brazzaville, and in the process to raise the general level of its aid to the MPLA.[23] Several factors seem to have played a role in this decision. First, Alvaro Cunhal, Secretary-General of the Portuguese Communist Party and a long-time acquaintance of Neto, apparently advised the Soviets to renew their support.[24] Second, the USSR lost faith in Chipenda's ability to win out in the internal MPLA struggle. Third, Moscow saw the Portuguese and Angolan situations as linked and evidently believed that mutually reinforcing processes of radicalization would take place in the two countries.[25] Finally, the manifestations of growing Chinese influence in Angola generated a compelling need for a means of exerting a counterweight.

Despite this decision, however, the Soviets had every reason to be aware of the MPLA's weaknesses. It is therefore probable that they urged Neto to work, at least for the time being, toward a political solution in Angola.

January–August 1975

On January 10–15, 1975, the three nationalist movements met at Alvor in southern Portugal. There they pledged to form a transitional government and to hold free elections in October 1975. The transitional government would exercise power under Portuguese supervision until the day of independence, scheduled for November 11, 1975. At this time, the Portuguese would withdraw their last remaining troops.

The Soviet media hailed the Alvor accord as "an important step along the path to decolonization"[26] and ceased attacks on the MPLA's rivals, the FNLA and UNITA. Such evidence suggests that at this point the USSR favored some sort of coalition among the nationalist movements. Nonetheless, the Soviet leadership, concerned about the mounting military capabilities of the FNLA, decided to step up its weapons deliveries to the MPLA. As already noted, China and the

United States had begun to supply the FNLA with military hardware. (Indeed, on January 22, 1975, the U.S. government's Forty Committee authorized the CIA to pass another $265,000 to the FNLA for the chief purpose of purchasing weapons and ammunition.[27]) Then in February 1975 Chipenda, Neto's prime rival within the MPLA, and his army of 3,000 guerrillas joined the ranks of the FNLA.

The previous December, the Soviet-supported Organization of Afro-Asian Solidarity had declared 1975 the "year of practical aid to the peoples of the former Portuguese colonies," and in February 1975 an executive secretary of the Soviet committee of this organization, A. Dzasokhov, headed the first Soviet delegation to Angola. This was followed by a second one in April which discussed with MPLA leaders the question of "specific material aid" and the "training of cadres for Angola in African, socialist and other countries."[28] About the same time (in March), the Soviets began to increase their own independent arms deliveries to the MPLA.[29] Heretofore, most Soviet aid to Angola had gone through either the Organization of African Unity (OAU) or such "friendly" intermediary states as Libya and the Congo-Brazzaville.

Soviet arms arrived in Angola by various channels. The USSR and its allies sent some heavy equipment (including armored vehicles) by sea to Angolan ports. During the months of April, May, and June, for example, a total of two Yugoslav ships, four Soviet ships, and two East German ships reportedly made stops in Angola. Other heavy equipment was airlifted by Soviet AN-12 and AN-22 aircraft to Brazzaville and was then sent by surface to Pointe Noire; from there it was either reshipped or airlifted to MPLA bases on the Angolan coast. About 100 tons of arms found their way to southern Angola by these routes in the month of April alone.[30] Although officially neutral, the Portuguese authorities, some of whom favored the MPLA, did not impede the deliveries.

As a result of this influx of weapons, the MPLA was able to arm several thousand additional men in Luanda, some of them boys 12 to 15 years old. Under Neto's leadership, the MPLA also began to strengthen its support among the masses by establishing new district popular committees.[31]

About the same time that the Soviet arms arrived, Cuban military advisers commenced to show up to work with the MPLA. In early April, MPLA official P. Jorge made a trip to Cuba, and on May 7, the Cuban ambassador to Zaire reportedly visited Luanda.[32] According to

Cuban leader Carlos Rafael Rodríguez, Havana in the late spring decided to send 230 military personnel to Angola.[33] By the end of May, Cuban advisers had reportedly assisted the MPLA in a military skirmish in the town of Caxito, during which the MPLA had first employed tanks; and Cuban artillerymen had reportedly participated in clashes between the MPLA and its rivals, the FNLA and UNITA, in Lobito, Quibala, Cola, and Sa da Bandeira.[34]

This Soviet and Cuban military assistance unquestionably emboldened the MPLA and contributed to the breakdown of the transitional coalition government. However, the evidence indicates that other factors were at play as well. Both the FNLA and UNITA, increasingly truculent as the result of U.S. and Chinese backing, initiated many of the local military clashes that occurred during the spring of 1975. The FNLA in particular was responsible for some of the outbreaks of fighting in Luanda. In March 1975, for example, it decided to send a motorized column to Luanda to dislodge the MPLA from the capital.[35]

Indeed, the skirmishes in the spring of 1975 and the eruption of civil war the ensuing summer grew fundamentally out of the intense mistrust between the rival leaders (in particular, Neto and Roberto), ethnic and racial animosities, and the ongoing power struggle among the liberation movements. As one of the officials of the FNLA reportedly stated, "Ideology is secondary. . . . It's really just a power struggle. We have all been fighting [the Portuguese] so long, we have too much invested in blood to allow the others to win."[36]

And the signs of the strength and popularity of the leaders of the FNLA and UNITA (especially Savimbi, whose arrival in Luanda, according to some sources, made "a spectacular impact" on the city's population[37]) caused the MPLA to feel especially insecure. For instance, during several negotiations with the two other factions, the MPLA tried to thwart the holding of elections, pushing for the creation of a "socialist council of state" instead.[38]

As a consequence, the MPLA finally brought matters to a head by moving to force the FNLA and UNITA units out of Luanda. In May, the MPLA expelled the FNLA from the suburbs. The following month, it gained momentum and drove both organizations entirely out of the capital, finally taking control of the city on July 9. Gradually, it also assumed command of 12 of the 15 provinces.[39]

During this period, the Soviet leadership, while clearly concerned about the situation, did not appear to view it as serious. After all, the escalation of Soviet military aid and the arrival of Cuban advisers had given the MPLA an edge against the FNLA and UNITA, and the MPLA was winning the undeclared civil war. Moreover, until June Soviet reports of the "trouble" in Angola, while continuing to voice support for the MPLA, attributed the difficulties to the machinations of the "imperialists." Thus, the Soviets sought to avoid placing the blame entirely on the FNLA and, especially, UNITA.[40] This evidence suggests that they probably were still willing at this juncture to endorse some kind of coalition government for Angola. At the same time, their complacence about the offensive of the MPLA tends to indicate that they hoped this offensive would provide the MPLA with sufficient clout to compel its rivals to accept a compromise giving it the leading role in any future coalition.

August–September 1975

The months of August and September were critical ones with respect to Soviet decision-making on Angola, for although a small number of Cuban military personnel had arrived in Angola as early as May 1975, Soviet-Cuban military intervention did not assume major proportions until late September and early October, when Cuban and Soviet ships and aircraft began to ferry the first of thousands of Cuban soldiers to Angola. It would appear that the Soviets and Cubans in the late summer of 1975 took steps to ensure that they could launch a massive invasion on short notice by negotiating an agreement with President Marien Ngouabi of the People's Republic of the Congo to use Brazzaville, his capital, as the staging base for Cuban military personnel sent to Angola,[41] but the Soviet decision to go for broke in Angola seems to have been the product of a reassessment of the Angolan situation sometime in late August or early September.

One can identify several specific factors that Moscow evidently felt compelled it to take a new decision as well as a number of factors that influenced the character of the decision that it reached. Let us look first at the former considerations. These can be grouped under four general headings.

External Signals and Involvements. The collapse of the Portuguese dictatorship in 1974 had brought about changes in the perceptions and behavior of many nations with respect to Angola, and during 1975 several of these nations had in varying degrees become actively involved there. From the Soviet point of view, however, the most worrisome actors were the United States, China, and South Africa.

All three of these powers had lined up behind the FNLA and UNITA, and during the summer of 1975 their commitment seemed to become more pronounced. In late July 1975, for instance, the U.S. government's Forty Committee and subsequently President Gerald Ford, at the urging of Zaire and Zambia, approved a $14 million paramilitary program to assist the FNLA and UNITA. Shorty thereafter, this covert program got under way via the airport in Kinshasa (Zaire).[42] Although China formally agreed to respect the call of the Organization of African Unity (OAU) for neutrality among the three rivals in Angola in July 1975, its military personnel remained at the FNLA's bases in Zaire until October 24, 1975.[43] Indeed, alarmed by the MPLA offensive in June and July, Peking in mid-July reportedly authorized Zaire to release to the FNLA Chinese military equipment held by the Zairian army.[44] Moreover, despite a number of MPLA attempts toward rapprochement with the Chinese, Peking continued to be hostile.[45] While South Africa did not undertake an extensive intervention in Angola until October—i.e., *after* the launching of the Soviet-Cuban operation—it did carry out a limited intervention (as the Cubans had been doing since May) on August 8, 1975, in the southern part of the Portuguese colony. The ostensible purpose of this secret venture was to secure the safety of a hydroelectric complex on the Cunène River serving South African-controlled Namibia, but the undertaking came in response to a request from UNITA's Savimbi and was plainly a move to provide military advisory personnel and military equipment to UNITA and the FNLA. Savimbi's request for aid followed consultation with several moderate African regimes (Zaire, Zambia, the Ivory Coast, and Senegal)[46] and perhaps encouragement from the United States (although firm evidence on this point is lacking).

There are substantial indications that Moscow not only was aware of but was perturbed by these developments. By mid-August, the Soviet media began to indicate concern about intensified Chinese and U.S. military aid to the FNLA and UNITA, and by early September the media were speaking of U.S.-Chinese coordination of covert assistance.[47] They gave particular prominence to a story by Leslie Gelb published in *The New York Times* on September 25 which reported, among other things, that the United States and China were cooperating on behalf of the FNLA and UNITA.[48] Shortly after the Soviet-Cuban invasion got under way, V. Solodovnikov, director of the USSR Academy of Sciences' African Institute, charged that in Angola "the present leadership of the People's Republic of China, in its struggle against the MPLA, actually entered into a conspiracy with the United

States. . . ."[49] To some extent, of course, Soviet comments toward the end of 1975 were simply justifications for the Soviet-Cuban intervention, but it would be a mistake to dismiss them as only that. They also reflected long-standing Soviet fears of a Chinese-American entente. Soviet analysts had for years expressed concern over the possibility of such a development in the Third World in general and in Africa in particular.

With regard to South Africa, the Soviet media in the latter part of August commenced to discuss the threat of large-scale intervention in Angola by South African forces and to assess the implications of such a move. Although the South African army for the time being refrained from advancing deeper into Angolan territory than the area of the hydroelectric complex, it would appear from the reports of Soviet observers that by early September Moscow had probably become convinced that a major South African invasion was likely in the near future.[50]

The Situation in Angola. Events in Angola took an adverse turn for the USSR during August and September. In July, it had grown clear that there could be no peaceful solution to the internal political struggle, and Moscow had increasingly identified itself with the MPLA's push for power. For example, in contrast to Soviet reporting on the clashes between the rival factions in the spring, the Soviet media during and after the heavy fighting in June and July openly attacked first the FNLA and later UNITA, accusing them of hampering the process of decolonization in pursuit of "narrow tribal interests."[51] Any lingering hope that Moscow may have had about UNITA's remaining neutral in the civil war vanished on August 20, when UNITA, meeting in Silva Porto, essentially declared war on the MPLA and commenced fighting alongside the FNLA.[52] (It can be argued that the informal FNLA-UNITA alliance had evolved gradually from the skirmishes that had taken place in the big cities in the spring, when the MPLA had decided to chase the other movements out of its zone of influence. Yet until the summer at least some MPLA officials had still believed that UNITA—an organization with seemingly irreconcilable ethnic differences with the FNLA—might stay out of the conflict between the MPLA and FNLA.[53] There were indications that the Soviets shared this belief.[54])

At the same time that Soviet fortunes were getting more and more closely intertwined with those of the MPLA, however, the MPLA was experiencing reverses on the battlefield. During August and early September, the limited intervention by South Africa in southern Anogla and the growing U.S. and Chinese military aid to the FNLA-UNITA coalition helped halt the MPLA's advances, and the movement's armed elements even found themselves driven from a number of positions. The most serious state of affairs developed in the north, where FNLA forces came within 20 miles of the capital of Luanda. Although the MPLA (with the help of Cuban military personnel) briefly regained the initiative in the north in early September, the tide again turned in favor of the FNLA during September 11–17. Then, after two battalions of Zairian elite commandos joined the FNLA forces, the MPLA began to retreat toward Luanda.[55]

While the military situation remained fairly fluid, it was becoming increasingly obvious that the presence of a few hundred, or even several hundred, Cubans might not suffice to stop the U.S.-Chinese-South African-Zairian-backed counteroffensive of the FNLA-UNITA coalition before Angola was scheduled to receive its independence on November 11. By late August or early September, Soviet reports were picturing the state of affairs in the colony as quite critical.[56]

Circumstances in Portugal. Moscow had long seen definite linkages between developments in Portugal and developments in Angola,[57] and the ouster of the leftist government of Prime Minister Vasco dos Santos Gonçalves in Lisbon on August 28 represented a distinct complication in Angola from the Soviet perspective. It is important to bear in mind a number of things in this regard. First, not only the Portuguese Communist Party but also some elements of the Revolutionary Council of the *Movimento das Forças Armadas* (Armed Forces Movement or MFA) had taken the position that the MPLA's strong ties with the USSR did not constitute an impediment to handing over power to it along with the other liberation groups. Indeed, for a combination of ideological, political, and personal reasons, several figures in the MFA—notably, Prime Minister Gonçalves; General Otelo Saraiva de Carvalho, commander of the MFA's elite security force, the Continental Operations Command or COPCOM; Brigadier Pezarat Corrêia, commander of the southern military region in Portugal; and Navy Admiral Antonio Alva Rosa Coutinho, until January 1975 Portuguese High Commissioner in Angola—supported the desire of the MPLA for a dominant role in Angola.[58] With such political forces in the ascendancy after a domestic crisis in Portugal in March 1975, the MPLA had reaped many benefits. While the Portuguese army in Angola did not as a whole come out openly in favor of the MPLA, the Gonçalves government, as pointed out earlier, did not discourage the

Soviets from providing the MPLA with massive supplies of weapons in the spring of 1975. More significant, many MFA members who backed the MPLA and occupied key posts in Angola displayed overt sympathy with the MPLA and tried to help it by both direct and indirect means.[59] After the March shakeup, there were even unconfirmed reports that some Portuguese units in Angola were going to be replaced by others "devoted to defending the progressive line."[60] By early August, then, MPLA Chairman Neto could describe the MFA as playing the role of the "fourth liberation movement" in Angola while giving "quasi-total support" to the MPLA.[61]

In light of these considerations, the Soviets appeared to expect that the Gonçalves government would at least provide indirect military and political aid to the MPLA to assist it in winning an eventual victory in Angola.[62] But the fall of the Gonçalves government radically altered these calculations, for the MFA subsequently backed away from its partisanship toward the MPLA and adopted a more moderate position favoring a transitional government composed of the three national liberation movements. This shift left the radicals within the Portuguese units in Angola little option but to remain passive observers of the civil war and thus deprived the MPLA of a crucial source of aid. To make matters worse, the change in the MFA position seemed to harden the resolve of the FNLA and UNITA to press forward with their cause.

The imminence of Angolan independence. On November 11, the Portuguese armed forces would turn over rule of Angola to whichever national liberation movement or coalition of movements happened to control the capital city of Luanda. In this context, the faction that succeeded in mustering "sufficient support" to win the battle of Luanda *before that deadline* would emerge the victor in the power struggle or would at least gain a major and perhaps insurmountable advantage over its competitors. Since all three movements lacked modern equipment, a logistical system, and internal lines of communication, "sufficient support" in practical terms meant a limited amount of sophisticated weapons and a commensurate number of experienced soldiers capable of handling them.

These various considerations pushed the Soviet leadership toward a new decision vis-à-vis Angola. Basically, two options were open to Moscow. Either it could continue to try to balance off the FNLA and UNITA with modest military aid and Cuban advisers and run the risk of total military defeat of the MPLA, or it could intervene decisively on behalf of the MPLA.

Several factors seem to have entered into the choice that the Soviet leadership made. These fall into three main categories:

Soviet national security interests. Obtaining a strong position in Angola by helping the MPLA establish itself in power held a number of potential benefits for the USSR. To begin with, Angola itself had some distinct attractions as a client state. As Soviet commentators were fond of noting, it possessed important oil and mineral resources. Indeed, according to one Soviet observer, "it has not been ruled out" that Angola "is the richest country on the African continent, not counting South Africa."[63] Increased Soviet access to these resources would not only weaken Western economic ties with the territory but also might afford economic gains for the USSR, at least over the long run. Moscow must also have been aware that relatively free use of Angolan ports such as Luanda would facilitate its efforts to maintain a naval presence along the west coast of Africa.[64]

In the larger context, the situation afforded the USSR an opportunity to deal a setback to its two main rivals, the United States and China. Checking the growth of the latter's influence in Africa had become of particular concern to Moscow during the course of the 1970s, for, as pointed out previously, China had launched a concerted drive to expand its links with African countries after it had emerged from the relative isolation that it had imposed upon itself during the Great Proletarian Cultural Revolution.[65]

Perhaps most critical, a significant Soviet presence in Angola would enhance the USSR's ability to win a major voice in the affairs of Southern Africa because of Angola's strategic geographic location. As the Soviet leadership had already recognized, the situation in the region was undergoing fundamental alteration in the wake of the collapse of the Portuguese empire. Such a circumstance created potential hazards and potential openings for the USSR, and Angola figured in a key way in both. If an FNLA-UNITA government took power in Luanda, South Africa's détente policy toward moderate Black African states like Zambia and Zaire might proceed apace, thus diminishing the chances for Soviet penetration of the area. Moreover, an MPLA defeat might destroy the African liberation movements' image of the USSR as a worthwhile ally and cause them to look to China as their main source of support. As a TASS commentator put it, an MPLA loss could produce "a very grave negative aftermath in the destiny of the national liberation movements in the whole of Southern Africa."[66] If, on the other hand, the MPLA assumed control of Angola with Soviet help, Moscow might then be well fixed to disrupt the contacts between the moderate African countries and the remaining white rulers of the area and to encourage a step-up in guerrilla activities to overthrow the white regimes. In the words of V. Sidenko, a long-time Soviet African specialist,

> If independent Angola were to follow the example of Mozambique this would be for the imperialist-backed regimes a blow from which they would be hardly likely to recover. The triumph of the patriotic forces in Angola would give a new powerful impulse to the liberation struggle in the last strongholds of racism, the Republic of South Africa and Namibia.[67]

As for the risks entailed in an intervention on behalf of the MPLA, Moscow seems to have assessed these as fairly low. Its main concern, of course, was how the United States would respond and what the repercussions on U.S.-Soviet relations would be, but it appears to have concluded that, in the aftermath of the Vietnam debacle of April 1975, domestic constraints on Washington's actions would prevent the United States from making a major issue of Angola. Certainly, Soviet analysts argued publicly that Vietnam and the Watergate scandal had had far-reaching effects on the mood of the American people and the U.S. Congress. "The Vietnam tragedy," they declared, had provided "a serious lesson for the majority of Americans."[68] In fact, they went on, it had caused a crisis in the American political system that had created political instability and vastly increased the power of Congress, which was "regaining rights which were taken away from it during the 'cold war' period." To buttress this last point, they cited the Congressional role in cutting off military aid to South Vietnam and Cambodia during the spring of 1975.[69]

Moreover, the Soviet leadership had plenty of evidence from American behavior on the ground in Angola that the post-Vietnam domestic mood constituted a barrier to forceful U.S. action. For example, instead of openly challenging the initial Soviet-Cuban involvement in Angola in the spring and summer of 1975, the U.S. government, as mentioned earlier, had furnished covert paramilitary aid to the FNLA and UNITA through Kinshasa (Zaire). Even in the summer of 1975, this paramilitary aid was still quite limited and designed primarily to restore a power balance between the FNLA-UNITA coalition and the MPLA after the latter's summer offensive, for a more extensive program would have required Congressional approval. (Despite the restricted character of this aid, it should be noted, not all U.S. government officials approved of it. The most prominent dissenter was Nathaniel Davis, Assistant Secretary of State for African Affairs, who resigned in August 1975 because of his opposition.)[70]

Bureaucratic Politics. Forces within the Soviet hierarchy favoring a tough stand in Angola gained ascendancy. It would appear likely that divisions of opinion about Angola had existed within the Soviet leadership for some time. Such divisions would help to account for the hesitation, uncertainty, and shifting character of the USSR's policy between 1973 and 1975. By the summer of 1975, divisions of this sort were clearly present. Intelligence reports suggest, for instance, that elements in the Ministry of Foreign Affairs and the Ministry of Defense opposed an intervention on the grounds that it would endanger détente and might prove highly expensive.[71] Yet, as events ultimately attested, the hard-liners won the day.

Aside from rational calculations of Soviet national interests, a number of things may have played a role in tipping the balance. Some powerful segments of the Soviet bureaucracy may have looked upon Angola as offering opportunities for them to perform their organizational missions. The International Department of the Central Committee of the Communist Party of the Soviet Union (CPSU), for example, may have regarded a major intervention in Angola as a way of showing the revolutionary forces and national liberation movements of the Third World the depth of the USSR's commitment to them, and the Soviet navy may have wanted to acquire access to strategically located Angolan ports. Similarly, the KGB (state security) and the GRU (military intelligence) may have perceived an MPLA victory as essential to the expansion of intelligence operations in Southern Africa.

Probably more influential, however, were the bureaucratic and domestic considerations that flowed from the fact that the Angolan civil war had erupted only shortly before the 25th CPSU Congress, the first congress since the inauguration of détente with the United States in 1972. If Leonid Brezhnev and his supporters had taken a weak stand on Angola, they would have provided ammunition to the critics of détente, for the latter could have argued that détente inhibited the USSR's global activism and prevented it from assisting its clients in the Third World. A tough stand, on the other hand, afforded Brezhnev and his supporters a convenient demonstration to critics at home and abroad that détente was not a "one-way street," that the USSR did not "betray" the revolutionary forces in the Third World, and that

Angola would not become another Chile. In a more positive sense, such a stand not only would brighten the USSR's tarnished image as the leader of the world revolutionary movement but also would help the USSR regain momentum in world politics after the setbacks it had suffered recently in Chile, Egypt, and Portugal.

The Cuban dimension. Fidel Castro would appear to have encouraged an intervention and to have indicated a willingness to supply the troops for the venture. In this connection, it is important to remember that Cuba had been dispatching military personnel to Africa on a limited basis for a decade. During 1965–66, Cuban advisers went to Guinea and the Congo-Brazzaville to provide military assistance, and Cuban soldiers fought briefly with the forces opposing the government of Moise Tshombe in the Congo-Leopoldville (now Zaire) in 1965. After Castro became disillusioned about the prospects for "revolutionary changes in Latin America" during the late 1960s and early 1970s,[72] his attention turned increasingly to Africa. According to his own assessment, "Africa is the weakest link of imperialism today. . . . Imperialist domination is not as strong there as in Latin America. Therefore, the possibility for fundamental changes on the African continent is real."[73] Thus, Cuban military personnel in the 1970s became involved in several African countries: Guinea, Tanzania, Somalia, Guinea-Bissau, and Mozambique. Moreover, as we have already seen, a small number of Cuban military advisers served with the MPLA forces in Angola from May 1975 onward. In short, Cuba had long manifested a readiness to engage in military undertakings in African countries in the service of revolution on the continent. Such military undertakings, in Castro's eyes, represented the natural "result of our principles, our ideology, our convictions and our own blood."[74]

Moreover, Castro had been a backer of the MPLA and a close friend of Neto for a number of years. Cuban support for the MPLA had not gone through the kinds of ups and downs that had characterized Soviet support, and even during the spring and summer of 1975 Cuba seemed more eager to render vigorous backing to the MPLA than did the USSR.

Finally, the Cubans were far from oblivious to the concrete rewards that they might reap from participation in an intervention. Some of Castro's comments suggest, for example, that he saw involvement in such an enterprise as a good way to refurbish his image as a revolutionary leader of the nonaligned world (perhaps replacing Tito) and to enhance the prestige and influence of his regime in the Third World prior to the conference of nonaligned nations to be held in Havana in 1979.[75] There is also circumstantial evidence that he may have viewed it as helpful to Cuban efforts to obtain increased economic aid from Moscow or a rescheduling of the repayment of Cuba's enormous debt to the USSR. Shortly before the massive Soviet-Cuban intervention began, the Soviets reportedly promised "a considerable increase" in economic and technical assistance to Havana.[76]

It would be far-fetched, of course, to look upon Cuba as the main impetus behind the invasion or to think that the Cubans compelled the USSR to act against its will. Nonetheless, Havana's conviction that an operation should be mounted and particularly its willingness to provide the forces for that operation constituted important inputs into Soviet decision-making. In light of the declining fortunes of the "progressive" elements of the MFA in Portugal, it was obvious that radicals within the Portuguese military in Angola could not serve as Soviet proxies or even indirect supporters of the MPLA; therefore, if the USSR intervened in a major way, it needed to deploy combat troops capable of handling sophisticated weapons for the MPLA. Since the use of Soviet forces might elicit a firm response from the United States and have a detrimental impact on U.S.-Soviet détente, an alternative source of troops was essential, and Cuba filled the bill in this regard. Furthermore, the similarity of the physical environment of Angola to that of Cuba and the presence of a substantial number of black and mulatto soldiers in the Cuban armed forces would enable Cuban troops to get acclimated quickly and function effectively with MPLA soldiers.

In light of these various considerations, the Soviet leadership chose to launch a massive effort to rescue the MPLA from defeat in Angola. This decision, the evidence indicates, came sometime in late August or early September. Reports from Cuban prisoners reveal that the actual dispatch of Cuban forces must have gotten under way before the South Africans opted to intervene toward the end of October,[77] and the timing of the arrival in Angola by ship of Cuban troops points to a decision a few weeks earlier. Other evidence tends to confirm such a judgment. For example, Radio Moscow announced on September 29 that the Presidium of the World Peace Council, an organization with links to the International Department of the Central Committee of the Communist Party of the Soviet Union (CPSU), had called for a "week of solidarity with the people of Angola" to begin the following day. In supporting this call, the Soviet commentary declared that "solidarity with fighting Angola is *now* solidarity with the MPLA."[78] It is significant that this statement was made about the time that officials of the three Angolan liberation movements were expected to arrive in Kampala for a meeting of the OAU Conciliatory Committee on Angola. Also on September 29, Fidel Castro, addressing a meeting in Havana, stressed Cuba's duty to offer assistance to "other people" in their "path toward liberation."[79] In mid-October, then, a World Peace Council meeting issued a declaration that the MPLA was "the only true legal representative of the Angolan people"—thus implying that it was worthy of assuming power on independence day, November 11.[80]

October–November 1975

Throughout October and November, Moscow's prime concern was to help the MPLA hang on to Luanda and to turn the military tide that by late October was running strongly against it. In August–September, UNITA's Savimbi, dissatisfied with the military situation in the south and pressed by Zambian President Kenneth Kaunda to open the Benguela railroad by November 11 so that Zambia could resume use of it for vital copper exports, had accepted increasing South African military assistance, and on October 23 South African armed forces intervened directly in the civil war. Two columns of armored cars, trucks, light planes, and helicopters and roughly 3,000 regular South African troops (counting those who provided logistic support around the borders) teamed up with UNITA elements to try to eliminate MPLA forces in southern Angola.[81] On October 29, one column took Moçãmedes; by November 7, its conquests also included Benguela and Lobito. Meanwhile, the other column captured Luso in the east. Both then began pressing toward Luanda. In the north, moreover, the FNLA continued its cautious advances toward the capital's northern boundaries. Despite the fact that more regular troops of the Cuban army were landing in the country via Cuban and Soviet ships, the area of Cuban-MPLA control as the day of independence approached shrank to Luanda, Cabinda, and three of the 15 provinces—i.e., a rather narrow band of territory stretching across north-central Angola. Even here, the MPLA position became so tenuous that the movement's panicked leaders commenced sending their families out of the country.[82] In fact, as a Soviet eyewitness has reported, they even weighed the possibility of proclaiming independence on November 5 instead of November 11,[83] for this would provide them with a legal basis for requesting massive Soviet-Cuban aid while Luanda was still in their hands.

To stop the South African-backed offensive of the FNLA and UNITA, the Soviets and Cubans stepped up their assistance to the MPLA both quantitatively and qualitatively. No doubt mindful of the setback that it had suffered in the Congo-Leopoldville in the early 1960s because of poor coordination and limited airlift capabilities, the USSR mounted the Angolan operation with a good deal of finesse, committing substantial aircraft to the venture and deploying naval covering forces in adjacent waters. Soviet and Cuban planes began almost daily airlifts of Cuban combat troops and Soviet and East German advisers to assist the MPLA, while the Soviet air force and navy combined efforts to transport weapons and military equipment from the USSR through the Congo-Brazzaville directly to Luanda. These arms included surface-to-surface missiles, the hand-held SAM-7 antiaircraft missile, 122mm "katyusha" rockets, T-34 and T-54 tanks, PT-76 amphibious tanks, armored reconnaissance vehicles (BRDM-2), trucks, helicopters, gunships, heavy artillery, light aircraft, and (eventually, in January 1976) MIG-21 aircraft. By late November, according to CIA estimates, the total Soviet outlay in Angola had reached $225 million, as compared with $25 million for the United States. To protect the supply operation, the USSR maintained a naval squadron in West African waters, with its base at Conakry in Guinea.[84]

By independence day (November 11), roughly 2,800 Cuban troops had reached Angola, and their initial mission was defense of the capital. This they succeeded in accomplishing in fairly short order. On November 12, only one day after a frightened MPLA leadership had declared the establishment of the People's Republic of Angola, Cuban forces managed to halt the FNLA drive just short of the capital.

Thereafter, the military balance gradually tipped in favor of the MPLA as both the quantity and quality of the Soviet-Cuban military intervention escalated. For a while, South African and UNITA forces continued to score some victories and to advance toward Luanda, but by early December the MPLA, with Cuban combat troops doing most of the effective fighting, had moved onto the offensive and was pushing its rivals back on all fronts. Since the FNLA and UNITA had few men trained in mobile mechanized warfare, the ability of Cuban military specialists and combat soldiers to handle sophisticated weapons gave the MPLA a military edge. It also provided a psychological advantage, for when Cuban forces began to use the famous "katyushas" in their attacks on towns and troops concentrations of the FNLA and UNITA, these weapons had devastating effects on FNLA and UNITA morale.[85]

The Soviets, however, did not confine themselves to bringing about a reversal of the MPLA's situation on the battlefield. They also launched a major diplomatic campaign on behalf of the MPLA. In this undertaking, they capitalized greatly on South African involvement in Angola in support of UNITA. Predictably, the South African intervention stirred up much pro-MPLA sentiment in Black Africa and prejudiced the UNITA-FNLA coalition's case. Indeed, a number of African countries that had previously taken a neutral stand on the civil war now threw their backing to the MPLA.

Where the USSR encountered reluctance to recognize the MPLA regime, it did not hesitate to apply pressure. Allegations that it tried to bribe certain African leaders to get them to extend recognition remain unconfirmed, and evidence suggesting that it may have employed economic means to influence the positions of countries such as Ghana and Nigeria is fragmentary and inconclusive. But there can be no doubt that Soviet officials made strong representations in many African states. In Uganda, for example, a bizarre uproar occurred in November as a result of the intensity of Soviet prodding. When the Soviet ambassador to Uganda, A. V. Zakharov, demanded recognition of the MPLA government, Idi Amin called him a "criminal," and the severity of Amin's attacks led the USSR to suspend relations with his regime temporarily.[86]

December 1975–January 1976

By early December 1975, the Soviet-Cuban rescue operations had worked, and the military picture in Angola had altered in favor of the MPLA. Nonetheless, Moscow appears to have paused briefly before it approved a broad offensive against the UNITA-FNLA forces. Between December 9 and 25, for instance, the Soviets ferried no new Cuban troops to Angola.[87]

This pause evidently grew out of Moscow's desire to assess the reactions of outside powers to the changed circumstances on the ground in Angola. As mentioned earlier, the Chinese had totally disengaged militarily from the Angolan civil war in October. At that juncture, Peking may have believed that the combination of U.S. and South African support for the UNITA-FNLA coalition would ensure the MPLA's defeat without further Chinese action, and that too close an identification with South Africa would harm the Chinese cause on the continent. In any event, China now found itself unable to affect the situation meaningfully from its standpoint, although it is rumored to have urged the United States to intervene against the Soviet-backed MPLA. Thus, Washington's response was the critical one for the Soviets—especially in light of the Ford administration's public warnings that the USSR's actions in Angola threatened U.S.-Soviet relations. Presumably, the vote of the U.S. Senate on December 19 to cut off covert aid to the FNLA and UNITA (because of fears of a "new Vietnam") convinced Soviet leaders that the domestic constraints on U.S. policy-makers were so formidable that the USSR had nothing to worry about from the American quarter. With the cessation of U.S. aid to the UNITA-FNLA coalition, South Africa in early January decided to discontinue its assistance to the coalition. Consequently, the way was clear for the MPLA and its allies to push on militarily.

In late December, Cuban and MPLA troops opened a big offensive aimed at achieving a decisive victory before the convening of an extraordinary summit conference of the OAU in late January 1976 in Addis Ababa. To sustain this operation, the Soviets and Cubans reportedly went so far as to pressure several Caribbean countries (Trinidad, Guyana, Barbados, and Jamaica) to permit planes carrying Cuban troops and war matériel for Angola to use local airport facilities.[88]

By February, there were 12,000 Cuban combat troops in Angola, and the Soviet Union had poured in a total of $400 million in arms and assistance since the onset of the civil war (as compared with an estimated $54 million worth of aid to the MPLA over the previous 19 years). The Cubans even had jets and heavy armor at their disposal.[89] Against such forces, the FNLA and UNITA soldiers were no match, and those not killed in the onslaught retreated into the bush.

With the gradual defeat of the FNLA, the withdrawal of South African troops, the scattering of UNITA elements, and Soviet diplomatic exploitation of the emotional South African issue, the positions of a number of key African states altered. In December, Idi Amin reversed his earlier decision to expel Soviet diplomats from Uganda, and Uganda and other African countries such as Nigeria and Tanzania began to shift their backing to the MPLA. Subsequently, on February

11, 1976, the OAU, after some initial hesitation, recognized the MPLA regime as the legitimate government of Angola.[90]

Conclusions

As we have seen, then, Soviet decision-making on the Angolan intervention of 1975 was by no means a simple or straightforward process. This case study, moreover, suggests some generalizations about Soviet decision-making in the broader African context.

First, Soviet leaders have not in recent years operated with a carefully thought out master plan vis-à-vis Africa. In fact, events have tended to shape their behavior more than their behavior has shaped events. It was clearly the dissolution of the Portuguese empire, the pressure from the Chinese to play the influence game, and the distribution of power among the competing forces in Angola, for example, that prompted the USSR to resume aid to Neto and strengthen its ties with the MPLA. By the same token, there is no evidence that Moscow fomented the civil war and the breakdown of the Alvor accord signed by the three rival Angolan factions. If such an important Soviet undertaking as the Angolan enterprise reflects no broad scheme for the continent, then it hardly seems likely that such a scheme underlies Soviet ventures of lesser consequence.

Second, the courses that Soviet leaders have chosen to pursue in specific African situations have not reflected assessments of just local African factors. There has been a large element of global politics in Moscow's calculations. Competition with the United States and China, for example, had a great deal to do with the USSR's involvement in Angola. Not infrequently, great-power considerations may weigh more heavily in the minds of Soviet decision-makers than concrete African circumstances.

Third, Soviet decision-making in the African context has in recent years been influenced, at least marginally, by Cuba's policy on the continent. It is true that Cuba's major military involvements have been undertaken in a global policy context determined largely by the USSR and that these involvements have been made possible primarily by Soviet logistical support, military cover, and weaponry. However, as the Angolan case demonstrates, Moscow has also been dependent on the willingness of Castro to provide Cuban ground forces for the USSR's large military ventures in Africa. Thus, it has not been in a position to totally ignore Havana's views.

Fourth, Soviet decision-making with respect to Africa has seemed to be subject to the sorts of domestic "pulling and tugging" that Graham Allison posits in *Essence of Decision*.[91] That is, it has reflected not only national security interests but also perceived needs on the part of some elements of the national-security bureaucracy to fulfill their organizational roles. It seems highly likely, for instance, that a combination of (a) the concern of Brezhnev and his supporters to stave off potential repercussions in the Soviet hierarchy of a policy of nonintervention and (b) the desires of portions of the Soviet bureaucracy to take advantage of the opportunities that a major intervention in Angola would afford them to carry out their particular functions helped overcome the opposition to such an intervention within the leadership. Inherently, of course, this "pulling and tugging" varies from case to case, as well as over time.

Finally, Soviet leaders have proved to be acutely conscious of power considerations in reaching decisions about Africa. They have been quite cautious about committing themselves in a direct military fashion, but when they have determined to make a firm military commitment, they have not spared resources in implementing that decision. In Angola, for instance, the USSR took a major hand in the conflict only after it found its MPLA clients with their backs to the wall shortly before independence day on November 11, 1975, and after it had concluded that strong domestic constraints would probably prevent the United States from responding in kind. Then the Soviets jumped into the fray in a massive way, using their newly acquired long-range sea- and air-lift capabilities to provide effective military support.

On balance, it seems likely that these features of Soviet decision-making vis-à-vis Africa will continue to prevail in the future as they have in the past. Hence, Moscow's decision-making with respect to the continent in the years ahead will probably be shaped by a combination of the opportunities that present themselves in Africa, global politics, the Cuban factor, bureaucratic and domestic politics in the USSR, and, last but not least, the willingness of the West to employ the power at its disposal to heighten the risks for the Soviets in exploiting the opportunities that confront them.

5

The Theory and Practice of Marxism-Leninism in Mozambique and Ethiopia

Marina Ottaway

SINCE THE MID-1970s, several Black African countries have chosen Marxism-Leninism as their official ideology. At the same time, "African socialism," the ideology of reconciliation which was much in vogue in Africa during the 1960s, has not gained new adherents. But how significant is this development? What does the adoption of Marxism-Leninism mean in African countries? Are they Soviet satellites upon which choices are being imposed, or countries autonomously making their choices? This chapter will attempt to answer some of these questions in relation to Ethiopia and Mozambique.

At the outset, it is essential to clarify some of the premises on which this analysis is based. The first is that Marxism-Leninism has historically been open to many interpretations, and that none of these interpretations is correct by definition. From this perspective, the issue of whether Ethiopia and Mozambique are truly Marxist-Leninist countries is irrelevant, while the question of how the ideology is being interpreted in each country becomes central. A second, related premise is that the fundamental question about interpretations of Marxism-Leninism is whether they stress dialectics and participation or central planning and control. This question must be answered not only by looking at ideological writings and policy declarations, but also by analyzing the functioning of the institutions being created. A third premise is that while the choice of ideologies, institutions, and policies can be—and in Third World countries most often is—a voluntaristic one, by fiat of the rulers, the process of implementation is inevitably influenced by existing socioeconomic conditions, which can frustrate the efforts of even the most well-intentioned and committed leaders. Thus, it is important to consider the extent to which a society is divided and conflict-ridden, rather than united and acquiescent. Both extremes can in fact encourage the evolution of a socialist system toward centralization and bureaucratization. A final premise is that the international situation can have a strong influence on the way in which a certain ideology gets translated into practice, but that it is one among many factors.

Although Ethiopia and Mozambique have made a common ideological choice, they are quite different countries, in terms of both their histories and their social structures. Ethiopia, which experienced colonialism for only a very short period, came to Marxism in an attempt to deal with the class divisions and conflicts deeply embedded in its society, rather than simply because of the ideological commitment of its leaders. The most important policy decisions taken in Ethiopia after the overthrow of Emperor Haile Selassie in 1974 were efforts to solve the immediate problems the state faced, and preceded any commitment to Marxism-Leninism. Yet, all these policies are quite compatible with the ideology. Both policies and ideological choices, in other words, are closely related to the characteristics of the society. In Mozambique, with its long history of colonialization, the ideological choice was part of the struggle against Portuguese colonialism, and it was based more on a desire to prevent the development of a class society than on an attempt to resolve already clearly delineated class conflicts. Thus, the ideology is a much more artificial implant in Mozambique, but there is a high degree of coherence between ideology, institutions, and policy decisions, because conflict has interfered less with policy-making.

Despite the important differences between them, however, Ethiopia and Mozambique are encountering some similar problems in the process of implementation of the ideology. These have to do with the internal dynamics of the two countries and the pressures deriving from their international positions.

To provide greater insight into the differences and similarities between these two African countries which call themselves Marxist-Leninist, this chapter will explore four aspects of their experiences and situations in depth. These include: (1) the processes leading to the adoption of the ideology; (2) the interpretations of the theory and the character of the institutions set up to translate the theory into reality; (3) the pressures created by socioeconomic conditions; and (4) the international positions of the two countries.

The Adoption of the Ideology

The embrace of Marxism-Leninism as official ideology took place at virtually the same time in both Ethiopia and Mozambique—in 1977—but against quite different backgrounds. In Mozambique, it was the result of a long, rather gradual process involving little conflict, except briefly within the top ranks of the *Frente de Libertação de Moçambique* (Liberation Front of Mozambique—FRELIMO). In Ethiopia, the adoption of the ideology was the outgrowth of a process compressed into the space of two years and marked by great strife, on occasion even large-scale violence. In neither country was the process a democratic one, reflecting a clear understanding of the issues and a choice on the part of a significant segment of the population. While there was less obvious compulsion and violence in Mozambique than in Ethiopia because of the much greater degree of unity among the country's leaders, this very unity in a sense made the process more strikingly "from the top down" there.

The transformation of FRELIMO from a front of different movements fighting for independence into a Marxist-Leninist party committed to continuing the revolution after the demise of the colonial regime is closely connected with events in the liberation struggle. FRELIMO succeeded early in the war in establishing control over the northern provinces and hence had to face the question of how to administer these liberated zones. This led to a split between two factions of FRELIMO and subsequently to the triumph of the more radical one, eventually led by Samora Machel. FRELIMO's second congress, held in July 1968 in the liberated zones, marked the victory of the radical faction. In the words of a FRELIMO document:

> Its [the Congress's] importance resides in the confirmation of the revolutionary political line of Frelimo and the condemnation and rejection of the counterrevolutionary positions represented at the Congress by a group headed by Uria Simango and Lazaro Kavandame. . . . This group rejected the policies of emancipation for women, clemency toward the captured Portuguese soldiers, mobilization in depth of the population, the creation of a people's army, the strategy of prolonged war, etc.[1]

The victory of the radical faction was confirmed in April 1969 and May 1970 at two meetings of the party's Central Committee. A document on "the process of the democratic people's revolution in

Mozambique" issued after these meetings clarified the new, quite elaborate position of the Front.[2] While the document made no explicit references to the ideology of Marxism-Leninism, it was unmistakably influenced by it, both in content and style. Central to the document was the idea that the revolutionary process is a dialectical one, in which a period of unity is succeeded by one of criticism, through which a new unity is reached. In other words, the revolutionary process requires periodic reconsideration of strategies and policies in view of new developments. The unifying factor guiding this process is the "interest of the masses." According to the document, two periods of "criticism" had taken place in the history of FRELIMO up to that time. The first had had to do with whether or not to launch the armed struggle; the second had concerned the organization of the liberated zones. What the document defined as the issues discussed during the second period of criticism indicated that the movement of FRELIMO toward Marxism was sealed. It said:

> How production should be organized, how the population should be administered, which type of relationships of production should exist in the liberated zones, which relations should be established between the population and the leadership of FRELIMO, between the army and the population, these were the urgent problems, requiring immediate, clear and concrete solutions.[3]

The solutions offered to these issues stemmed from two equally significant decisions: the rejection of the "bourgeois solution" and the rejection of a return to tradition. FRELIMO chose to oppose the authority of the chiefs, to stress collectivization of agriculture, to promote mobilization and political education of the population in order to develop a participatory system, and to assign a political as well as a military role to the army. All these measures were seen as efforts to prevent the growth of "the embryos of the bourgeoisie and the survivors of feudalism,"[4] who had found fertile ground in the liberated zones. The definition of traditional society as feudal is quite significant, showing that FRELIMO had already rejected the *ujamaa* concept of socialism (to use Julius Nyerere's term for it), based on the romantic vision of primitive communalism in precolonial African societies. FRELIMO policies in the liberated zones were directly aimed at destroying the remnants of tradition. The stress on the emancipation of women, the rejection of the authority of the chiefs, the reliance on the mobilization of the population through its education to an "advanced, scientific, objective and collective ideology,"[5] all had this underlying purpose.

While the term "Marxism-Leninism" did not appear in FRELIMO documents at this stage, and FRELIMO did not stress the support of socialist countries as crucial to the war of liberation, the direction had already been set—although obviously the implementation still fell far short of the ideal. The proclamation of Marxism-Leninism as Mozambique's ideology at the Third Party Congress in February 1977 was thus simply the logical extension of a process begun well before independence.

The introduction of Marxism-Leninism in Ethiopia came about in a very different manner, characterized by much more haphazardness and by much greater conflict. From the very beginning of the Ethiopian revolution, there were two major forces fighting for change; the military and the leftist intellectuals. The military had the force and thus seized power, but they had no clear ideology and indeed no clear concept of what they would do with the power they had seized. The intellectuals, representing various shades of Marxism, had strong ideological convictions but no power and no clear concept of how the ideology should be translated into practice.

When the military deposed the Emperor in September 1974, they floundered for a few months before proclaiming in December of that year the birth of *hebrettesebawinet,* or "Ethiopian socialism," which they proudly announced was a homespun ideology owing nothing to the experience of other countries or the ideas of other people.[6] The land reform was the major accomplishment of this early phase of the revolution. However, the Land Reform Proclamation, which called for the organization of peasants into self-governing associations, was drafted by some of the Marxist intellectuals who had started gravitating toward the military council or Dergue.

The reliance of the military on Marxist intellectuals was inevitable under the circumstances. Having eliminated the top officers of the imperial army in the process of the revolution, the military could not draw from its own ranks sufficient numbers of educated cadres to run the country and formulate new policies. Moreover, there was a real need to widen the base of power and support in the country. The Marxist intellectuals were the obvious group to which to turn for support and expertise.

Two problems soon emerged, however. The civilians did not accept the idea of a military government, but demanded an immediate transition to a civilian government and the formation of a party. Furthermore, they did not accept the vague ideology of Ethiopian socialism but pressed for the adoption of Marxism. The alliance of the military and the leftist intellectuals was thus very uneasy, a partnership of necessity between two groups which neither trusted nor particularly liked each other. To make the situation more complicated, both the Dergue and the Marxist intellectuals quickly split into various factions.

It is through this many-sided struggle for power, the details of which we cannot examine here, that Marxism came to replace *hebret-tesebawinet* as the country's ideology. Paradoxically, it was never proclaimed as such officially. There is no single document one can point to as marking the turning point in the Ethiopian revolution, although there are several landmarks in this process. The first one was the proclamation in April 1976 of a "national democratic revolution" by Lt. Col. Mengistu Haile Mariam, at that time first vice-chairman of the Dergue and after February 1977 the country's leader.[7] His speech was an unmistakably Marxist document, sealing the alliance between one faction of the Dergue, headed by him, and one of the civilian factions, led by Haile Fida, a former activist in the movement of Ethiopian students in Europe and a Marxist with a clearly pro-Soviet orientation. The second landmark was an internal coup within the Dergue in February 1977, whereby Mengistu seized power and eliminated his opponents in the military council. This coup was followed by growing Soviet and Cuban military assistance to Ethiopia, then deeply enmeshed in wars against a secessionist movement in Eritrea and against Somalia in the Ogaden.

Thereafter, Marxiam-Leninism was undoubtedly the country's ideology. It was taught in the University of Addis Ababa by Soviet professors and explained in newspapers by Soviet and Ethiopian writers. However, for all its ideological orthodoxy, Ethiopia still did not have a political party to carry the ideological banner. An attempt by Mengistu's civilian allies to wrest power from the military resulted in their political demise during the summer of 1977, dashing all hopes for the quick formation of a party. Only a Political Office for Mass Organizational Affairs (POMOA) existed as late as 1979, and while it was supposed eventually to become the leading party, it was still firmly subordinated to the military.

The Theory and the Institutions

The differences in the processes through which Mozambique and Ethiopia came to consider themselves Marxist-Leninist countries have inevitably been reflected in the interpretations of the ideology in the two countries. In Mozambique, the formulations of theory focus on specific organizational problems that the country faces, and there is a close link between theoretical positions and the solutions advanced for these problems. In Ethiopia, the ideological debates reflect almost exclusively the concern of each of the opposing factions to show that its position is correct and those of its adversaries are wrong. Thus, while theoretical debates are clearly related to politics, they are almost completely unrelated to policy issues.

In looking at the ideological documents produced in the two countries, even a casual reader cannot fail to be struck by the sharp contrast in form and style. The Mozambiquan writings reveal a concern for clarity and for making the ideology and the policies it inspires understandable to a large segment of the population, while the Ethiopian writers are complex and often obscure, belying any claim that they are intended for the "broad masses" to which they constantly refer. This difference is not accidental. In Mozambique, the ideology was elaborated and refined in the process of organizing the population; in Ethiopia, it was elaborated in student circles, particularly those in Europe and in the United States, without much regard for the population's level of intellectual sophistication. Yet, there were probably more people involved in the debate in Ethiopia than the debate in Mozambique.

In the Mozambiquan interpretation, Marxism-Leninism is seen not as a rigid, given formulation but as a set of ideas to be continually reexamined and developed. FRELIMO, according to the party statutes of 1977, is guided by a synthesis of the revolutionary experience of the Mozambiquan people and the universal principles of Marxism-Leninism.[8] "What we are saying," explained Machel, "is that our movement's revolutionary ideology was forged in each of the political battles which it was necessary to wage, in each of the options it was necessary to choose."[9] Machel has, in fact, harshly criticized those who are afraid of formulating ideas in an original fashion:

> Educated Mozambiquans and government officials always find excuses
> to remain attached to old values. They are still mentally colonized, they

show that they are enslaved to foreign ideas, they lack confidence in themselves, they do not trust the capacity of our vanguard, FRELIMO, to develop Marxism-Leninism in an original form, on the basis of our experience. Only that which is imported is good. We do not despise other people's experiences, but we must first of all evaluate our own experiences, and evaluate other people's critically.[10]

However, he has warned, this reformulation of Marxism-Leninism must not degenerate into an ideology of "African socialism": "It is necessary for us to be always on guard against the chauvinistic deviations of 'specific socialisms.' We reject the idea that there can be an 'African socialism' or a 'Mozambiquan socialism.' We consciously affirm that there can be no socialism other than scientific socialism."[11]

The ideology which has emerged from this synthesis of the revolutionary experience of the Mozambiquan people and the universal principles of Marxism-Leninism has a definite Maoist tinge to it. Mao is often mentioned alongside Marx and Lenin as one of the authors whose work is of inspiration to Mozambique, and the ideology is at times even referred to as Marxism-Leninism-Maoism.

Three ideas stand out most clearly in analysis of the ideological writings in Mozambique: the idea of participation and mobilization, and consequently the rejection of "commandism";[12] the idea of class struggle; and, finally, the idea of the need to create a new man in order to achieve the goals of socialism. The stress on participation probably resulted from FRELIMO's experiences during the war of national liberation, when it required the support of the population and had only a limited number of cadres to organize and mobilize the people. Rejection of commandism was as much a necessity as an ideological choice.

The Mozambiquan emphasis on class struggle differentiates Mozambique most clearly from "African socialist" countries, but it also owes the most to the universal principles of Marxism-Leninism and least to the experience of the Mozambiquan people. In fact, class struggle is defined not as battle against a distinct and established group, an enemy which the majority of the population has encountered in its daily life and clearly perceives as such, but rather as an effort to prevent the growth of such a class enemy. Class struggle, FRELIMO explains, means struggle against all exploiters. These exploiters consist of three groups. The first is the colonial bourgeoisie. It was the mainstay of the colonial regime and ultimately responsible for the war. The second group of exploiters is composed of "certain individuals, although not possessing many assets, who have tried desperately to replace the colonial bourgeoisie and to occupy the positions left vacant by them." But this group was thwarted by FRELIMO, so that it is not an enemy with which the majority of the population has had a direct experience. The third group is made up of individuals who "although born of the people, became corrupted and betrayed the people." It includes collaborators during the war and "all lawless, professional criminals, thieves, murderers, drug addicts, prostitutes, gamblers and others."[13] By FRELIMO's own admission, these class enemies are small and weak. But Machel has maintained that they cannot be ignored, for "This class enemy does not act in isolation. It is a connecting link.We cannot consider him a weak and isolated enemy. We must measure his dimensions, his world connections, that is, we must constantly see in our enemy imperialism, and think of ways of fighting imperialism."[14] Because of this linkage between the internal class enemies and imperialism, he has added, class struggle in Mozambique must take the form of violent confrontations.[15]

Thus, in the final analysis, it would appear that class struggle has two aspects. It is an external struggle against imperialism and an internal struggle for change in which the leading role is to be played by the working class. This stress on the working class is not clearly related to the Mozambiquan experience, since the backbone of FRELIMO was the peasantry of the liberated zones rather than the urban workers, with whom FRELIMO had a minimum of contact during the war. Nevertheless, this working class is now expected to play the leading role, on the ground that the experience of industrial workers is by definition collective because of the conditions under which they work. FRELIMO, however, recognizes the demographic and historical reality of the country by stating that while the working class is the leading force of the revolution, the peasantry, by virtue of its numbers and experience during the war, is the principal force.[16]

The preoccupation with the creation of a new man is much more closely related to the experience of FRELIMO, in particular to the wartime opposition of the traditional chiefs of the liberated zones, who saw in the end of colonial domination an occasion to strengthen their positions. Creating a new man, in Sergio Vieira's words, means getting rid of the colonial mentality, but without going back to tradition.[17] The mentally colonized individual is the one who has lost his spatial and cultural dimensions, so that he thinks of the Algarve rather than of the Indian Ocean coast when visualizing a beach, "fills himself full of Aragon and Dostoyevsky," and has forgotten the word used for peanuts in Mozambique. Tradition cannot create the new man. The "traditional-feudal" society (while the appropriateness of the term "feudal" in relation to Mozambique may be open to question, this issue need not concern us here) is a "conservative, immobile society with a rigid hierarchy. . . . It is a society which excludes youth, excludes innovation, excludes women. The correct term is gerontocracy." Thus, the new man can only be created by moving away from both tradition and colonialism. Ideology plays a role in this process; however:

> The creation of the New Man is not principally a subjective factor, but the change in objective conditions. If it were to the contrary, we would fall into idealism. We have to change the economic and social base, we have to change the infrastructure of society in order to create the New Man. If not, we would be like the priests and would fall for the thesis of the internal transformation of the person and we would have a saint.

A very important aspect of this process of transformation from which the new man will emerge is the emancipation of women and their full integration into society. The position of FRELIMO has long been that:

> The emancipation of women is not an act of charity, it does not stem from a humanitarian act or from compassion. The liberation of women is a fundamental necessity of the revolution, a guarantee that it will continue, a condition for its triumph. The main goal of the revolution is the destruction of a system of exploitation, the building of a new society which frees the potentiality of human beings and which reconciles them with work, with nature. The issue of the emancipation of women arises within this context.[18]

There is no doubt, in conclusion, that Marxism-Leninism has been interpreted, at the theoretical level, in a democratic, decentralized, participatory, flexible way in Mozambique. It is seen not as a dogma but as a set of ideas to be adapted to the reality of the country, and the whole population is supposed to participate in this process. The crucial issue is inevitably whether the institutions being created in Mozambique and the policies being implemented there correspond to this interpretation of the ideology. In seeking to answer such a question, one must look at the party, the "dynamizing groups," and the communal villages as the institutions which should ensure participation and the creation of the "new man," and at the policy of holding criticism sessions in all organizations to identify, criticize, and reeducate "class enemies," as the embodiment of the idea of class struggle.

The party and the dynamizing groups, so closely related that they must be discussed jointly, are best understood by considering both the pre-independence and the post-independence periods. Before independence, the party was everything. It mobilized people, administered the liberated zones, and waged war. The main technique that it used to mobilize the population was the formation of dynamizing groups, which party leaders saw as the link between the organized party and the mass of unorganized people. Underlying this method was the idea that the party could not, and presumably should not, do everything from the top down. Rather, the population should organize itself to bring about local change. Thus, the inhabitants of a village or the workers of an enterprise selected the members of their dynamizing group from their own ranks. Party officials were on hand to provide the initial incentive and to explain the functions of dynamizing groups, but not to select their members. These dynamizing groups, in other words, were not party cells. Instead, they fulfilled two functions: they supplemented the work of the party cadres, and they gave meaningful content to the idea of participation, since they were not part of a bureaucratic structure.[19]

After independence, the role of the party inevitably changed, for independence meant taking over the apparatus of the administration. FRELIMO began to stress the difference between administrative and political tasks, and hence the separation of state and party:

> . . . there must be no confusion between the functions of the party and those of the state, they are quite distinct. It is true that in the past some party structures took it upon themselves to solve social problems, juridical problems, problems concerning marriages. . . . There was a phase during which it was the party and the dynamizing groups which performed those functions. . . . Why? Because we were not structured, the state apparatus was not structured. It was still the colonial state apparatus. The population started immediately to turn away from it and to FRELIMO to solve their problems. This shows how much confidence they had in FRELIMO. Today, the functions are quite distinct. The function of the party is that of establishing the broad lines of our development. The party gives an overall direction to the society, sets priorities, issues statements concerning the main tasks. The state exercises sovereignty and authority. Defending territorial integrity is a state function. Representing the Mozambiquan people in the world, on the international level, is a task for the state.

The state exercises above all the political and administrative power.
. . .
The state is an instrument of the party. The state does not replace the party, nor the party the state. They are quite distinct.[20]

As of mid-1979, it remains quite difficult to judge the extent to which this idea has been implemented. There is some evidence that the party is still carrying out functions which appear to be clearly administrative in nature. For example, the party establishes the detailed production plans in some peasant cooperatives, although it is not supposed to do so in theory.

It is even more difficult to determine what the continued overlapping in the functions of state and party means. One possible explanation is simply that Mozambique is in a period of transition. Since both the party and the state administration are still being reorganized, not all areas, particularly outside the cities, have both party cadres and administration officials. In such circumstances, the distinction between party and government functions inevitably becomes blurred, and anybody who is there, be it a representative of the party or the government, ends up doing what needs to be done. If this is the case, then the failure to clearly separate party and state is not particularly significant. However, other, politically more significant, interpretations are possible. The failure of FRELIMO to relinquish administrative tasks could above all indicate a trend toward the merging of party and state and toward the obliteration of the dialectical relationship between the two. Experiences of other socialist countries strongly suggest that the lack of a dialectical relationship between state and party is more likely to mean centralization and bureaucratization than to mean the withering away of the state in favor of a system of pure mobilization and participation. Whether the separation of party and state will take place, as Machel has announced it will, or whether the two will continue to overlap is therefore a question of great political importance, but one that is impossible to answer at present.

Just as there are unresolved issues concerning the relationship of party and state, there are likewise unresolved issues concerning the relationship of party and dynamizing groups. With the party congress of February 1977, which not only endorsed Marxism-Leninism as the official ideology but adopted new party statutes as well, the role of the dynamizing groups started merging with that of FRELIMO itself.[21] This development was inevitable, for the more organized the party became, the less it needed to rely on outside groups in order to mobilize the population. Moreover, the new statutes clearly define FRELIMO as a vanguard, and not a mass, party—that is, as a party composed of carefully selected cadres. One of the principal duties of party members is to "explain the Party's political line to the masses, unite them around the Party, mobilize and organize them to undertake tasks defined by the Party."[22] If this is the task of FRELIMO, the dynamizing groups lose any *raison d'être.* As of the summer of 1979, it appears that in the villages the dynamizing groups will be allowed to disappear as soon as party cells are formed there, but that they will be maintained in the cities as neighborhood committees in charge of dealing with the petty, day-to-day problems of each neighborhood.

FRELIMO's commitment to participation and mobilization is also reflected in the effort to organize the peasants into communal villages. However, there are still very serious, unanswered questions about what these communal villages are supposed to be and do. The policy of creating such villages was first undertaken during the war in the liberated zones and has since been extended to the rest of the country, with varying degrees of success. As of mid-1979, there are just over 1,000 communal villages, with an estimated population of about 1.6 million people. The villages vary widely in terms of history, size, degree of collectivization, and organization. Some of them are just villages where people reside next to each other but cultivate individually. Many of the villages established to relocate flood victims in 1976 and 1977 fall into this category. Since the Mozambiquan peasants formerly lived in scattered homesteads rather than in villages, coming together is already a significant change. Other communal villages are just the old Portuguese *aldeamentos* (strategic hamlets), into which peasants were herded during the war to keep them away from the guerrillas. These villages, too, are often just residential areas. At the other extreme are some villages where people not only live but also work together in cooperatives. Other communal villages are inhabited by workers of state farms. The most common situation is probably that in which people reside in the village and cultivate a small collective field but devote most of their time to their individual plots.[23]

In addition, it is by no means clear what character these villages will assume in the long run. Mozambiquan officials in charge of the communal villages argue that they must be political, social, and economic units. Politically, they should have a party cell, a people's assembly, and—in the case of the larger ones—an appointed local administrator. In terms of social infrastructure, they should have a school, a clinic, and a communal store as minimum services. The issue of the economic organization of the villages is much more ambiguous. It is plainly stated that all communal villages should have a production unit, but this production unit does not necessarily have to be a communal field or a cooperative. The idea is accepted that having a production unit may simply mean that there is a state farm near the village on which people get wage employment. In fact, at least some officials in the government believe that the state farms represent a higher phase of economic organization than cooperatives and thus the most desirable solution, although obviously not one that can be implemented in the entire country in the foreseeable future. But this idea is very controversial and rejected by others as leading to an excessively centralized and bureaucratic system.

One of the reasons why these matters continue to be unsettled is that the communal villages still do not have juridical status. In June 1979, a process of discussion of the organization of communal villages began throughout the country. The issue is supposed to be covered at the local, district, provincial, and national levels successively over a six-month period. This process should culminate in early 1980 with the publication of the statutes for the communal villages. Some of the questions which are open at present should be answered by then.

As pointed out earlier, the idea of class struggle is somewhat artificial in Mozambiquan conditions. Awareness of the existence of class enemies cannot be taken for granted, as it can, for example, in Ethiopia, where peasants do not need political education to know that their former landlords are the enemy. In order to heighten consciousness of the existence of these class enemies FRELIMO has used criticism sessions, in which the past and present attitudes of members of a group, and particularly of individuals holding or running for office, are discussed. The policy is aimed above all at identifying former collaborators. While these people were initially then placed in "reeducation" camps, the policy in 1979 is to keep them in their jobs but under public scrutiny for two years, during which time they have to prove they are reformed. The new leniency is due in part to the fact that these former collaborators often have technical skills that the government cannot spare at the moment, and in part to a political decision that this constant scrutiny serves to create class consciousness among the population.

Perhaps the most impressive manifestation to date of FRELIMO's

willingness to promote not only participation but also criticism and
"class struggle" came in late 1977, when Mozambiquans were called
upon to select representatives to local, district, municipal, and provincial assemblies and to a National People's Assembly.[24] FRELIMO
promoted public meetings at which those in attendance were
encouraged to review openly the qualifications of the candidates. At
the local level, participation was especially effective, resulting in the
rejection of about 10 percent of the candidates, despite the fact that
these had been selected by the dynamizing groups. Many of those
rejected were traditional chiefs; others were former collaborators or
simply individuals whose personal and political conduct was considered questionable by the population.[25]

Discussing how Marxism-Leninism has been interpreted in Ethiopia
is more difficult. First of all, most ideological discussions in Ethiopia
are contained in nonofficial publications. Moreover, the frequent
splits within the Dergue and between it and its civilian allies raise the
question of whether any document can be considered to represent the
Dergue's point of view. To compound this difficulty, the ideological
differences between groups close to the Dergue and those overtly
against it are minimal. For this reason, we will consider ideological
writings only briefly here, and focus instead on the new institutions,
which give a clearer idea of what Marxism-Leninism means in
Ethiopia.

There have been roughly three periods in the ideological evolution
of the Dergue since the onset of the revolution in 1974. Until late
1975, the ideology was the non-Marxist *hebrettesebawinet*. Official
statements summed this up as "equality, self-reliance, the dignity of
labor, the supremacy of the common good, and the indivisibility of
Ethiopian unity."[26]

The second period, up to February 1977, was marked by acrimoni-
ous disputes among two factions of Ethiopian Marxists, with the
Dergue an uneasy ally of one of them. Debate focused mainly on two
issues: (1) the right of nationalities to self-determination, and (2) the
pace of the transition from feudalism to socialism. Both theoretical
issues were closely linked to the immediate political problems of the
country—that is, policy toward the secessionist movement in Eritrea
and the question, burning for the civilian Left, of whether a military
regime could possibly usher in socialism.[27] Each faction claimed that
its position represented the correct Marxist-Leninist point of view.

The group seeking an alliance with the Dergue, and implicitly

Mengistu as well, recognized the right of nationalities to self-determination, but within the overall framework of Ethiopian unity. Moreover, it held that there could be no immediate transition from feudalism to socialism, for socialism had to be preceded by a national democratic revolution "under proletarian leadership in close collaboration with farmers and support of the petty bourgeois, anti-feudal and anti-imperialist forces."[28] What no document stated yet was clear from the political context was that the military had a key role to play in this national democratic revolution. By contrast, the Dergue's Marxist opponents, while stressing the same two points, argued that the right of nationalities to self-determination should include the right of secession and that the military had no role to play in the period of transition.[29] Interestingly enough, the idea of class struggle appeared in all documents but was not greatly emphasized by any. The likely reason is that conditions in Ethiopia at that time, when the land reform had pitted peasants against landlords and when members of the former aristocracy were being imprisoned and executed, made class struggle enough of an everyday reality to be taken for granted.

The third period, after the internal coup which brought Mengistu to power in February 1977, saw Ethiopia accept the Soviet interpretation of Marxism-Leninism. Although the Dergue's embrace of the ideology became explicit, theory became quite detached from reality. To paraphrase FRELIMO, the focus was on the universal principles of Marxism-Leninism and not on the revolutionary experience of the Ethiopian people. For example, during the spring of 1977, students at the University of Addis Ababa taking a compulsory course on Marxism-Leninism were studying from mimeographed handouts consisting of translations from Soviet textbooks. The ideological school also relied heavily on Soviet publications.

As has already been suggested, however, theoretical formulations reveal far less about the character of the new Ethiopia than do the institutions set up since the onset of the revolution. At the institutional level, there is much contradiction. An extremely authoritarian leadership at the top coexists with extremely decentralized institutions at the local level. The party, which presumably should be the connecting link, does not exist. This anomalous situation for a Marxist-Leninist country has led to some strife between the Dergue and its Soviet and Cuban advisers, who on at least one occasion have sought to push Mengistu to speed up the process of party formation.[30]

The major obstacle to the creation of a party has been the tense relations between the military and the civilians. Establishing a party implies a transition to a civilian government, or at least a much greater sharing of power between the military and the civilians. But all attempts at a rapprochement have been thwarted by mutual suspicions. When the Dergue allowed the civilians to play a prominent role, as was the case during the first half of 1977, they tried to use their position against the Dergue.[31] The repression that followed, in which hundreds of civilians met their deaths, set back the formation of a political party even further.

Of substantial importance, too, has been the fact that the civilian Left suffers from great internal cleavages. In mid-1977, there were five Marxist-Leninist parties in Ethiopia, joined in an uneasy alliance known as the Union of Marxist-Leninist Organizations. Only two of these need be mentioned here: MEISON, which was the most influential at that time but disgraced itself within a few months by trying too openly to work against the Dergue, and Revolutionary Seded, an organization that the Dergue had created as a countervailing force to MEISON and that hence had a predominantly military membership. A year later, only three of the original five parties were left in the Union (MEISON was one of those eliminated). Moreover, while the three claimed to be moving toward greater unity, their joint communiqués continued to be vague, and power remained in the hands of the Dergue.

As mentioned earlier, the major policy decisions taken and the most important institutions established after the overthrow of the Emperor all antedate Ethiopia's explicit commitment to Marxism-Leninism but do not conflict with it. In early 1975, the Dergue nationalized banks, insurance companies, and major industries. In March 1975, it announced the most sweeping land reform yet promulgated in Africa. This not only nationalized all land but also created some 24,000 peasants' associations to carry out the reform. In July 1975, all urban houses, except those occupied by the owner, were nationalized, and the urban population was organized into neighborhood associations or *kebeles*. These decisions spelled out an unmistakable commitment to socialism and laid the foundations for popular participation.

The most important institutions set up to date are the peasants' associations, which came into being at the time of the Land Reform Proclamation. Unlike the Mozambiquan communal villages, the Ethiopian peasants' associations have clear juridical status. Their powers were first defined in a proclamation in March 1975 and subsequently expanded and clarified in December 1975. These powers are quite extensive, ranging from the implementation of the land reform to the founding of cooperatives and collective farms and even to the performance of significant judiciary functions. The ultimate purpose of the peasants' associations is deemed to be to bring about collectivization, but after considerable strife the view has prevailed that this is a long-term goal, and that to push for it immediately would be counterproductive.

Although the juridical position of the peasants' associations is quite well defined, they have become somewhat controversial from a political standpoint. Here it is necessary to understand that even in the time of Emperor Haile Selassie, the central Ethiopian government had a problem in controlling the rural areas. The size of the country and its population, the difficulty of communication stemming from the absence of roads and the extremely rugged nature of the Ethiopian plateau, a tradition of local autonomy deriving from the country's social structure, and the weakness of the state bureaucracy contributed to this problem. In a sense, the creation of the peasants' associations exacerbated the situation. Therefore, there is a growing feeling within the Mengistu regime at the end of the 1970s that the autonomy of the peasants' associations is excessive, that the central government has too little control, and that the associations are putting their own interests before that of the nation, thereby displaying all the worst "petty bourgeois" tendencies of the peasants.

The central government's efforts to control the peasants' associations have taken two forms. First, it has sought to strengthen the political and administrative structures at the district and provincial level by forming assemblies made up of elected representatives of the peasants' associations, representatives of the various ministries, and appointed administrators. Such a step, it should be noted, is quite compatible with respect for participation. At the same time, the government has attempted to manipulate the peasants' associations themselves, trying to put hand-picked individuals in positions of power. This endeavor has been the work not only of the Provincial Office for Mass Organizational Affairs, but of many of the rival groups competing at the central level. As a result, the peasants' associations have in some cases been caught up in the national struggle for power. This has been particularly true in the more accessible areas.

The neighborhood associations or *kebeles* in the cities, the urban parallel of the peasants' associations, have been even more heavily involved in the national power struggle. Lacking the protection afforded by rural isolation, they for a period became veritable battlegrounds in the struggle between military and civilian factions; thus, they lost much of their autonomy. Nevertheless, the potential for participation and initiative at the local level still exists in the cities as well as in the countryside.

What is missing most in Ethiopia as of mid-1979 is not channels for participation but an instrument for coordinating and mobilizing the local, grass-roots organizations behind an overall plan or policy of development. In other words, Ethiopia suffers from an excess of centralization and authoritarianism at the top and an excess of decentralization at the local level—a situation which will probably not change in the absence of a political party.

While the level of conflict existing in Ethiopian society has so far prevented the development of a very centralized and bureaucratic system, Ethiopia has not solved the problem of maintaining a dialectical element in the process of transformation. Conflict has not been clearly accepted as a positive element and institutionalized. The government simply has not been able to suppress it. Although it seems unlikely that the Dergue will succeed in completely eliminating conflict in the foreseeable future, the Dergue nonetheless betrays a definite repressive tendency. This is constrained only by the deep divisions in Ethiopian society and the isolation of rural areas.

The Pressures

Both Mozambique and Ethiopia, then, have attempted—fairly successfully, under the circumstances—to promote a high degree of participation on the part of the population and to set up decentralized institutions. Material conditions and ideology have encouraged the two countries to move in this direction. As for the former, the lack of trained personnel, the difficulty of communications (in Ethiopia, for instance, the majority of the population lives hours of walk away from a road), and the general confusion which arises in a period of rapid change would have made it impossible to set up centralized, tightly planned and controlled systems. The ideological commitment to participation is very explicit in Mozambique, particularly among the top leaders. That on the part of the Dergue in Ethiopia is much more ambiguous, as the recent trend toward the appointment of officers to top positions in the provincial administration demonstrates. In any event, the new governments in both countries have created institutions that make participation possible.

Nevertheless, as we have seen, there have been indications of the emergence of a more bureaucratic tendency. The question is which trend is likely to prevail in the future. To try to answer this question, it is necessary to look at changes in the material conditions of the two countries, for such changes will not only remove the obstacles to centralization which have existed so far but also create pressures for it.

Elimination of obstacles to centralization is closely tied to the process of development. The difficulty of communications and the shortage of cadres are bound to decrease as these countries develop. Although the poverty of Ethiopia and Mozambique suggests that change will be slow and painful, it is taking place. Ethiopia has already embarked on a program of rural road construction and Mozambique is gradually overcoming the transport problems which arose because the Portuguese took with them, or destroyed, large numbers of vehicles when they left. Although there is a serious shortage of cadres and technicians in both countries—particularly acute in the case of Mozambique, which lost most of its educated population with the departure of the Portuguese—the two countries are training people. Ethiopia has greatly increased admissions to the university and has organized an ideological school. Progress in Mozambique has been less dramatic thus far, for the country must increase the number of high school graduates before it can embark on an expansion of higher education. But even here, it is only a matter of time before the number of cadres starts growing.

As the shortage of trained personnel eases, centralization becomes possible, although not inevitable. In Mozambique in particular, there are already signs that the availability of trained personnel may lead to substantially greater centralization. For example, in some areas provincial officials in the Ministry of Agriculture have been preparing production plans for peasant cooperatives.

One reason that the training of more cadres may bring about more centralization is that these cadres will at first be in very short supply. Neither Ethiopia nor Mozambique, after all, can go from having no agronomists to having an agronomist working with each small cooperative or each peasants' association. This state of affairs means that initially there is bound to be strong pressure for the organization of large units of production, so that the few technicians can be put to most efficient use. For instance, Mozambique has in some areas formed peasant cooperatives with hundreds of members, for it is easier, when there are few cadres, to provide help and advice to a few large units than to many small ones.

In addition, the chaos that has plagued both countries is abating, and the administrative and political structures are getting better organized. Although this trend is positive (chaos is certainly not an absolute good), the question is whether there will still be a high level of participation on the part of the population once the institutions become stronger. Here we need to consider the two countries separately.

In Mozambique, the leaders are committed to participation, and so far they have succeeded in promoting it. The policies that FRELIMO pursued in the liberated zones, the creation of the dynamizing groups, the establishment of administrative commissions and production councils in the factories,[32] all have resulted in involving the population, not just the party cadres, in political tasks.

However, the situation is likely to change in the future. FRELIMO is now a ruling party—indeed, a vanguard party. Consequently, it is tightening its organization and the selection of cadres. It is also absorbing the dynamizing groups. By its own statutes, FRELIMO is a strongly hierarchical organization adhering to the principles of democratic centralism, but the stronger FRELIMO becomes, the more the democratic challenge rests essentially on what happens within the party itself. Lately, the criticism sessions which are continuing within all organizations have been directed above all at former collaborators. Whether criticism and conflict will be allowed to continue once the collaborators have been dealt with is a matter which remains to be seen.

The importance of criticism within the party is all the greater since class struggle is more an artificial concept than a reality in Mozambique. Formation of a national bourgeoisie and resurgence of a traditional-feudal oligarchy are potential rather than actual threats. More real is the possibility of the creation of a new bureaucratic class in Milovan Djilas' sense, a privileged class rooted in the party and government bureaucracy. Here again, only democracy within the party can prevent such a development.

In Ethiopia, the situation is quite different. The commitment of the leadership to participation is much less clear. Little open debate of the choices facing the country takes place, decisions are announced after they are made, and any consultation that goes on is covert. Finally, violence has played an important part in resolving conflicts of opinion. A large number of dissenters, both military and civilian, have been killed. To be sure, the blame for this violence does not rest entirely with the winners, for they would probably have found themselves treated in the same fashion had they been on the losing side. Still, one cannot speak of democracy, no matter what definition of the term one chooses to use.

At the same time, the ruling group in Ethiopia faces more severe domestic challenges than does that in Mozambique. There is a considerable amount of opposition, both on the part of civilian groups and within the military. While the wave of "red terror" which swept the country in 1977–78 weakened this opposition, it still persists, and the Dergue has to come to grips with it and the reasons for it if the Dergue is ever to succeed in forming a party. The opposition is more important in the cities, but not confined to there.

In many ways, the dangers of excessive centralization and bureaucratization are less serious now in Ethiopia than in Mozambique. Ethiopia could become centralized only if all opposition groups were destroyed—a threat which hardly seems imminent. Of course, what we find in Ethiopia is not an example of successful democratic centralism; rather, the existence of conflict guarantees that the process of change will remain dialectical.

One of the major pressures for centralization in both Ethiopia and Mozambique comes from economic conditions, and particularly from the problems of the rural sector, which constitutes the backbone of the two countries' economies. The new regimes in both states have in theory chosen a decentralized model of development, relying on the formation of peasants' associations and communal villages to spur production and participation. In practice, however, both governments have been investing large amounts of money and effort in the creation of state farms, thus significantly departing from the model espoused in theory. The reasons are very simple. There has been no dramatic increase in agricultural production since the establishment of peasants' associations and communal villages. In fact, the disruption caused by change has led to a decrease in production which has severely affected urban food supplies. In Mozambique, the Portuguese plantations had provided food for the cities as well as export crops. After the Portuguese departed at independence, the government had to import food out of a dwindling reserve of foreign currency. In Ethiopia, the cities had obtained their food supplies from commercial farms and from the stocks of grain that landlords collected from peasants as feudal dues and sold on the urban market. After the proclamation of the land reform, the peasants started eating more and producing less, thereby creating a severe shortfall in the marketed amount of grain. The problem was compounded by the disruption of production on the nationalized commercial farms. Initially, the government was uncertain whether these farms should be broken up, with the land distributed to the peasants, or should be transformed into state farms, and it did a little of each.

The food shortages in the cities seem to have induced both governments to give a lot of attention, and priority in financing, to the state farm sector. Ethiopia has stopped breaking up the large estates and has even opened more large, mechanized state farms in parts of the southwest, an area historically underpopulated because of the prevalence of sleeping sickness. Mozambique has invested most of its agriculture budget in state farms, although much controversy has surrounded this decision. In August 1978, the Minister of Agriculture, Joaquin de Carvalho, was dismissed on charges of, among other things, having neglected the peasant sector in favor of state farms. Yet, as of the summer of 1979, it does not appear that policies in the field of agriculture have altered significantly since his dismissal. The lion's share of funds continues to go to the state farms, and even the new plans being elaborated for the early 1980s apparently neglect the peasant sector.

One explanation of this neglect of the peasant sector in Mozambique is that communal villages are supposed to be self-sufficient initially. Some officials believe that for the first four or five years the communal villages will be able to pull themselves up by their own bootstraps, and that only at the end of that period will they require government help. It is difficult to know in mid-1979 whether this judgment will prove valid. One of the problems is that once state farms are set up, they will continue to make large funding demands on the Ministry of Agriculture, thus rendering it more difficult for the Ministry to channel funds to help the communal villages.

Ethiopia to date seems to have found a somewhat better balance between state farms and peasants' associations. In part, this state of affairs reflects the establishment during the last years of the imperial regime of a network of extension services aimed at reaching the peasants. This network could be converted to serve the peasants' associations. A major effort is now being made to train at least one member from each association to serve as extension worker in his home area, and loans are available to the associations. However, as already noted, new, mechanized state farms are being created even in Ethiopia.

Thus, there is a great deal of ambiguity in the agricultural policies of both countries, and a real possibility exists that the persistent problem of feeding the cities will encourage reliance on state farms. This is particularly true because even increases in production in the peasant sector may not generate a marketable surplus, for the peasants are generally undernourished and therefore likely to increase their own consumption before selling their output.

International Relations

So far, we have discussed events in Mozambique and Ethiopia from a strictly internal perspective, but one cannot simply dismiss out of hand the possibility of international linkages. To what extent, for example, have the choices made by the new regimes in the two countries to date been affected by outside forces, particularly the USSR? To what degree are international factors likely to have an impact on such choices in the future? It is to these issues that we now turn.

In Mozambique, the ideological choice was quite unrelated to Soviet influence. As mentioned previously, this choice resulted initially from events within the liberated zones, at a time when FRELIMO was receiving some arms and training from socialist countries but was indebted above all to Tanzania and Zambia, which were offering hospitality to FRELIMO guerrillas on their territory. In fact, the document called "The Process of the People's Democratic Revolution in Mozambique," which constituted FRELIMO's ideological charter during this period, listed as FRELIMO's major allies other liberation movements and progressive African countries, the Organization of African Unity, the working masses of NATO countries which opposed their governments' support for Portugal, and antifascist organizations in Portugal itself. The socialist states were cited last.[33] Above all, FRELIMO warned that "our fight for national independence requires a strong defense of our autonomy in the formulation of our foreign policy and the complete respect of the principles of equality and nonintervention in our internal affairs in our relations with other countries and other organizations."[34]

The party program of 1977 defined the "international workers' movement and Marxist-Leninist parties" as FRELIMO's "natural allies,"[35] but it stressed again the principle of independence in the conduct of the country's foreign affairs. Political reality thus far has facilitated respect for this principle, for Mozambique is not dependent on any one country for aid, but receives it from a variety of sources. The Soviet Union provides most arms, and the two states signed a treaty of friendship and cooperation during former USSR President Nikolay Podgornyy's visit to Mozambique in April 1977. Cuba, the Soviet Union, and various East European nations furnish technicians, but so do Portugal and other Western countries. The economic aid the country needs comes overwhelmingly from the West. Sweden extends a considerable amount of this assistance, particularly in the field of agriculture. Although the Mozambique government has been leery of involvement with the World Bank, it has obtained a number of loans from American banks. Mozambiquan authorities emphasize that they have no prejudices about dealing with the West. Indeed, Mozambique is even carrying on economic relations with the Republic of South Africa, which has committed itself to make more use of the port of Maputo and to improve Maputo's port facilities and railroad links as part of the bargain.

While there is little doubt about the Mozambiquan leadership's determination to maintain its autonomy, the political situation in Southern Africa poses a threat to that autonomy. Mozambique has been seriously affected by the war in Rhodesia, economically and, increasingly, militarily. In fact, the Rhodesian army has repeatedly bombed camps of the Zimbabwe African National Union (ZANU) in Mozambique and on some occasions even Mozambiquan military targets. If these attacks, which Mozambique is not equipped to oppose, should escalate, the country would be forced to become very dependent militarily on the Soviet Union, with all the problems of political interference which can derive from military dependence. Aside from enhancing the possibility of foreign interference, a continued and worsening war situation would probably encourage more centralization and authoritarianism in the country. The legislation passed in early 1979 that, among other things, introduced the death penalty for acts which threaten the security of the state, is just a sign of what the future may hold.[36] Thus, Mozambique's autonomy in international affairs and the fate of its internal policies of decentralization and participation to a considerable extent lie hostage to developments in the Rhodesian conflict.

Ethiopia, too, began its process of political transformation completely autonomously. Prior to 1977, the USSR played no significant role in Ethiopia. In fact, the United States until this time constituted the principal supplier of military aid to the country. Nevertheless, the policies adopted by the Dergue were, as we have seen, unmistakably socialist.

In early 1977, however, the military government, faced with the threat of disintegration of the state and with reluctance on the part of the United States to furnish the military aid that the Ethiopian regime urgently needed, turned to the USSR and Cuba. The Soviet Union provided Ethiopia with about a billion dollars' worth of arms, and Cuba sent it military personnel—up to 20,000 men at the peak. Hand in hand with this heavy dependence on Soviet and Cuban military aid went open commitment to Marxism-Leninism, in the most orthodox Soviet interpretation, and an almost slavish acceptance of the Soviet position on international issues such as Vietnam and China.

Nonetheless, the acceptance of the ideology did not lead to any significant changes in the Dergue's domestic policies. Moreover, Western economic aid has somewhat counterbalanced Ethiopia's military dependence on the USSR. The World Bank, the European Economic Community, Sweden, and even the United States have remained the major sources of economic assistance.

As to the future, Ethiopia's military dependence on the Soviet Union is likely to continue. Although the immediate threat to the African state's territorial integrity has been checked, the conflicts which brought about the dependency are by no means settled. Nor is the Dergue yet in a position to handle these conflicts on its own.

Conclusions

Because of all the unresolved issues in Mozambique and Ethiopia, it is impossible to conclude with a firm statement as to what Marxism-Leninism in these countries will amount to in the long run. While the governments of the two countries have attempted to pave the way for a decentralized and participatory system, there are economic and political factors at work in each which could bring about the opposite outcome. Furthermore, until the Rhodesian conflict is settled, relations between Ethiopia and Somalia are ameliorated, and a solution is found to the Eritrean problem, both countries will be open to foreign interference.

However, it is unlikely that in either case the Soviet Union will be able to determine policies. At most, Soviet involvement will be one of many factors operating. Socialism in Ethiopia and Mozambique is not simply the transplant of a foreign ideology. It reflects a complex process of social, political, and economic change shaped not only by ideological choices but also by power struggles and hard economic necessity.

6

Cuba, the Soviet Union, and Africa

Edward Gonzalez

SINCE IT LAUNCHED its Angolan operation in 1975, Cuba has emerged as a major actor in Africa. As of mid-1979, Havana had committed combat forces not only to Angola but also to Ethiopia, and it had sent military advisers, medical teams, and technical personnel to several additional African states.

Cuba has not acted alone, however. While the Castro government has dispatched combat troops and fighter pilots to Africa, it has had to rely directly or indirectly upon Soviet weaponry and logistical support to carry out its large-scale military operations in Angola and Ethiopia. That it has acted in concert with the USSR tends to be overlooked or dismissed by Cuba's defenders, but the fact that it has operated in tandem with the Soviet Union is seized upon by others as proof of their argument that Cuba is essentially an extension of Soviet global power. In my view, both of these perspectives are faulty. The first ignores the Cuban-Soviet relationship and the way that relationship affects Cuban policy in Africa; furthermore, it discounts the political, economic, and military payoffs Havana obtains from its African policy. The second perspective grossly oversimplifies the Soviet-Cuban relationship by reducing it to one of dominance and subordination. In so doing, it misses the dynamics of the interaction between Havana and Moscow and the leverage Cuba may obtain over the USSR as a result of its African successes.

This study assesses Cuba's expanding role in Africa in the context of the Cuban-Soviet relationship and of Soviet policy toward Africa.

Research for this article was facilitated by grants from the Social Science Research Council and from the Committee on International and Comparative Studies, and the Academic Senate, at the University of California, Los Angeles. The author also wishes to thank Martha Cottam and Isidro Sepulveda for their research assistance.

145

It begins by examining three views regarding Cuba's African role and their assumptions about Soviet policy on the continent. Next, it looks more closely at Soviet policy in Africa at the time of Angola, analyzing the implications of that policy for Cuba's own policy on the continent and for the Cuban-Soviet relationship. It then focuses on the impact of Angola on Soviet policy, and on the heightened international leverage and privileged relationship with Moscow that Cuba's role in Angola enabled Havana to acquire. Finally, the study concludes with a speculative analysis of the possible interactions between Cuban and Soviet elites and the resulting direct and indirect influence Cuba may exert on future Soviet policy in Africa.

At the outset, however, a brief caveat is in order regarding the analysis of Cuban foreign policy. Like those who work on other Communist regimes, the student of Cuba and its foreign policy is faced with a number of imponderables, owing in large measure to the closed and highly centralized nature of the Cuban political system and to the resulting absence, in most instances, of public debates within the regime itself. Hence, my analysis relies to a considerable extent on inferential evidence gleaned from the official Cuban press and particularly from the speeches of Fidel Castro and other Cuban leaders. In addition, it employs a "rational actor" approach to Cuban foreign policy. That is, I impute certain policy dispositions to specific Cuban elite elements on the basis of their previously observed policy preferences and of their likely stances on policy issues in light of their particular leadership positions, organizational interests, and so forth. Obviously, this type of approach can distort political "reality" because it may leave out other factors at work in the Cuban policy-making process, such as Soviet influence on Havana or personal interactions and bureaucratic politics within the top echelons of the Castro regime. Still, I have used these methodologies in the past to successfully predict Cuban political behavior, and predictive capability does remain a principal test for any political analysis.

Cuba: Surrogate, Internationalist, or Paladin?

Cuba's large-scale military presence in Angola, Ethiopia, and elsewhere in Africa, totaling an estimated 38,000 troops by the spring of 1978, has given rise to different interpretations of the expanding political and military role of Cuba in Africa. In the eyes of many of its critics, Cuba is seen as an indebted, compliant client state of the USSR, and thus as a Soviet-directed *surrogate* in Africa.[1] Accordingly, Cuba is less of an autonomous global actor than an instrument of Soviet foreign policy. That is, Cuba actively promotes Soviet political and strategic objectives in the region, while receiving necessary Soviet logistical support in return for its major operations in Angola, Ethiopia, and elsewhere.

A contrary view, put forth by Cuba's admirers as well as by the Castro regime itself, holds that Cuba is a self-directed revolutionary *internationalist* committed to combatting imperialism and to promoting national liberation and socialism in the Third World.[2] The dispatch of Cuban combat soldiers to Angola in 1975–77 and later to Ethiopia in 1977–78 thus represents an extension of Cuba's earlier, but more modest, military operations in Algeria in the early 1960s, Vietnam in the mid-1960s, and Syria in early 1974, along with lesser overseas missions elsewhere prior to Angola.[3]

Still another view, which I myself have advanced elsewhere, is that Cuba is a self-motivated international *paladin* which must necessarily operate within the parameters of Soviet political and strategic interests in Africa but which nevertheless pursues its own objectives in the region. This interpretation sees Cuban motivations as far more complex than does the internationalist thesis, as involving not only ideological drives but also the organizational interests of the Cuban armed forces and Fidel Castro's desire for heightened international status and increased leverage with the Third World and especially the Soviet Union.[4]

Although these three interpretations differ in their explanations of Cuban foreign policy, they share a set of implicit assumptions regarding Soviet policy toward Africa and Cuba's role in that policy at the time of Angola. The first assumption is that the Soviet Union had a grand design for Africa or that it was at least pursuing an expansionist strategy in the region. Thus, the surrogate thesis posits a highly activist Soviet strategy of penetration designed to achieve major political, economic, and strategic gains on the African continent.[5] For different reasons, the internationalist interpretation also maintains that the USSR was following an activist policy in Africa, as indicated by Soviet material as well as moral support for national liberation movements, progressive regimes, and socialist forces on the continent.[6] Although less explicit on the subject, the paladin thesis assumes that the Soviet Union had expansionist aims in mind in Africa.[7]

A correlative assumption is that Cuba's role in Africa was more or less dependent upon and supportive of Soviet policy in the region. This assumption clearly underlies the surrogate thesis, which sees Cuba's mounting presence in Africa as the outcome of established Soviet policy, with the Cubans serving as the cutting edge of the Soviet advance.[8] While the internationalist view assigns complete independence to Cuba's actions in Africa, it also inadvertently shares the same assumption. This view defends Soviet material support for Cuban operations in Africa on the grounds of Soviet solidarity with Cuba *and* the progressive or revolutionary forces in Africa.[9] As in the surrogate thesis, therefore, Cuban behavior is deemed to have been fully in phase with and supportive of established Soviet policy. The paladin argument explicitly adopts the same position. Although Cuba was pursuing its own ends in Africa, this line of thought argues that Havana must necessarily capitalize upon Soviet interests and objectives in the region in order to generate increased international leverage with the USSR.[10]

An expansionist Soviet policy, in turn, would have allowed Cuba some degree of influence over Soviet policy toward Africa if only because of Cuba's instrumental value to the USSR. This value lay in two related considerations. First, Cuba had developed a military presence in Africa long before Angola. In 1961, the Cubans set up a guerrilla training base in Ghana, and that base stayed in operation until Kwame Nkrumah's overthrow by the military in 1966. Cuban combat troops were deployed in Algeria in 1963–65 during that country's border conflict with Morocco. Ché Guevara led a contingent of Cuban guerrillas into Zaire and then into Congo-Brazzaville in 1965–66, prior to taking up the struggle in Bolivia. During 1965–66, Cuba established a large advisory military mission in the Congo-Brazzaville. This mission was credited with helping to quash a Congolese army revolt in June of the latter year. In 1966, Havana began to furnish military aid to the regime of Ahmed Sékou Touré in Guinea, including personnel to man Sékou Touré's Presidential Guard. Although Cuba's military involvement in Africa declined in the late 1960s, it picked up again after 1971. Thus, Havana dispatched new military missions to Sierra Leone in 1972, Somalia in 1974, and Algeria in 1975—all prior to the large-scale troop buildup in Angola that took place in the late summer of 1975.[11]

Second, Cuba's political, technical, and military missions in the region enjoyed far greater legitimacy than did those of the USSR.[12] For example, President Sékou Touré of Guinea, who had expelled the Soviet ambassador in late 1961, evidently for making contact with opposition groups within the country, five years later requested Cuba's assistance in setting up a popular militia to protect his regime against internal and external enemies. Indeed, the militia was later credited with playing a key role in repulsing a Portuguese attack on Conakry in November 1970. Also in 1966, as already noted, Sékou Touré established a Presidential Guard and staffed it with Cubans. As of the mid-1970s, it remained partially composed of Cuban officers.[13] Such acceptance of Cuba prior to Angola stemmed from a number of factors: Cuba was a small, revolutionary state in the Third World; its Afro-Cuban population had historic roots in Africa; and, although aligned with the Soviet bloc, Cuba behaved as a committed, selfless internationalist without big-power designs on the continent.[14]

Soviet Policy: Expansionist or Reactive?

For a Soviet Union pursuing an expansionist strategy in Africa, then, Cuba would constitute both a useful and influential ally. Upon closer inspection, however, it is by no means clear that Moscow was embarked upon an expansionist strategy in Africa, or even that it had clear-cut goals, at the time of Angola. To be sure, various observers have amassed evidence for the expansionist case.[15] Thus, they see Soviet material support for Marxist and liberation movements such as the Popular Movement for the Liberation of Angola (*Movimento Popular de Libertação de Angola* — MPLA) and the exiled African National Congress of South Africa, and for such unlikely regimes as those of Mu'ammar Gadhafi in Libya and Idi Amin in Uganda, as evidence of a drive to expand the Soviet Union's political influence. Southern Africa, in particular, they consider an invaluable economic prize for the USSR, as the entire region is rich with such mineral resources as petroleum, iron ore, diamonds, gold, uranium, and titanium.[16] Finally, they argue that the USSR pursues strategic advantage in Africa, as indicated by the fact that it has secured anchorage and air landing privileges along the African coast, thereby extending Soviet blue-water and airlift capabilities and providing the Soviet military with potential chokeholds over strategic routes in the Red Sea and the Indian and Atlantic Oceans.[17]

Nevertheless, other analysts of Soviet policy contend that aside from the Horn and North Africa, the African continent had assumed peripheral importance to the USSR by the 1970s. Beginning in the late 1960s, they maintain, the primary target of Soviet activity in the Third World became the belt of states to the south of the USSR that stretches from North Africa through the Middle East to South Asia. In this region, according to Richard Lowenthal, the Soviets embarked upon a new "strategy of counterimperialism" designed to stake out and consolidate a hegemonial position. As part of this strategy, Moscow concentrated its activities on states that were intrinsically important because of their geographic proximity, strategic position, and possible economic contribution to a future international division of labor—regardless of their political coloration or revolutionary potential. Moreover, it relied heavily upon Western-style economic linkages between the USSR and the target countries as a principal means by which to secure the Soviet zone of influence and to limit future Western encroachments. As a result, Iran, Pakistan, and Turkey, along with such traditional foreign aid recipients as India and Afghanistan, became favored objects of Soviet economic attention.[18] Significantly, this view not only assigns a low Soviet priority to much of Africa but also depicts Soviet strategy toward the Third World as highly conventional and conservative in its thrust.

These and other observers see Soviet policy within Africa itself prior to Angola as one of selective engagement rather than expansion, and, above all, as reactive and opportunistic.[19] The policy of selective engagement, they argue, stemmed initially from previous Soviet disappointment in supporting "revolutionary democratic" regimes in the early 1960s in the hope of effecting a transition to socialism in the countries over which these regimes ruled. In some crucial instances, such radical regimes proved unstable and were succeeded by more conservative ones: thus, President Ahmed Ben Bella of Algeria was overthrown by Colonel Houari Boumediene in mid-1965; in early 1966, President Kwame Nkrumah of Ghana suffered a similar fate at the hands of his military; and in 1968, Modibo Keita of Mali was also overthrown by a military coup. The downfall of these three "radical democrats"—all of whom, incidentally, had earlier been recipients of the Lenin Peace Prize—led to a fundamental reassessment of Soviet perspectives on Africa. In Soviet eyes, revolutionary advances in the region—to say nothing of the transition to socialism—now lay in the far distant future.[20] This more realistic if not pessimistic assessment was reinforced by the high volatility and unreliability that still other progressive governments later displayed in their foreign as well as domestic policies. In the Sudan, for example, Moscow in the late 1960s and early 1970s urged the local Communists to adopt a "national Communist" course in support of the regime of General Ja'far Muhammad Numayri, which at the time was strongly pro-Soviet; but after an abortive coup by Communist dissidents in 1971, Soviet relations with the Sudan deteriorated drastically as Numayri swung sharply toward the United States and the conservative Arab bloc.[21] Furthermore, in Egypt President Anwar al-Sadat, who succeeded Gamal Abdel Nasser in 1970, soon deviated from Nasser's strategy of close ties with the USSR, first by ousting Soviet military advisers in mid-1972 and then by turning full circle to the United States after 1974. Even where "revolutionary democrats" were firmly committed to a "socialist orientation" for their country, the Soviets conceded that structural constraints would force them to remain within the "orbit of the world capitalist economic system."[22]

These and other considerations, according to this school of thought, inclined the Soviets toward a basically selective, nonexpansionist policy in Africa prior to Angola. Moscow focused its attention on such economically and politically important states as Nigeria and on such strategically situated ones as Somalia, Algeria, and Tunisia, regardless of their political orientations. Elsewhere, the Soviet Union's material backing of national liberation movements—even Marxist ones—was by no means as steadfast as commonly assumed. A month prior to the Portuguese coup of April 1974, for instance, the Soviets for the second time abandoned Agostinho Neto, founding leader of the MPLA, and withheld support from that faction-ridden organization for more than six months; they did not resume it until the late summer or early fall of 1974, after Neto had regained control of his party and the Chinese had begun arming rival groups in Angola.[23]

In addition, these analysts go on, Soviet policy seemed reactive and opportunistic, with Moscow responding to developments in Africa and to U.S. and Chinese activities in the region. Moscow's renewed support for the liberation struggle in Angola, for example, was in large measure the outgrowth of the rapid decolonization process that followed the Portuguese coup of April 1974. In particular, the pro-Soviet and pro-MPLA orientation of the government of Vasco Gonçalves in Lisbon opened the way for Moscow to vastly increase its material support to the MPLA between March and July 1975—specifically, to ship armaments worth an estimated $20–30 million to the African group.[24] But the intensified Soviet (and Cuban) commitment to the MPLA at this time may also have been aimed at countering the United States and China, especially the latter since the Chinese were the principal backers of the MPLA's two rivals.[25] In fact, a desire to stem rising Chinese influence among guerrilla groups and regimes in Southern Africa had been a prime factor behind the step-up in Soviet material assistance to liberation movements beginning in the early 1970s.[26]

This general interpretation of Soviet motives and behavior—i.e., that Africa held only peripheral importance for Moscow, and that Soviet policy was essentially reactive and opportunistic—delineates a setting that would not be particularly advantageous for Cuba. To begin with, Cuba's political and military presence in Africa would have but marginal importance for the Soviet Union's global strategy. Consequently, were Moscow to call upon Cuba's services in the region, Cuba would become merely a "surrogate," operating at the discretion of its patron and employed for the furtherance of the latter's objectives. Africa's low priority, moreover, would mean that Cuba's instrumental value would be confined strictly to those few African countries of some importance to the USSR, either because of their intrinsic merit or because of their value in the international competition with China and the United States. Cuba's activity as an "internationalist" actor would therefore be restricted by limited Soviet ambitions in the region. Finally, the political influence that Cuba would gain with the Soviets because of its successful ventures in Africa would tend to be transitory, owing to the region's low priority in Soviet eyes. Thus, even as a purposeful "paladin," Cuba would be able to generate but limited, short-term international leverage vis-à-vis the Soviets as a result of its African activities.

Angola: A Watershed

The joint Cuban-Soviet operation in Angola that began in the summer of 1975 by no means settled the question of whether the Soviets were at the time pursuing an expansionist or an opportunistic, reactive policy, for there is evidence to support both interpretations. For example, the expansionist thesis gains credence from the fact that Soviet support had enabled Cuba's Revolutionary Armed Forces (FAR) to attain new levels of organizational, combat proficiency by the mid-1970s. This enhanced proficiency, together with the reduced use of the FAR for domestic developmental tasks and the lessening of the external threat to Cuba as a result of the Soviet-U.S. détente, greatly increased Cuba's capabilities for carrying out overseas missions.[27] Furthermore, the close coordination of Soviet logistical support with the large-scale Cuban troop buildup in Angola that commenced in the late summer of 1975 suggests that Moscow (and Havana) were indeed adhering to an expansionist design.

However, there were also elements of an opportunistic, reactive, and even incremental policy in the ever-growing Cuban-Soviet commitment to the MPLA. Thus, the Cubans and Soviets upped their level of support for the MPLA at the very time that the Chinese were disengaging from the Angolan civil war.[28] Somewhat later, the South African invasion into southern Angola in late October, coupled with the Zairian incursion from the north, threatened to entrap the 1,000 Cuban military personnel already stationed in Angola and led to the hurried airlifting of still more Cuban troops to repel the invaders.[29] In turn, the South African invasion helped Havana and Moscow justify the large Cuban presence in Angola—estimated at 15,000 troops by February 1976—to many African goverments. Finally, the disinclination of the United States to intervene, made evident by strong Congressional opposition to such action in December 1975, cleared the way for Cuba and the USSR to commit the necessary personnel and matériel to win militarily in Angola.[30]

Whatever the case may be, the success of the Angolan venture immediately gave Soviet policy in Africa a fresh impetus. In Angola itself, a friendly Marxist government was now seated in Luanda and consolidating its power. Elsewhere, the USSR made significant strides in combatting Chinese influence in Mozambique and Guinea-Bissau by means of loans and credits in the post-1975 period, although stepped-up Soviet aid to Tanzania had little impact on that country's close ties with Peking.[31] In the meantime, working closely with Cuban military and political advisers, the Soviets also became the principal supplier of military aid to the guerrilla forces based in Mozambique and Zambia that were seeking to liberate Zimbabwe from white Rhodesian rule and that had previously relied heavily on the Chinese.[32] To the north, on the Horn of Africa, the USSR began supplying arms to the radical military regime of Mengistu Haile Mariam in Ethiopia under a secret accord signed in December 1976. Eleven months later, not only Soviet material aid but also Cuban combat troops started to arrive en masse in Ethiopia to help the beleaguered

Mengistu repel the Somali invasion of the Ogaden and to shore up his government in its struggle with the Eritrean secessionist movement. By the spring of 1978, the Mengistu regime appeared relatively well entrenched owing largely to the presence of an estimated 16,000 or more Cuban military personnel, who had proved to be the decisive factor in the routing of Somali forces.[33] Meanwhile, although they lost their political influence and military facilities in Somalia by their backing of Ethiopia, the Soviets had secured an even stronger foothold on the Horn because of the direct Cuban-Soviet military presence in Ethiopia.[34]

These and other developments indicate that Soviet activities in Africa have gained a political momentum, and a military dimension, that did not exist prior to Angola. In this connection, one observer suggests: ". . . the step-up of Soviet activities on the continent since 1975 probably reflects an increase in opportunities rather than any change in approach. . . . [I]n recent years Africa has afforded Moscow more openings to expand its influence than has any other area of the Third World."[35] In turn, it has been to Cuba's own advantage to exploit if not create these new "openings" in Africa in order to maintain and enhance its leverage with the Soviet Union, as well as with the Third World in general.

In the context of the Cuban-Soviet relationship, international leverage here means Cuba's ability to influence Soviet policy to Cuba's own advantage by actively exploiting the Soviet Union's big power interests and its military and economic resources.[36] Cuba first obtained such leverage in Angola by demonstrating to Moscow that it had become an indispensable ally in Africa, capable not only of installing a pro-Soviet, Marxist regime in power but also of advancing Soviet prestige and influence elsewhere in Southern Africa. As a result, Cuba obtained highly favorable economic and trade accords from the USSR in April 1976, followed by new arms shipments from the Soviets to equip the FAR with more modern, sophisticated weaponry.[37] In addition, the Cuban regime gained a privileged status within the socialist camp. That status has been demonstrated by the deferential Soviet treatment of Fidel Castro at the 25th Congress of the Communist Party of the Soviet Union (CPSU) in February 1976 and by the frequent trips of consultation that he, his brother, and other Cuban officials have made to Moscow in subsequent years.

Since its Angolan exploits, therefore, Cuba has gone on to mount its own diplomatic, economic, and military offensive in Africa. For instance, Castro made a month-long triumphal tour of several African states in the spring of 1977, and he followed up this tour with still another visit to North Africa in the late summer of 1978. Havana has received delegations led by Neto, Mengistu, Joshua Nkomo, and other African leaders, and is offering education and technical training to Angolan and other African school children. Cuba has stationed new economic and technical aid missions in several African states in a further demonstration of its commitment to internationalism. It has also dispatched military advisers to Mozambique, Zambia, and Angola to train guerrilla contingents for the armed struggles over Zimbabwe and Namibia. Havana increased its military presence in Angola to an estimated 19,000 to 20,000 during 1977, after a partial pullout, in order to shore up the Neto government in the face of mounting internal resistance. By late March 1978, Cuba had dispatched some 16,000 combat troops and other military personnel to Ethiopia to help the Mengistu regime repel the Somali invasion and consolidate its hold on Ethiopia (excluding Eritrea).[38]

These and other activities further Cuba's own policy aims in Africa, such as the promotion of liberation and socialist movements, the creation of political alliances with radical African regimes, and the assertion of Castro's leadership over much of the Third World. But such activities are obviously congruent with and highly supportive of Soviet interests. It is noteworthy, for example, that while Cuba's Expenditionary Forces that spearheaded the successful offensive against Somalia in February–March 1978 were led by Division General Arnaldo Ochoa, they were under the overall command of Lt. General Vasiliy Ivanovich Petrov of the USSR.[39] Through its political as well as military activities, Cuba has thus assumed a unique role in advancing Moscow's big power aims and ambitions in Africa, thereby greatly enhancing Cuba's value as a strategic ally of the Soviet Union.

Accordingly, Cuba has since the mid-1970s become an international "paladin" rather than a compliant "surrogate" of the USSR or an ideologically-driven "internationalist." In this new role, Cuba promotes its own as well as Soviet interests in Africa, while actively deriving leverage with Moscow because of its effectiveness there. Indeed, Cuba's enhanced leverage is evident not only from the stepped-up Soviet arms deliveries to the FAR but also from the extraordinarily large subsidies that Moscow has been bestowing on the Cuban economy since the mid-1970s.[40] In addition, Cuba's new leverage may enable it to maintain some degree of independence from

Moscow in its own policy toward Africa and even to exercise some influence over Soviet policy on the continent.

Because of its increased leverage as a paladin, Cuba may at times be in a position to assert the priority of its own national interests in its African policy even though it must necessarily operate within the broad parameters of Soviet objectives. In Angola in May 1977, for example, Cuban troops were employed by Agostinho Neto to quash an attempted coup by an extremist, pro-Soviet faction within the MPLA. While it is not certain that the attempted coup was backed by Moscow, Neto's supporters are convinced of the fact.[41] If their suspicions are in fact correct, then Cuba's support of Neto ran counter to Soviet inclinations. Even if these suspicions are unfounded, Cuba's involvement nevertheless contrasts sharply with Soviet efforts to subvert Neto in the pre-1975 period.[42] In Ethiopia, Cuba's position on the Eritrean issue may have diverged from the initial Soviet inclination, and may perhaps have influenced Moscow's subsequent stance regarding a negotiated settlement. During the first part of 1978, Soviet public pronouncements implied that Moscow would back Mengistu on the use of military force to crush the Eritrean insurgents.[43] As early as February 26, however, Cuban Vice-President Carlos Rafael Rodríguez publicly insisted that Cuban troops would not be deployed against the rebels on grounds that Cuba had helped the Eritreans in their fight for self-determination from Ethiopia from the time of Haile Selassie onward, and that a "political solution" now had to be pursued by means of talks between the two sides.[44] Castro himself reaffirmed this perspective in late April during Mengistu's visit to Havana.[45] Faced with Arab as well as Cuban opposition to a military solution, Moscow the ensuing June began pushing actively for a negotiated settlement of the Eritrean issue.[46]

If the Cuban position on Neto and Eritrea did in actuality deviate from initial Soviet inclinations, Castro had the leverage with which to maintain his stance. To begin with, Moscow was totally dependent upon the employment of Cuban ground forces for the furtherance of Soviet gains in both Angola and Ethiopia. Hence, any initial Soviet preference for an anti-Neto faction or for a military solution in Eritrea would have had to yield to the Cuban position. On the Eritrean issue, the Cuban stance was also bolstered by the opposition of most Arab states to a military approach. Castro may have gained further leverage in both cases from the need to maintain some independence of action in the two countries in order to preserve Cuba's credibility as an autonomous Third World actor, free of Soviet control. The imperative of keeping up an image of independence among sensitive nationalist circles in the Third World thus redounds to Castro's advantage in dealing with Moscow on African questions.

Cuba's paladin role also may at times permit Cuba to influence— both directly and indirectly—the African policy of the Soviet Union. Havana's position on the Eritrean question in early 1978 is an example of how the Cubans can conceivably affect Soviet decisions on purely local or tactical matters. But the Castro regime may be able to influence Soviet policy on an even larger scale as well. In this connection, the necessity for Cuba to capitalize on Soviet aims in Africa in order to enhance its leverage position suggests that the Castro regime will press the Soviets to maintain their activist policy in Africa and to exploit new openings on the continent. From Havana's perspective, of course, such activism should be consonant with Cuba's foreign policy aims and limitations in Africa. Thus, the Cubans would seek to avoid appearing as a "proxy" of the Soviets in future overseas operations, while ensuring that the latter were within Cuba's material and manpower capabilities (to be discussed later).

For their part, the Soviets are certain to weigh a number of factors before deciding upon whether to maintain or intensify their activist policy in Africa. These include considerations relating to domestic politics, the United States and Western Europe, the SALT negotiations, the local African scene itself, and Soviet priorities and openings elsewhere, as in the increasingly turbulent Middle East. But the point is that, unlike in the pre-1975 period, *neither the Cuban position on Africa nor the Cuban factor in Africa can be ignored by the Soviets in their policy deliberations.* Accordingly, we need to look at how the Cubans might interact with and have impact on Soviet foreign policy elites in the course of the USSR's formulation of its African policy. Such impact is likely to take both direct and indirect forms.

Direct Cuban Influence

Direct Cuban effects on Soviet policy-makers will stem from lobbying activities by Cuban leaders in joint consultations and strategy sessions and as a result of other direct communications with Moscow regarding African affairs. These activities are likely to be spearheaded by Fidel himself, by his brother Raúl, and by the Cuban military, all of whom are the principal advocates within the Castro regime of high levels of Cuban-Soviet involvement in Africa. These Cuban elites likewise appear to enjoy far greater access to the Soviet political and military leadership than do other elite groupings or individuals within Cuba, save perhaps Vice-President Carlos Rafael Rodríguez.[47]

As has been argued, it is in Fidel's interest to influence Soviet policy on Africa along activist lines, since an activist Soviet policy optimizes Cuba's international status and its leverage position with Moscow and the Third World. Thus, he has reiterated time and again that Cuba itself will not forego its internationalist obligations in Africa as a condition for the normalization of relations with the United States.[48] Indeed, the fact that Havana is to host the Sixth Conference of Nonaligned States in September 1979 could provide a further incentive for Cuba to adhere to a highly activist foreign policy.[49]

Moreover, Fidel himself can be expected to carry considerable weight in Soviet foreign policy circles. After all, he has enabled the USSR to register important advances in Africa; he received a triumphant reception in several African states in the spring of 1977 and remains in close contact with African leaders; and he has become an effective broker between the socialist camp and Africa, serving in effect as a Third World link between the two. His influence is especially bound to be felt in Moscow given the fact that he enjoys direct access to the top Soviet leadership. Thus, after his African tour in March 1977, he flew to the USSR in early April for high-level strategy sessions and was greeted at the airport by Leonid Brezhnev, General Secretary of the Communist Party of the Soviet Union (CPSU); Premier Alexey Kosygin; then-President Nikolay Podgornyy; and Foreign Minister Andrey Gromyko.[50]

Strong supporters of Fidel's activist stance in Cuban foreign policy are his brother, Raúl Castro, and the Revolutionary Armed Forces (FAR). As General of the Army and head of the Ministry of the Revolutionary Armed Forces (MINFAR), Raúl expanded the military mission of the FAR to include not only internal defense but also support of Cuba's foreign policy objectives. The result of this new overseas mission, and the capabilities developed to fulfill it, was Cuba's large-scale military involvement in Angola and Ethiopia.

The FAR, for their part, have received both symbolic and tangible rewards following their successful operations in Africa. For instance, a new nomenclature system was promulgated for the FAR at the end of 1976. This established for FAR-MINFAR general officers the ranks of

General of the Army, Army Corps General, Division General, and Brigadier General; it increased the numbers of ranks for still other officers, thereby improving the opportunities for career advancement; and it placed Cuba's officer corps on an equal footing with the military of other countries.[51] In addition, Division Generals Senén Casas and Abelardo Colomé were appointed to the newly created Council of State at the end of 1976 in recognition of their key roles in the Angolan operation. The FAR also became the recipients of material payoffs from the USSR in the wake of Angola. Most of the Cuban military equipment used in Angola was replaced by new inventories and upgraded weapon systems within two years of that operation. For instance, the Soviets supplied newer T-62 tanks to replace the Korean-vintage T-34 tanks, as well as ZSU 23–4 self-propelled antiaircraft guns.[52] Later, in the spring of 1978, with Cuban pilots flying MIG-23s over Ethiopia, Cuba itself received several of these advanced aircraft. The MIG-23 augments Cuba's basic inventory of MIG-21s and presumably will replace the MIG-17s and MIG-15s that are being phased out.[53] On still another dimension, the victories won by Cuban troops in Angola and Ethiopia appear to have infused the Army with a heightened sense of military professionalism and *esprit de corps,* all the more so since these operations have brought the FAR new international recognition.[54] Moreover, the FAR have achieved their military successes without incurring high losses. Indeed, casualty rates thus far apparently have been relatively low within regular army ranks, as reservists accounted for 70 percent of the Cuban troops in Angola in 1975–76 and have since comprised 50 percent or more of the Cuban forces serving in Africa.[55]

One can expect, therefore, that the recent military successes in Africa have set in motion an array of organizational dynamics and interests within the FAR that will further impel Raúl and other MINFAR generals to push for the continuation of activist postures on the part of both Cuba and the USSR. In this connection, Africa looms as the logical choice for Cuba's future military involvement. Not only do the FAR currently have a military momentum and logistical backup system in Africa, but they have also become *the* decisive military factor in much of Africa. They do not enjoy such an advantage in the Middle East, for example, where Cuba's military prowess could be matched by that of the Arab states and where Cuba would encounter a formidable enemy in Israel.

In turn, it is through the Soviet military that Raúl and the MINFAR will most probably try to influence Soviet policy in Africa. The Cuban and Soviet military have had ongoing and institutionalized contact since 1960, when the USSR first began to supply armaments and training to Cuba. Indeed, the subsequent development of ties between the Cuban and Soviet military establishments constituted the most important institutional linkage between the two countries during the 1960s, far overshadowing the relationship between the CPSU and the Communist Party of Cuba (PCC), whose official existence dates only from October 1965.[56] In the 1970s, the increased proficiency and professionalism of the FAR, coupled with the success of the joint Cuban-Soviet ventures in Angola and Ethiopia, have most probably strengthened the professional and institutional bonds between the two military establishments. In any event, Soviet military specialists have long been stationed in Cuba under the command of a Soviet general; high-ranking Soviet officers, including the Minister of Defense, have visited Cuba; Raúl Castro routinely meets with his Soviet counterpart, Defense Minister D. F. Ustinov; and Soviet and Cuban generals reportedly worked closely in coordinating the Cuban offensive in Ethiopia.[57] Thus, through both formal and informal ties, the Soviet military establishment will surely serve as the principal conduit by which the MINFAR strives to influence Soviet policy in Africa. For its part, as will be elaborated below, the Soviet military may well have its own reasons for supporting the Cubans.

Indirect Cuban Influence

The nature of Cuba's indirect impact on Soviet policy will depend on Soviet assessments of the likely effect that Cuba's military, political, and technical presence will have on Africa, and of the way in which the existence of this Cuban factor can advance, obstruct, or complicate Soviet aims on the continent. Favorable assessments of the Cuban factor can bolster Cuba's own efforts to influence Soviet policy directly, i.e., can render the direct and indirect influences mutually supporting; conversely, negative Soviet assessments of the Cuban factor will tend to limit the effectiveness of Cuban lobbying activities.

But given Cuba's track record in Africa thus far, assessments of the Cuban factor most likely will continue to be favorable among most elite elements in the Soviet foreign policy community.[58] If that judgment is correct, four considerations suggest that Cuba's indirect effect will be to push these elites in an expansionist direction with regard to Africa.

First, the Cuban successes in Angola and Ethiopia would appear to reinforce the arguments of those civilian and military elements in the USSR who in general advocate a more aggressive international strategy to extend the Soviet Union's political, economic, and military influence in the world and to accelerate the revolutionary process abroad. According to Joan Barth Urban, Moscow's foreign policy establishment has for a substantial number of years been dominated by the "conservative sectarians." Most visibly led by Boris Ponomarev, head of the International Department of the Central Committee of the CPSU, they have prescribed a highly orthodox and cautious approach to the revolutionary process abroad, particularly in Western Europe, and they have subordinated the goal of world revolution to the demands of Soviet foreign policy, including the priority of détente. But Urban also identifies three other contending groups, the most important of which is the "revolutionary sectarians." The "revolutionary sectarians" believe in the possibility of uninterrupted revolution leading to socialism, they advocate an activist Soviet foreign policy for accelerating the revolutionary process abroad, and they contend that détente can be exploited to achieve revolutionary advances in Western Europe and elsewhere. This group appears to have been joined by Konstantin Zarodov, editor-in-chief of *Problems of Peace and Socialism* (or *World Marxist Review,* in the English version), who gained considerable public prominence in the late summer of 1975.[59] While the "revolutionary sectarians" in the mid-1970s were most concerned with Western Europe, particularly Portugal, the breakthroughs in Angola, Ethiopia, and elsewhere in Southern Africa must have strengthened their position within Soviet policy-making circles. In turn, they may well have become alerted to Africa's potential as a new theater for revolutionary advances and to Cuba's role in accelerating the revolutionary process.[60]

Second, the Angolan and Ethiopian outcomes most likely have intensified the Soviet military's backing of Cuba as an effective international paladin. One reason for such support lies in the fact that through Cuba's military and political role in Africa the Soviets may now be in a position to establish their own military presence on the Horn and in Southern Africa. For example, they signed a 20-year treaty of friendship and cooperation with the Neto government in October 1976 which stipulates that both the USSR and Angola "will continue to develop cooperation in the military sphere," although it does not spell out the nature of such cooperation.[61] Still another reason for the Soviet military to back the FAR can be found in the new military image that the USSR has acquired as a consequence of Cuban exploits in Africa. Previously, in the Middle East, the international reputation of the Soviet Union, and perhaps the self-esteem of the Soviet military itself, suffered as a result of the military defeats inflicted upon Egypt, Syria, and other Arab states by Israel despite massive Soviet military aid and training.[62] But now in Africa, Cuban troops, directly supported by the USSR and armed with Soviet equipment, have routed opposing forces in Angola and Ethiopia, thereby demonstrating the effectiveness of the Soviet military as well as the new global reach of the Soviet Union as a world power. Hence, it would appear that the Soviet military has a strong interest in seeing the FAR maintain their high level of involvement in Africa for both practical and symbolic reasons.

Third, Soviet strategists may now see increased possibilities for future breakthroughs in Africa not only because the USSR has greater capabilities for global outreach but also because Cuba's political and especially military presence can become the decisive factor in determining the outcome of political-military struggles and in assuring the consolidation of power by pro-Soviet regimes.[63] This new perception of the correlation of forces in Africa, and of the prospects for revolutionary and socialist advances on the continent, is far different from the one that existed prior to Angola. As noted earlier, the Soviets in the mid-1960s experienced a number of political-strategic reversals, and setbacks in their expectations, that subsequently led them to a pessimistic assessment of African realities. Specifically, the Soviets found the African political process to be highly volatile and unpredictable owing to the region's precapitalist stage of development, the resultant absence of a large, class-conscious proletariat, and the political unreliability of the ruling bourgeoisie and nationalist leaders.[64] But now these existing structural impediments to the socialist revolutionary process and to the rise of pro-Soviet regimes have to a large extent been offset by, in particular, the Cuban military presence. Indeed, it is possible that the Soviets may perceive Cuba as potentially capable of performing the same role in Africa that the Red Army played in the consolidation of Communist regimes in Eastern Europe after World War II. Such a role, in turn, is made all the more possible by the development of the Soviet Union's own capabilities for providing logistical support to the Cubans in Africa.[65]

Finally and relatedly, because of the Cuba factor Soviet ideologues and policy-makers alike may now believe not only that socialist-oriented regimes in Africa are viable, but also that they will adopt domestic policies deepening the revolutionary process and will adhere to external postures favorable to the USSR. To be sure, Africa today seems, in Soviet eyes, to lack the requisite conditions for "socialist revolution" as well as for the ascension of bona fide Marxist-Leninist regimes to power. Furthermore, the Soviets in the past have had disappointing experiences with progressive or revolutionary democratic regimes in Africa, such as those in Ghana and Mali, which embarked on noncapitalist paths of development, only to founder and give way to conservative governments. Yet, despite these negative considerations, Soviet writers now appear to view the emergence and development of socialist-oriented regimes in Africa with optimism. While they are non-Communist in their leadership, these regimes are socialist-inclined in their policies even while they remain in the stage of a national-democratic revolution. In fact, such regimes are headed by "revolutionary democrats," and their socialist orientation constitutes "a stage of transition from precapitalist or early capitalist phases to socialism via several intermediate stages; it is the highest stage of the national-democratic revolution."[66]

Precisely because of underdevelopment and dependence, the socialist-oriented regimes in Africa could become all the more responsive to Soviet and especially Cuban efforts to construct stable, transitional political orders. In societies lacking educational, organizational, and technical skills, the Cubans can make a decisive contribution—as they already have begun to do in Angola and Ethiopia—to the building of party, mass organization, governmental, and military structures so essential to the survival of otherwise fragile socialist-oriented regimes.[67] Also, the presence of Cuban and Soviet military and civilian personnel in the African countries, along with the latter's military, economic, and technical ties to the socialist camp, can provide the USSR with the means of exercising direct or indirect influence over the policies of the socialist-oriented regimes. Thus, the Soviets may now believe that they are assured of pro-Soviet allies on the continent, and that in the more distant future the socialist-oriented regimes could develop the requisite conditions for genuine socialist revolutions.[68]

In contrast, the Soviets now appear less likely to exercise the same degree of influence over revolutionary and Communist movements in Western Europe. Despite initial Soviet euphoria over events in Portugal in 1974–75, the revolutionary process in that country as well as in Italy and Spain now appears stalled, in part because of the very complexities of these more advanced capitalist societies and the absence of a single decisive factor equivalent to Cuba's presence in Africa. Moreover, the Soviets in recent years have had to contend increasingly with the ideological deviation posed by the Italian and Spanish Communist parties in the form of Eurocommunism, while the fledgling Communist movement in Africa has thus far proved to be far more manageable. In this respect, the very presence in Africa of party cadres and advisers from Cuba, itself a developing Third World country, is likely to provide a useful bridge between the CPSU and the African Communist parties and leftist movements.[69]

Prospects

The preceding discussion has pointed up the various ways in which Cuba's direct and indirect influence could contribute to the maintenance or intensification of the USSR's activist policy in Africa. Left out of this discussion has been the direct or indirect effect that Cuba might have on Soviet *internal politics* as these relate to Moscow's African policy. Some observers have suggested that Soviet intervention in Angola stemmed in part from Brezhnev's need to achieve a major foreign policy victory in the face of domestic economic difficulties and pressure from militant circles within the Soviet regime for a reaffirmation of the Soviet commitment to revolution.[70] If this judgment is accurate, then Brezhnev's departure from the political scene and the ensuing succession problem could very well increase the likelihood of Soviet adventurism in Africa. For instance, the Soviet military, in the absence of strong civilian control in the immediate post-Brezhnev period, might press for new interventions on the continent, or a contender for the top leadership might attempt to win power through a new foreign policy exploit. Under such circumstances, Cuba might conceivably provide direct or indirect reinforcement for elements favoring greater activism. Nevertheless, there are too many uncertainties about Soviet domestic politics after Brezhnev to venture even a tentative assessment of the probable Cuban impact on them.

In any case, it is important to stress that Cuba by itself will not necessarily bring about, directly or indirectly, the adoption of an expansionist policy by the USSR in either the Brezhnev or the post-Brezhnev period. As was mentioned earlier, there are a number of domestic and foreign policy considerations that may cause the Soviet leaders to choose a more cautious approach toward Africa. Indeed, the Soviets might prefer to level off their involvement in Africa and to concentrate instead on the more strategically important and politically volatile region of the Middle East, where new targets of opportunity have emerged in the wake of the Iranian revolution. What the foregoing analysis does suggest, however, is that the constraints on Soviet policy will have to come from sources other than Cuba—specifically, from within the Soviet system and from the West and Africa itself.

At the same time, of course, there are intrinsic limits to Cuba's overseas capabilities. The island has an economy that continues to rest essentially on sugar and sugar exports, so it must depend heavily upon the Soviet bloc and Western nations for most industrial products and technology. Its population numbers but 9.5 million, and it boasts an estimated per capita GNP of only $1,115 (1976).[71] Cuba thus remains a developing nation with a limited industrial capacity and economic-technical outreach. Accordingly, Cuba's economic and technical assistance programs in Africa may be more important politically than they are economically. That is, they may be of symbolic value to African states and useful in providing the latter with leverage for obtaining Western assistance, but economically they may have only marginal impact on those underdeveloped countries in desperate need of Western technology and capital, as Angola has begun to discover.[72] In sum, although Cuba's Third World credentials make it appealing to a number of African regimes, those very same credentials severely limit the kinds of contributions Cuba can make to Africa's economic modernization.

This leaves Cuba's capacity for military involvement in Africa as its most potent instrument for promoting Cuban objectives on the continent. Here, too, Cuba's overseas capabilities are constrained by several factors. Not only do the FAR continue to depend on Soviet weaponry and logistical support, but there are finite limits to the manpower at their disposal. The Cuban regular army stands at 120,000 officers and enlisted personnel; in addition, the country has 60,000 ready reservists. As observers have pointed out, these reservists must be called upon for active duty overseas if Cuba is to commit any significant number of combat troops abroad, as it has done in Angola and Ethiopia, without seriously weakening the island's defenses.[73] But the deployment of the reservists siphons off manpower from the Cuban economy, thereby creating potential production and morale problems on the home front.[74]

These limitations or deficiencies, however, should not be overemphasized. To begin with, Cuba has a relatively youthful population; in fact, young Cubans are expected to start entering the labor force at a rate of about 100,000 a year by the end of the 1970s. The Cuban economy at present does not have the capacity to fully absorb all of these young people, including those with skills and specialized education. Thus, assigning a number of them to "internationalist duty"—either in military service abroad or in foreign aid missions—becomes one way in which Cuba can diminish the prospect of underemployment for its young labor force as well as instill greater revolutionary consciousness in the younger generation.[75] Furthermore, the dominant elites within the Cuban leadership, Fidel and Raúl Castro and the military, have thus far not been deterred from overseas operations by the island's limited resources and production problems, or by the risk of civilian disaffection. On the contrary, they have shown a disposition to commit whatever forces may be necessary to shore up the MPLA militarily in Angola, to dispatch still additional troops to repel Somalia and stabilize the Mengistu regime in Ethiopia, and to increase even further the number of technicians, specialists, and political advisers working in Angola.[76]

Looking ahead, it therefore seems reasonable to expect that the Castro regime will be ready to undertake new large-scale military operations in Africa, particularly if Cuban forces are not engaged in the developing conflict between South Yemen and Yemen and if the number of Cuban troops in Angola or Ethiopia can be reduced.[77] If these conditions do arise, then Cuba's future military involvement in Africa will probably be guided by three considerations. First, the new Cuban military commitment most likely will occur where Soviet priorities run high, as in Southern Africa and the Horn, in order to assure optimal levels of Soviet logistical and military support and to generate added leverage with Moscow. Second, the new military involvement probably will be undertaken where Cuba would enjoy international legitimacy if not legality in Third World circles for its actions. Thus, instead of being accused of serving Soviet ends, Cuba could likely win widespread Third World support by dispatching large troop contingents to defend Zambia from Rhodesian attacks or to protect Angola from renewed South African and Rhodesian incursions. Third, Cuba can be expected to minimize the military risks of its operations not only by making certain of Soviet backing but also by selecting targets of opportunity that are within the range of Cuba's military capabilities. For example, Cuba most probably will eschew a direct, full-scale confrontation with South Africa over Namibia; however, it might be prepared to join with African states in a war against Rhodesia, whose newly elected government is perceived throughout most of Africa as white-dominated even though headed by black politicians and where the military situation would be more favorable. Cuba's participation in such a joint international venture against the Rhodesians, in turn, would both enhance and legitimize its paladin role in Africa and further heighten its value to the Soviet Union.

7

Sino– Soviet Rivalry in Africa

George T. Yu

AFRICA IN THE 1970s has become a major battleground of the Sino–Soviet conflict. The struggle there between the two Communist giants takes place on two distinct but interconnected levels. On the first plane, the People's Republic of China (PRC) and the USSR seek to "win friends and influence people" through formal and informal political interaction, economic aid, military assistance, and other activities. On the second, more abstract plane, each actor attacks the other's motives and role related to Africa.

From Moscow's standpoint, then, China poses a distinct challenge in Africa, and that challenge constitutes an important aspect of the context in which Soviet policy toward the continent takes shape. This study will look at the dimensions of the Chinese challenge and the precise nature of the threat that it poses to Soviet interests. More specifically, it will examine overall Chinese activities on the continent, the image that the Soviet Union has sought to project in Africa and Moscow's perceptions of how Chinese behavior tarnishes that image, Peking's critique of the USSR's intentions and actions in Africa, and the impact that China has apparently had on Soviet policy toward the continent in the past and is likely to have in the future.

Chinese Activities

Initially, China's interaction with Africa developed in the context of the Sino–American confrontation that followed the Korean War. In the wake of the Bandung Conference of Afro-Asian States in 1955, the PRC launched an effort in Africa, similar to its diplomatic offensive in South and Southeast Asia, to win increased international recognition

and support as a means of breaking out of the political "encircle-
ment" that the United States had attempted to establish. As the
number of independent countries on the continent grew, Peking intensified this effort, and Africa remained a battlefield in the
Chinese–American cold war through the early 1960s.

With the emergence of open Sino–Soviet discord in the early 1960s,
however, China's African policy began to be more and more directed
against the Soviet Union. As the conflict escalated from a political-
ideological dispute to a semimilitary confrontation in the late 1960s
and early 1970s, the USSR replaced the United States as the main foe
in Peking's eyes, and the Chinese as a result stepped up their campaign to combat Soviet influence in Africa. Indeed, Africa soon assumed major importance as an arena of Sino–Soviet competition.
This competition has become especially strong in the period since the
end of the Great Proletarian Cultural Revolution in 1969, which has
witnessed a major expansion of Chinese activities on the continent.

To appreciate the extent of Chinese undertakings in Africa at the
end of the 1970s, it is useful to compare China's relations with Africa
through 1966 with those since 1970. While Sino–African interaction
did not cease between 1966 and 1970 (the period when China was
preoccupied with the Cultural Revolution), it fell off substantially.

As the primary indicator of Chinese activity, we shall use economic
credits and grants that the PRC has extended to African states.
Viewed alone, these data tell us little about Sino–Soviet rivalry.
Therefore, we shall assess them in light of the credits and grants that
the USSR has provided African countries during the same two
periods.

Through 1977, the PRC offered a total of nearly U.S. $2.5 billion in
economic credits and grants to African countries—a figure representing about 55 percent of all its aid commitments to the non-Communist
world.[1] As Table 1 indicates, $428 million worth were extended during
the 1954–66 period. When one compares these Chinese credits and
grants with Soviet credits and grants during the same years, one finds
several noteworthy things. First, China ran a poor second to the
Soviet Union in terms of aid commitments to Africa. Not only did the
USSR offer aid to a greater number of African states—17, against 11
for China—but its aid commitments also amounted to more than four
times those of China. Second, there was Sino–Soviet competition in
10 instances, with the Soviet Union being the major Communist donor
in 8 of the 10 cases. China constituted the leading donor with respect

to the Congo-Brazzaville and Tanzania. Third, except for Algeria and Egypt, Chinese commitments were south of the Sahara, including concentrations in East and West Africa. The Soviet Union, in addition to major commitments in North Africa, was active in West Africa and Ethiopia and Somalia. Neither China nor the Soviet Union had established an economic presence in Southern Africa. Fourth, Peking's individual aid commitments were in general smaller projects than those of the USSR, and nowhere did China's foreign aid program finance a "flagship" project of the grandiose scale of the Soviet-financed Aswan Dam in Egypt.

TABLE 1
Chinese and Soviet Aid Commitments
to Africa, 1954–66 and 1970–77
(in millions of U.S. dollars)

	1954–66		1970–77	
	China	USSR	China	USSR
Algeria	52	236	40	479
Angola	—	—	—	10
Benin[a]	—	—	44	—
Burundi	—	—	20	—
Cameroon	—	8	71	—
Central African Empire[b]	4	—	—	2
Chad	—	—	50	2
Congo[c]	25	10	—	4
Egypt	85	1,001	28	299
Equatorial Guinea	—	—	—	1
Ethiopia	—	102	85	3
Gambia	—	—	17	—
Ghana	42	93	—	1
Guinea	56	106	11	3
Guinea-Bissau	—	—	17	14
Kenya	18	48	—	—
Liberia	—	—	10	—
Madagascar	—	—	66	—
Mali	55	59	4	—
Mauritania	—	—	59	1
Mauritius	—	—	35	—
Morocco	—	44	32	44
Mozambique	—	—	59	3
Niger	—	—	51	2

TABLE 1 continued

	1954–66		1970–77	
	China	USSR	China	USSR
Nigeria	—	—	—	7
Rwanda	—	—	22	1
Senegal	—	7	49	2
Sierra Leone	—	28	30	—
Somalia	22	66	111	87
Sudan	—	22	82	—
Tanzania	54	20	305	19
Togo	—	—	45	—
Tunisia	—	34	97	55
Uganda	15	16	—	—
Upper Volta	—	—	52	1
Zaire[d]	—	—	100	—
Zambia	—	—	290	—
TOTALS	$428	$1,900	$1,882	$1,040

[a]Prior to 1975 known as Dahomey.
[b]Prior to 1977 known as the Central African Republic.
[c]Prior to 1969 known as Congo-Brazzaville.
[d]Prior to 1971 known as the Democratic Republic of the Congo or Congo-Leopoldville or Kinshasa.

SOURCES: The data for 1954–66 are drawn from U.S. Department of State, *Communist States and Developing Countries: Aid and Trade in 1974*, Washington, D.C., February 1976; the data for 1970–77 are adapted by the author from *ibid.* and from U.S. Central Intelligence Agency, *Communist Aid to the Less Developed Countries of the Free World, 1976*, ER 77–10296, Washington, D.C., August 1977; and U.S. Central Intelligence Agency, *Communist Aid to Less Developed Countries of the Free World, 1977*, ER 78–10478U, Washington, D.C., November 1978.

The relative smallness of Chinese aid commitments should not be taken as a sign that Peking lacked interest in Africa, or as a reflection of Africa's unimportance in the Sino–Soviet conflict. While use of the years 1954–66 is desirable from the standpoint of covering Soviet activity from its beginning, such a periodization does tend to skew the comparison. Chinese aid to Africa did not in fact commence until 1956 (Egypt was the first recipient), and it did not reach truly significant proportions until after 1961, peaking at $195 million in 1964. As has already been pointed out, the early 1960s witnessed the development of overt Sino–Soviet conflict.

The importance of Africa in Chinese foreign policy during the 1960s also manifested itself in the visits of Premier Chou En-lai and Foreign Minister Ch'en Yi to the continent in 1963–64 and 1965 respectively.

One objective of these trips was to round up African support for barring the USSR from participation in the "second Bandung" conference scheduled for June 1965 (but later abandoned after an abortive attempt to convene it).

However, China's turn "inward" during the Cultural Revolution temporarily halted its budding African policy, and the PRC did not return to Africa as a major actor until 1970. Table 1 shows the degree of Chinese "reentry" onto the African scene in terms of economic aid in this and subsequent years. Comparison of Chinese and Soviet aid commitments during this period leads to a number of observations. First, there was a reversal of Chinese and Soviet roles from the pre-1966 period. China now became the chief Communist aid donor to African countries. Not only did China offer almost twice the amount of economic assistance that the Soviet Union did, but the PRC also extended aid to 29 states as opposed to 22 for the USSR. Second, there were 16 instances of direct Sino–Soviet competition, and China constituted the leading donor in 12 cases. Third, China's economic presence now extended to most of Africa. New commitments included Morocco and Tunisia in the north; Liberia, Mauritania, Niger, Senegal, and Togo in the west; the Sudan in the northeast; Cameroon and Zaire in Central Africa; and Mozambique and Zambia in the south. With the exception of Somalia, Soviet economic aid continued to be concentrated in North Africa, with a scattering of minor commitments south of the Sahara. Fourth, more African countries received aid from China for the first time than obtained initial assistance from the USSR. Whereas China extended aid to 23 new African recipients, the Soviet Union offered assistance to only 11 African states for the first time. Fifth, the average amount of Chinese aid per recipient increased from $39 million in the 1954–66 period to $65 million in the 1970–77 period, while the average figure for Soviet assistance per recipient for the same periods declined from $112 million to $51 million. Finally, China during the 1970–77 period undertook its first "flagship" project—the construction of the massive Tanzania–Zambia railway at a cost in excess of $450 million.[2]

TABLE 2
The People's Republic of China's
New Diplomatic Relations in Africa, 1970–79

Year	State
1970	Equatorial Guinea
1970	Ethiopia
1971	Cameroon
1971	Nigeria
1971	Rwanda
1971	Senegal
1971	Sierra Leone
1972	Chad
1972	Malagasy Republic
1972	Mauritius
1972	Togo
1972	Zaire
1973	Upper Volta
1974	Gabon
1974	Gambia
1974	Guinea-Bissau
1974	Niger
1975	Botswana
1975	Comoros
1975	Sao Tome and Principe
1975	Mozambique
1976	Cape Verde
1976	Seychelles
1977	Liberia
1978	Libya[a]
1979	Djibouti

[a]Libya had unilaterally announced recognition of China in 1971 but had continued to maintain relations with the Republic of China on Taiwan.

SOURCE: Compiled from New China News Agency releases.

Other indicators also attest to China's major effort in Africa since 1970. During this period, for example, Peking carried out an intensive campaign to broaden its diplomatic relations with the continent. By early 1979, it had forged official ties with 26 countries with which it had not previously had formal links (see Table 2), thus bringing the total of African states with which it maintained diplomatic relations to 42. Over the same period, China's leaders have entertained an impressive number of African leaders in Peking (see Table 3). During these visits, the Chinese always reminded the Africans of the struggle against "imperialism and hegemonism"—i.e., against the influence of both superpowers.

TABLE 3
Major African Delegations to China,
1971–79[a]

Year	Leader of Delegation
1971	President of the Liberation Front of Mozambique
1971	Deputy President of Sudan
1972	President of the Supreme Revolutionary Council of Somalia
1972	Vice-President of Zambia
1973	President of Zaire
1973	President of Cameroon
1973	President of the Congo
1973	President of Sierra Leone
1974	President of Zambia
1974	President of Tanzania
1974	President of Senegal
1974	Vice-President of the Supreme Military Council of Niger
1974	President of Togo
1974	Head of the Federal Military Government of Nigeria
1974	President of Mauritania
1974	President of Gabon
1975	President of the Liberation Front of Mozambique
1975	President of Gambia
1975	President of Sao Tome and Principe
1976	President of Malagasy Republic
1976	President of Benin
1976	President of Botswana
1976	President of the Central African Republic
1976	Vice-President of Tanzania
1977	President of Mauritania
1977	President of Gabon
1977	President of Sudan
1977	Prime Minister of the Congo
1977	Vice-President of Somalia
1977	General Secretary of the Zimbabwe African National Union
1977	President of the Supreme Military Council of Niger
1977	President of Cameroon
1978	Deputy Prime Minister of Egypt
1978	Minister of the Supreme Military Council of Ghana
1978	President of Somalia
1978	President of Seychelles
1978	President of Mozambique

TABLE 3 continued

Year	Leader of Delegation
1978	President of the Congo
1978	President of Rwanda
1978	President of Liberia
1978	President of Gabon
1979	President of Burundi

^aThrough March 1979 only.

[a]Through March 1979 only.

SOURCE: Compiled from New China News Agency releases.

In only one respect—arms transfers—do Chinese activities in Africa appear to have been relatively limited. Table 4 sets forth Chinese and Soviet arms transfers to African countries during the 1967–76 period. Several features of these transfers stand out. First, the U.S. $142 million in arms that China provided was minuscule in comparison with the USSR's more than U.S.$4 billion worth. Second, China supplied arms to only 15 African states, whereas the Soviet Union furnished arms to 21. Third, African recipients of Chinese arms got an average of only $10 million worth of weapons, as against the average of $210 million that recipients of Soviet arms obtained. Fourth, China's arms transfers to the continent were overwhelmingly confined to a small number of countries south of the Sahara, while the USSR provided arms to a politically diverse and geographically widespread group of countries. Tanzania and Zaire were the major recipients of Chinese weapons; the Soviet recipients included such states as Algeria, Angola, Central African Empire, Guinea, Libya, Nigeria, Uganda, and Zambia. Finally, of the eight cases in which China and the Soviet Union competed directly as arms suppliers, in just one—Tanzania—was China the leading supplier. Tanzania, it should be pointed out, has gotten 53 percent of China's arms transfers to Africa.

This general state of affairs with regard to arms transfers, however, has reflected the disadvantages under which the Chinese have had to operate rather than any inherent lack of desire to challenge the Soviets in Africa. A closer examination of the patterns of Chinese (and Soviet) arms transfers to the continent sustains such a conclusion.[3] If one looks at the 1961–76 period—a period which corresponds roughly to that of Sino–Soviet competition in Africa—two things emerge. First, while the dollar volume of Chinese arms transfers has been small in comparison with that of Soviet arms transfers,

TABLE 4
Chinese and Soviet Arms Transfers to Africa,
1967–76
(in millions of U.S. dollars)

African State	China	Soviet Union
Algeria	—	315
Angola	—	190
Benin	—	1
Burundi	1	—
Cameroon	5	—
Central African Empire	—	1
Chad	—	5
Congo	10	10
Egypt	5	2,365
Equatorial Guinea	—	5
Gambia	1	—
Guinea	5	50
Guinea-Bissau	—	5
Libya	—	1,005
Malagasy Republic	—	1
Malawi	1	—
Mali	1	25
Morocco	—	10
Mozambique	1	15
Nigeria	—	70
Rwanda	1	—
Somalia	—	181
Sudan	5	65
Tanzania	75	30
Tunisia	5	—
Uganda	—	65
Zaire	21	—
Zambia	5	10
TOTALS	$142	$4,424

SOURCE: U.S. Arms Control and Disarmament Agency, *World Military Expenditures and Arms Transfers 1967–1976*, Washington, D.C., 1978.

China has furnished weapons to African countries since practically the beginning. Second, Chinese and Soviet arms transfers to the continent have tended to go up at about the same time. As with Chinese economic aid commitments, one can discern two major periods of Chinese arms transfers to Africa: (a) from the early 1960s through the Cultural Revolution and (b) the post–Cultural Revolution years. During the first period, the number of African recipients was small (a total of six), and the annual dollar volume of the transfers remained fairly constant (amounting to around U.S.$80 million in toto). By and large, Soviet activities on the continent during these years displayed the same characteristics, although the value of Soviet transfers was much greater. The post–Cultural Revolution years, however, witnessed an increase in both the number of recipients and the dollar volume of Chinese arms transfers to Africa. During 1973–76, there were 11 new recipients of Chinese weapons (Burundi, Cameroon, Egypt, Gambia, Malawi, Mali, Mozambique, Rwanda, Sudan, Tunisia, and Zaire), and the transfers to these new recipients totaled about $50 million. In addition, China upped its arms transfers to some past recipients— particularly Tanzania. During these same years, the Soviet Union also expanded its activities on the continent. For example, it provided arms to nine new recipients (Angola, Benin, Central African Empire, Chad, Equatorial Guinea, Guinea-Bissau, Malagasy Republic, Mozambique, and Zambia). Altogether, these transfers amounted to about $250 million.

In sum, while arms transfers have not been China's "card" in its competition with the USSR, Peking's persistent supply of arms to Africa, even if at a low level, has represented China's acknowledgment of the importance of this form of interaction. Though the Chinese have denounced the superpowers as "arms merchants," they have felt compelled, despite their inability to furnish large quantities of modern weapons, to offer what they could manage in light of the urgency with which African countries have often sought arms.

Clearly, then, Africa in the 1970s has emerged as an area of strong contention between China and the USSR, and China has managed to bolster its position on the continent considerably—at least in terms of establishing an economic presence and winning increased formal acceptance from Africans. This situation has posed problems for the Soviet Union. To understand the character of these, we need to look first at the state of affairs as Moscow has viewed it.

The Soviet Perspective

At the opening session of the 1965 Moscow Conference on the Historic Relations of the Peoples of the Soviet Union and Africa, a Soviet spokesman underlined the "tradition of friendship" and the importance of Marxism-Leninism in the USSR's relations with Africa. According to him, the "tradition of friendship" derived from contacts in the 19th century between Russian travelers and Africans in areas ranging from Libya to the Congo, and it reflected the fact that relationships had been founded on "mutual respect and strong mutual interest." As for the influence of Marxism-Leninism, this had manifested itself in the Soviet Union's representation of and devotion to the working masses and oppressed peoples—including being "on the side of the oppressed nations" and extending assistance to national liberation movements. In short, he maintained that the USSR had a long and deep interest in Africa and had served as supporter of the weak and helper of those seeking national liberation.[4]

Such themes mirrored a Soviet desire to portray Moscow as the foremost champion of the international revolutionary movement, and that desire has remained constant over the years. Yet despite Soviet assistance to the "national liberation and revolutionary struggles" in Algeria, the Congo-Leopoldville, Angola, Mozambique, etc., there have been those, Soviet writers say, who have sought "to denigrate the Leninist foreign policy of the world's first socialist state."[5] China stands at the forefront of these denigrators.

According to one Soviet source, China has been "fanning anti-Soviet sentiments and undermining friendly ties" between the USSR and Africa, while seeking to establish "a dominant position in the African liberation movement" and to impose Chinese hegemony on Africa.[6] China, the same source goes on, launched its drive to develop relations with Africa in the 1950s, and even during these early years Peking employed "special ways" of building such relations— stressing the "traditional ties" between China and Africa, supporting African nationalism, linking the Islamic community in China with Islamic communities in Africa, and appealing for African friendship on the basis of racial prejudice. But it was not until the 1960s that China began to show its true colors by pursuing a hegemonic policy toward Africa.

As part of this policy, runs the Soviet interpretation, China attempted to achieve dominance over African national liberation and revolutionary movements. During the 1960s, Peking called on Africa "to adopt violent armed struggle as the only effective revolutionary method," promulgating the idea that "quick and easy victory over imperialism was possible." The insurrectionary course followed by the National Liberation Front (*Front de Libération Nationale*—FLN) in Algeria was selected as a "model" for African revolutionary struggle and as an example of the application of the Chinese pattern of national liberation. Other African insurgent movements which received Chinese support included ones in the Congo-Leopoldville, Cameroon, Angola, and Mozambique. In all cases, Peking insisted "on armed struggle irrespective of change of the internal political and international situations."

Such methods, in the Soviet view, constituted "pseudo-revolutionary tactics" and "adventuristic actions" and often resulted in dividing and weakening the revolutionary forces. Furthermore, Chinese assistance to the liberation struggles consisted of little more than verbal support, with little or no practical help forthcoming.

Another aspect of China's hegemonic policy toward Africa, Soviet commentary maintains, was to launch direct attacks against the USSR. For example, Peking questioned the effectiveness of Soviet aid and support to the FLN in Algeria, and it criticized the USSR for the Soviet role in the Congo-Leopoldville—now Zaire—in the 1960s. It even tried to exclude the Soviet Union from Africa by preventing the USSR from participating in the projected Second Conference of Afro-Asian States in 1965. The objective of all these efforts was to weaken Soviet ties with Africa, especially with the African revolutionary movements, while enhancing China's links.

China's bid for leadership in Africa, Soviet analysis insists, had distinctly chauvinistic characteristics. These became evident especially during the period of the Chinese Cultural Revolution. Beginning in 1965, China sought to interfere in the internal affairs of African states "to plant the experience of the 'cultural revolution' in African soil." During the same years, Peking supported the secessionist Biafran forces in the Nigerian civil war and accused the Soviet Union of betraying the African revolutionary movement for failing to do likewise. In sum, China's activities pointed to a "Peking brand of neocolonialism."

During the 1970s, according to Soviet contentions, the PRC persisted in its campaign against the USSR and for Chinese hegemony in Africa. However, Peking adopted a "soft," more flexible line in its foreign policy. That is, it no longer called for "people's wars" in Africa; rather, it endeavored to rally African countries, as well as those in the rest of the Third World, against the two superpowers, the Soviet Union and the United States. Thus, China identified itself with and sought the leadership of the Third World, while it tried to link the Soviet Union, as a "social-imperialist," with the imperialist United

States. Such a policy was "clearly designed to whitewash imperialism, to divert the peoples of the developing countries from the
struggle against neocolonialism and to turn them against the socialist
community."[7]

From the Soviet standpoint, then, China has come to constitute a
serious obstacle to the USSR's efforts to win recognition as the patron of the national liberation and revolutionary movement in Africa.
But Moscow has nonetheless remained determined to pursue that
end. This determination has manifested itself in "positive actions" to
assist the "anti-imperialist struggle" on the continent—e.g., the extension of military aid to the Popular Movement for the Liberation of
Angola (*Movimento Popular de Libertação de Angola*—MPLA) and to
the Ethiopian military regime headed by Mengistu Haile Mariam.

The Chinese Charges

Having looked at the Chinese challenge from the Soviet perspective, it is now essential to explore in detail precisely what the Chinese
have been saying to African audiences about the USSR. Chinese
statements concentrate on the motives behind Soviet actions vis-à-vis
the continent and the role that the USSR plays there.

According to the Chinese, the Soviet Union has had three primary
objectives with respect to Africa. First, it has wanted access to the
rich natural resources of the continent, including copper, diamonds,
gold, and uranium. It has needed these to supply its industries, and in
return it has sold machinery and other finished products to Africa.
While Moscow has called the exchange of Soviet industrial products
for African natural resources the "international division of labor,"
this exchange has in fact been quite different in nature. It has constituted nothing more than a device to keep the African countries "always dependent economically" by turning them into raw materials
producers and finished products markets for the USSR.[8]

Second, the Soviet Union has hoped to advance Soviet global
strategic interests in Africa. That is, Moscow has wished to gain control of the continent to further its efforts to compete with the United
States for world hegemony. Soviet control of Africa would inherently
strengthen the USSR's position in this contest. Moreover, control of
Central and Southern Africa, specifically, would enable the USSR to
dominate "important strategic waterways," the Indian Ocean and the

Atlantic Ocean. As one Chinese source has put things, "in its ambitious scramble for world hegemony, the Soviet Union seeks to take over Africa for the purpose of cutting the sea-transport lanes, the lifelines of West Europe and the United States."[9]

Third, Moscow has tried to undermine Africa's unity. For example, the USSR has sowed dissension among liberation movements by classifying them as "revolutionary, non-revolutionary and even 'counter-revolutionary'" groups.[10] It has also espoused the "reactionary theory" that African states fall into two categories, "the reactionary and the progressive."[11] Such behavior, according to the Chinese, has been designed to interfere directly in the continent's affairs and to set Africans against Africans, and has clearly produced setbacks for Africa's struggle against imperialism.

As for the Soviet Union's role in Africa, the Chinese contend that Moscow's actions on the continent have revealed the USSR to be an aggressive, expansionist imperialist power. A 1976 *Jen-min Jih-pao* editorial stated bluntly: "On the pretext of opposing imperialism and colonialism . . . [the Soviets] stretch their tentacles into other countries to carry out colonialist domination and colonialist exploitation."[12] From this conclusion, the Chinese draw far-reaching implications—namely, that the USSR has replaced the Western powers as the key imperialist in Africa. In the words of one Chinese source, as the "Western wolf" was being repelled, the "Soviet tiger" was entering Africa.[13]

To Peking, Soviet behavior has been especially deceptive because Moscow has conducted its activities on the continent under the banner of "international duties" by a "socialist country."[14] The Chinese utterly reject this characterization. Could a "real socialist country," asked China's ambassador to the United Nations at a meeting of the U.N. Security Council in 1976, engage in a "policy of expansion?"[15]

In debunking the way in which the USSR portrays its activities in Africa, the Chinese attempt to set the record straight on what they regard as two key aspects of the Soviet approach to the continent. The first has to do with Soviet attitudes toward African liberation movements. Contrary to Soviet claims, the Chinese maintain, the USSR has "always bitterly resented and opposed war[s] of national liberation." Indeed, the Soviet Union has turned "away from revolution" and denied others "the right to make revolution."[16]

Consider the record, the Chinese say, of the USSR on the question of liberation struggles. The position of Nikita Khrushchev and Leonid

Brezhnev is known to all: "They have harped on a now well-known theme that 'even a tiny spark can cause a world conflagration' and that the next world war will be a thermonuclear war which would mean the end of mankind. They therefore developed a morbid fear of and hatred for any war of national liberation."[17]

Furthermore, Soviet operations reflect this perspective. For instance, the Soviet Union refused to support the Algerian national liberation struggle of the 1950s for fear that "any small war might spark off a big one." It called the struggle "an internal affair of France."[18] Similarly, the USSR in the 1960s failed to assist the Congolese liberation struggle and even did "all [it] could to snuff out this 'spark' "[19] by approving, along with the United States, the dispatch of U.N. troops to suppress the liberation movement in the Congo-Leopoldville.[20] Soviet behavior since then has been "no less ugly." In 1973, Moscow prevented the Arab people "from waging a just war against the Israeli aggressors."[21]

To be sure, the Chinese argue, the Soviet Union's basic opposition to wars of national liberation has not precluded a willingness on its part to try to manipulate national liberation struggles for its own gain. In instances where Moscow has seen a struggle for national liberation going on in a region whose location and resources it deemed vital to the USSR, and where Moscow considered control of the liberation movement a means to win control of the region, the USSR has not hesitated to "support" the liberation struggle as a cover for its own expansionism. But, say the Chinese, such Soviet behavior does not amount to genuine support of wars of national liberation. Rather, it constitutes armed invasion. Indeed, the USSR "would not hesitate to unleash a war to achieve its ambition of world domination."[22]

According to Peking, then, Soviet policy and behavior toward national liberation struggles has in the final analysis been both reactionary and aggressive. The USSR, which styles itself "socialist," has "done all the evils of the imperialists."[23]

The second aspect of the Soviet approach to Africa regarding which the Chinese seek to dispel Moscow's "myths" concerns Soviet economic and military aid. In Chinese eyes, the USSR's economic aid really amounts to economic plunder, for its purpose is to penetrate and gain control of the "key economic departments" of the recipient countries. Furthermore, Peking insists, Moscow has been far from generous in providing aid to African countries. Between 1959 and 1973, the USSR extended less than U.S. $1.3 billion in credits to African states, and it actually furnished less than one-third of that total.[24] To top things off, much of the machinery and equipment that the Soviet Union has supplied to African countries has been out of date.

A similar situation prevails, according to the Chinese, with respect to Soviet military aid. Moscow has treated military assistance as a means of obtaining a foothold in the "vital departments" of the recipient African countries, and it has also used military aid programs to dispose of its obsolete arms. More important, the USSR has demanded air and naval bases from African states in return for military assistance. Indeed,

> The Soviet Union has built military airfields, floating docks, oil depots, radar stations, and other military facilities at some strategic sites on African coasts along the Mediterranean, the Indian Ocean and the Atlantic. Its warships wantonly ply the territorial waters of other countries' airspace [sic] at will. These are facts known to all.[25]

This kind of Soviet involvement in Africa, Peking asserts, leads to Soviet "military occupation and colonial rule."[26]

Angola and the Horn

The Angolan crisis of 1975–76 and developments in the Horn of Africa in 1977–78 helped solidify these Chinese perspectives, and they likewise afforded China an opportunity to hammer home to Africans some of the themes that grow out of them. Therefore, there is utility in focusing briefly on the Chinese response to these crises.

As Peking saw things, Soviet interest in Angola stemmed from the country's rich resources and strategic location. With regard to the former, Angola under the Portuguese had long been known as the "jewel of Africa," rich in cotton and sugarcane, and in oil, diamonds, gold, uranium, iron, copper, manganese, and other minerals. Moreover, the USSR had for some time cast "covetous eyes" on these resources and hoped to replace the Portuguese as the masters of this African "jewel."[27]

Angola's location appealed to Moscow for two reasons. First, the country was situated in Southern Africa. Thus, it would provide a springboard for Soviet expansion into Central and Southern Africa. This consideration, of course, meant that Soviet activities in Angola constituted "a prelude to further [Soviet] division and control of the whole of Africa."[28] Second, Angola lay on the Atlantic Ocean along sea lanes vital to Western Europe and the United States. This consideration reduced Africa to a "peripheral" status and made Angola a factor in the USSR's larger global designs, especially those connected with Europe and North America.[29]

It was these factors and not a desire to support liberation movements, the Chinese charged, that accounted for the Soviet decision to get involved in Angola. Indeed, the Angolan crisis "proved" Moscow's opposition to liberation movements. The Chinese interpreted the sequence of events in the following fashion:

The Angolan people had carried out a protracted armed liberation struggle for national independence. While differences had existed among the three Angolan liberation organizations, those differences "were something normal and could have been fully settled through consultations without outside interference." As a matter of fact, the three groups had as early as January 1975—well before Angola's independence—jointly concluded the Alvor Agreement with the Portuguese on the formation of a transitional government to prepare for independence. The following June, the three signed the Nakuru Agreement committing themselves to a cease-fire. Thus, Angola was looking forward to independence under the banner of unity supported by the Organization of African Unity.[30]

It was at this point, Peking held, that the Soviet Union intervened, thereby weakening not only Angola's unity and independence but also Africa's struggle against imperialism:

> After the signing of the Alvor Agreement on Independence of Angola, the Soviet Union hurriedly stepped in before the old colonialists withdrew their forces. First it set its propaganda machine in motion to sow discord among the three liberation organizations, and then sent large quantities of arms to Angola and even dispatched military personnel for direct maneuvering. Thus it provoked the civil war there in a deliberate attempt to undermine the Angolan cause of independence and Africa's united struggle against imperialism.[31]

Moreover, the Chinese pointed out, these were not the only consequences of the Soviet step. The Angolan civil war initiated by the USSR brought about the intervention of South Africa. South African involvement, Peking stressed, came only *after* Soviet intervention. Hence, the USSR inflicted further imperialist pressure on Angola. At the same time, Moscow capitalized upon the South African incursion to further its own aggression and expansionism in the African country.[32]

The ultimate outcome of Soviet policy and behavior, from the Chinese standpoint, was to propel Angola "into the orbit of Soviet social-imperialism." This outcome came about first through Soviet support of one Angolan organization against the two other liberation movements and then through the dispatch of Soviet military personnel and foreign mercenaries (Cubans) and the presence of Soviet warships off the Angolan coast. "All this," commented *Jen-min Jih-pao,* "clearly reveals the vicious features of the Soviet revisionists as a conqueror."³³ In short, the USSR had occupied Angola.

In asserting this conclusion, China rejected Moscow's claims that its role in Angola derived from "revolutionary conscience"—a term attributed to Brezhnev. How, asked Peking, could Brezhnev speak in this manner when the "Soviet social-imperialists took military action against two [Angolan] liberation organizations" and thereby strangled the Angolan transitional government? The USSR had even brushed aside the appeals of African states to the three Angolan liberation movements to join hands. In doing these things, the Soviet Union showed its disregard for the rights of the Angolan people. Thus, "revolutionary conscience" was nothing more than another cover for Soviet expansionism.³⁴

The Chinese also derided the notion that the USSR had merely extended military aid to the MPLA forces. During the independence struggle of the Angolan liberation movements, the Chinese argued, Moscow had never provided any real support to them; it was only on the eve of the country's achievement of independence that the USSR suddenly became a "generous" donor. It then transported several hundred million dollars worth of arms, along with 1,000 Soviet military officers and 10,000 foreign mercenary troops (Cubans), "across the oceans" to Angola. Such assistance did not have as its aim the liberation of Angola; instead, the Soviet Union simply wanted to replace Portugal as Angola's "overlord." After all, "150,000 black brothers in Angola were killed with the Soviet weapons, and many towns and villages were razed to the ground by the Soviet bombshells."³⁵

Nor did the Chinese believe that Angola constituted the limit of Soviet ambitions. To the contrary, they saw Angola as a potential base of operations from which further Soviet expansionist adventures on the continent could be launched. Early in 1976, Peking pointedly asked: "Would there be a second or third Angola on the African continent? Would the Soviet revisionists repeat their old trick and stretch their tentacles to central Africa or even southern Africa under the signboard of 'supporting the national liberation movement'? This is a serious but realistic question."[36]

Subsequent events confirmed to the Chinese the validity of their suspicions on this score. Peking interpreted the 1977 invasion of Zaire's Shaba Province by Angola-based Zairian exiles as an instance of "premeditated and planned" Soviet expansion into other portions of Africa. The USSR, the Chinese maintained, had hired and equipped mercenary troops in Angola to carry out the invasion, thus creating "another Angola-type incident." This undertaking had once again "torn to shreds the Soviet banner of 'supporting the national liberation struggle.'"[37]

China saw the 1978 invasion of Shaba Province by the same forces as a continuation of the 1977 attack, as "a new crime committed by Soviet social-imperialism."[38] Peking charged that Moscow had recruited and armed the ex-Katangan gendarmes, and that the USSR and its proxy, Cuba, had trained and controlled them. Soviet purposes, the Chinese claimed, were as follows:

> Zaire, situated in the heart of Africa and with rich strategic resources, is a piece of juicy meat in the eyes of the Soviet Union. Especially after its success in Angola, the Soviet Union intends to further control the sea passages to Europe. This is a component part of the Soviet strategic objective in its global rivalry with the United States.[39]

In assessing the implications of the invasion, Peking maintained that direct military intervention "has become the main force of Soviet expansionism in Africa."[40]

Although the Horn was further removed from Angola than Zaire was, the Chinese regarded Soviet behavior in the Horn as indicative of a similar armed expansionism. According to one Chinese writer, the Soviet Union was playing the role of an armed arsonist, sending "an endless stream of Soviet military equipment and personnel" to the Horn. It had at first resorted to the "tactics of straddling two boats," but after one of the two African countries (Somalia) had frustrated it, it had finally supported the other (Ethiopia).[41] In these maneuvers, it had had several "evil aims." Among these were:

(1) To seize strategic regions. The importance of the Horn lay in its strategic location, facing both the Red Sea and the Indian Ocean. The Soviet Union sought to gain a base in the region to control "the lifeline" from the Atlantic to the Indian Ocean via the Red Sea.

(2) To sow dissension and to "fish in troubled waters." These were favorite policies of the Soviet Union, which incited one African coun-

try against another. Such policies also offered the Soviet Union "good excuses for infiltration."

(3) To regain a position of preeminence. After its expulsion from Egypt, Sudan, and Somalia, the Soviet Union sought to "retrieve its defeats" in the Horn. The Soviet Union also had an interest in reinforcing its position in nearby Arab countries.[42]

In Chinese eyes, then, the Soviet Union has plainly emerged as the root cause of Africa's turmoil. Speaking at a banquet in honor of the President of Rwanda in June 1978, Vice Premier Teng Hsiao-p'ing summed up the Chinese perspective in accusing the Soviet Union of sowing discord and creating trouble in Africa by dispatching arms and mercenaries and kindling war flames.[43]

Influence and Prospects

There remains, finally, the question of the concrete effect of China on Soviet policy. While the USSR has plainly displayed great sensitivity to the Chinese challenge in Africa, has the challenge caused Moscow to do something that it might not otherwise have done, or to fail to do something that it might otherwise have decided to do? If so, to what extent?

At the verbal level, the USSR has clearly felt compelled to refute Chinese charges that it has betrayed the national liberation and revolutionary movement and become an aggressive and expansionist power, and it has even attempted to besmirch the Chinese image in African eyes by issuing countercharges against Peking. In the context of the Sino–Soviet conflict, the USSR has taken seriously the defense of "the Leninist foreign policy of the world's first socialist state." But when it comes to Soviet actions, the Chinese impact has been far more limited.

The Chinese factor in Soviet policy has been most evident in instances where Moscow has perceived that the PRC might seriously damage the USSR's claims to be the chief supporter of African liberation and sovereignty. Angola affords the classic illustration. Peking had developed close ties with the FNLA prior to the military coup in Portugal in April 1974, and, as Moscow viewed things, the FNLA and UNITA—the two most compatible allies among the three competitors—might wind up dominating any coalition government in Angola. Consequently, China might be in a position to gain an important foothold in Southern Africa for itself and to deny the USSR a role in the area. Such considerations played a major part in the Soviet decision to lend its backing to the MPLA.[44]

China's ability to pose this kind of challenge, of course, has depended on the needs of African states and groups, on one hand, and Peking's capacity to meet those needs, on the other. By and large, the number of cases in which Africans have recently experienced dramatically pressing needs has been fairly small. Most of these, moreover, have involved armed conflict of one sort or another. The struggles of the liberation movements in Southern Africa and the conflict in the Horn constitute the prime examples. With the heavy internal demands on its scarce resources, its shortage of modern arms, and its limited capacity to project its power abroad, China has found itself severely restricted in trying to fulfill what Africans regard as their requirements—especially in the military sphere.[45] Hence, one can point to relatively few instances of direct Chinese impact on Soviet policy.

This general picture carries some implications for the future. As long as the Sino–Soviet conflict persists—and there have as yet been no signs of even a moderating trend—Chinese denunciations of Soviet intentions and actions in Africa are likely to continue, and Moscow, in turn, will probably deem it essential to wage an ongoing propaganda campaign to "correct" Peking's version of things. Furthermore, the USSR might even decide to try to maintain a rough parity between its economic aid commitments to African countries and those of the Chinese—an effort which, as we have seen, Moscow to date in the 1970s has not judged necessary—and thus reduce Soviet vulnerability to Chinese charges in this realm. Yet because China's limited capacity to support African causes in straightforward power terms will not in all likelihood increase much, China will not constitute a very formidable alternative to the USSR as a source of succor for Africans; hence, Peking's influence on Soviet behavior will probably remain quite restricted in the foreseeable future.

8

The African– American Nexus in Soviet Strategy

W. Scott Thompson

IN THE TRIANGLE of influences acting among the Soviet Union, the United States, and Africa, the simplest, best documented, and most discussed side is the effect of Soviet African policy on U.S. policy. The impact has been not only on U.S. African policy but on U.S. foreign policy in general. It was the Soviet-Cuban intervention in Angola that led the American president in 1976 to drop the use of the word "détente" and that accelerated the American reassessment of Soviet goals worldwide as the massive Soviet buildup in strategic and conventional power and the capacity to project that power abroad gained momentum.

But what about the converse? Has U.S. African policy affected Soviet strategy—either toward Africa or on a broader plane? The answer is necessarily a speculation about a speculation. Nonetheless, there can be some agreement that the Soviets do concern themselves with American policy in a quite serious—sometimes obsessive— way.[1] And given the rising importance of Africa to both superpowers, it would seem reasonable to assume that, under scrutiny, one would discern varying sorts of American "inputs" to Soviet strategy toward Africa. The conclusion to which this essay comes is that U.S. African policy has in fact affected Soviet strategy not only toward Africa but toward all the "intermediate zones," as Soviet writers are wont to call the regions of the Third World. The relationship has indeed been a powerful one—yet of a wholly unexpected sort. For the origin of American influence on Soviet African policy has been essentially the opposite of that of Soviet influence on U.S. African policy. While the latter has resulted from unprecedentedly strident action, the former has for the most part stemmed from inaction.

The Pre-Angola Situation

At the outset of an examination such as this, it is tempting to try to explain Soviet African policy without reference to American actions—at least through the Angolan civil war. The argument would be that Soviet African policy has in every major way unfolded to opportunities created by its own ideological limbering and by what the Soviets would call the "objective conditions" in Africa, and that American-offered opportunities have at best been short-term, a dimple on the face of a very tall body of policy development. After all, Soviet involvement in Africa—and Russian before that—was minimal, if not nonexistent, prior to 1950 (an important exception being Ethiopia);[2] thereafter, Moscow had opportunities with regime after regime, in a steadily enlarging number of African countries, to cement ties of varying depth. It was, for a time, all gain, since for every Soviet connection there was a corresponding lessening of the proportionate importance of the ex-colonial ties (which is why Patrick McGowan in the late 1960s quite appropriately used African relations with the Soviet Union as an analytical measuring stick of the functional independence of African states[3]). When France withdrew from Guinea in 1958 in a huff, the Soviet Union moved in swiftly. When Kwame Nkrumah sought to radicalize the Ghanaian polity in 1961, he did so by opening relations with Moscow. This led to a rapid diminution of British and American influence in Accra, as was to happen elsewhere—from Tanzania to Benin, Libya to Zambia.

Moreover, the major *changes* (as opposed to opportunistic moves) in past Soviet African policy have come from a combination of internal Soviet developments and reverses/successes on the ground in Africa—rather than as a response to American moves (or the absence of American moves). Thus, the early Soviet initiatives in Africa in the late 1950s resulted from the unaided "discovery" that all African leaders were not unredeemable colonial stooges, and that there were possibilities for education and development in Africa which might reinforce the USSR's broad objectives. In other words, a change occurred in the "subjective" environment in Moscow, not in the "objective" conditions in Africa.

Another major change came in the mid-1960s as a result of too much success, followed by too many reverses. The Soviets had discovered that Nikita Khrushchev's strategy of legitimizing the leapfrogging of steps on the African path to socialism would not work; they began to suspect—in Robert Legvold's words—that "Africa's revolutionary democrats may not be up to the struggle."[4] Strategy toward Africa would therefore have to be more deliberate, and diplomatic relations, more general—especially with the important states like Nigeria.

Although the United States was making some alterations of its own policy that were oddly parallel in the same period, Moscow was undertaking changes in its African policy for its own internal reasons. For their part, the Americans were becoming obsessed with—and bogged down in—Southeast Asia, and when in late 1964 they were able to intervene in the eastern Congo rebellion (to rescue trapped Western nationals) without eliciting a meaningful Soviet reaction, they concluded that Africa was strategically unimportant, thus failing to perceive that Moscow, incapable of responding, was expending its energies developing the means for precisely such contingencies in the future. The new Nixon administration at the end of the decade downgraded the importance of Africa in U.S. policy still further by relegating Africa to the bottom of the geographic list of American priorities.

Whether the Soviets were conscious of the increasingly deliberate American diffidence toward Africa is not apparent. What they were aware of was, in the first instance, the degree to which the United States still enjoyed economic and political ties throughout the continent, giving Washington capabilities which they sought to emulate and equal. The Soviets had manifestly not written off Africa and presumably saw the U.S. problem in Asia as providing Soviet opportunities in Africa, but there is little evidence that the more realistic Soviet strategy of the late 1960s and early 1970s emerged from either American omission or commission. Soviet policy is better understood in terms of the unfolding learning process that the USSR went through in dealing with such undeveloped societies, and in terms of Moscow's not illogical conviction that radical change would eventually occur in many parts of the continent—particularly the white redoubt of the South, where it was plainly inevitable.

There is one way, however, in which American policy *had* held real importance for Moscow prior to mid-1970s—at the strictly military level. The Soviets were always impressed with the American ability to project power far afield.[5] After all, in 1960, the year the present act of the African drama began, the United States was able to obtain the solution that it desired in the Congo (now Zaire) because it could ferry the troops of the moderate African states (and of the radical states desiring a moderate solution) back and forth to Leopoldville, and because it had the matériel, intelligence, and diplomatic network on the ground with which to coordinate its effort. The attempted Soviet intervention—some trucks and transport planes to help the nascent opposition and radical government in Stanleyville—was a humiliating failure. It was small wonder that the Soviets refused to pay their special U.N. assessment for the operation and caused the closure of the General Assembly in 1965: the U.N. Congo Command, among other things, had forcibly removed the Soviet ambassador from Leopoldville in the fall of 1960.[6]

Other U.S. interventions and démarches in Africa also made an impact on Moscow. For example, the British-Belgian-American landings in Stanleyville in late 1964, to which reference has already been made, showed a capability that was at once awesome and threatening.[7] As late as 1975, the Soviets were still not completely sure of themselves, as they began involving themselves heavily and militarily in Angolan affairs. True, they had been aiding their Angolan Marxist allies, the Popular Movement for the Liberation of Angola (*Movimento Popular de Libertação de Angola*—MPLA) for almost two decades, and they knew the Angolan ground well. But we know that in October of 1975 they kept a close eye on American intentions, specifically with reference to the disposition of the Sixth Fleet, and that the General Staff took its sudden and dramatic decision to organize a massive airlift only *after* it had become apparent that the United States was politically and militarily immobilized.[8] The General Staff would have been more aware than most Americans that a small contingent from the Sixth Fleet could have blown the Soviet naval task force of six ships out of the water. Or, in a mere show of power, as Michael MccGwire has pointed out, it could simply have sailed around the Soviet convoy, showing all who needed reminding that the United States *could* intervene and simply had chosen to skip this one.[9]

So American military capabilities up to late 1975 were a serious and practical inhibition to Soviet moves in Africa. But that changed very rapidly with the Angolan civil war—or so we will argue. In the post-Angolan period, U.S. policy toward Black Africa became a direct part of the Soviet calculus. We find that in one set of cases—notably the Horn, "Shaba I," and "Shaba II" crises—U.S. omission has been the critical factor from the Soviet standpoint, while in another set—

involving Southern Africa—the precise character of the policies that the United States has devised has had significance for Moscow.

U.S. Omission

American unwillingness to take a decisive stand on African issues does not begin with the Angolan civil war. Indeed, U.S. omission—as a result of domestic pressures—had worked in the Soviet favor before. During the Nigerian civil war, the Federal Military Government felt snubbed on several accounts by Washington. At the very outset of the war, for example, Secretary of State Dean Rusk undiplomatically referred to Nigeria as primarily a "British responsibility."[10] But the real issue was arms supply. In Lagos, American neutrality in the civil war was construed, not unfairly, as helpful to the rebels. The Soviets were happy to move into the vacuum, and supplied Lagos with increasingly sophisticated matériel and aircraft in the quantities that were requested. As the struggle wore on, the United States, because of the Biafra lobby, could not change its stance—although the professional assessment in Foggy Bottom was that this stance only prolonged a war whose outcome was not in doubt.[11]

The great difference between the Nigerian and Angolan civil wars for the two superpowers lay in the nature of the relationship between the adversaries in Africa and their respective allies outside the continent. In the Nigerian case, there was no parallel ideological or strategic split between the Federal Military Government and Biafra, on the one hand, and the superpowers, on the other. Thus, both Great Britain and the USSR aided Lagos, while an even more dissimilar set of nations, from China to South Africa, aided Biafra. But Angola, at least as many Africans saw it,[12] was a test case of superpower will, with Moscow and its allied lined up on one side and the Western powers on the other.

On the American part, however, Angola was a game only half played out. The dealer, a secretary of state about whom there was a growing controversy which made the U.S. Congress disinclined to approve an overt strategy for exploiting the cards he held, chose at first to hide his moves behind Zairian cover. Such a strategy produced positive results initially. By the autumn of 1975, MPLA fortunes were waning—especially after October 23, when a mechanized column of troops of the National Union for the Total Independence of Angola

(*União Nacional pro Independencia Total de Angola* — UNITA), South Africans, and Portuguese mercenaries crossed into Angola from South-West Africa. This made UNITA, the largest, most effective, and most pro-Western guerrilla force, and the Zaire-backed Front for the Liberation of Angola (*Frente Nacional de Libertação de Angola* — FNLA), long supported by the United States, the likely winners in the civil war. But by the fall, Congress, having become aware of the covert American activities, was saying "never again" to U.S. military involvement in civil war–type situations. Equally pertinent, the launching of the Soviet intervention in October was so swift that it caught even the American executive off guard. Thus, by February the Soviets and their Cuban allies had won this particular game. Nevertheless, they obviously knew that they had triumphed by default. The fact that it took 20,000 Cuban troops to do so and then to sustain the victorious MPLA hardly bolstered the legitimacy of the outcome.[13]

While American omission emerged as a serious factor in Soviet policy with the USSR's triumph in Angola, only with the conflict in the Horn of Africa did this factor play a critical role in the development of Soviet policy toward specific African conflicts. Like the Nigerian civil war, but unlike the one in Angola, the conflict in the Horn had cross-cutting relationships to the external powers. With the Soviet Union and Israel—concerned that the Red Sea not become wholly Arab dominated—backing Ethiopia and with Somalia fighting with Soviet arms and Saudi cash while receiving marginal help from Morocco, Sudan, and Egypt, there was anything but a neat contest from the standpoint of international alliances.[14] Yet the analogy with Angola is stronger than that with Nigeria, for the great powers figured directly and prominently in the strife in the Horn. Thus, an examination of this strife is critical to an understanding of the evolution of the Soviet approach to Africa.

The Horn

To render the conflict in the Horn understandable, a brief review of American and Soviet involvement in the region is essential. Let us begin with Ethiopia. Until 1974, Ethiopia was the United States' closest ally in Africa. At the height of the relationship, Ethiopia permitted several thousand agents and technicians of the U.S. Central Intelligence Agency and National Security Agency on its soil to operate one of the most important American communications monitoring stations in the world.[15] Ethiopia also served as a restraining influence on African radicalism and helped out friends of the United States. U.S. officials have claimed, for example, that Ethiopian bases played a role in the Israeli air force's initial attack on Egyptian airfields in the 1967 war.[16]

Yet when the Emperor was overthrown, in the "creeping coup" of 1974 that brought an unknown but incipiently radical group to power, the United States used little of its still-considerable influence to affect the direction of developments, other than to attempt to save the Emperor's life. This was an "abandonment," according to John Spencer, an authority on modern Ethiopia.[17] But it occurred during and after the exposure of the Watergate cover-up, the source of so many foreign policy problems of this period.

Over the ensuing three years in Addis Ababa, the new military regime's initial lofty intentions of reform degenerated into a sordid feast on the revolution's own children, as one of the world's most vicious dictators, increasingly encouraged by his Soviet backers, captured the central reins of power at the expense of what responsible cadre were left. The United States exercised no influence throughout this period, allowing its arms supply program to dwindle and then finally suspending that program, on "human rights" grounds, in April 1977.

Col. Mengistu Haile Mariam, like so many other leaders of unstable regimes in unstructured states, needed an ideological justification to legitimize what he sought to do, and he found it in Marxism-Leninism. Moreover, as attested by the secret aid agreement that Soviet officials signed with him in December 1976, before he had fully consolidated power, he received Soviet backing in the factional struggles that raged in Ethiopia.[18] Whether this blend of local needs and "scientific socialism" set him on a course that was largely principled or largely opportunistic is impossible to say, though clearly his Marxist rhetoric increased in intensity as the months progressed.

What is more important than motive, however, is result. Only after Mengistu consolidated his power in February 1977—most significantly, through a shootout in Addis Ababa in which most of his cabinet colleagues were killed (reportedly by him)—did the Soviets escalate their commitment to him to a high level. The military government as a whole had, like the early Leninists, got rid of a monarchy, quashed the nobility, decimated a church, and (in theory) divided up the land for the peasantry,[19] but no single leader had emerged who was hard and tough enough to be willing to exercise sufficient ruthlessness to permit the "revolution" to be thoroughly consolidated. After February 4, the Soviets had in Mengistu the first Third World leader since Fidel Castro with such qualities. They therefore began showering lavish praise on him and made a gigantic pledge of military aid—reportedly $400 million—that was to grow still further in the months ahead.[20]

Hitherto, the Soviets had held back in important respects from wholly embracing the Ethiopian leadership for yet another reason—their own military stake in Somalia. According to a highly credible account by a U.S. government official, who based his analysis on discussions with Soviet diplomats as well as on more arcane intelligence, the Soviet military and the Politburo were by this point (early 1977) locking horns over which side to back.[21] By this account, the military wished to keep the bird in the hand in Somalia (the naval complex at Berbera and access to several airfields around the country); the Politburo, frustrated in general by Third World leaders committed to local socialisms, religions, and other impediments to "scientific socialism," made the critical decision to avoid a choice in the Horn if possible, but if forced to make a choice, to opt for Ethiopia.

There were other reasons for choosing Ethiopia. Not only was it ten times as populous as Somalia; it could dominate the Red Sea as well as serve as a satisfactory staging post for any mission in the area of the Persian Gulf. Furthermore, the Ethiopian air space would be as invaluable to the Soviets as it had been to the Americans for the previous quarter century.

And, meantime, Mengistu's need of the Soviets grew apace. Bitter factional struggles in Addis Ababa, between varying hues of radicals, further weakened the regime. In turn, the regime's preoccupation with the internecine warfare in the capital created new openings for the secessionists in Eritrea and the Ogaden. Eritrean revolutionaries had long held the upper hand in their struggle and now began consolidating their hold. In the Ogaden, as we will see in a different context, the Somalis thought the time ripe for launching an attack and soon had gained control of all but the highest ground in the region. Small wonder, then, that Mengistu talked a very revolutionary line, or that the Soviets viewed his very dependence on them and their allies as an opportunity of historic moment. It is a truism that revolutionary powers like the Soviet Union thrive on disorder, for it assists them in trying to spread their influence and reduce that of the powers which benefited from the previous status quo.

The Soviet position in and toward Somalia, like that of the United States, was always conditioned by the underlying ethnic conflict of the Horn, although there were considerable differences in how this cut across the evolving policies of the two superpowers. Africa, it should be noted, is plagued by unstable borders, the heritage of boundaries drawn up, mostly in the late 19th century, for European convenience and splitting tribes, clans, and even families. Hence, there has been widespread opposition on the continent to any alteration of borders on the grounds that if this Pandora's box is opened, it will be virtually impossible to close. But the Horn encompasses the two states that do not fit the general African mold, thereby rendering—powerfully, from the Somali viewpoint—the modern African rule against the alteration of borders of dubious relevance to them.[22] Somalia is the only homogeneous African state north of the Limpopo; indeed, it may well be the only true African nation. Moreover, Somalia is the only African state with a substantial component of its dominant ethnic group outside its borders. The Ogaden, at present a part of Ethiopia, is populated by one of the five principal Somali clans, and it has been the central aim of Somali policy to regain that territory. Ethiopia, for its part, was until recently termed an "empire." And empire it is—an amalgam of peoples conquered by Emperor Menelik II, Haile Selassie's grandfather, and reconquered (or reacquired) by Haile Selassie himself in the 20th century. The Ogaden was won from the Italians (who had held it only briefly) at the battle of Sadowa in 1897 and was gradually brought under Amharic administration in the early years of the century. But between 1935 (when Haile Selassie went into exile following his defeat at Italian hands) and the late 1940s, the Ogaden was administered by Italians and British, both of whom conjoined it administratively to other ethnic Somali territories.

To Moscow at least, U.S. policy with respect to the ethnic conflict in the Horn no doubt reflected strategic considerations—i.e., the United States followed Haile Selassie's lead throughout the 1950s as part of a drive to secure allies in the outer tier of states around the increasingly Soviet-influenced heartland of the Middle East. Thus, to ensure the Emperor's cooperation, Washington provided arms for his military. More important, it supported his claims to both Eritrea and the Ogaden. Eritrea, a former Italian colony turned U.N. trust territory, was ceded to Ethiopia by U.N. vote. This was a great achievement for the Emperor, given the lack of historical precedent for Amhara rule over the Eritreans and given the outlet to the sea which the territory was to confer on the empire. But it was to be a mixed blessing, as rebellion began not long after Ethiopia ended Eritrea's special federal status in 1962 by annexing it completely. By 1974 Eritrean rebels, divided though they were among themselves, controlled most of Eritrea. As for the Ogaden, Great Britain had transferred control of the territory to Ethiopia in the late 1940s, but Somalis there and in Somali-populated territories under British and Italian jurisdiction continued to protest that move throughout the 1950s. When the new state of Somalia, formed from British Somaliland and the U.N. Trust Territory of Somaliland under Italian administration, gained its independence in 1960, it set reunification with the Ogaden as the first order of business. Within less than four years, Ethiopia and Somalia were to fight on the battlefield over the area.

As far as Mogadiscio was concerned, Washington's backing of Ethiopia made the United States, not unreasonably, an object of suspicion. Given Washington's unwillingness to see the Ogaden issue in Somalia's way, moreover, the United States could not dispel that suspicion and improve its relations with Somalia, even though by the early 1970s the importance of American ties with Ethiopia had diminished, as satellites had assumed the most critical of the functions once carried out at the great Kagnew communications base in Eritrea. Washington over and over cited the argument of most Black African states, that colonial boundaries must be kept intact, as precluding support for the Somali position. In Somali eyes, however, that very rule in fact favored the Somali claim, for the Ogaden had been administered by European colonial powers with Somalia. Continuation of rule by the Ethiopian empire was, to the Somalis, a local form of imperialism.

This state of affairs rendered relatively simple Moscow's task of wooing Somalia in order to establish a foothold in the Horn to counter the American presence there. Taking advantage of Somalia's fears of, and ambitions toward, Ethiopia, the USSR began aiding the new African state as early as 1961, and throughout the 1960s the Soviets built up Somali power. This buildup understandably whetted Mogadiscio's appetite for the separated lands of the Ogaden. As time passed, the Soviets could have had fewer and fewer illusions as to why they were welcome in Somalia.

But then in 1969 Somalia's Moscow-trained military leadership overthrew the existing democratic government—one of the few in Africa—and started to work much more closely with the Soviets.

Two external developments heightened Somalia's importance to the USSR still further. First, Moscow's increasing difficulties with Egypt made an alternative Middle Eastern/Indian Ocean base of operations attractive. Indeed, Michael MccGwire has argued that the Soviets were shifting their focus in this period toward Somalia in any event, so "it seems likely that [Anwar al-] Sadat's request [for Soviet military advisers to leave Egypt] suited the Soviets' purpose."[23] This shift, MccGwire maintains, reflected the USSR's intensifying conflict with China, which necessitated a strong Soviet position in the Indian Ocean to safeguard Moscow's alternate line of communication between its Asian and European realms. Secondly, there was the Arab oil embargo during the 1973 Arab–Israeli war, along with the fourfold increase in world oil prices that followed. Because of the heightened vulnerability of the industrial West to the oil weapon, the Soviets had all the more incentive to improve their position in Somalia, for Somalia affords ready access to the sea lanes to and from the oil-rich Persian Gulf. By 1975, the Soviets sat astride the Western jugular, with a missile handling and storage facility, a strategic air strip, and all manner of support facilities under their own control on Somali territory or in Somali waters at Berbera.[24]

Thus, as it became clear that in Ethiopia there was a potentially genuine Leninist revolution—in Moscow's rather narrow understanding of this term—the USSR faced a possible dilemma. On one hand, it could continue to back the Mogadiscio regime to preserve the Soviet military position in Somalia, even though it was increasingly obvious that the relationship was largely opportunistic, with the Somalis motivated more by a desire to arm themselves to regain the Ogaden than by a search for succor for the home-grown and Islam-reinforced socialism which the regime proclaimed and honored. On the other hand, the USSR might seek to develop ties with Ethiopia's ideologically more compatible revolutionaries only to find that it had thereby sacrificed its military position in Somalia.

At the same time, however, there was no inherent reason (something which contemporary commentary inevitably failed to note) why the Soviets might not succeed in having things both ways. After all, the United States for 25 years had held the balance between Greece and Turkey, while remaining allied to both, before overt conflict broke out between them. Why could Moscow not achieve a *pax Sovietica* in the Horn?

If in Ethiopia the United States threw away its own good cards and failed to trump its adversary's, in Somalia it missed every signal from a would-be partner and wholly misplayed the hand, thereby substantially mitigating Soviet problems. At least as early as late 1975, Washington's two most important friends in the Persian Gulf region—Iran and Saudi Arabia—began separate efforts to persuade the Somali leadership to follow in Anwar al-Sadat's footsteps and lessen his dependence on Soviet arms.[25] But the Somali condition was an alternative source of arms that was dependable. The Iranians proposed use of their own channels; the Saudis, with increasing insistence, indicated that they would pay for Western arms if they could find a supplier. The U.S. Defense Department, having become convinced that a threat to Western shipping lanes existed—indeed, that grave peril was involved—was willing to play. In 1976, the Saudi Defense Minister, Prince Abdullah, visited his counterparts in America and reiterated his government's generous offer.[26] The Saudis, it was clear, would pay any bill involved in getting the Soviets out of the Red Sea and away from the Indian Ocean littoral. Given the more benign perceptions of Soviet intentions in the State Department, however, it was not possible for the Defense Department to do anything about this matter during the remainder of the Ford administration.

The issue slowly percolated through the bureaucracy independent of administration in late 1976 and early 1977 as, at a glacial pace, one after another senior official began to see the implications of a disintegrating Ethiopia increasingly dependent on the Soviets at the center and a continued Soviet military presence in Somalia. But the realization did not reach everywhere. Incredibly, when Saudi Crown Prince Fahd visited Washington in the spring and renewed the Saudi offer, he was piously turned down, by one account, on the grounds that the United States was no longer to be an arms merchant.[27] Apparently, the White House did not even perceive the strategic issue.

By the summer of 1977, however, the rapid Soviet buildup in Ethiopia after Mengistu's seizure of full power in February, had alarmed the administration. A decision was made—and announced—in July that Washington would arm Somalia. What ensued attests that the handling of this question must be ranked among the most glaring cases of bungled government decision-making in recent American diplomatic history. According to Arnaud de Borchgrave, Washington had been told that Mogadiscio was ready and able to move into the Ogaden, pending the assurance of an arms supply, and Washington reached the decision to arm the Somalis in full knowledge of the order

of battle. Thus, the Somalis "claim that they began their all-out invasion of Ethiopia's Ogaden region last July because of the prospect of
U.S. arms aid—and because they had received secret U.S. messages
which they interpreted as a go-ahead to conquer the area." These
messages, de Borchgrave reported, came from "the very top" and
indicated that Washington was "not adverse to further guerrilla pressure in the Ogaden."[28] Moscow, too, seems to have assumed that
Washington had given Somalia a "green light." In a characteristic reference, Radio Moscow subsequently observed that "the promise of
arms virtually pushed Somalia into the aggression against Ethiopia."[29]

Whether or not American officials intended to give Mogadiscio a
green light, they at minimum displayed great naiveté in making their
decision, for such a decision was bound to encourage the Somalis to
attack. Clearly, the Americans underestimated the ease with which
the Somalis could gain control of the Ogaden as long as they had only
the Ethiopian army with which to contend.

In any event, when Somali forces began driving the Ethiopian army
out of the region, Washington immediately drew back. Those factions
in the administration less concerned about Soviet advances in the
Third World and/or eager to cut back on American arms sales to the
Third World and to please sub-Saharan regimes now had a new handle
with which to beat an old issue. U.S. diplomats around the world
conveyed the new line: American aid to Somalia was impossible because of that country's "aggression."[30]

It was evident that the Carter administration thought it could avoid
commitment and simply watch the Soviets stumble. As Richard Burt
of *The New York Times* put things, Washington based its policy "on
the assumption that Moscow's efforts are bound to fail."[31] With considerable consistency, the senior members of the administration spoke
of the "quagmire" into which the Soviets had purportedly fallen.
High administration spokesmen—including those who shortly were to
take precisely the opposite line—scoffed at the notion that the
Soviets knew what they were doing. As the year progressed, events
gave further encouragement to this viewpoint. By the end of
November, not only had Somali forces occupied all of the Ogaden
save for two strategically located cities, but the Somalis had also
thrown out all Soviet advisers from their country and denied the
USSR continuing access to Berbera and other local facilities of military import.

The Soviets, while beginning their massive arms buildup in

Ethiopia, kept the pressure on Washington, accusing it—curiously—
of trying to "internationalize" the conflict by allowing American-
supplied arms from Iran to come to Mogadiscio. "In this way the
U.S. is preventing a peaceful settlement of the conflict, for which the
Ethiopian Government has repeatedly called."[32]

What caused the administration suddenly to notice that it had been
playing the fool is not clear. But at the end of the year, Bernard
Gwertzman, a senior correspondent of *The New York Times*, revealed
that the White House and State Department had "conceded" their
inability to induce the Russians to cut their involvement in the
Horn[33]—as if there had ever been a chance of "convincing" the
Soviets of this through unarmed diplomacy.

The Soviet leadership, ignoring its internal critics (especially now
that it had arrived at a clear policy), was attending to the realities of
the order of battle and was completing one of the most monumental
arms transfers in history. With Washington standing by, simply watching, the Soviets poured more than a billion dollars of military aid into
Ethiopia, overflying Turkey, Iran, and other countries without permission in order to reach the Horn. Such illegal and unfriendly acts
were in fact yet another signal to the world of Moscow's resolve and
Washington's feebleness.[34] How could Turks or Iranians face down
the USSR and demand that its military aircraft land for a search if, as
happened, their own ally refused to back them up? The Soviets also
used their gunboats to subdue opposition in the ports of Eritrea so as
to unload matériel from ships before rebels in that province had cut
access roads.[35] On the diplomatic front, Moscow continued to
"stonewall" Washington, which found it difficult to understand why
the Soviets did not wish to apply the modalities of détente to this
newest battlefield.

In February began the biggest military operation in Africa since
World War II's battles in Libya and Egypt. With the guidance of the
First Deputy Commander of Soviet Ground Forces, a 12,000-man
Cuban force, with the assistance of the Ethiopians, launched a
blitzkrieg across the Ogaden desert, using tanks helicoptered in from
Addis Ababa and squadrons of MIG-21s and -23s. Within 10 days, the
Somalis were decimated, the back of their armed forces broken.[36]

In the aftermath of the debacle, tragedy became farce as far as U.S.
policy was concerned. With respect to the past, one American foreign
service officer with extensive experience in the Horn had already
said, "the administration couldn't have bungled things more if it had
tried—and at every step of the way."[37] Soon quarreling within the

administration became virtually open. State Department spokesmen sought to minimize the impact of events in the Horn, while the President's national security adviser, Zbigniew Brzezinski, made strong speeches in public and hawkish talks in private, arguing that the Soviets were risking a breakdown of détente and a possible collapse of the strategic arms negotiations themselves. His antidote, stated privately, was to use "diplomatic and strategic power—but not military power." This proposition stunned those who had always associated strategic power with a willingness to take military risks of a high order. What Brzezinski in fact wanted to do was to move an aircraft carrier into the region, without, however, giving it the ability to act—as if anyone would have been fooled by such a bluff.[38] He also raised the notion of linkage, to the horror of American liberals and Soviet writers in about the same degree.[39]

The President only compounded the farce by publicly taking credit, at a press conference, for the withdrawal of the Somali army from the Ogaden—days after it had been decimated by Soviet armor.[40] In a further example of the naiveté and wishful thinking coloring American policy during this period, he suggested that, as the Somalis had left the Ogaden, the Soviets and Cubans could now depart from the Horn, there being no further occasion for their presence. Even more absurd was the administration request "for Soviet help in establishing corps of international observers to monitor a cease-fire arrangement" to protect against reprisals[41]—as if an alien occupation of the Ogaden *could* be sustained without reprisals.

Of far greater pertinence to the realities of the situation than the mere fact of the Somali withdrawal was what followed in Somalia—namely, an attempted *coup d'état* by Soviet-oriented elements among the remnants of the army. Although it did not succeed, there was little basis for optimism as to the outcome of the next effort.

Meantime, what of Ethiopia and Colonel Mengistu's grim regime? In the late summer of 1977, even as the big Soviet arms buildup got under way, Carter administration officials had bragged that Mengistu had toned down his attacks on the United States, but a delegation of senior Washington officials to Addis Ababa in early 1978, led by Deputy National Security Adviser David Aaron, only succeeded in advertising their inability to affect the underlying realities.[42] By every analysis, Mengistu had grown wholly dependent on Soviet, Cuban, and East German arms. Ethiopia had arguably become, at least for the moment, the first real Soviet satellite in Africa.

It was late 1978, however, before the issue of Eritrea was more or less resolved. The revolutionary movements there had long struck observers as among the most impressive ever to appear in Africa;[43] thus, mowing down the insurgents required enormous force. This objective the Ethiopian army was finally able to accomplish in the summer and fall of 1978 with Soviet assistance in the form of matériel, advisers, and apparently actual participation in the bombardment of ports and rebel positions.[44] The importance that the Soviets attached to Eritrea, which sits not only near the Persian Gulf but across the narrow Red Sea from Saudi Arabia, emerged clearly at about the same time with the near-simultaneous assassination of the president of North Yemen and the coup against, and death of, the president of South Yemen on June 23–24, 1978. Both were moderates within the constellation of the forces within their countries, and both were evidently eliminated by means that required outside assistance— specifically, from the Soviets and Cubans.

Thus, at the close of 1978 Soviet strategy in the region looked like a tremendous success. Nevertheless, the USSR was going to have to continue to commit resources to Ethiopia on a large scale to enable Addis Ababa to persist in suppressing so much of the domain which Haile Selassie had packaged together into what had been, briefly, the Ethiopian empire.

The Shaba Crises

While American omission was operating as a factor in Soviet policy in the Horn, it was also working, albeit more subtly, in Zaire, in the case of the incursion into Shaba (formerly known as Katanga) from Angola in the spring of 1977. The first important point to note about this incursion is an ironic one. It was carried out by the old Katangan gendarmes, mercenaries of the agents of the "neocolonialist stooge" incarnate, Moise Tshombe, who had left their homeland with their patron's demise in 1965 and had earned favor in the Marxist MPLA camp 10 years later during the Angolan civil war by fighting alongside the winning party. However, their "return" to Shaba can hardly be considered an unplanned or private affair. They did not infiltrate back in guerrilla style with the weapons which they had brought with them to Angola almost 12 years earlier; rather, they advanced through identifiable routes in conventional formation with fairly new AK-47s and assorted other weaponry. Moreover, many had been trained by

Cubans and East Germans.[45] The extent to which the Soviets concerned themselves with the venture is not clear, but if it was something less than a high priority item of business, it was not irrelevant to them. Their own obsession with Zaire over 17 years, their continual harping on its criticality to the Western economies, and their awareness of the extensive American investment there certainly suggest otherwise.

The vehemence of the USSR's reaction to and warnings about the Moroccan-Egyptian-Saudi-French move to counter the intervention reinforces this judgment. "The deeper the United States and other NATO countries are becoming involved in Zaire's affairs," a Soviet analyst declared, "the greater danger arises for the peace and well being, not only of the African nations, but also of the peoples of those NATO countries." And Brezhnev himself said much the same, warning the "interveners" of the "consequences" if they persisted.[46]

Ironically, it was the "other" set of interveners, the ones who had intervened in fact, who ultimately occasioned "consequences." As a result of Shaba II—the second incursion by rebel forces, in May 1978—U.S. policy almost ceased to be a policy of omission. Indeed, the whole concept of détente on which American (though obviously not Soviet) policy had been built came into serious question. If Shaba I had been a farce—with the United States laughing on the sidelines[47]—then Shaba II, as Crawford Young has written, was indisputably a tragedy.[48] In the latter case, 4,500 irregulars seized Kolwezi, causing thousands of deaths and the flight of almost all the 2,000 European residents on whose skills the mining industry was dependent. Furthermore, the atrocities inflicted on Europeans tended to insure that the attraction of replacements would be difficult. Although a French-Belgian counterintervention eventually turned back the invasion, the rebels succeeded in their minimum objective of making the survival of the Zairian economy (and hence the polity) more problematical. At the same time, however, the invasion, following on the heels of Soviet successes in the Horn and elsewhere, finally (if briefly) outraged the Carter administration, once it became convinced of Cuban-Soviet complicity in the affair.[49]

As a result, Moscow now perceived distinct limits on its actions. U.S. public opinion was manifestly changing, and though administration thinking lagged far behind it, there could be no more easy Soviet interventions as in Angola and the Horn, where the American response had at best been equivocal. Indeed, the United States had

provided logistical support in Shaba II for the French-Belgian counterintervention.

For almost three years, American omission had caused the Soviet
leadership at least to try to declare the continent "off limits to the
West"—or so it would appear if the head of the Community Party of
the Soviet Union, while taking satisfaction from what was happening
in Zaire in 1977 as a consequence in part of Soviet moves, could attempt to frighten Western powers away from efforts to restore the
status quo ante there. But as France emerged with a tough and forward African policy, Moscow was left simply to threaten and bluster
in the Shaba case. Nonetheless, it is important to remember that the
actual undertakings of the U.S. government in Zaire came about only
as a result of European leadership and a dramatic change in American
public opinion, and it was by no means certain that the Soviets would
regard the U.S. reaction in this instance as requiring a lowering of the
USSR's profile in independent Black Africa, much less in the white
redoubts of Southern Africa, to which we now turn.

Southern Africa

As we have observed, a failure of American will may well have
opened many doors for the Soviets in Africa. Or perhaps it might be
more appropriately described as the "so-what school of foreign policy," as some architects of the Carter administration's policy have
labeled their approach to international affairs, in light of their lack of
concern about Communist influence in the Third World.[50] But there
has been no lack of initiative in Southern Africa since the advent of
the Carter administration.

Tracing how the various U.S. initiatives there—from Zimbabwe to
Namibia—have affected Soviet policy is vastly more complicated
than looking at the opportunities created by omission—not least because of the very flux of the situation. The USSR, with its new alliances with Angola and Mozambique, is, in certain senses, becoming
something of a "status quo" power in Southern Africa, needing to
calculate its policy carefully in view of the substantial political interests at risk. And the United States, despite its many economic interests in the region, has increasingly acted unfettered (and uncon-
cerned) by these interests. But the basic situation remains unaltered:
the United States is in no position to organize a revolution in South-

ern Africa, however much some of its leaders might like to, while the Soviet Union has every interest in continuing to use at least South Africa as a whipping boy of the West and presumably in fomenting revolution in the region as well. (It would not be fair or responsible, though, to describe Soviet policy as purely opportunistic, for the USSR's opposition to racism—beyond its own borders anyway—has been largely consistent.)

The Soviets presumably have learned that at least at the superficial level, virtually every Southern African issue works in their favor, particularly in view of how the Americans have played their cards. But at a more profound level, as I shall argue, it may well be that the Soviets are less optimistic—or at least less than heady—about their own prospects.

Let us begin with the positive side from Moscow's perspective. Up until Shaba II, as we have seen, the Soviets could deal with the dé-tente issue as they desired. During the Ford administration, whenever American opinion grew inflamed by new advances of an ally—for example, in Angola—the USSR could throw a sop to the administration by speaking favorably of negotiated solutions (and thereby, as in the Angolan case, buy its allies a few more weeks to consolidate their military conquests).[51] And of course before long, the Ford administration was gone, and a new one had come to office that took precisely the opposite tack. The American ambassador to the United Nations, and a few months later, the President of the United States, declared that the very Cuban troops who a year earlier had been said to "threaten" détente were now a "stabilizing" influence in the war-torn territory[52] (something which, of course, was strictly true, in the sense that Soviet troops in Hungary in 1956 and thereafter were, most certainly, a stabilizing influence). So the Soviets, in the short run, won either way.

Prior to the internal settlement attempted by Prime Minister Ian Smith and three black leaders in Rhodesia/Zimbabwe, Carter administration policy had ostensibly been to press for a negotiated settlement involving *all* parties, including the Zimbabwe African People's Union (zapu), which had guerrilla forces training in Zambia with Soviet help. Except in the unlikely event that this approach would work, the Americans were in a competition with the Soviets that they could not win, for with every further disintegration of the situation, the Soviet "revolutionary" position would increase in credibility.[53]

Once the internal settlement was devised, the administration had a new problem. Here was a multi-racial, moderate (if potential) solution to a thorny problem. There was no assurance that it would work, but it was certainly the sort of solution to problems that America had traditionally sought.

Nonetheless, the Carter administration put itself in outright opposition to the internal settlement, arguing that real peace could not be achieved until the black revolutionary groups, and their military arms, were brought into the government and military. It was, of course, something of a self-fulfilling prophecy. As Henry Kissinger has frequently pointed out, this position was bound—at the very least—to make Joshua Nkomo of ZAPU more truculent in his demands.

Initially, Washington made no differentiation between the two main guerrilla groups—i.e., ZAPU and the Zimbabwe African National Union (ZANU)—but in time a private preference for the ZAPU forces became evident. For one thing, moderates within the ruling American elite saw Nkomo as essentially a bourgeois, malleable, and ultimately moderate leader—perhaps a Jomo Kenyatta. But those supplying the drive behind the Carter administration's African policy, it would appear, were motivated by something different, something that must be seen by way of Soviet policy. These strategists were increasingly concerned that the Soviet-Cuban strike force would move from the Horn down to Rhodesia, and they believed that if the Rhodesian group which Moscow backed and trained was brought into the government, Moscow's presumed intentions would be thwarted. Their anxiety was reinforced by the administration's knowledge that even the most prestigious of the left-wing, but still nonaligned, leaders of Africa were growing more and more fearful of a Soviet-Cuban "hit" themselves, precisely because of their own successes in establishing socialist models for Africa as a whole. "After the Soviets clean up in Eritrea, I will be next on their hit list," a publicly anti-American African leader said privately—but so as to reach Washington.[54]

But regardless of the extent to which the Americans may have favored Nkomo of their own accord and regardless of the extent to which their own diplomacy had reduced their alternatives to supporting him, what they advertised was that the credibility of the Soviet strike force had become so great that the USSR no longer needed to use it. Once the fear of a Soviet-administered solution entered Western hearts, the Americans canted their diplomacy, in effect, to achieving the USSR's purpose for it, for getting Nkomo and his forces into the government would be impossible without giving them a position of leadership. With all the dangers entailed, this was not something which the internal Rhodesian leadership was apt to contemplate.

Washington's own conception of its position was of course, different. "Hard-liners" like Brzezinski appeared to see U.S. strategy as the only realistic way of sustaining influence in Southern Africa. Those on the other side, like U.N. Ambassador Andrew Young, considered themselves wholly on the revolutionary side (whatever qualifications the revolutionaries would have added notwithstanding). Young stated that "there was no difference between the American position and that of the Patriotic Front (of ZAPU and ZANU) except on the position of a United Nations Force."[55]

Moscow's approach was to continue training guerrillas while awaiting further American concessions. For example, when U.S. Secretary of State Cyrus Vance went to Moscow in late April 1978 to, among other things, appeal for Soviet cooperation in Africa, only a few hours after his departure the Cubans and Soviets published a communiqué calling for continued burning of the revolutionary fires in Africa.[56]

U.S. diplomacy, as seen in mid-1979, seemed to have fared no better with respect to Namibia—though for a while possibilities looked brighter there. It had been, after all, something of an achievement for the five NATO partners in the Security Council to work together to force South Africa into a settlement on South-West Africa that had a chance of sticking. But at all times the South Africans were suspicious of Western intentions, and in the end when the painfully negotiated solution began to fall apart, John Vorster, in his last act as Prime Minister of South Africa, declared that his country would launch the territory to independence on its own terms.

It was still too early to foretell the outcome, but it appeared that American policy had at least been consistent. Extraordinary pressure—including explicit threats of support for economic sanctions and the like—was put on South Africa to make previously unheard-of concessions, while much less pressure was put on the Carter administration favorite, the Marxist Sam Nujomo, who through the South-West Africa People's Organization (SWAPO) commands what is probably a minority segment of the largest ethnic group in the territory. Even with respect to Walvis Bay, juridically a part of South Africa, State Department negotiators favored the provocative position of SWAPO—namely, that the enclave must come to independence with Namibia—although they counseled SWAPO leaders, as one State Department official put it, "not to jeopardize independence by insisting on it, since they will get it afterwards in any case.''[57] Small wonder, then, that the South Africans finally, as so often in their history, elected to go it alone.

Though the situation in South Africa had not yet become one of revolutionary war, U.S. policy applied, *mutatis mutandis*, the same logic used in Rhodesia and Namibia to South Africa itself. Here too, however, American concessions designed to preclude Soviet advances had set a pattern. Consider, for example, the case of Moscow's report of a planned South African nuclear test in mid-1978. The ironies in the American attempt to forestall this alleged venture are several. Even if one is of the same persuasion as the present American leadership with respect to South Africa, one can take small comfort from the successful outcome of U.S. representations, for as Richard Bissell has pointed out:

> The Soviet Union demonstrated its role as the guardian of the black states in southern Africa, a role affirmed by the willingness of the United States to undertake measures against South Africa at the initiative of the Soviet Union. The United States has not prevented the proliferation of nuclear weapons, since all now believe that South Africa possesses "bombs in the closet."[58]

If one's persuasion lies in the realist's direction—that is, if one is concerned by the Soviet expansion in Southern Africa and would prefer not to bring down the South African regime before something stable and ultimately pro-Western can be mounted in its place—then the irony is compounded. Why (from this vantage point) should the United States congratulate itself on joining with the Soviets in condemning the weapons test of a country as avowedly hostile to Moscow as it is solicitous of Western interests (however little its attitude is welcomed in the West)? Nuclear proliferation, it might be added more generally, has by and large been the work of *American* friends and allies, primarily those near—or with particular reason to be fearful of—the Soviet Union and made anxious by the United States' worldwide pullback from its forward commitments during the 1970s and by the USSR's simultaneous establishment of new commitments around the globe.

The Soviets have been careful not to give the Carter administration any credit for its shifts in policy in Southern Africa. In fact, Moscow portrays the new U.S. African policies in precisely the same light that it does the U.S. embrace of détente—as something to which Washington has been driven by the shift in the correlation of forces. In reaction to a conciliatory speech by U.S. Secretary of State Vance, for example, Radio Moscow said that it was clear "that the U.S. ruling circles now have to consider more and more the changes that have taken place in Africa as a result of the successes of the national liberation movement of the peoples on the continent in the struggle for the liquidation of the colonial system." Washington, the broadcast went on, was simply making a virtue of necessity:

> The failure of the intervention against Angola [sic], the growing armed struggle of Africans in Zimbabwe and Namibia, the active support for national liberation movements by the OAU and, above all, the "frontline states" . . . and the growing international isolation of the racist regimes are all factors which the U.S. ruling circles, which not so long ago regarded the south of Africa as a rear zone, have been forced to take into account.[59]

Another commentary expanded upon this point:

> "The course of events," the *Washington Post* writes, "is dictating a new African policy to the Carter administration." Although locally it is now focused on formulating the so-called "Rhodesian settlement plan," its real framework and strategic aims are far broader: with the help of compromise decisions with respect to Zimbabwe and Namibia to let steam out of the South African broiler, which has been overheated to a critical point, and ultimately to preserve the Republic of South Africa . . . the chief link in the triple chain of the "white belt". . . . [60]

But beneath the euphoria that the Soviets derive from the conviction that the correlation of forces is moving their way with a vengeance, I sense that a certain unease still lingers about how all this will turn out. Consider the way in which the Soviet media have dealt with Ambassador Andrew Young. From the start, the Soviets were uncertain as to how to regard him. As they see things, he is surely an objective force in their favor—after all anyone who would try to lecture the United States out of its "paranoid fear of communism" (much less declare that the U.S., like the Soviet Union, has many political prisoners) would seem likely to warm their hearts.[61] But of course Young has also called the Soviets "racists," which complicates matters for them. At first, therefore, the Soviets simply classified Young as another—though "earnest"—shuttle diplomatist in the Kissinger tradition, trying to preserve "what is in effect the white minority's domination" in Rhodesia. By April 1977, the Soviets were saying that Young's slips of the tongue were "tolerated for propaganda purposes" and that "it can't be ruled out completely that they might even be well calculated" since Washington was trying to develop a new African policy owing to increased pressure from Black Africa, and since Washington had to keep its whole policy consonant with its "so-called human rights campaign."[62] In June, Young was compared to Erostrate, who burned down the temple to Artemis to attract attention. He was tolerated "because he really had no power."[63] (Could the Soviets really have been blind to the fact that Young was, at the pertinent time, perhaps the most influential American in establishing the parameters of U.S. policy in Africa? It hardly seems possible.) And Young's adoption of an analogy between the American south and Southern Africa and his prescription of tactics in the latter parallel to those which had been employed in the former—i.e., the exclusion of armed violence—offered further proof to Moscow that Young was a tool of the capitalist interests. Indeed, the Soviets viewed his praise for free enterprise as confirmation that he was simply helping the "pragmatically minded representatives of business circles in . . . South Africa . . . to 'slacken the reins'" on apartheid in order to preserve their interests.[64]

Soviet writers, in sum, seem to feel that Young is being used precisely as some American adherents of *Realpolitik* hoped (or believed) he is being used.[65] That is, the United States intends to capitalize on his rhetoric to seduce radical states away from the Soviet Union, rebuild the American image in the Third World, and to disguise—from them as well as from Young himself—the true interests being protected under this cover. These interests involve continued access to the critical minerals from Southern Africa upon which many Western industries depend—a dependency so little commented upon in the United States but so frequently in the Soviet Union.

Soviet treatment of President Carter's trip to Nigeria in March 1978 fits into the same picture. The Soviet media presented the trip not as something new and different, but as something "in the context of Washington's overall policy. This policy is determined by the efforts of American monopolies to consolidate their positions in the developing countries and to oppose the growth of the national liberation movement."[66]

The problem with the Soviet analysis, of course, is that it squares with no realities of the *moment*. Carter's policy might wind up serving the purposes that Moscow attributes to it if it continues to falter at every turn, but that result would represent a massive defeat for the administration in terms of the policy's original aims. To interpret Carter's policy as have the Soviets and some Americans is entirely to miss the new thrust of U.S. diplomacy, for it cannot be doubted that Carter and his principal associates (except, possibly, Brzezinski) genuinely do seek the collapse of the present system in Southern Africa and have sought to effect that as rapidly as possible. There is little evidence that they would regret, more than in passing, the assumption of power by Marxist-Leninist cadre in Salisbury and Johannesburg as in Maputo and Luanda. To be sure, they may not have thought out the consequences of their line, but that is no-matter. Even if their more moderate number have reached this conclusion *faute de mieux,* that hardly affects the outcome of the policy.

Is it possible that Soviet analysts have missed this historic and momentous shift in the thrust of American policy in the Third World? One could construct an argument for such a position. It would state, first, that Moscow has been exceedingly sensitive about Carter's human rights policy (i.e., that the Soviet leadership has seen in it, incorrectly, more international design than domestic piety) and that Moscow has therefore become convinced of a new American animus against the Soviet regime. Then it would go on to observe that, ideologically, it is nearly impossible for the Soviets to believe that the United States could ever support the downfall of something which *they* see as critical to the sustenance of the industrial West (regardless of whether or not the American governing elite is capable of recognizing its importance).

On the other hand, one must ask whether a regime which could so skillfully manipulate official American opinion during the Angolan intervention[67] could conceivably be oblivious to so basic a reversal in U.S. policy. At the very least, one might contend, the Soviets were simply taking advantage of the "free goods" presented them by the Carter administration, for surely by mid-1978 they had seen a pattern of unilateral concessions developing in Carter's overall foreign policy: Young's favorable characterization of the Cuban role in Angola; the decision to withdraw ground forces from Korea without negotiations for reciprocal concessions by North Korea's suppliers and backers; the cancellation of the B-1 bomber despite the continued construction of the Soviet equivalent, the Backfire; the initial decision, later slightly modified, to cancel the neutron bomb; and, finally and most pertinent to Southern Africa, the U.S. support for the Soviet favorite in the Rhodesian imbroglio. Under such circumstances, according to this line of argument, it would only be rational from the Soviet standpoint to take every new American position as a basis from which to exact further concessions, without giving anything in return. Thus, Moscow would have every reason to insist that these U.S. decisions were merely attempts to make a virtue of necessity or were not genuine, and to press Washington for more of the same.

But such an assessment still begs the question of whether the Soviets have perceived the extraordinary character of U.S. foreign policy under the Carter administration. Moreover, there is an alternative explanation of Soviet analysis which might offer a better fit for the contradictory data. This would be that the Soviets do see the change in U.S. policy but consider it largely irrelevant in light of the deeper and more powerful currents which, traditionally, have determined U.S.—and Western—policy in Africa. That is, Moscow believes that West European interests remain committed to a conservative policy framework and are waiting for the day when Carter's policy has failed or when Carter is no longer around to reassert such a framework, but are in the meantime endorsing Andrew Young's efforts to make Western policy more palatable to Africans.

Other commentary in the Soviet media lends credence to this interpretation. Thus, there has been much mention (and condemnation) of alleged Western calls for the formation of a South Atlantic Treaty Organization (SATO)[68]—calls of which this writer at least had been ignorant until he read about them in the Soviet press. There has been even more strident denunciation of the Western-African forces deployed in Shaba to reestablish security and stability there in the wake of the invasion by elements of the former Katangese gendarmes now residing in Angola. *Novoye Vremya,* for instance, has quoted with approval the argument in an Italian Communist publication that Carter's "ultimate aim" is "to replace the old racist and antinationalist bastion . . . with a moderate bloc from Cape Town to Kinshasa to isolate the two former Portuguese colonies and merge completely with the world capitalist system." The United States, *Novoye Vremya* goes on, would not join the new bloc created; rather, it would control the grouping through "subimperialist" powers.[69] From the Soviet perspective, the lack of direct U.S. participation would not make the bloc less dangerous, but, on the contrary, would render it more so. Consider, for example, an important analysis in *Izvestiya* in late March 1978 after the Soviet gamble in the Horn had paid off. The

Americans, the newspaper declared, had become chary of foreign adventures with their own troops and thus were relying—as General Alexander Haig, commander of NATO forces, had phrased things—on "'regional military potentials.'" It then proceeded to claim that "although the U.S. ruling circles officially declared that they did not intend to supply Somalia with arms while Somali troops were on Ethiopian territory, they provoked the Somali–Ethiopian conflict and supplied Somalia with arms through 'strawmen'—Saudi Arabia, Iran, Egypt and Sudan."[70]

The interesting point here is that while the Soviets presumably knew full well of U.S. reluctance even to give green lights to friends, they were also aware of the local eagerness to act. At least since the Shaba I crisis brought them together, the French, Moroccans, Sudanese, and Egyptians—along, until 1979, with the Egyptians' Saudi bankers—have by a number of accounts closely cooperated at several levels in an increasingly institutionalized manner.[71] Whether or not the Carter administration has been kept adequately apprised of such activity is irrelevant as far as Moscow is concerned. Soviet leaders take the possibilities of Western action in Southern Africa seriously and will do what they can to put the West on the defensive with respect to its purported aims while allowing time for their own plans to mature. In light of the depth of conviction among senior officials of the Carter administration about the proper approach to Southern African issues, such a Soviet view might seem fantastic, but the Soviets have always been better at taking a long view of Western policy than have Westerners themselves.

Soviet Purpose in Africa

There is a final, and possibly the most important, link connecting Africa, the Soviet Union, and the United States, and this has to do with Soviet *purpose*. To be sure, one could maintain that it is hard enough to discern the objectives of one's own country, given the contrary pulls and competing interests, and hence even more difficult, as well as highly self-serving, to try to divine those of an adversary. However, it is well understood that the Soviet bureaucracy is more purposeful than its West European and American counterparts. Furthermore, the Soviet bureaucracy, because of its nature and organization (as was hinted at earlier), looks to long-term goals, and it is not affected by the sort of *predictable* redefinition of goals that occurs quadrennially in the United States. True, the fortuitous and the unforeseen have jarred Soviet objectives and policies, but they have done the same to American objectives and policies. In light of the purposefulness of the Soviet brand of Marxism-Leninism and the administered character of the Soviet polity and economy, it does not seem unreasonable to ascribe goals to the USSR.

Then what are Moscow's aims in Africa? Why have the Soviets persisted in trying to establish centers of influence on the continent despite the numerous reverses they have suffered from Cairo to Accra? What has driven them on in Africa, even when the United States perceptibly lost interest in the continent in the mid-1960s and shifted its concern to Southeast Asia (insofar as it was concerned with events outside Europe)? Has it been simply a combination of local interests, the opportunities that various regimes like those in the Congo-Brazzaville or Libya have afforded, a logical and compelling desire to capitalize on Western involvement in Southern Africa, and a "principled" wish to end racism in that part of the world? Or is there some higher, overarching scheme that would help to explain why, for example, the USSR armed Field Marshal Idi Amin of Uganda with $50 million worth of arms while at the same time it was opposing racism in Southern Africa?

It has become fashionable to set up as a straw-man argument the notion that the Soviet Union possesses detailed and long-range "game plans" for world conquest and then to refute that notion. Such an approach, however, misses the point.

What must be remembered, first of all, is that the Soviets see world politics in terms of the overall correlation of forces. And at the strategic level, the USSR has over the last two decades gone from inferiority to parity, and now, it would appear, to superiority. Certainly, there can be no doubt about parity. A recent study sponsored by the Carter administration indicates that whereas the United States in 1962 had been ahead of the Soviet Union on 41 key indices, that figure had dropped to 11 by 1978, with the lead on those 11 also likely to vanish before long.[72] Another study, in which I myself had a hand, goes further. It suggests that, in light of the forces which the Carter administration seemed to have conceded in the SALT II negotiations by late 1978, the United States would have only "alternative ways to lose" in any conflict with the USSR.[73]

With such improvements in the USSR's broad strategic capabilities, the Soviets have undoubtedly been reassessing their ability to act regionally. And it is hardly credible that they do not have a clear idea of the degree of Western dependence on the minerals in Africa and on the sea lanes around the continent, along which the amount of oil alone flowing to the West has risen 3,600 percent since the late 1960s.[74] After all, the most notable difference between Soviet reporting on American interests in Africa and American reporting on its own interests on the continent is the Soviet emphasis precisely on oil and critical minerals. Indeed, the Soviets have something of an obsession with the subject.[75]

The real question is whether this obsession provides a clue to the purpose behind Moscow's enormous investment in Africa in recent years. Certainly, one can reasonably contend that in implanting its influence along vital Western sea lanes and in or near states which produce important minerals, the USSR achieves a dual goal. On the one hand, it ensures the availability of supplies of the minerals for itself. It should be noted in this connection that even though the Soviet Union will not soon become as dependent on imports of minerals as the United States is, the USSR's dependence will continue to grow in the future.[76] On the other hand, the USSR puts itself in a position to cut off (or slow down, or otherwise affect the delivery of) shipments of crucial minerals to the West.[77] The Soviets, by acting as they have in the Horn, have from a strategic standpoint outflanked the Middle East, which is critical to Western survival. That this outcome of the Soviet effort was intentional on Moscow's part seems quite clear. In March 1978, for example, an *Izvestiya* analyst argued that the center of American policy in the region was not Cairo but Saudi Arabia. "World oil prices," he said, "depend to a considerable degree on Saudi Arabia's stance. Saudi Arabia is the bulwark of the most reactionary forces in the Arab world."[78] Those who would deride such an assessment of Soviet purpose must recognize that at the very minimum the burden of proof would appear to lie with them.

Perhaps the saving grace for the West will be, oddly, that the Soviets may come to feel a stake—at least in certain areas—in the status quo in Africa. In this regard, it should be noted that the only apprehension that they evinced about their course in the Horn concerned Washington's obvious delight at their dilemma there prior to the loss of their position in Somalia. Whole paragraphs of Soviet comments about Western glee on this issue could be applied, *mutatis mutandis,* to the USSR's own reaction to the Western dilemma in

Southern Africa.[79] The point here is very simple. Where the Soviets have interests, their policy may have to be supple and based on compromise; where they do not, their stand—like that of any state and especially like that of the United States in the Horn once it had virtually withdrawn from contention—can be bold and clear.

Do the Soviets see the irony? One must wonder. When Soviet commentators during the period of the crisis in the Horn continually sounded the theme that any conflict situations that arose around the world could be settled by peaceful negotiations, they seemed unaware of the contradiction between such statements and the USSR's posture in Southern Africa. Nor did a Soviet writer appear any less oblivious in charging the United States with "Vietnamizing" the Horn—that is, with setting African against African as it had allegedly set Vietnamese against Vietnamese. He observed: "The fact that there are deep contradictions between the states [in the Horn] does not mean that they can only be settled by armed struggle. . . . The only reason why this old conflict, inherited from the colonial past, has become so intense is that the United States has openly and actively interfered in it."[80] This was written, incidentally, after the *volte face* in U.S. policy toward Somalia in July 1977, of which any serious Soviet analyst must have known.

It was only from such small matters as a potential Soviet vested interest in an increasingly complicated status quo that Western strategists could take comfort at the end of the 1970s. Against the growing Soviet involvement in all the facets and levels of international relations, throughout the world and not just in Africa, was the still more impressive fact that the Soviet Union was becoming steadily more powerful, in actuality and in the perceptions of others. If caution was apt to be one consequence of the greater Soviet involvement, an accommodation by actors throughout the world to that increasingly powerful state, as foreshadowed herein, was surely the more impressive possibility. Action, in the end, might cease to be necessary for Moscow to achieve its objectives.

Conclusion

David E. Albright

IN LIGHT OF the foregoing analyses, what can be said in sum about the dynamics of Soviet-African relations in the 1970s? And what import does this have with regard to the prospects of communism in Africa in the foreseeable future?

Addressing the first question is a fairly complex undertaking, for as noted at the beginning of this volume, the analyses of specific facets of the recent dynamics of Soviet-African relations do not add up to a wholly consistent and integrated perspective. Therefore, in trying to characterize these dynamics in general terms, it is essential to take explicit account of the differences in judgment as well as the elements of consensus that emerge.

The Dynamics of Soviet-African Relations

As for the African environment, there is agreement on several key points. First, the 1970s have ushered in a new era in African politics that has significantly enhanced the opportunities for Communist powers outside the continent, and especially the USSR, to expand their roles there. This era is marked by quite pronounced increases in the level of conflict in Africa. The conflict has three separate dimensions—intrastate, interstate, and black vs. white. As for the first sphere, the situation that existed in most African countries in the 1960s as the continent shook off the bonds of colonialism no longer pertains. The broad national fronts that assumed governmental control initially have in most places given way to more narrowly based, often authoritarian, regimes. With this development, politics has tended to take the form of an extralegal contest between the "outs" and the "ins," and the result has been a substantial escalation in

The views expressed in this essay are those of the author and do not necessarily reflect the perspectives of the U.S. International Communication Agency or the U.S. government.

219

internal violence and a search for outside support to wage the battle effectively. In the interstate realm, the African commitment of the 1960s to eschew force to settle border disputes and other disagreements has weakened considerably. The 1977–78 war between Somalia and Ethiopia over the Ogaden region provides the most outstanding example, but it by no means exhausts the list. Indeed, actions such as Uganda's invasion of Tanzania in 1978 during the final months of Idi Amin's rule and Tanzania's counterattack to topple the erratic Ugandan dictator, or the occupation and carving up of the Spanish Sahara by Morocco and Mauritania in 1975, would probably have been unthinkable in the atmosphere of the 1960s. Moreover, the Organization of African Unity has proved highly ineffectual in handling contentious issues between states. Under such circumstances, African countries have increasingly looked for backing outside the continent to bolster their positions on matters in dispute among them. With regard to the black vs. white struggle the collapse of the Portuguese empire in Africa in the wake of the April 1974 military coup in Lisbon has had profound consequences. On the one hand, it enabled the Portuguese colonies on the continent and particularly those in the white redoubt region of Southern Africa to gain independence under black majority rule, thereby heightening black African anticipations of ending white domination everywhere on the continent in fairly short order. On the other hand, the emergence of black governments in both Angola and Mozambique reduced the white-controlled enclave to South Africa, Namibia, and Rhodesia. These three entities have substantial numbers of whites in their populations, and those whites have traditionally displayed a high degree of resolve to maintain their political dominance. This combination of rising expectations on the part of black Africans and stiff resistance to majority rule by whites in the areas still under their control has caused mounting strife in Southern Africa. Furthermore, the frustration produced by the sense of growing possibilities for change coupled with white recalcitrance has sent black Africans looking for allies to help hasten what they see as the inevitable denouement of the drama.

Second, African wariness about dealing with the Communist states in general and the USSR in particular has diminished greatly in the 1970s. During the anticolonial struggles of the 1950s and 1960s on the continent and the initial years of independence that followed, the prevailing attitude toward the Soviet Union among African nationalist leaders was watchful reserve bordering on suspicion. Even radical

African rulers such as Kwame Nkrumah of Ghana, Gamal Abdel Nasser of the United Arab Republic, and Ahmed Sékou Touré of Guinea took care to distinguish their political doctrines from those of Moscow, and they also tended to shy away from entanglements that significantly tied their hands or enabled the USSR to meddle in the internal political affairs of their countries. With sustained contact over the years, however, many Africans have come to view the Soviet Union as simply another great power rather than a peculiarly dangerous one. Consequently, the old leeriness has faded. To be sure, the degree to which Africans are willing to associate themselves with Moscow varies widely. Leaders such as Agostinho Neto of Angola and Mengistu Haile Mariam of Ethiopia have displayed no qualms about accepting massive military aid as well as economic assistance from the USSR, while others such as Kenneth Kaunda of Zambia and Julius Nyerere of Tanzania prefer to obtain the bulk of their military and economic aid from China or the West but do not automatically reject help from the Soviet Union. Nevertheless, few today even approach the kind of hostility that Félix Houphouët-Boigny of the Ivory Coast or Dr. H. K. Banda of Malawi still evince toward Moscow.

Third, ideological developments on the continent have played a role in the changes in African outlooks toward the Communist powers and notably the Soviet Union, but these developments have not been the dominant factor behind the shift in African perspectives. The emergence of avowedly Marxist-Leninist regimes in several African countries, it is true, has laid some foundations there for a sense of common purpose with the Soviet Union in the world revolutionary struggle. At the same time, the Marxist-Leninist rulers on the continent have not displayed a uniform willingness to cooperate with the USSR. Their openness to such cooperation, like that of their more conservative African counterparts, has depended essentially on their individual needs and on the capacity and readiness of the Soviet Union to meet those needs. Moreover, if the USSR has appeared to be inclined to act in ways that run counter to the interests of a Marxist-Leninist African state, the latter has not let ideological affinities with Moscow deter it from manifesting its displeasure to the Soviet leadership. Somalia's expulsion of Soviet advisers in 1977 provides the most glaring illustration.

In fact, ideology has proved to be a source of tension as well as a bond between the African Marxist-Leninists and Moscow. While the African Marxist-Leninists have firmly disassociated themselves from the notion of African socialism, local realities have strongly colored their versions of Marxism-Leninism. As a consequence, their theory and especially their practice differ markedly from the "scientific socialism" of the USSR. In light of these differences, the Soviet Union has demonstrated great reluctance to accept any of the African variants of Marxism-Leninism as the genuine article, and it has prodded the self-proclaimed Marxist-Leninists on the continent to embrace its own vision of socialism. The condescension inherent in this position has not set well with the African Marxist-Leninists. Indeed, it has not infrequently produced friction between them and Moscow.

Diversity of interpretation begins to creep in, however, as the evidential base weakens and the scope for speculation increases. It turns up fundamentally in appraisals of the depth of the changes that have occurred in Africa in the 1970s. The predominant judgment on this matter has several distinct elements. Africa, according to this view, remains in a state of great political flux. Most countries on the continent have governments which lack strong popular roots and face challenges from competing internal forces. Moreover, few African nations boast institutions capable of managing political transitions in an orderly fashion. Thus, political upheavals and abrupt shifts in course continue to be the rule throughout the bulk of the continent. These features of the African scene, coupled with the idiosyncratic outlooks of even those on the continent who profess allegiance to Marxism-Leninism, tend to render any convergence of interests of the USSR and individual African states as temporary today as it was in the past. With the fall of a regime or with an African leader's decision to modify his diplomatic posture, a divergence of interests can take place and can generate a desire on the part of the specific African country to reduce the degree of its involvement with the Soviet Union. Confronted with such a situation, Moscow still has little choice but to acquiesce. To do otherwise would seriously endanger its position on the continent as a whole. In this perspective, then, African factors retain a crucial role in the determination of the USSR's behavior toward the continent.

A minority school of thought, however, takes implicit or explicit issue with at least portions of this general assessment. One variant of it calls attention to the possibility of a qualitative change in the situation on the continent. Specifically, the presence of Cuban troops in Angola and Ethiopia may permit the Marxist-Leninist regimes in these states to consolidate their rule and to ensure their long-term survival. Moreover, with the growing capabilities of the USSR to carry out military activities in Africa, "socialist-oriented" forces in other countries could seek to employ Cuban-Soviet, or simply Soviet, military aid to similar ends. Another variant goes somewhat further. It holds that the result of the Soviet-Cuban military interventions in Angola and Ethiopia in the 1970s is likely to be the permanent implantation of radical, essentially anti-Western governments there, and it foresees additional military forays by the USSR on the continent that could wind up having the same consequences in other nations. Indeed, it maintains that a looming imbalance at the global strategic level will encourage adventurism on Moscow's part. That is, the USSR will actively look for and perhaps even foster opportunities to assist political elements in Africa favorably disposed toward it to win and retain power.

The pattern of assessments of circumstances on the USSR's side contrasts markedly with that related to the African environment. On all critical matters, one can discern a common denominator of opinion, but beyond that disagreement prevails. There is general concurrence, to begin with, that the Soviet Union has had a long-standing interest in Africa. In part, the line of analysis runs, this interest has derived from revolutionary concerns. According to Leninist precepts, the triumph of socialism will take place in the course of a world revolutionary process that brings about the abolition of all imperialist exploitation. Thus, the Bolshevik leadership in the early days after the 1917 Russian revolution took up the cause of independence for the African colonies as well as other territorial possessions of the West European powers, and Moscow continued to lend support to this cause well into the post–World War II era, although with ebbs and flows in intensity and with shifting positions on what combination of local elements should head the struggle for liberation. When the bulk of the African colonies achieved sovereignty in the 1950s and 1960s, the USSR, despite some initial hesitation in the early 1950s, hailed this development as a major step forward; nevertheless, it contended that true freedom from imperialism would come only with the eradication of all vestiges of economic, military, and cultural dependence upon the West, including the United States. At the same time, the interest has had a geographic dimension. For any major power located on the land mass which the Soviet Union occupies, portions of Africa—notably, those countries bordering on the Mediterranean and Red Seas plus the Gulf of Aden—would constitute a natural preoccupation. The enterprises of the Tsarist government in these areas clearly underscore this fact. During the interwar period and the early years after World War II, the Soviet regime lacked the physical wherewithal to assert itself here as its Tsarist predecessor had, but since the mid-1960s it has acquired the means to make a distinct impact. Hence, increased Soviet involvement in Africa in the 1970s has to some extent been the inevitable outgrowth of the rise of a strong power (especially in a military sense) on the soil of traditional Russia.

A minority assessment, however, sees more extensive historical roots for the USSR's recent behavior toward Africa than just a long-term Soviet interest in the continent. It views Moscow's fundamental approach to Africa in the 1970s as a revival of the 19th-century *Realpolitik* of the Tsarist government. While this school of thought does not argue that the Soviet leadership would have been unable to devise such a policy on its own, the school does believe that the precedent conditioned the adoption of the policy.

Second, everyone accepts the proposition that in the 1970s the USSR has regarded Africa as of some importance to it. Certainly, Moscow has given plenty of evidence to sustain such an evaluation. During the early part of the decade, the USSR provided the arms and training that turned the Somali army into one of the most effective military forces on the continent, although the Soviets subsequently helped rout that army when it sought to wrest the Ogaden region from Ethiopian control. In the mid-1970s, Moscow went to considerable expense and effort to enable the Popular Movement for the Liberation of Angola (*Movimento Popular de Libertação de Angola* — MPLA) to triumph in the Angolan civil war. A few years later, the USSR committed an estimated $1 billion or more to the military government of Ethiopia to ensure the integrity of the former Ethiopian empire. Toward the end of the decade, the Soviets greatly stepped up the flow of arms to the guerrilla movements in Southern Africa, especially to the Patriotic Front of Rhodesia. In the economic sphere, the USSR in 1978 concluded a huge 30-year phosphate deal with Morocco that called for Soviet aid in building extraction and processing facilities in exchange for a guaranteed supply of phosphate rock. It has also consented to assist Nigeria in the construction of a major iron and steel complex.

Just what priority the Soviet leadership has attached to Africa in recent years, on the other hand, is a subject of dispute. According to the majority perspective, the continent as a whole has rated fairly low on the USSR's list of concerns. True, Moscow has tended to distinguish between North Africa and sub-Saharan Africa and has included the former among the regions of primary interest to it in the Third World. Yet in Soviet eyes, even such regions have not enjoyed the same significance in the 1970s that they had in the 1960s. A minority appraisal, in contrast, suggests that Africa has figured rather prominently in Moscow's concerns. The main reason for this Soviet attention to the continent, this school of thought contends, lies in Africa's overall strategic value. Not only does it contain minerals and other natural resources of importance to the West, but it also offers ready access to sea lanes along which flow goods vital to Western economies—particularly oil.

Third, there is unanimity that Moscow has perceived new opportunities in the 1970s to enhance the position of the Soviet state in Africa. The intervention in Angola in 1975–76, for instance, permitted the USSR to replace China as the main champion of the national liberation movements in Southern Africa, and it gave the Soviet Union a territorial base from which to operate to influence other events in that region. Provision of economic and particularly military aid to Somalia in the early 1970s afforded the USSR a foothold in the strategically significant Horn of Africa; moreover, Moscow's switch to support of Ethiopia in 1977–78 confirmed the Soviet Union as the dominant outside power in the area. It is worth mentioning, too, that the USSR's phosphate deal with Morocco in 1978 not only served Moscow's economic ends but also made the Soviet Union a long-term factor in the economy of a strategically located African country.

A minority interpretation, however, raises the additional possibility that Moscow may have come to see chances for furthering revolution on the continent. Such an assessment, this school of thought concedes, probably did not figure in the initial reasons for Soviet involvement in Angola, but the school holds that as it grew more and more evident that the combined Soviet-Cuban military presence there offered a shield behind which the radical MPLA regime could consolidate its gains, this consideration may have entered Soviet calculations apropos of Africa. To be sure, Moscow does not recognize even the Marxist-Leninist governments of Angola or Ethiopia as full-fledged "scientific socialist" regimes. Nevertheless, it does regard the "revolutionary democratic" programs that these governments propose to carry out as major steps toward socialism.

Fourth, everyone agrees that the Soviet decision-making process with respect to the continent has been complex. This process has been affected by the behavior of a number of factors outside as well as in Africa. The former have included, most notably, the United States, the West European countries, China, and Cuba. Furthermore, domestic politics and bureaucratic cleavages within the USSR itself have entered into the process.

But differences of opinion exist as to exactly what types of behavior or circumstances of non-Soviet actors have affected Moscow's decision-making in the 1970s. One, and apparently the predominant, view is that no single sort of behavior or circumstance has proved consistently the most critical. That is, the importance of individual kinds of behavior or circumstances has varied from case to case. Portugal's political choice to hand over the reins of government in its African colonies to the extant liberation groups there, for example, brought about Moscow's resumption of aid on a significant scale to the faction-ridden MPLA in Angola toward the end of 1974. (Several months earlier, it will be recalled, the USSR had drastically curtailed its help to the organization, and Moscow had even totally suspended assistance to the forces headed by the MPLA's nominal leader, Agostinho Neto, despite a long previous association with him.) Somalia's expulsion of all Soviet advisers in November 1977 and the subsequent refusal of the Western powers to furnish arms to Mogadiscio caused the USSR to mount a huge air- and sealift of Soviet arms and Cuban troops to Ethiopia to help drive the invading Somali army out of the Ogaden. And Morocco's linkage of a phosphates deal economically attractive to the Soviet Union with Moscow's attitude toward the Algerian-backed Polisario Front apparently induced Soviet leaders to give Rabat private assurances that they would not aid the Front— even though such assurances risked offending Algeria.

Another school of thought advances the contrary judgment. It singles out behavior or circumstances bearing upon Moscow's power calculations as paramount. While it does not deny that other factors have contributed to Soviet decisions, it sees these factors as secondary. Moreover, it feels that they have been getting increasingly less significant as the USSR's global strategic position has strengthened.

Fifth, there is consensus that Moscow looks at Africa through the prism of its larger, global concerns. The most obvious signs of this in the 1970s have derived from the fierce competition that the USSR has waged with both the United States and China on the continent. For instance, the Soviet Union supported the MPLA against two rival groups backed by the United States and China in the 1975–76 Angolan civil war. It established itself as the chief patron of Samora Machel's government in Mozambique in the mid-1970s, thereby displacing China. Although Moscow has endorsed the cause of the Patriotic Front of Rhodesia, it has in practice supplied the great bulk of its military aid to Joshua Nkomo's Zimbabwe African People's Union rather than to Robert Mugabwe's Zimbabwe African National Union, which has ties to China. The USSR has denounced Egypt for concluding a peace treaty with Israel under U.S. auspices.

Exactly how much impact global strategic factors have had on Soviet behavior on the continent, however, is a matter of contention. According to the majority judgment, the growing strategic might of the USSR has certainly made it more willing to throw its weight around in Africa. The Soviet interventions in Angola and Ethiopia constitute the classic illustrations. Nevertheless, the USSR still has reasonably limited capabilities to project its power onto the continent.[1] Thus, it continues to confront an essentially unfavorable military balance in most regions. Aware of this disadvantage, Moscow has been cautious in committing itself militarily in Africa. As a matter of fact, it has held back on large-scale involvement until it has had a fair degree of confidence in the probability of the success of the venture. In addition, it has followed a fundamentally political course on the continent. That is, it has endeavored to exploit its new military capacities to achieve political goals in Africa and has sought to avoid provoking a direct face-down with the United States.

A minority school of thought, in contrast, perceives an underlying thrust to recent Soviet policy on the continent that flows directly from the global strategic situation. It contends that Moscow has opted to try to capitalize on the shifting global balance to pursue expansionist objectives in Africa. Furthermore, it insists that Moscow's assertiveness will probably grow more pronounced as the USSR achieves the superiority that the school anticipates in the 1980s.

As to the inputs into Soviet-African relations by third parties, those of China evoke the least controversy. Indeed, there is general concurrence on all major points here. During the 1970s, according to the common appraisal, China not only has persisted in carrying on the competition with the USSR in Africa that the Peking leadership launched in the 1960s, but has even stepped up efforts to undermine Soviet prestige and influence on the continent. This rivalry has had two dimensions. On one level, the Chinese have tried to destroy the

USSR's credentials as a revolutionary mentor by depicting Soviet rulers as big-power chauvinists cynically attempting to manipulate African countries for Moscow's own expansionist purposes. At the level of practical politics, the Chinese have sought to widen their diplomatic contacts on the continent and to present China as an alternative source of economic and military aid as well as an alternative development model to the USSR.

Such endeavors have plainly had some impact on Soviet behavior in Africa. The Chinese challenge seems to have played a role in Soviet ventures like the intervention in Angola in 1975–76, the subsequent supply of military aid to the black guerrilla forces fighting to overthrow Rhodesia's white government, and the courtship of Tanzania in the late 1970s. Furthermore, the USSR in its media output to Africa has strongly refuted Chinese charges and striven to impugn Chinese motives for leveling them. It has also tried to enlist African leaders and governments in this counterattack.

Nonetheless, Peking has found it exceedingly difficult to mount a serious threat to the Soviet Union's position on the continent. To be sure, the Chinese have succeeded in broadening their diplomatic ties with Africa, and they have had no trouble discovering recipients of economic aid among African countries. In fact, their commitments of economic assistance to the states of the continent have exceeded those of the USSR in the 1970s. But China's capacity to meet African needs has had severe limits. Although the level of Chinese economic aid to African states has compared favorably with that of Soviet economic aid in recent years, this situation has mirrored Moscow's growing reluctance to extend credits to nations on the continent at least as much as it has Peking's inherent ability to compete as a donor. More telling, China has been unable to supply military assistance in either the quantity or the form that most African countries or liberation movements have desired. Certainly it has proved a fairly ineffective ally against Soviet-aided African forces, such as the MPLA in Angola during the 1975–76 period.

For this reason, Chinese activities in the 1970s have essentially affected the intensity of Soviet enterprises on the continent and not their basic nature. Peking's denunciations of the USSR, for instance, have prompted Moscow to work assiduously to validate its claims to be the prime champion of African liberation. The volume of Soviet propaganda directed at the continent on this theme as well as the behavior of the USSR in various countries, and particularly in Angola during the civil war there, provide ample testimony. Yet there have been no signs that China has caused the Soviet leadership to act in some fashion that it did not wish to act, or has prevented the Soviet leadership from undertaking some project that it wanted to undertake.

On the contributions of Cuba and the United States to Soviet-African relations, however, the extent of consensus narrows considerably. Concerning those of the former, there is unanimity on a few basic points on which the evidence is strong. Cuban interest and involvement in Africa, everyone agrees, antedate the 1970s. Indeed, they began in the early 1960s, even before Fidel Castro's regime had fully consolidated its internal control. Moreover, the years in which this interest and involvement originated were one during which Havana's approach to the Third World had a more militant cast than Moscow's—despite Cuba's own heavy dependence on the USSR's largesse and backing.[2]

At the same time, Cuba's role in Africa has expanded enormously in scope in the 1970s, and that expansion has taken place within the context of increased Soviet involvement on the continent. It would have been impossible, for example, for Havana to supply the number of troops that it dispatched to Angola and Ethiopia if it had not been able to count on the USSR for weapons and logistical support. By the same token, it would have found the task of sustaining the troops that remain in these two African countries quite difficult without Soviet help.

Still, Cuba has had reasons of its own for close collaboration with the USSR in recent years. The Angolan operation greatly enhanced Fidel Castro's stature as a Third World leader, for it demonstrated his willingness and ability to extend his endorsements of "anti-imperialist" and "revolutionary" causes from the verbal realm to the sphere of concrete military action. Even those in the Third World who did not particularly approve of the Cuban intervention had to reckon with its implications. Subsequent Cuban activities in Ethiopia further bolstered Castro's position. In addition, the success of the Angolan and Ethiopian enterprises seems to have strengthened Havana's hand in its bilateral dealings with Moscow. The result has been more generous economic and military aid from the Soviet Union.

Assessments diverge, however, as the evidence becomes more tenuous. The fundamental disagreements have to do with the linkage between Cuban and Soviet policies in Africa. In the majority perspective, Cuban and Soviet policies toward the continent have been largely congruent, but not entirely so. Where they have differed, Moscow has at least had to take account of Cuban views in reaching decisions about its own course of action. The period just before the full-scale Cuban-Soviet intervention in Angola in the fall of 1975 affords perhaps the best illustration. It would appear that Havana quite early commenced to contemplate major assistance to the MPLA, while Moscow initially held back on the matter. Nevertheless, Cuba's eagerness to play a role in events clearly figured in Soviet calculations about what to do as the MPLA's situation deteriorated. In some cases, Havana may even have compelled the USSR to shift its tactical line. For instance, Soviet officials in Angola evidently had some prior knowledge of the abortive coup against Agostinho Neto in May 1977 and did not move to stop it or warn Neto about it, but Cuban troops apparently were instrumental in putting down the coup and saving Neto. And in Ethiopia the USSR evinced some signs of an inclination to meet the Mengistu regime's requests for all-out military support in Eritrea until Cuba adamantly refused to allow its combat troops to be employed there. Most significantly, Havana has acquired mounting leverage to influence Soviet policy in directions of its own choosing as the 1970s have progressed. Cuba's manifest utility as an ally in military ventures in which the USSR does not wish to assume a highly exposed position has rendered consultation and coordination with Havana on actions in Africa of some moment for Moscow, and Cuba's new standing in the councils of the Third World not only makes Cuba a potential channel through which to try to shape Third World attitudes but also increases the hazards of ignoring Cuban views. While this leverage will probably not suffice to enable Havana to get its way in all cases, it could prove effective in some instances.

A minority school of thought, on the other hand, looks upon the linkage between Cuban and Soviet policies as essentially unidimensional. That is, it regards Cuba as a Soviet proxy. It tends to doubt that Cuban and Soviet policies have genuinely clashed. Furthermore, it holds that if they have come into serious conflict, Moscow has succeeded in imposing its will on Havana.

With respect to the inputs of the United States, there is broad acceptance of several propositions. During the 1970s, according to the common judgment, the United States has retained its 1960s role as the USSR's chief rival in Africa, and Soviet-American competition has continued to encompass a wide range of activities—economic, cultural, social, scientific, political, and military. But as the USSR's military capabilities have improved and as the American-Soviet strategic balance has reached actual parity, the military aspect of the competition has become more and more prominent.

Also, American behavior in Africa in recent years has sometimes given the Soviets increased room to maneuver on the continent. The Angolan civil war and the conflict between Ethiopia and Somalia in the Ogaden constitute the classic examples. In the first case, the United States furnished substantial clandestine aid to the MPLA's rivals until late 1975, but then the U.S. Congress forbade such assistance, thereby leaving the way open for Soviet and Cuban forces to install the MPLA in power. In the second case, the United States declined to provide arms to Somalia after it invaded the Ogaden, and when Somalia expelled its Soviet advisers because of Moscow's military aid to Ethiopia, the USSR and Cuba carried out a massive military buildup in Ethiopia that permitted the Ethiopians to drive the Somali army from the Ogaden.

Beyond these propositions, though, disputes arise. These disputes stem from differing conclusions about the effects on Soviet activities in Africa of changes that Washington has allowed to occur in the U.S.-USSR strategic balance. According to the dominant outlook, the USSR may have become increasingly assertive on the continent as the global strategic balance has moved toward parity, but the regional correlation of forces remains unfavorable to the Soviet Union. That is, the United States and its allies still have the capabilities to deter the USSR from military adventures on the continent. However, the analysis goes, the relevance of such capabilities to precise circumstances may be limited, for African desires and needs continue to be the prime factor determining whether Soviet military involvement is welcome. If an African government or movement—especially one with substantial backing on the continent—requests Soviet military help, the ability of the United States to combat the forces that the USSR may deploy in response to that request has little bearing on the situation.

A minority interpretation, in contrast, contends that the alterations in the U.S.-USSR strategic balance have produced a qualitatively new state of affairs in Africa. They have convinced Moscow of an impending shift in the regional correlation of forces. It is this, the assessment runs, that the USSR has aggressively been seeking to exploit. This school of thought goes on to argue that Moscow may well step up these efforts as the strategic superiority that the school foresees for the USSR in the 1980s develops. From such a perspective, then, the growing inability of the United States to deter Soviet military actions in Africa has emerged as the crucial determinant of the USSR's relations with the continent.

The Future

In turning now to the prospects for communism in Africa, it is important to recognize one thing at the outset. Those prospects really have two distinct aspects—the outlook for indigenous African forces and the outlook for the involvement on the continent of outside Communist powers. Each requires examination in its own right.

Apropos of the first, the preceding discussion suggests several conclusions. By and large, the political climate on the continent in the 1980s seems likely to be conducive to the emergence of some new Marxist-Leninist regimes. The fragile national unity that prevailed in a good many African countries in the 1960s as they moved toward and achieved independence has now all but disappeared. As a consequence, a variety of groups vie for power in just about every state and territory, and each tends to see its interests as at odds with those of others. Moreover, the general absence of institutions through which orderly political change could take place has made violence the common *modus operandi* of the political "outs" in their competition with the political "ins." Under such circumstances, radical forces, even if small in number, have a substantial chance to assume control of the reins of local authority here and there.

Just where these new Marxist-Leninist regimes might appear is, of course, virtually impossible to predict. The level of conflict in lands in which whites still cling to at least a measure of power in the late 1970s—Rhodesia, Namibia, and South Africa—may render the probabilities highest in these countries. Yet an unexpected turn of events in many other places could permit local radical elements to establish sway there.

Whether the existing Marxist-Leninist regimes or any new ones that come into being will develop sufficiently deep social roots and strong enough administrative structures to ensure their long-term survival, however, remains open to serious question. It is instructive to recall in this regard that as of the end of the 1970s, only Ethiopia has experienced a genuine social upheaval, and even there the benefits of the revolution for underprivileged groups have been at best mixed. Thus, none of the current regimes rides a wave of widespread popular enthusiasm for its programs. Furthermore, the lack of trained cadres to carry out the tasks that the regimes have set for themselves imposes great dangers to these regimes over the long haul. If they cannot consolidate their rule, they run the risk of ultimately being swept aside by other forces.

To be sure, the presence of Cuban troops and extensive organizational help from the USSR could conceivably enable the Marxist-Leninist regimes in Angola and Ethiopia to entrench themselves permanently, and the same would apply for any other governments with which Havana and Moscow might become intimately associated. But such an outcome is by no means assured. Much will depend on the tenacity and skill of the present Angolan and Ethiopian leaderships. Of perhaps greater significance, Cuba and the Soviet Union do not at the moment play a major role in some countries with self-proclaimed Marxist-Leninist regimes, and they do not appear too likely to acquire such a role in the foreseeable future. The government of Mozambique, for instance, has kept both at arm's length, despite its willingness to sign a treaty of friendship and cooperation with the USSR.

What seems a good deal more certain is that the Marxist-Leninists on the continent will continue to have attributes that displease Moscow and make it reluctant to accept them as genuine representatives of the species. To date, all the existing Marxist-Leninist governments in Africa have devised policies tailored to their own local realities and not geared to Soviet prescriptions. Not even those in Angola or Ethiopia have hesitated to follow their own courses, despite their heavy dependence on the Soviet Union to stay in power. And there is little reason to suppose that their inclinations will change in the years ahead or that any new Marxist-Leninist regimes on the continent will differ greatly in their attitudes. While the Soviet presence in countries like Angola and Ethiopia does afford some potential for reshaping outlooks, the USSR's recent setbacks in Egypt and Somalia highlight how easily the Soviets can offend African sensibilities and damage their own position; thus, Moscow does not appear likely to endanger its relationship with either state by pushing very hard on ideological matters.

As far as the role of outside Communist powers in African affairs in the 1980s is concerned, the atmosphere on the continent will in all probability be favorable to increased Communist involvement. Strife has been on the upswing in Africa in recent years, and no reversal of the trend seems to loom on the near horizon. If anything, conflict is likely to increase in both scope and intensity. In the absence of effective African mechanisms for resolving disputes, this tendency, in turn, will probably send Africans in search of help from forces outside the continent. Moreover, the earlier African leeriness about looking to Communist states for succor has diminished in the 1970s, even if it has not entirely vanished. Therefore, it would appear likely that African petitions for support from such quarters will grow in the years ahead.

What role the Communist nations will actually play in the continent's evolution, however, depends upon a number of variables. For both Cuba and China (as well as the remaining smaller Communist states), the critical factor will be the extent of the USSR's involvement in the process. Havana has a definite interest in trying to expand Cuban activities in Africa, for greater Cuban influence on the continent would serve Fidel Castro's aspirations to become the leader of the Third World and would also reinforce the island's importance in Moscow's eyes. Nevertheless, Cuba has limited capabilities to pursue such a course on its own. To be more than modestly successful in enhancing its stature in Africa, Cuba must operate in tandem with the USSR. Whether or not Havana has some capacity to induce Moscow to follow a parallel approach, there can be no doubt that the ultimate decision about the USSR's policy will rest with the Soviet leadership. In this sense, then, the precise nature of the future Cuban role on the continent will lie in Moscow's hands.

Peking, too, has reasons for wanting to enhance its position in Africa. Not only would an enlarged role on the continent bolster China's claim to status as a global power, but it would likewise pose an additional challenge to the USSR, which remains China's chief enemy in Peking's perspective. At the same time, China has limited resources to devote to competing in the African milieu. The drive for rapid economic modernization that Peking launched at home in the late 1970s will require major resource inputs to sustain, and the military threat from Vietnam in the wake of the brief Sino–Vietnamese border war in early 1979 has placed new demands upon China's already thinly stretched military resources. Thus, the nature of the Chinese role on the African continent in the years to come will be determined in large part by how active the USSR is there and how expensive rivalry with Moscow gets for Peking.

The factors that will govern the USSR's role in Africa are much more complex than those that will shape the roles of Cuba and China. Quite clearly, Moscow has had a long-standing interest in Africa, and it is hard to imagine that this interest will disappear in the foreseeable future. But that Soviet involvement on the continent will stay at the level it has been during the 1970s—whatever the true characterization of that level may be—is by no means a foregone conclusion. If changes do occur, they will reflect the interaction of four variables: (1) what payoffs Moscow believes it has derived from its past activities and may gain from altering the intensity of them; (2) what opportunities the Soviet leadership sees for involvement elsewhere, and their relative attractiveness in comparison with the opportunities in Africa; (3) what constraints Moscow deems outside forces impose; and (4) internal political developments within the USSR.

On the first matter, much depends on two considerations. Does a state of flux still prevail in Africa, and will the interests of the USSR and particular African countries and movements continue to diverge as well as converge? If African regimes or movements with which the USSR now has close ties fell or suffered serious defeats or if these regimes or movements curtailed their links with the Soviet Union, then Moscow might decide that it had overcommitted itself. By the same token, if the regimes or movements with which the USSR enjoys intimate relations as of the late 1970s strengthen their positions and do not become estranged from the Soviet Union, Moscow might come to feel that it should step up its involvement. As the previous discussion has indicated, the evidence is too skimpy and the future too murky to venture definitive judgments on either of these matters. The most that one can say is that they will bear careful watching.

With respect to the second issue, it is essential to recognize that Africa constitutes only one piece in the global mosaic of Soviet priorities. Like all international actors, the USSR has finite resources, and how it elects to allocate those resources at any given juncture is largely a function of what openings are available to it, and precisely where they are. In this connection, it is of some possible consequence that the late 1970s have brought Moscow major new opportunities in the Third World outside of Africa. The most significant of these have been in the countries forming an arc around the USSR's southern borders.

Concerning the third question, one should note that the USSR has plainly enhanced its overall military prowess during the 1970s, and it could move from parity with the United States to some degree of superiority in the global strategic balance during the 1980s.[3] Just how such a situation would affect Moscow's evaluation of the constraints on its behavior in Africa, however, is cloudy. Despite the recent demonstrations of the USSR's capacity to carry out new forms of military activities in Africa, the balance of forces with regard to the continent has not yet shifted decisively toward the Soviet Union. Furthermore, the United States and its Western allies would appear to have the means to preserve a favorable balance if they choose to employ those means. What the United States and its Western partners do about the continental balance in the years ahead, then, will probably have as much impact on how Moscow views the constraints under which it must operate in Africa as changes in the global strategic balance will. If there is a failure of will on the Western side, of course, Moscow could abandon caution and seek to take maximum advantage of the situation.

With regard to the fourth issue, evidence has accumulated in the late 1970s that a political succession is nearing, and such a development will inevitably overshadow simple bureaucratic rivalries as an influence on the role of the USSR in Africa. Just what effect it will have on that role is impossible to foresee. In combination with the problems of sustaining economic growth, for example, it could lead to a focus on domestic matters and a decline in attention to the outside world; on the other hand, it could also produce factional conflict that would in turn generate increased pressure for foreign adventures. And these scenarios by no means exhaust the list.

Despite all the uncertainties surrounding the role of the USSR in Africa in the 1980s, it does not, on balance, appear too hazardous to venture one broad judgment on the matter. In light of the outcome thus far of the Soviet Union's expanded involvement on the continent in the 1970s as well as the many signs of Moscow's desire to flex its increasingly powerful military muscles, the Soviet role in Africa seems unlikely to diminish in the first half of the decade. If it alters at all, it will probably grow.

Notes

Introduction

1. See, *inter alia,* the excerpts from the question-and-answer session that he conducted at a Spokane Town Meeting on May 5, 1978, in *Department of State Bulletin,* July 1978, p. 21, and his commencement address at the U.S. Naval Academy on June 7, 1978, in *ibid.,* p. 16.

2. On the Soviet and Cuban roles in the Angolan and Ethiopian situations, see Jiri Valenta, "The Soviet-Cuban Intervention in Angola, 1975," *Studies in Comparative Communism* (Los Angeles), Spring/Summer 1978, pp. 3–33, and my chapter on "The Horn of Africa and the Arab–Israeli Conflict," in Robert O. Freedman, ed., *World Politics and the Arab–Israeli Conflict* (Elmsford, N.Y.: Pergamon Press, 1979).

3. For the texts, see *Pravda* (Moscow), Oct. 9, 1976; Moscow TASS in English, Nov. 20, 1978, in Foreign Broadcast Information Service, *Daily Report: Soviet Union* (Washington, D.C.), Nov. 21, 1978, pp. H/6–8.

4. For the latest information on the strength of the Cuban military forces in Angola and Ethiopia, see the semimonthly issues of *African Confidential* (London).

5. See George T. Yu, "The USSR and Africa: China's Impact," *Problems of Communism* (Washington, D.C.), January–February 1978, pp. 40–50; U.S. Central Intelligence Agency, *Communist Aid to Less Developed Countries of the Free World, 1977,* ER 78–10478U (Washington, D.C., November 1978); *The Washington Post,* June 6, 1979.

6. See Zbigniew Brzezinski, ed., *Africa and the Communist World* (Stanford, Calif.: Stanford University Press, 1963).

7. See Robert Legvold, *Soviet Policy in West Africa* (Cambridge, Mass.: Harvard University Press, 1970).

1. African Outlooks toward the USSR

1. These new requirements have been amply described by Soviet Admiral of the Fleet Sergey Gorshkov in his 1976 volume *Morskaya moshch' gosudarstva,* published in English as *The Sea Power of the State* (London: Pergamon, 1979).

2. George Padmore, *Pan-Africanism or Communism?* (London: Dobson, 1956).

3. See Hugh Seton-Watson, *Nationalism and Communism* (London: Methuen, 1964).

4. See Colin Legum, *Pan Africanism* (London: Pall Mall, 1962), pp. 104 ff.

5. See Julius Nyerere, *UJAMAA: Essays on Socialism* (London: Oxford University Press, 1968); also, William H. Friedland and Carl G. Rosberg, Jr., *African Socialism* (Stanford, Calif.: Stanford University Press, 1964).

6. Quoted in Aimé Césaire, "The Political Thought of Sékou Touré," *Présence Africaine* (Paris), No. 29, 1960.

7. See *ibid.*

8. Kwame Nkrumah, *I Speak of Freedom* (London: Heinemann, 1961); and *idem, Ghana: An Autobiography* (London: Nelson, 1957).

9. Whether, indeed, the USSR was seeking to overthrow Sékou Touré or merely wished to use contacts in the official trade union organization to urge the Guinean president to adopt more radical policies remains open to question. On this, see William Attwood, *The Reds and the Blacks* (New York: Harper and Row, 1967).

10. For an important survey of the USSR's relations with both the Egyptian and Algerian Communist parties, see Mohammed Heikal's *Sphinx and Commissar* (London: Collins, 1978).

11. See Colin Legum, "Africa's Contending Revolutionaries," *Problems of Communism* (Washington, D.C.), March–April 1972, pp. 2–15.

12. See Heikal, *op. cit.*

13. The reprinted texts of the comments that Obasanjo and Sékou Touré made at Khartoum on this subject may be found in *Africa Currents* (London), Autumn/Winter, 1978/79, pp. 8–11 and 17–19.

14. See *ibid.*, pp. 21–23.

15. See Colin Legum and Tony Hodges, *After Angola: The War Over Southern Africa* (London: Rex Collings, 1976).

16. Ghana News Agency, Accra, Mar. 9, 1976.

17. For a balanced evaluation of Soviet economic aid, see Christopher Stevens, *The Soviet Union and Black Africa* (London: Macmillan, 1976).

18. Data derived from U.S. Central Intelligence Agency, *Communist Aid to the Less Developed Countries of the Free World, 1976*, ER 77–10296 (Washington, D.C., August 1977); *idem, Communist Aid to the Less Developed Countries of the Free World, 1977*, ER 78–10478U (Washington, D.C., November 1978); U.S. State Department, Bureau of Intelligence and Research, *Communist States and Developing Countries: Aid and Trade in 1974* (Washington, D.C.: Jan. 27, 1976), Table 8 in Appendix; *The International Transfer of Conventional Arms, A Report to the Congress from the U.S. Arms Control and Disarmament Agency, April 12, 1974* (Washington, D.C.: U.S. Government Printing Office, 1974); and the annual report of the U.S. Arms Control and Disarmament Agency on world military expenditures and arms transfers, published since 1975. Figures for Soviet military aid do not include a $1,000 million arms sales agreement between the USSR and Libya signed in 1974. During 1954–77, the USSR and Eastern Europe extended a total of $5,660 million in economic aid to African states, of which $3,280 million came from the Soviet Union. These figures compare with $2,476 million in economic aid extended by the People's Republic of China. See U.S. Cen-

tral Intelligence Agency, *Communist Aid to the Less Developed Countries of the Free World, 1977.*

19. See Colin Legum, ed., *Africa Contemporary Record 1976–77* (London: Rex Collings; New York: Africana Publishing Co., 1977), pp. B/681 and B/687.

20. *New Nigerian* (Kaduna), Mar. 2, 1979.

21. Legum and Hodges, *op. cit.*

22. Colin Legum, ed., *Africa Contemporary Record 1975–76* (London: Rex Collings; New York: Africana Publishing Co., 1976), p. B/365.

23. Radio Omduhrman, June 27, 1977.

24. *Africa Contemporary Record 1975–76,* p. B/332.

25. Gorshkov, *op cit.*

26. Although these figures hold prominent government positions, they do not necessarily reflect the majority view of their regimes. They should rather be seen as pro-Moscow pressure groups within the ruling parties.

27. *Africa Contemporary Record 1975–76,* p. B/333.

28. *Ibid.,* p. A/28.

29. Radio Cairo, May 25, 1976.

30. Radio Omduhrman, May 18, 1977.

31. Khartoum TV, June 27, 1977.

32. Radio Rabat, Apr. 15, 1977.

33. On the conclusion of the accord, see Moscow TASS in English, Mar. 10, 1978.

34. See Colin Legum and Bill Lee, *Conflict in the Horn of Africa* (London: Rex Collings; New York: Africana Publishing Co., 1978).

35. See the citation in note 13.

36. *Africa Research Bulletin* (Exeter, England), No. 11, Dec. 15, 1977, p. 4651.

37. Conversations of the author with diplomats in Mogadiscio and Khartoum.

38. See Legum and Lee, *op cit.*

39. *New Times* (Moscow), No. 24, June 1977, p. 25.

40. See Legum and Lee, *op cit.*

41. See "Ethiopian Transformations," *Zycie Warzawy* (Warsaw), as translated by the Polish news agency, Oct. 13, 1978.

42. For the text, see *The African Communist* (London), No. 75, Fourth Quarter, 1978.

2. Moscow's African Policy of the 1970s

1. For the text, see *Pravda* (Moscow), Oct. 9, 1976.

2. See the TASS version of the text in Foreign Broadcast Information Service, *Daily Report: Soviet Union* (Washington, D.C.—hereafter, *FBIS-SOV*), Apr. 4, 1977, pp. H/2–5.

3. See *The Washington Post,* May 7, 1977, and Mar. 11, 1978; Moscow TASS in English, Nov. 20, 1978, in *FBIS-SOV,* Nov. 21, 1978, pp. H/6–8. The 1978 treaty, it should be noted, replaced a less formal mutual declaration on

"the foundations for relationships and cooperation," issued during a visit that Mengistu made to Moscow in May 1977. For the text of the declaration, see the TASS translation in *FBIS-SOV,* May 9, 1977, pp. H/8–9.

4. On Soviet military might, see, for example, the annual volumes of *The Military Balance* and *Strategic Survey,* published by the International Institute for Strategic Studies in London.

5. For a sampling of the diversity of views, see the comments by Andrew Young, U.S. Ambassador to the United Nations, in *The New York Times,* May 22 and June 5, 1978; by Zbigniew Brzezinski, Assistant for National Security Affairs to the U.S. president, during an interview on "Meet the Press" on May 28, 1978, published in the *Department of State Bulletin* (Washington, D.C.), July 1978, pp. 26–28; by British Foreign Secretary David Owen, as reported in *The New York Times,* Apr. 6, 1978; by U.S. Senate Majority Leader Robert Byrd, in *ibid.,* May 31, 1978; by Tanzanian President Julius Nyerere, in *ibid.,* June 9, 1978; and by U.S. Senator George McGovern, in *ibid.,* June 26, 1978.

6. The analysis in the ensuing pages draws upon work done for the author's *The Dilemmas of Courtship: The Soviet Union, China and Ghana,* forthcoming. See also Robert Legvold, *Soviet Policy in West Africa* (Cambridge, Mass.: Harvard University Press, 1970).

7. Report of the Central Committee to the 20th Party Congress, in Leo Gruliow, ed., *Current Soviet Policies—II: The Documentary Record of the 20th Communist Party Congress and Its Aftermath* (New York: Frederick A. Praeger, 1957), p. 33. For a more extensive exposition of the new perspective, see E. Zhukov, "The Eastern Peoples and World's Destiny," *International Affairs* (Moscow), April 1956, pp. 45–51.

8. To trace this evolution in Soviet outlook, see, for example, S. Datlin, "Africa through Colonialist Eyes," *International Affairs,* December 1956, pp. 110–20; I. I. Potekhin, "The Reviving Significance of Africa in World Economics and Politics," *Kommunist* (Moscow), No. 6, April 1957, pp. 100–13; *idem,* "The Collapse of the Colonial System in Africa," *ibid.,* No. 17, December 1958, pp. 99–112; and an editorial on "African Renaissance," *New Times* (Moscow), No. 4, January 1959, p. 4.

9. With regard to Africa, for example, S. Datlin wrote in *Pravda* on Feb. 17, 1958: "The African nations have not all been equally successful in the struggle for freedom. . . . And there are some who juggle lightheartedly with the concepts of sovereignty, little realizing what forces and efforts will be required before the people achieve their cherished goal."

10. Report of the Central Committee to the 20th Party Congress, *loc. cit.,* p. 33.

11. Khrushchev himself capsulized Soviet outlook in his remarks at the 21st CPSU Congress in January–February 1959. See Leo Gruliow, ed., *Current Soviet Policies—III: The Documentary Record of the Extraordinary 21st Congress of the Communist Party of the Soviet Union* (New York: Columbia University Press, 1960), pp. 55, 201.

12. For analysis of the Congo affair and its ramifications, see Catherine Hoskyns, *The Congo since Independence, January 1960–December 1961* (London: Oxford University Press, 1965); and W. Scott Thompson, *Ghana's*

Foreign Policy, 1957–1966 (Princeton: Princeton University Press, 1969), pp. 119–61.

13. For the Soviet government's bitter statement of Dec. 7, 1960, see *New Times*, No. 51, December 1960, p. 39.

14. For more detailed discussion of these developments, see the author's *The Dilemmas of Courtship . . .* , Chs. 4 and 6; Legvold, *op. cit.*, Chs. 4–7.

15. For more extended treatment of this point, see the author's *The Dilemmas of Courtship . . .* , Ch. 6; Legvold, *op. cit.*, pp. 194–201; Uri Ra'anan, "Moscow and the 'Third World,'" *Problems of Communism* (Washington, D.C.), January–February 1965, pp. 22–31.

16. This was the language that Khrushchev used in what purported to be an interview with the editors of two Algerian newspapers, a Ghanaian one, and a Burmese one, in December 1963, as reported in *Pravda* and *Izvestiya* (Moscow), Dec. 22, 1963.

17. For an explicit statement of the notion that the USSR could function as a "vanguard," see Georgi Mirsky, "The Proletariat and National Liberation," *New Times*, May 1, 1964, p. 9.

18. See, for example, Viktor Mayevskiy's report on a trip around Africa under the auspices of the World Peace Council in *Pravda*, Mar. 31, 1965; Akademiya Nauk SSSR, Institut Afriki, *Nezavisimyye strany Afriki: ekonomicheskiye i sotsial'nyye problemy* [The independent countries of Africa: economic and social problems] (Moscow: Nauka, 1965); A. Vladin, "Professional Education in Ghana," *New Times*, July 8, 1965; L. Aleksandrovskaya, *Gana* [Ghana] (Moscow: Mysl', 1965).

19. See, for instance, K. Ivanov, "National-Liberation Movement and Non-Capitalist Path of Development," *International Affairs*, May 1965, pp. 59–60; K. N. Brutents, "Several Peculiarities of the National-Liberation Movement," *Voprosy filosofii* (Moscow), June 1965, p. 36; Fyodor Burlatskiy's article in *Pravda*, Aug. 15, 1965; "The National-Liberation Movement and Social Progress," *Kommunist*, No. 13, September 1965, pp. 20–24; R. Ul'yanovskiy, "Several Questions of Non-Capitalist Development of the Liberated Countries," *ibid.*, No. 1, January 1966, pp. 113–15; and K. Ivanov, "The National-Liberation Movement and Non-Capitalist Path of Development," *International Affairs*, February 1966, pp. 20–21.

20. For a particularly biting capsulization of the thinking on this matter, see the comments of Lufti El Kohli, an Egyptian Communist, at a seminar held in Cairo in October 1966 on "Africa's national and social revolution." The seminar was sponsored jointly by *Problems of Peace and Socialism* (Prague) and *At-Talia* (Cairo), a monthly that El Kohli edited. El Kohli's comments may be found in *The World Marxist Review* (Toronto—the North American edition of *Problems of Peace and Socialism*), January 1967, pp. 18–19. That these comments accurately conveyed Moscow's disillusionment with "revolutionary democrats" was made amply clear by Soviet reactions to events preceding and following the fall of Modibo Keita's regime in Mali in November 1968. See Legvold, *op. cit.*, pp. 290–302.

21. K. Brutents, "African Revolution: Gains and Problems," *International Affairs*, January 1967, p. 21.

22. See, for instance, Yuri Bochkaryov, "The Outlook in Africa," *New*

Times, Apr. 27, 1966, p. 9; N. Gavrilov, "Africa: Classes, Parties and Politics," *International Affairs,* July 1966, p. 43.

23. Richard Lowenthal, "Soviet 'Counterimperialism,'" *Problems of Communism,* November–December 1976, pp. 52–63. See also his "Epilogue" in *Model or Ally? The Communist Powers and the Developing Countries* (New York: Oxford University Press, 1977), pp. 359–76.

24. For more extended treatment of the various elements of the revised Soviet approach, see Fritz Ermarth, "The Soviet Union in the Third World: Purpose in Search of Power," *Annals of the American Academy of Political and Social Science* (Philadelphia), November 1969, pp. 31–40; Legvold, *op. cit.,* pp. 275–344; Elizabeth Kridl Valkenier, "New Trends in Soviet Economic Relations," in Erik P. Hoffmann and Frederic J. Fleron, eds., *The Conduct of Soviet Foreign Policy* (Chicago: Aldine, 1971); Valkenier, "The USSR and the Third World," *Survey* (London), Summer 1973, pp. 41–49; and Lowenthal, "Soviet 'Counterimperialism,'" *loc. cit.*

25. *Pravda,* Apr. 7, 1971. The economic aspects of the strategy, it should be noted, received explicit endorsement in Kosygin's report of Apr. 5, 1966, to the 23rd CPSU Congress (*ibid.,* Apr. 6, 1966); however, no top Soviet official articulated both the political and economic dimensions of the strategy until Kosygin's address to the 24th Congress.

26. For a good analysis of the evolution of Soviet attitudes toward the unfolding Nigerian crisis, see Legvold, *op. cit.,* pp. 311–30.

27. These figures are the author's calculations based on data given in Leo Tansky, "Soviet Foreign Aid: Scope, Direction, and Trends," in U.S. Congress, Joint Economic Committee, *Soviet Economic Prospects for the Seventies* (Washington, D.C.: U.S. Government Printing Office, 1973), p. 775; and in Orah Cooper, "Soviet Economic Aid to the Third World," in U.S. Congress, Joint Economic Committee, *Soviet Economy in a New Perspective,* (Washington, D.C.: U.S. Government Printing Office, 1976), p. 194. In evaluating the figures for the 1954–64 period, it is important to bear in mind that most of sub-Saharan Africa did not attain independence until the 1960s. Figures for both periods represent aid offered by the USSR, not aid actually drawn by Third World countries.

28. See, for instance, the conflicting positions set forth by Sh. Sanokoyev and N. Kapchenko in their contributions at a "scientific conference," held in May 1976 under the joint auspices of the Department of Marxist-Leninist Political Economy of the Academy of Social Sciences under the CPSU Central Committee and the Editorial Board of *International Affairs,* on "the present stage in the general crisis of capitalism and world relations," *International Affairs,* August 1976, pp. 13 and 33, respectively. From the late 1950s until the mid-1970s, the standard Soviet thesis had been that the correlation of forces was changing to the advantage of the USSR.

29. For a review and analysis of some of the literature on this subject, see Joan Barth Urban, "Contemporary Soviet Perspectives on Revolution in the West," *Orbis* (Philadelphia) Winter 1976, pp. 1359–402.

30. V. Solodovnikov and N. Gavrilov, "Africa: Tendencies of Non-Capitalist Development," *International Affairs,* March 1976, p. 33.

31. *Pravda,* Aug. 26, 1978. Emphasis added.

32. V. Solodovnikov, "Elimination of the Colonial System, an Expression of the General Crisis of Capitalism," *International Affairs,* August 1976, p. 24. For later statements in a similar vein, see K. Brutents in *Pravda,* Feb. 10, 1978; Y. Primakov, "Neo-colonialism: Essence, Forms, Limits," *International Affairs,* November 1978, p. 66; Anatoly Gromyko, "Africa in the Strategy of Neo-colonialism," *ibid.,* p. 85.

33. For relevant discussion of these various aspects of the socialist-oriented states, see K. Brutents in *Pravda,* Feb. 10, 1978; Y. Tarabrin, "The National Liberation Movement: Problems and Prospects," *International Affairs,* February 1978, pp. 65–66; Radio Moscow in English to Africa, Apr. 21, 1978, in *FBIS-SOV,* May 4, 1978, pp. H/1–2; V. Kudryavtsev, "Africa Fights for Its Future," *International Affairs,* May 1978, p. 32; B. Pilyatskin and S. Linkov, "Mozambique in Work and Struggle," *ibid.,* July 1978, pp. 108–15; *Izvestiya,* Dec. 5, 1978.

34. *Pravda,* Aug. 26, 1978.

35. O. Orestov, "Independent Africa in the Making," *International Affairs,* November 1975, p. 75.

36. Solodovnikov and Gavrilov, "Africa: Tendencies of Non-Capitalist Development," p. 36.

37. A. Iskenderov, "Unity of the World Revolutionary Process—A Factor of Stronger Peace," *International Affairs,* December 1978, p. 70.

38. See the private remarks of Soviet officials reported by Kevin Klose, *The Washington Post,* Nov. 16, 1977.

39. Radio Moscow in English to Africa, Apr. 21, 1978, in *FBIS-SOV,* May 4, 1978, p. H/3. For comparable assessments, see Alim Keshokov, "A Country of a Young Revolution," *Kommunist,* No. 6, April 1978, pp. 106–14; Kudryavtsev, *loc. cit.,* p. 32; the commentary by Nikolay Petrovich Khokhlov on Radio Moscow Domestic Service in Russian, Sept. 12, 1978, in *FBIS-SOV,* Sept. 13, 1978, p. H/3.

40. Solodovnikov and Gavrilov, "Africa: Tendencies of Non-Capitalist Development," p. 32.

41. *Ibid.* For a more recent appraisal of a similar order, see the commentary of Viktor Sidenko, Radio Moscow in English to Africa, May 9, 1978, in *FBIS-SOV,* May 11, 1978, pp. H/4–5.

42. Orestov, *loc. cit.,* p. 81. For acknowledgments of the state of flux on the continent in the late 1970s, see K. Brutents in *Pravda,* Feb. 10, 1978; Kudryavtsev, *loc. cit.,* pp. 33–34; Iskenderov, *loc, cit.,* pp. 70–71.

43. Sidenko commentary, Radio Moscow in English to Africa, May 9, 1978, in *loc. cit.*

44. Orestov, *loc. cit.,* p. 81.

45. *Ibid.* For more recent Soviet or Soviet-endorsed assessments to the same effect, see Tarabrin, *loc. cit.,* p. 68; *Pravda,* Aug. 26, 1978.

46. Indeed, although Soviet analysts have unequivocally asserted that "the most serious political and economic subversion in Africa today is aimed at the countries who proclaim socialist orientation as the principle of their development," they have highlighted the wide variations in standards of social and

economic development within this group. For typical references to the socialist-oriented countries as the principal targets of "imperialist subversion," see V. Vorobyov, "Colonialist Policies in Africa," *International Affairs*, September 1978, p. 40; and V. Kudryavtsev, "A Policy of Aggression, Threats and Conflicts," *ibid.*, November 1978, p. 82. The quotation in the preceding sentence comes from the first source. On the diversity among the states with a socialist orientation, see Kudryavtsev, "Africa Fights for Its Future," p. 34.

47. These figures are taken from U.S. Central Intelligence Agency, *Communist Aid to the Less Developed Countries of the Free World, 1976*, ER 77–10296 (Washington, D.C., August 1977), pp. 11–13, and *idem, Communist Aid to Less Developed Countries of the Free World, 1977*, ER 78–10478U (Washington, D.C., November 1978), pp. 5–6. Both documents are available through the Documents Expediting Service of the U.S. Library of Congress.

48. *Pravda*, Feb. 25, 1976.

49. *Communist Aid . . . 1977*, p. 37. For more detailed discussion of Soviet policy toward India in the last half of the 1970s, see William J. Barnds, "The USSR, China, and South Asia," *Problems of Communism*, November–December 1977, pp. 44–59.

50. See *Communist Aid . . . 1977*, pp. 29–30.

51. For the text, see *The Washington Post*, Oct. 2, 1977.

52. For a sampling of Soviet commentary along these lines, see *Izvestiya*, Sept. 19 and 20, 1978; *Pravda*, Sept. 21, 22, and 24, 1978; Leonid Brezhnev's remarks conveyed by Radio Moscow in Arabic to the Arab World, Sept. 23, 1978, as reported in *FBIS-SOV*, Sept. 25, 1978, pp. F/6–7.

53. For the text of the "political document" as issued by TASS, June 23, 1978, see *FBIS-SOV*, June 26, 1978, pp. G/1–3. The agreement to enter into a long-term trade arrangement, the first such accord between Moscow and Ankara in the post–World War II era, was mentioned in the joint communiqué put out on June 25, 1978, at the end of Ecevit's visit, and the projected volume of trade was reported by Radio Anatolia in Turkish to Turkey on the same day. See *FBIS-SOV*, June 26, 1978, pp. G/8–9; and *ibid.*, pp. G/10–11. The trade protocol was signed in the autumn. See Radio Moscow, TASS in English, Nov. 24, 1978, in *FBIS-SOV*, Nov. 27, 1978, pp. G/1–2.

54. For overviews of Soviet-Afghan relations in 1978, see Don Oberdorfer and Jonathan C. Randal in *The Washington Post*, May 29 and Nov. 7, 1978, respectively. The text of the treaty may be found in *FBIS-SOV*, Dec. 6, 1978, pp. J/10–13.

55. *Communist Aid . . . 1977*, p. 31.

56. Radio Moscow in Persian to Iran, Apr. 11, 1978, and Moscow Domestic Service in Russian, Apr. 12, 1978, in *FBIS-SOV*, Apr. 13, 1978, pp. F/4–5.

57. For a good summary of Soviet behavior during Iran's growing crisis in 1978, see Kevin Kose in *The Washington Post*, Nov. 15, 1978. On the ensuing Soviet propaganda campaign, see the coverage in *FBIS-SOV* from mid-November 1978 to early February 1979.

58. A. Skorodumov, "Soviet-African Trade," *International Affairs*, May 1977, pp. 117–20.

59. V. Rymalov, "Newly Free Countries: Problems of Economic Development," *International Affairs*, July 1978, pp. 57–58.

60. *Ibid.*, p. 56.

61. *Ibid.*, pp. 57–59.

62. Space limitations preclude a country-by-country discussion of Soviet activities in Africa here, but the following analysis grows out of detailed research of this sort that the author has conducted in connection with a larger study in progress. In tackling the issue of whether the Soviet Union has a grand design for Africa, it seems fruitless to this author to attempt to proceed from general theory or doctrine. If there is a grand design, one must assume that what the Soviet Union is doing in Africa relates to it; hence, it ought to be possible to put the various pieces of Soviet policy together into some sort of coherent mosaic. For an elaboration of this view, see John C. Campbell, "The Communist Powers and the Middle East: Moscow's Purposes," *Problems of Communism*, September–October 1972, especially pp. 41–43.

63. For a discussion of this decision and the factors influencing it, see Michael MccGwire, "The Evolution of Soviet Naval Policy: 1970–74," in Michael MccGwire *et al.*, eds., *Soviet Naval Policy: Constraints and Objectives* (New York: Praeger, 1975), pp. 505–46.

64. See Robert G. Weinland, "Egypt and the Soviet Mediterranean Squadron," *Österreichische Militarische Zeitschrift* (Vienna), November–December 1977. The USSR in 1958 had established a Mediterranean naval presence consisting entirely of submarines. These submarines, and a tender, were based in Vlore, Albania. As a result of developing discord between the Soviet and Albanian leaderships, however, Tirana canceled the base arrangement in 1961. Unsuccessful in obtaining an alternative base, Moscow temporarily withdrew all its combat forces from the area.

65. U.S. House of Representatives, Committee on International Relations, *The Soviet Union and the Third World: A Watershed in Great Power Policy?* (Washington, D.C.: U.S. Government Printing Office, 1977), Supplement. This document was prepared by the Senior Specialist Division, Congressional Research Service, Library of Congress. For evidence of continuing Soviet activity of this sort in more recent years, see, for example, the reports of visits by Soviet warships to Algeria in April 1978, to the Seychelles in June 1978, and to Mozambique in April 1979, carried in *FBIS-SOV*, Apr. 6, 1978, p. F/1; Apr. 10, 1978, p. F/7; Apr. 17, 1978, p. F/1; May 31, 1978, p. H/7; Apr. 22, 1979, p. J/5.

66. On the USSR's access to Guinean facilities during much of the 1970s and the subsequent limitations placed on that access, see U.S. House of Representatives, Committee on International Relations, *The Soviet Union and the Third World: A Watershed in Great Power Policy*, Supplement; *The New York Times*, Nov. 19, 1977; *Le Monde* (Paris), May 31, 1978; Jim Hoagland and Sanford J. Ungar in *The Washington Post*, May 31 and June 18, 1978, respectively. For authoritative discussion of the new thrust of Guinea's foreign policy, which has involved reconciliation with France and even reception of French President Valéry Giscard d'Estaing in Conakry, see the interview with Sékou Touré broadcast by Radio Paris Domestic Service in French, Nov. 30,

1978, as reported in Foreign Broadcast Information Service, *Daily Report: Sub-Saharan Africa* (Washington, D.C.—hereafter *FBIS-SSA*), Dec. 1, 1978, pp. D/2–3; and the interview with the Guinean president published in *Le Monde*, Dec. 5, 1978.

67. Weinland, *loc. cit.*

68. International Institute for Strategic Studies, *Strategic Survey 1976* (London, 1977), p. 60. See also U.S. Senate, Committee on Appropriations, *Report to the Committee on Appropriations, U.S. Senate, by Members of the Fact-Finding Team Sent to Somalia at the Invitation of the President of Somalia: Visit to the Democratic Republic of Somalia*, 94th Cong., 1st sess., 1975 (committee print); U.S. Senate, Committee on Armed Services, *Soviet Military Capability in Berbera, Somalia: Report of Senator Bartlett to the Committee on Armed Services, U.S. Senate*, 94th Cong., 1st sess., 1975 (committee print).

69. See the expulsion statement issued by Minister of Information and National Guidance Abdi Kassim Salad on behalf of the Central Committee of the Somalia Revolutionary Socialist Party on Nov. 13, 1977, in *FBIS-SSA*, Nov. 14, 1977, pp. B/2–3; and the Nov. 20, 1977, speech of President Mohamed Siad Barre on the expulsion, in *FBIS–SSA*, Nov. 21, 1977, pp. B/5–7.

70. For the treaty, see the source cited in note 1. The information on the forms of "cooperation" comes from conversations with officials of the U.S. Department of State in April 1979.

71. For the relevant clause in the treaty, see *FBIS-SOV*, Nov. 21, 1978, p. H/7. On the "floating base," see Elmo Zumwalt and Worth Bagley in the *Detroit News*, July 9, 1978.

72. For a concise exposition, see Admiral Stansfield Turner, "The Naval Balance: Not Just a Numbers Game," *Foreign Affairs* (New York), January 1977, pp. 339–54.

73. See Robert Weinland, "Analysis of Admiral Gorshkov's 'Navies in War and Peace,'" in MccGwire *et al., op. cit.*, pp. 547–62; and *idem*, "The Changing Mission Structure of the Soviet Navy," *Survival* (London), April–May 1972, pp. 129–33.

74. *Cf.*, for instance, David Rees, *Soviet Strategic Penetration of Africa*, Conflict Studies, No. 77 (London: Institute for the Study of Conflict, November 1976); and Colin Legum's discussion in *The Observer*, Mar. 20, 1977. These conflicting interpretations of Soviet purpose, it should be stressed, reflect not merely personal idiosyncracies but also the ambiguity of the available evidence. On one hand, Soviet analysts have given plenty of indication that they understand the importance to the West of the sea lanes around Africa. See, for instance, V. Sofinskiy and A. Khazanov, "The Horn of Africa in Imperialism's Strategy," *Novoye Vremya* (Moscow), Feb. 10, 1978, pp. 4–6. On the other hand, the USSR has thus far employed its naval forces in the area essentially to serve its diplomatic ends in Africa. See, for example, James M. McConnell and Bradford Dismukes, "Soviet Diplomacy of Force in the Third World," *Problems of Communism*, January–February 1979, pp. 14–27.

75. See Weinland, "Egypt and the Soviet Mediterranean Squadron."

76. On the latter point, see, for instance, *ibid.*

77. This figure is my own calculation based on yearly figures for average daily strength given in *ibid,* and, in the case of 1977, provided personally by Robert Weinland.

78. For illustrations, see Alvin Z. Rubinstein, "Moscow and Cairo: Currents of Influence," *Problems of Communism,* July–August 1974, pp. 17–28, and *idem, Red Star on the Nile: The Soviet-Egyptian Influence Relationship since the June War* (Princeton: Princeton University Press, 1977).

79. For analysis of this linkage, see, for example, Chester A. Crocker, "The African Dimension of Indian Ocean Policy," *Orbis,* Fall 1976, pp. 650–56.

80. For a clear, if tacit, Soviet admission of such a motivation, see V. Vorobyov, *loc. cit.,* pp. 41–42. Although Vorobyov's article appeared several months after Moscow took the decision, his remarks on this subject are consistent with what the Soviets had been saying in less explicit fashion all along. See for instance, V. Matveyev's article in *Izvestiya,* Sept. 18, 1977; and Moscow Radio Peace and Progress in English to Africa, Oct. 28, 1977, in *FBIS-SOV,* Oct. 31, 1977, pp. H/4–5.

81. For a more detailed discussion of the evidence regarding Moscow's likely motivations for helping the MPLA, see Colin Legum, "The Soviet Union, China and the West in Southern Africa," *Foreign Affairs,* July 1976, pp. 747–53. Indirect confirmation of Legum's conclusions may be found in V. Sofinsky and A. Khazanov, "Angolan Chronicle of the Peking Betrayal," *International Affairs,* July 1978, pp. 60–69. These two authors maintain, among other things, that "an attempt to isolate the national liberation movement from the common anti-imperialist front and subordinate it to Maoist guidance . . . determined Peking's policy toward the national liberation movement *in Angola and other Portuguese colonies.*" (Emphasis added.) See p. 60.

82. For more details, see Colin Legum, ed., *Africa Contemporary Record: Annual Survey and Documents 1975–76* (New York: Africana Publishing Co., 1976), pp. 799–800, 803; *Communist Aid . . . 1976,* p. 21, and *Communist Aid . . . 1977,* pp. 18–19; Radio Moscow in English to Africa, Nov. 23, 1977, in *FBIS-SOV,* Nov. 29, 1977, p. H/3; *Pravda,* Sept. 7, 1978.

83. On the tortured history of the agreement, see *Communist Aid . . . 1976,* p. 18, and *Communist Aid . . . 1977,* p. 14; Moscow TASS in English, Mar. 10, 1978, in *FBIS-SOV,* Mar. 13, 1978, p. F/4; *Pravda,* Mar. 14, 1978. On Soviet concessions with regard to the Saharan territory, see, for instance, Ronald Koven in *The Washington Post,* July 11, 1978.

84. See David Ottaway and Peter Osnos in *The Washington Post,* Apr. 16 and May 7, 1977, respectively; Murray Marder in *ibid.,* Mar. 11, 1978.

85. For typical African criticism of the Soviet Union and Cuba, see the debate at the Khartoum summit meeting of the OAU toward the end of July 1978, as covered in *FBIS-SSA* beginning July 19, 1978, and the accounts of the July 1978 meeting in Belgrade of the foreign ministers of nonaligned states, in *The Washington Post,* July 29 and 31, 1978. For representative Soviet statements opposing the emergence of "miniblocs," see *Pravda,* Mar. 24, May 12, June 12, June 23, and June 29, 1978; Moscow in English to Af-

rica, May 26, 1978, in *FBIS-SOV*, May 30, 1978, p. H/8; Moscow in English to Africa, June 4, 1978, in *FBIS-SOV*, June 5, 1978, pp. H/3–4; Moscow TASS in English, July 5, 1978, in *FBIS-SOV*, July 17, 1978, pp. H/3–4; Radio Moscow International Service in English, July 17, 1978, in *FBIS-SOV*, July 18, 1978, p. H/4; Moscow TASS in English, July 21 and 22, 1978, in *FBIS-SOV*, July 24, 1978, pp. H/3–5; *Izvestiya*, July 20 and 27, 1978; Vorobyov, *loc. cit.*, p. 47; Kudryavtsev, "A Policy of Aggression, Threats and Fanning Conflict," pp. 82–83.

86. See Tansky, *loc. cit.*; Cooper, *loc. cit.*; *Communist Aid . . . 1976* and *Communist Aid . . . 1977*.

87. A Radio Moscow broadcast in the summer of 1978, for instance, observed: "Experience shows that most African countries developing along noncapitalist lines succeed in finding ways of drawing privately owned foreign capital into national construction under strict government control. With this in view such countries as Tanzania or Ethiopia have set juridical limits with which foreign capital can operate. They've passed laws that define the forms of control over this capital, limiting its sphere of operations to positions that do not threaten these countries' noncapitalist orientation." Radio Moscow in English to Africa, Sept. [Aug.?] 30, 1978, in *FBIS-SOV*, Sept. 7, 1978, p. H/1.

88. For further discussion of this point, see Lowenthal, "Soviet 'Counterimperialism,'" pp. 62–63. Incomplete evidence for the late 1970s suggests that there has been no reversal of this trend in Western investment. According to the U.S. Conference Board, a nonprofit business research organization, analysis of the 329 private American foreign investment projects announced in 1977–78 showed that 58 percent were in Europe, 16 percent in Asia (mostly Japan), 12 percent in Canada, 9 percent in Latin America, and 5 percent in the Middle East and Africa. During the same period, non-U.S. manufacturing firms launched 629 investment projects in the United States. No dollar values were available, however, for either the American or the non-American investments. See *The Washington Post*, Apr. 8, 1979.

89. By late 1978, Soviet sources were openly proclaiming that "imperialist states have lost the possibility of suppressing other nations by armed force" because "the origination and consolidation of the world socialist system deprived the imperialist states of their monopoly position as the sole source of . . . arms . . . for the young independent countries." See Primakov, *loc. cit.*, p. 66.

90. On Soviet military assistance to Amin, see Colin Legum, *The Observer*, June 24, 1975; and *Communist Aid . . . 1976*, p. 22. For the reversal in Soviet policy, see Kevin Klose in *The Washington Post*, Apr. 30, 1979, and *Pravda*, Apr. 29, 1979.

91. *Communist Aid . . . 1976*, p. 17; and *Communist Aid . . . 1977*, p. 14.

92. See David Ottaway and Murray Marder in *The Washington Post*, Apr. 16, 1977, and Mar. 11, 1978, respectively.

93. On the relations of the Front for the National Liberation of Angola (*Frente Nacional de Libertação de Angola*—FNLA) and the National Union for the Total Independence of Angola (*União Nacional pro Independencia Total de Angola*—UNITA) with the United States, see John A. Marcum,

"Lessons of Angola," *Foreign Affairs*, April 1976, pp. 407–25; Colin Legum, "Foreign Intervention in Angola," in Legum, *African Contemporary Record: Annual Survey and Documents 1975–76*, pp. 3–39; and *idem*, "The Soviet Union, China and the West in Southern Africa," esp. pp. 747–53.

94. For further discussion of Chinese activities in Africa, see George T. Yu, "The USSR and Africa: China's Impact," *Problems of Communism*, January–February 1978, pp. 40–50.

95. David Ottaway in *The Washington Post*, Mar. 27, 1977; *Communist Aid . . . 1977*, p. 20.

96. *Communist Aid . . . 1976*, pp. 19–20; Legum, "The Soviet Union, China and the West in Southern Africa," pp. 754–55.

97. *Communist Aid . . . 1976*, pp. 12, 16, and 20; *Communist Aid . . . 1977*, pp. 5 and 21–22.

98. For more extensive treatment of the evidence on which this reconstruction is based, see Legum, "The Soviet Union, China and the West in Southern Africa," pp. 747–53; and *idem*, "Foreign Intervention in Angola." One can also gain some retrospective insight into Soviet thinking regarding the Angolan crisis of 1975–76 from Sefinsky and Khazanov, *loc. cit.*

99. See *Communist Aid . . . 1976*, p. 14.

100. For analysis of the evolving Soviet role in Somalia and of the Soviet relationship with the Eritrean secessionists, see Brian Crozier, *The Soviet Presence in Somalia*, Conflict Studies, No. 54 (London: Institute for the Study of Conflict, 1975); F. Stephen Larrabee, "Somalia and Moscow's Problems on the Horn of Africa," *Radio Liberty Research* (Munich), RL 158/77, July 5, 1977; David E. Albright, "The Horn of Africa and the Arab–Israeli Conflict," in Robert O. Freedman, ed., *World Politics and the Arab–Israeli Conflict* (Elmsford, N.Y.: Pergamon Press, 1979).

101. For discussions of this plan and the local reactions to it, see James Buston's account in *Financial Times* (London), Apr. 24, 1977; Colin Legum's report in *The Observer*, May 9, 1977; and David Ottaway's dispatches in *The Washington Post*, May 17 and 26, and June 9, 1977. Fidel Castro first broached the idea of a federation to Siad Barre and Mengistu Haile Mariam of Ethiopia at a secret meeting over which Castro presided in Aden in March 1977.

102. So, at least, Moscow seems to have concluded. See the accounts of a Somali opposition movement by Moscow TASS in English, Oct. 5, 1978, in *FBIS-SOV*, Oct. 6, 1978, p. H/2, and by Radio Moscow in English to Africa, Oct. 11, 1978, in *FBIS-SOV*, Oct. 12, 1978, pp. H/1–2; also the Soviet commentary on the January 1979 Extraordinary Congress of the Somali Revolutionary Socialist Party, Radio Moscow in English to Africa, Jan. 31, 1979, in *FBIS–SOV*, Feb. 1, 1979, pp. H/1–2.

103. On Israel's role in Ethiopia during 1974–78 even in the absence of formal diplomatic relations between the two countries, see my "The Horn of Africa and the Arab–Israeli Conflict," *loc.cit.* For Dayan's remarks, see *The New York Times* and *The Washington Post*, Feb. 7, 1978, and the *Christian Science Monitor* (Boston), Feb. 8, 1978. There is a public report of the departure of the advisers in *Newsweek* (New York), Feb. 13, 1978, p. 47. My in-

formation on the circumstances of the withdrawal derives from a private converstion with an Israeli official.

104. For a discussion of the evidence on this point, see my "The Horn of Africa and the Arab–Israeli Conflict," *loc. cit.*

105. Ethiopian forces captured the last major town held by the insurgents in late November 1978. However, the rebels still claimed control of the countryside, amounting to 85 percent of the territory. On developments in Eritrea, see Addis Ababa Domestic Service in Amharic, Nov. 28, 1978, in *FBIS-SSA*, Nov. 29, 1978, pp. B/1–2; Rome ANSA in English, Nov. 29, 1978, in *FBIS-SSA*, Nov. 30, 1978, pp. B/2–3; *The Washington Post*, Nov. 29 and 30, 1978; *Pravda*, Nov. 30, 1978; Paris AFP in English, Dec. 7, 1978, in *FBIS-SSA*, Dec. 8, 1978, p. B/1.

106. For the differing perspectives of Mengistu and Soviet officials on the "vanguard party" issue, see, for example, the Ethiopian leader's speech at a dinner in Moscow on Nov. 17, 1978, and his address at a rally in Addis Ababa on May Day 1979, as reported, respectively in *Pravda*, Nov. 18, 1978, and by Addis Ababa Domestic Service in Amharic, May 1, 1979, in *FBIS-SSA*, May 2, 1979, pp. B/1–2; the commentary of Radio Moscow in English to Africa, Dec. 15, 1978, in *FBIS-SOV*, Dec. 18, 1978, p. H/2. On Mengistu's relations with professed Marxist-Leninists in the civilian sphere, see Colin Legum and Bill Lee, *Conflict in the Horn of Africa* (New York: Africana Publishing Co., 1978), Part 2. There were also reports in the spring of 1978 of tension between Addis Ababa and Havana over Cuban involvement in the clandestine return to Ethiopia of a leader of a banned Marxist party. See, for instance, *The Washington Post*, May 30, 1978.

107. See Radio Addis Ababa Domestic Service in Amharic, June 28, 1978, in *FBIS-SSA*, June 29, 1978, p. B/1.

108. My information on the existence of this faction comes from Legum and Lee, *op. cit.*, Part 2, and from Israeli sources.

109. See, for instance, the press conference conducted by a representative of the Angolan Defense Ministry in Luanda on Nov. 9, 1977, as reported by Radio Luanda Domestic Service in Portuguese, Nov. 9, 1977, in *FBIS-SSA*, Nov. 11, 1977, pp. E/1–2; David Ottaway in *The Washington Post*, May 18 and Dec. 29, 1978; a press conference by President Neto, as reported by Radio Luanda Domestic Service in Portuguese, Sept. 11, 1978, in *FBIS-SSA*, Sept. 12, 1978, pp. E/1–4; the communiqué issued by the Angolan Directorate of Information and Security on Nov. 10, 1978, and carried by Radio Luanda Domestic Service in Portuguese, Nov. 11, 1978, in *FBIS-SSA*, Nov. 13, 1978, pp. E/1–6; Flavio Tavares in *O Estado de Sao Paulo*, Nov. 15, 1978, as reported in *FBIS-SSA*, Nov. 16, 1978, pp. E/1–2.

110. *The Washington Post*, Nov. 18, 1977.

111. See, for example, the report by Leon Dash in *ibid.*, Aug. 13, 1977; Radio Johannesburg International Service in English, Aug. 15, 1978, in *FBIS-SSA*, Aug. 16, 1978, p. E/1. The Dash article is the final installment of a fascinating account of UNITA activities based on a 2,100-mile trek through Angola with UNITA guerrillas that lasted seven and a half months. The full series ran in *The Washington Post*, Aug. 7–13, 1977.

112. On the expanding ties between Angola and Zaire, see Kinshasa AZAP in French, July 17, 1978, in *FBIS-SSA*, July 18, 1978, pp. E/1–2; Kinshasa AZAP in French, July 22, 1978, and Radio Luanda Domestic Service in Portuguese, July 22 and 23, 1978, in *FBIS-SSA*, July 24, 1978, p. C/1; Radio Kinshasa Domestic Service in French, Aug. 20 and 21, 1978, in *FBIS-SSA*, Aug. 22, 1978, pp. C/2–6; Radio Luanda Domestic Service in Portuguese, Oct. 16, 1978, in *FBIS-SSA*, Oct. 17, 1978, pp. E/1–3; Radio Maputo Domestic Service in Portuguese, Oct. 17, 1978, and Radio Luanda Domestic Service in Portuguese, Oct. 17, 1978, in *FBIS-SSA*, Oct. 27, 1978, p. E/1. On the effect of the rapprochement on insurgent activity in Angola, see, for instance, the report of a Neto press conference carried by Radio Luanda Domestic Service in Portuguese, Sept. 11, 1978, in *loc. cit.*

113. On these various aspects of the Namibia question, see Gerald J. Bender, "Angola, the Cubans, and American Anxieties," *Foreign Policy* (New York) Summer 1978, pp. 16–22; Robert G. Kaiser and Walter Pincus in *The Washington Post*, June 28, 1979; Radio Luanda Domestic Service in Portuguese, July 10, 1978, in *FBIS-SSA*, July 11, 1978, p. E/2; Radio Luanda Domestic Service in Portuguese, July 13, 1978, in *FBIS-SSA*, July 14, 1978, pp. E/1–2; David Ottaway in *The Washington Post*, July 17 and 22, Sept. 21 and 23, and Dec. 29, 1978; the report of a Neto press conference carried by Radio Luanda Domestic Service in Portuguese, Sept. 11, 1978, in *loc. cit.*; Neto's speech on Nov. 11, 1978, as broadcast by Radio Luanda Domestic Service in Portuguese, Nov. 11, 1978, in *FBIS-SSA*, Nov. 13, 1978, pp. E/2–6; Carlyle Murphy in *The Washington Post*, Mar. 2, 1979.

114. See, for example, Bender, *loc. cit.*, pp. 18–19; David Ottaway in *The Washington Post*, Dec. 29, 1978. I am also indebted to Gerald Bender for expanding upon his assessments of the security situation in Ovimbundu areas, based on his travels there, in a personal conversation in April 1979.

115. Bender, *loc. cit.*, p. 21.

116. On these openings to the West, see, for instance, Don Oberdorfer, Terri Shaw, and David Ottaway in *The Washington Post*, June 21, June 30, and July 22, 1978, respectively; Radio Luanda Domestic Service in Portuguese, Sept. 8, 1978, in *FBIS-SSA*, Sept. 11, 1978, p. E/1; the report of Neto's press conference carried by Radio Luanda Domestic Service in Portuguese, Sept. 11, 1978, in *loc. cit.*; David Ottaway in *The Washington Post*, Dec. 14 and 22, 1978; Neto's speech of Dec. 17, 1978, as broadcast by Radio Luanda Domestic Service in Portuguese, Dec. 17, 1978, and excerpted in *FBIS-SSA*, Dec. 18, 1978, pp. E/5–6.

117. See Radio Luanda Domestic Service in Portuguese, Dec. 9 and 10, 1978, in *FBIS-SSA*, Dec. 11, 1978, pp. E/1–2; Radio Luanda Domestic Service in Portuguese, Dec. 10, 1978, in *FBIS-SSA*, Dec. 12, 1978, pp. E/1–2; the Reuter dispatch and David Ottaway in *The Washington Post*, Dec. 10 and 15, 1978, respectively.

118. On the condition of the economy and the quality of Soviet and Cuban aid, see, for example, *Communist Aid . . . 1977*, pp. 16–17; Norman Kirkham's interview with one of the freelance pilots who ferried Cuban troops between Havana and Luanda during the period from October 1977 to March

1978, in *Sunday Gleaner* (Kingston), July 16, 1978, as carried in *FBIS-SSA,* July 21, 1978, pp. E/1–3; the report of David Lamb in the *Los Angeles Times,* Dec. 3, 1978.

119. For the views of Neto and his adherents, derived from extensive interviews in Angola, see Bender, *loc. cit.,* pp. 23–26. Other accounts of the coup may be found in *The New York Times,* May 29, June 5, and June 29, 1977; *The Washington Post,* June 24, 1977.

120. In this regard, one probably ought to differentiate the circumstances in the two African states. While Addis Ababa has far more effective local military forces at its disposal in the late 1970s than Luanda does, pacifying and ruling the disparate peoples of the former Ethiopian empire as well as guaranteeing national security in a local environment that is largely hostile may over the long run impose many more constraints on Ethiopia's actions than Angola will confront.

121. For representative recent commentary on Ethiopia, see Radio Moscow in English to Africa, Apr. 21, 1978, in *FBIS-SOV,* May 4, 1978, p. H/3; Keshokov, *loc. cit.,* pp. 106–14; Kudryavtsev, "Africa Fights for Its Future," p. 32; Radio Moscow Domestic Service in Russian, Sept. 12, 1978, in *FBIS-SOV,* Sept. 13, 1978, pp. H/2–4; *Izvestiya,* Dec. 5, 1978; Moscow TASS in English, Jan. 16, 1979, in *FBIS-SOV,* Jan. 17, 1979, p. H/2.

122. See Lowenthal, "Soviet 'Counterimperialism,'" esp. pp. 52–53, 60–63.

123. Gromyko, *loc. cit.,* p. 84.

124. In regard to outside powers, one point is worth underscoring. Even though Soviet commentators explicitly acknowledge American wariness in the post-Vietnam era about intervening abroad, they display a healthy respect for the capacity of the United States and its Western allies to carry out interventions. See, for instance, Kudryavtsev, "A Policy of Aggression, Threats and Fanning Conflicts," pp. 82–83.

125. For particularly suggestive Soviet commentary on these matters, see Primakov, *loc. cit.,* p. 70; Kudryavtsev, "A Policy of Aggression, Threats and Fanning Conflicts," pp. 82–83; Gromyko, *loc. cit.,* pp. 86–87.

126. For good illustrations, see Kudryavtsev, "Africa Fights for Its Future," pp. 32–33, and *idem,* "A Policy of Aggression, Threats and Fanning Conflicts," p. 83; Gromyko, *loc. cit.,* p. 85.

3.   Russia's Historic Stake in Black Africa

1. The second Romanov, Tsar Alexis (1645–76) considered enlisting the Christian Ethiopians in a joint military action against the Ottoman infidels. See D. Tsvetayev, "Snosheniya s Abissiniye" [Relations with Abyssinia], *Ruskiy Arkhiv,* 1888, No. 2, pp. 206–209, as cited in Edward T. Wilson, *Russia and Black Africa before World War II* (New York: Holmes and Meier, 1974), p. 9. I am indebted to Saone Crocker for her assistance in distilling the relevant portions of that volume for this chapter and for her insights on South Africa.

2. Letter of instruction from Peter I to Admiral Wilster, British Museum,

Addition No. 21259/71. Peter asked the Admiral to persuade the Madagascan king to visit Russia and "by all means to learn from him whether he wishes to have commerce with us."

3. Wilson, *op. cit.,* p. 6.

4. M. G. Kokovstov, *Opisaniye Arkhipelaga i Varvariyskego Berega* [Description of the Aegean and the Barbary Coast] (St. Petersburg: F. Tumanskiy, 1786), pp. 82, 127.

5. Wilson, *op. cit.,* pp. 7–8.

6. Most of Uspenskiy's writings on Ethiopia are contained in a four-part article, "Tserkovnoye i politicheskoye sostoyaniye Abissinii s drevneyshikh vremen do nashikh dney" [The ecclesiastical and political status of Abyssinia from earliest times until the present], in *Trudy Kiyevskoy Dukhovnoy Akademii* (St. Petersburg), Nos. 3–6, 1866.

7. See E. P. Kovalevskiy, *Puteshestviye vo vnutrennyuyu Afriku* [Travels in the interior of Africa] (St. Petersburg, 1849), Vol. 1, pp. 144–45.

8. Wilson, *op. cit.,* p. 27, starred footnote.

9. See L. Nikolaev (a member of the Ashinov expedition), in *Ashinovskaiya ekspeditsiya* [The Ashinov expedition] (Odessa, 1889).

10. Wilson, *op. cit.,* pp. 28–39.

11. "Russia in Africa—the Abyssinian Expedition" (Part 1), *The Times* (London), July 28, 1891, p. 5.

12. F. Volgin, *V strane Chernykh Khristian* [In the country of black Christians] (St. Petersburg, 1895), pp. 86–87.

13. See Archimandrite Efrem, *Poyezdka v Abissiniyu* [Journey to Abyssinia] (St. Petersburg: Universitetskaya Tipografiya, 1901), pp. 136–63.

14. See Wilson, *op. cit.,* pp. 58–59.

15. *Ibid.,* p. 63.

16. N. Notovitch to Gabriel Hanotaux, May 12, 1898, *Documents Diplomatiques Français* (Paris), Vol. 14, p. 283, reporting a conversation with Vlassov, who was en route to Addis Ababa.

17. Wilson, *op. cit.,* pp. 66–67.

18. *Ibid.*

19. See Artamonov papers, Library of Congress (Mss. Div.), Acc. No. 14,897.

20. A. I. Kokhanovskiy, "Imperator Menelik II i sovremennaya Abissiniya" [Emperor Menelik II and contemporary Abyssinia], *Novyy Vostok* (Petrograd), No. 1, 1922, p. 332.

21. "Nikolai Romanov ob Anglo-Burskoy Voine" [Nicholas Romanov on the Anglo–Boer War], *Krasniy Arkhiv* (Leningrad), No. 63, 1934, p. 125.

22. *Ruskaya vedomosti,* No. 29, Jan. 29, 1900, p. 3.

23. Wilson, *op. cit.,* p. 83.

24. See V. I. Lenin, *Imperialism: the Highest State of Capitalism* (New York: International Publishers, 1939).

25. Wilson, *op. cit.,* p. 124.

26. See, for instance, M. Pavlovich, *Bor'ba za Aziyu i Afriku* [The struggle for Asia and Africa] (Moscow, 1923).

27. *Gold Coast Independent* (Accra), Vol. 1, No. 2 (June 13, 1918), p. 23.

28. *Le Libéré* (Paris), Nov. 15, 1923, p. 4.

29. Houénou, "La Grande pitié des colonies" [The great pity of the colonies], *Les Continents* (Paris), Vol. 1, No. 2 (June 1, 1924), p. 1.

30. See Lenin, "Première esquisse des Thèses sur les Questions Nationales et Coloniales" [First draft of the thesis on national and colonial questions], *L'Internationale Communiste* (Moscow), Vol. 1 (1920), p. 1769; and his *Selected Works* (New York: International Publishers, 1938), Vol. 10, p. 243.

31. Wilson, *op. cit.*, p. 147.

32. Senghor, "Ce qu'est notre comité [What is our committee], *La Voix des Nègres* (Paris), Vol. 1, No. 1 (January 1927), p. 1.

33. See Wilson, *op. cit.*, p. 147.

34. On the congress, see the detailed analysis and sources in *ibid.*, pp. 160–75.

35. *Ibid.*, p. 186.

36. *Ibid.*, p. 187.

37. See, for example, Nguyen ai Quac (or Ho Chi Minh), "Colonialisme condamné: l'expérience de l'Afrique Equatoriale Française" [Colonialism condemned: the experience of French Equatorial Africa], *La Correspondance Internationale* (Moscow), Vol. 4, No. 73 (Oct. 28, 1924), pp. 811–12; M. Joubert, "L'Insurrection des Nègres de l'Afrique Equatoriale Française" [The insurrection of the Negroes of French Equatorial Africa], *ibid.*, Vol. 9, No. 11 (Feb. 6, 1929), p. 113.

38. For further discussion as well as citations, see Wilson, *op. cit.*, pp. 196–98.

39. "Report of Losovsky to the Fifth Congress of the RILU," *The Negro Worker* (Hamburg), Vol. 1, Nos. 4/5 (April–May 1931), p. 17.

40. On the Profintern Congress and its actions, see Wilson, *op. cit.*, pp. 199–202.

41. *Ibid.*, pp. 213–19.

42. *Ibid.*, pp. 232–33.

43. *Ibid.*, pp. 248, 286.

44. Padmore, "Au Revoir," *The Negro Worker* (Copenhagen), Vol. 3, Nos. 8/9 (August–September 1933), p. 18.

45. Edward Roux, *Time Longer than Rope* (Madison, Wis.: University of Wisconsin Press, 1964), pp. 198–217; and Gwendolen M. Carter, *The Politics of Inequality*, 3rd ed. (London: Thames and Hudson, 1962), pp. 161–62.

46. Roux, *op. cit.*, pp. 200, 214, 232.

47. *Ibid.*, pp. 255–56.

48. See David E. Albright, "The Horn of Africa and the Arab–Israeli Conflict," in Robert O. Freedman, ed., *World Politics and the Arab–Israeli Conflict* (Elmsford, N.Y.: Pergamon Press, 1979).

4. *Soviet Decision-Making on the Intervention in Angola*

1. See, for example, Walter Hahn and Alvin Cottrell, *Soviet Shadow over Africa* (Miami: Center for Advanced International Studies, University of Miami, 1976). For a similar assessment, see the brief discussion by the former

Director of the CIA, William E. Colby, in his *Honorable Men: My Life in the CIA* (New York: Simon and Schuster, 1978), pp. 421–23.

2. See, for instance, John Stockwell, *In Search of Enemies: A CIA Story* (New York: W. W. Norton & Company, 1978). Although I have found Stockwell's narrative useful in the preparation of this essay, his analysis of Soviet and Cuban behavior in Angola is dubious, to say the least. For an authoritative Soviet interpretation of events, see Oleg Ignatyev, *Secret Weapon in Africa* (Moscow: Progress Publishers, 1977). During the period leading up to and during the intervention, Ignatyev visited Angola twice (September 1974 and October–November 1975) as a *Pravda* foreign correspondent.

3. See, for example, the article by Colin Legum, "The Soviet Union, China and the West in Southern Africa," *Foreign Affairs* (New York), Vol. 54, No. 4 (July 1976), pp. 745–62.

4. This is even true in some degree of what has been perhaps the best study of the intervention to date. See Peter Vanneman and Martin James, "The Soviet Intervention in Angola: Intentions and Implications," *Strategic Review* (Cambridge, Mass.), Vol. 4, No. 3 (Summer 1976), pp. 92–103. The only analysis thus far which argues that the Cubans acted more or less independently is William J. Durch, *The Cuban Military in Africa and the Middle East: From Algeria to Angola,* Professional Paper No. 201, Center for Naval Analyses, Arlington, Virginia, September 1977. Durch's study is very perceptive but focuses mainly on Cuban rather than Soviet decision-making.

5. On this point, see John A. Marcum's definitive study of the Angolan national liberation movement: *The Angolan Revolution,* Vol. 1 (Cambridge, Mass.: MIT Press, 1969), p. 28.

6. Michael T. Kaufman, "The Three Men Who Control Angola's Warring Factions," *The New York Times,* Dec. 28, 1975; and *The Daily Telegraph* (London), June 23, 1975.

7. See "Angola's National Forces," *International Affairs* (Moscow), No. 3, March 1963, pp. 116–17; and V. Midtsev and P. Yevsyukov, *Pravda* (Moscow), Mar. 19, 1962.

8. Marcum, *op.cit.,* pp. 69, 181–87.

9. For a detailed analysis of the complex problem of the national liberation movements in Angola, see Charles K. Ebinger, "External Intervention in Internal War: The Politics and Diplomacy of the Angolan Civil War," *Orbis* (Philadelphia), Vol. 20, No. 31 (Fall 1976), pp. 669–99.

10. *Pravda,* June 16, 1961.

11. John A. Marcum, *The Angolan Revolution,* Vol. 2 (Cambridge, Mass.: MIT Press, 1978), p. 171.

12. *Noveyshaya istoriya Afriki* [Modern history of Africa] (Moscow: Nauka, 1968), p. 500.

13. Marcum, *The Angolan Revolution,* Vol. 2, pp. 160–61.

14. Ye. Tarabrin, "Peking's Maneuvers in Africa," *New Times* (Moscow), No. 6, February 1972, p. 19; G. V. Astafev and A. M. Dubinskiy, eds., *Vneshnyaya politika i mezdunarodnyye otnosheniya kitayskoy narodnoy respubliki, II, 1963–1973* [Foreign policy and international relations of the Chinese People's Republic, II, 1963–1973] (Moscow: Mysl', 1974), p. 185.

15. See E. Bogush, *Maoism i politika raskola v natsional'nom osvoboditel'nom dvizhenii* [Maoism and splittist policies in the national liberation movement], Moscow: Mysl', 1969), pp. 112–13.

16. John A. Marcum, "Lessons of Angola," *Foreign Affairs,* Vol. 54, No. 3 (April 1976), p. 408.

17. See his address to the International Conference of Support to the Nations of the Portuguese Colonies, in Rome, June 27–29, 1970, as cited in V. G. Solodovnikov, *Problemy sovremennoy Afriki* [The problems of contemporary Africa] (Moscow: Nauka, 1973), p. 388. A similar statement appeared in *Pravda,* July 5, 1970. See also an interview with Neto, "Angola's Fight for Freedom," *New Times,* No. 5, January 1973, p. 17.

18. Marcum, *The Angolan Revolution,* Vol. 2, pp. 245–46.

19. Stockwell, *op. cit.,* pp. 66–67.

20. Interviews with Neto, *Le Monde* (Paris), Feb. 5, 1975, and with H. Carreira, Supreme Commander of the MPLA armed forces, in *Borba* (Belgrade), Jan. 3, 1975.

21. O. Ignatyev, "Angola: On the Threshold of Change," *New Times,* No. 42, November 1974, p. 14.

22. Legum, *loc. cit.,* p. 749.

23. William E. Schaufele, Jr., Assistant Secretary of State for African Affairs, "The African Dimension of the Angolan Conflict" (Washington, D.C.: U.S. State Department, Bureau of Public Affairs), Feb. 6, 1976, p. 2; Marcum, *The Angolan Revolution,* Vol. 2, p. 253.

24. Ebinger, *loc. cit.,* p. 688.

25. See, for example, Y. Gavrilov, "An Important Victory in the Struggle against Colonialism," *International Affairs* (Moscow), No. 10 (October 1974), p. 98.

26. See, for instance, Radio Moscow, Jan. 24, 1975.

27. Stockwell, *op. cit.,* p. 54.

28. Radio Moscow, Feb. 5, 1975; an interview with Dzasokhov in *O'Seculo* (Lisbon), Apr. 17, 1975.

29. Marcum, *The Angolan Revolution,* Vol. 2, p. 259.

30. Radio Luanda, Apr. 30, 1975; Radio Nairobi, June 11, 1975; *Die Welt* (Hamburg), Aug. 27, 1975; *Comercio* (Lisbon), Aug. 28, 1975; *The New York Times,* Sept. 25, 1975; M. Kaufman, *ibid.,* Nov. 24, 1975.

31. S. Vydrin, "Angola Greets Its Heroes," *New Times,* No. 10, March 1975, p. 8.

32. Interview with P. Jorge, *O'Seculo,* Apr. 12, 1975; Radio Luanda, May 7, 1975.

33. *The New York Times,* Jan. 12, 1976. The CIA estimates were similar—250 men by the summer of 1975. See Stockwell, *op. cit.,* p. 170. In August, another 200 infantry instructors reportedly joined the Cuban advisory group. See Marcum, *The Angolan Revolution,* Vol. 2, p. 273.

34. Reported by Radio Kinshasa, Jan. 1, 1976.

35. Marcum, *The Angolan Revolution,* Vol. 2, p. 258.

36. Michael T. Kaufman, "Suddenly, Angola," *The New York Times,* Jan. 4, 1976, p. 7.

37. Interview with General S. Cardoso, Portuguese High Commissioner of Angola, *Expresso* (Lisbon), May 17, 1975.

38. Interviews with N. Kabangu, a member of the FNLA's Political Bureau, Radio Luanda, July 26, 1975; with Savimbi, *O'Seculo*, Feb. 22, 1975; with Neto, *ibid.*, Apr. 23, 1975; and with MPLA official S. Mingas, *ibid.*, Apr. 29, 1975.

39. Schaufele, *op. cit.*, p. 2.

40. See, for example, the interview with Dzasokhov in *O'Seculo*, Apr. 17. 1975; V. Kudryavtsev, "Angola's a Heavy Burden," *Izvestiya* (Moscow), May 22, 1975; and Radio Moscow, June 27, 1975.

41. See Legum, *loc. cit.*, pp. 750–51.

42. Schaufele, *op. cit.*, p. 2, and Stockwell, *op. cit.*, p. 55.

43. Stockwell, *op. cit.*, p. 191.

44. Ebinger, *loc. cit.*, p. 689.

45. These rebuffs led to the MPLA's condemnation of the Chinese rulers in October 1975 for supporting the FNLA and UNITA against it. See Radio Luanda, Oct. 5, 1975, and an interview with Neto in *Afrique-Asie* (Paris), Oct. 20–Nov. 2, 1975.

46. Stockwell, *op. cit.*, pp. 185–86, and *The Washington Post*, Jan. 6, 1976.

47. Radio Moscow, Aug. 16, 1975; TASS, Aug. 23 and 25, 1975; O. Ignatyev, "The True Face of Angola's Enemies," *Pravda*, Sept. 9, 1975; B. Pilyatskin, "NCNA Covers Up the Traces," *Izvestiya*, Sept. 9, 1975.

48. TASS, Sept. 26, 1975; V. Sidenko, "Angola: Peoples against Reaction," *New Times*, No. 43, October 1975, pp. 14–15.

49. TASS, Nov. 18, 1975.

50. See reports on the South African involvement by TASS, Aug. 18 and 23, and Sept. 5 and 7, 1975; and by F. Tarasov, "Mercenaries Again," *Pravda*, Sept. 22, 1975.

51. The first public Soviet criticism of the FNLA and UNITA was that of S. Kulik of Radio Moscow, June 11, 1975. Subsequently, the criticism grew in intensity. See Radio Moscow, July 16 and 18, 1975; S. Kulik, "Threat to Angola's Freedom," *Pravda*, July 24, 1975; "Conspiracy against Angola," TASS, Aug. 4, 1975.

52. Agence France Presse (AFP), Aug. 22, 1975. See also an interview with K. Marques, UNITA Deputy Secretary General for Foreign Affairs, *Le Soleil* (Dakar), Oct. 4–5, 1975.

53. See an interview with MPLA leader L. Lára, Radio Lisbon, June 9, 1975.

54. For instance, the main target of Soviet attacks before August 20 was the FNLA. See, among others, B. Lesnov, "The Plot against Angola," *Izvestiya*, Aug. 5, 1975.

55. Stockwell, *op. cit.*, pp. 128–37, 161–64.

56. See *Pravda*, Aug. 18, 1975; TASS, Sept. 2, 1975; V. Yermakov, "Portugal and Angola's Hour of Trial," *New Times*, No. 37, Sept. 8, 1975, pp. 14–15.

57. See *Pravda*, April 24, 1975.

58. For their views, see *O'Seculo Illustrado* (Lisbon), May 3, 1975; *Diario*

de Noticias (Lisbon), Nov. 10, 1975; Radio Havana, July 24, 26, and 30, and Aug. 23, 1975; Radio Lisbon, July 39 and Aug. 23, 1975; *Expresso,* Aug. 23, 1975.

59. Radio Luanda, May 19, 1975; Radio Lisbon, June 3, 1975; and an interview with a Portuguese officer who served in Angola at that time.

60. AFP, April 13, 1975.

61. Radio Lisbon, Aug. 7, 1975. H. Carreira, Supreme Commander of the MPLA armed froces, also praised the MFA for its "correct policy" and "progressive political orientation." See *Rabotnichesko delo* (Sofia), Aug. 26, 1975.

62. Indeed, Soviet spokesmen argued that the cooperation of progressive forces "would give a guarantee of success" both in Portugal and in Angola. See, for example, Radio Moscow, May 14, 1975, and Alexander Ignatov, "Clouds over Luanda," *New Times,* No. 23, May 1975, pp. 12–13.

63. This was pointed out by M. Zenovich in "On the Road to Independence," *Pravda,* Feb. 26, 1975. For a similar comment, see Radio Moscow, Nov. 21, 1975. For a serious analysis of Angola's economic potential, see A. V. Pritvorov, "The Economics of Angola," *Narody Azii i Afriki* (Moscow), No. 3, March 1975, pp. 122–30.

64. On these efforts, see James M. McConnell and Bradford Dismukes, "Soviet Diplomacy of Force in the Third World," *Problems of Communism* (Washington, D.C.), January–February 1979, pp. 17–19.

65. On this drive, see George T. Yu, "The USSR and Africa: China's Impact," *ibid.,* January–February 1978, pp. 40–50.

66. "Threat to Angola's Freedom," TASS, July 22, 1975.

67. V. Sidenko, "The Intrigues of Angola's Enemies," *New Times,* No. 30, July 1975, pp. 14–15.

68. Radio Moscow, June 20 and 21, 1975.

69. D. Kraminov, "Washington–Moscow: A Skirmish at the Crossroads," *Za Rubezhom* (Moscow), June 13–19, 1975, p. 16.

70. For a discussion of covert U.S. military activities in Angola, see Stockwell, *op. cit.,* pp. 40–56 and 157–75. For Davis's version of decision-making regarding these activities, see his "The Angola Decision of 1975: A Personal Memoir," *Foreign Affairs,* Vol. 57, No. 1 (Fall 1978), pp. 109–24.

71. Vanneman and James, "The Soviet Intervention in Angola," p. 97; *idem,* "The Lessons of Angola: A Global Perspective on Communist Intervention in Southern Africa," in Robert Pearson, ed., *Sino-Soviet Intervention in Africa* (Washington, D.C.: Council on American Affairs, 1977), pp. 10–37.

72. In an interview in Mexico City in January 1975, Castro stated: "We must be realistic. Changes similar to those of the Cuban revolution are not within sight in the Latin American countries." Radio Buenos Aires, Jan. 10, 1975.

73. An interview with Castro by Simon Alley, *Afrique-Asie (Paris),* May 16–29, 1977, p. 19.

74. Castro's speech at the First Congress of the Cuban Communist Party, Radio Havana, Dec. 22, 1975.

75. In September 1975, he predicted that in the future "the prestige of our revolution will increase" and "we will be having more influence in the international revolutionary movement." Radio Havana, Sept. 29, 1975.

76. See the protocol of coordination of national plans signed between the two countries for the period 1976–80, as described by Radio Havana, Sept. 19, 1975, and *Pravda,* Sept. 20, 1975.

77. Schaufele, *op. cit.,* p. 3. Indeed, the first contingent of several hundred uniformed, regular Cuban soldiers arrived toward the end of September. See Radio Paris, Oct. 24, 1975.

78. TASS, Sept. 29, 1975. Emphasis added.

79. Radio Havana, Sept. 29, 1975.

80. *O'Seculo,* Oct. 20, 1975.

81. Stockwell, *op. cit.,* pp. 164–65.

82. For descriptions of the military operations in Angola and the critical situation of the MPLA before Nov. 11, see Ignatyev, *Secret Weapon in Africa,* pp. 155–74, and Stockwell, *op. cit.,* pp. 164–65.

83. Ignatyev, *Secret Weapon in Africa,* p. 166.

84. Stockwell, *op. cit.,* p. 216; McConnell and Dismukes, *loc. cit.,* p. 20.

85. Ignatyev, *Secret Weapon in Africa,* p. 164, and Stockwell, *op. cit.,* pp. 162–63.

86. *The New York Times,* Nov. 12, 1975.

87. Schaufele, *op. cit.,* p. 3.

88. AFP, Dec. 30, 1975, and Jan. 10, 1976.

89. Stockwell, *op. cit.,* pp. 216–32.

90. *Ibid.,* pp. 192–93, 202.

91. *Essence of Decision* (Boston: Little, Brown and Co., 1971).

5. The Theory and Practice of Marxism-Leninism in Mozambique and Ethiopia

1. Samora Machel, *Le processus de la révolution démocratique populaire au Mozambique. Textes du President du Frelimo, 1970–74* [The process of the democratic people's revolution in Mozambique. Texts of the president of Frelimo, 1970–74] (Paris: Editions l'Harmattan, 1977), p. 11.

2. *Ibid.,* pp. 18–98.

3. *Ibid.,* p. 50.

4. *Ibid.,* p. 51.

5. *Ibid.,* p. 77. The same theme is contained in numerous other papers of the pre-independence period. See, for example, "Liberation of Woman Is a Necessity of the Revolution, a Guarantee of Its Continuation, a Condition of Its Triumph," in S. Machel, *op. cit.,* pp. 159–84.

6. Ethiopia Ministry of Information, "*Ethiopia Tikdem*: The Origins and Future Direction of the Movement" [in English], mimeographed, Dec. 20, 1974.

7. For the text of his remarks, see *The Ethiopian Herald* (Addis Ababa), Apr. 21, 1976.

8. Statutes of FRELIMO, Ch. 1, Art. 3.

9. Extracts from the Report of the Standing Political Committee to the Fourth Session of the Central Committee of FRELIMO, presented by President Samora Machel, in Mozambique Information Agency, *Dossier, 4th Session of*

the Central Committee of Frelimo elected by the Third Congress (Maputo, Aug. 7–16, 1978), p. 4.

10. Samora Machel, *"Notre Tache pour 1979." Entrevue accordée par le President Samora Machel a la presse nationale à la fin de l'année 1978* [Our tasks for 1979. Interview granted to the national press by President Samora Machel at the end of 1978] (Maputo: Mozambique Information Agency, n.d.), pp. 11–12.

11. Report of the Standing Political Committee . . . , *loc. cit.,* p. 6.

12. President Samora Machel's closing speech, in *Dossier, 4th Session of the Central Committee of Frelimo . . . ,* p. 21.

13. Thesis Number Two, in "Theses: What Are They and What Are Their Objectives?" mimeographed (Maputo, n.d.). These theses were issued at the time of the Third Party Congress in 1977 to elaborate the party's ideology.

14. *"Notre Tache pour 1979"* . . . , p. 6.

15. *Ibid.,* p. 7.

16. See Thesis Number Four, in "Theses: What Are They and What Are Their Objectives?" Also, Mozambique Information Agency, *Bulletin* (Maputo), No. 9/10 (Congress Special Issue), pp. 10–12.

17. Sergio Vieira, "The New Man Is a Process; Speech to the Second Conference of the Ministry of Education and Culture, December 1977," mimeographed (Maputo, n.d.). The following quotations in the text come from this speech.

18. "Liberation of Woman Is a Necessity . . . ," p. 164.

19. For a general discussion of dynamizing groups, see Carole Collins, "Mozambique: Dynamizing the People," *Issues* (Waltham, Mass.), pp. 12–16.

20. *"Notre Tache pour 1979"* . . . , pp. 3–4.

21. See Collins, *loc. cit.,* p. 15.

22. Statutes of FRELIMO, Ch. 2, Art. 9.

23. Personal communication with officials in the National Commission for Communal Villages, June 1979. Much information on the communal villages is also found in *Tempo* (Maputo), No. 418, Oct. 8, 1978; No. 419, Oct. 15, 1978; No. 434, Jan. 28, 1979; and No. 435, Feb. 4, 1979.

24. For details on the elections, see Allan Isaacman, *A Luta Continua: Creating a New Society in Mozambique,* Southern African Pamphlet No. 1 (Binghamton, N.Y.: Ferdinand Brandel Center, State University of New York at Binghamton, n.d.), pp. 42–46.

25. *Ibid.,* p. 45.

26. *"Ethiopia Tikdem:* The Origins and Future Direction of the Movement." For more details on this period, see David and Marina Ottaway, *Ethiopia: Empire in Revolution* (New York: Africana Publishing Co., 1978), Ch. 5.

27. For an analysis of the debate, see Marina Ottaway, "Democracy and New Democracy: The Ideological Debate in the Ethiopian Revolution," *African Studies Review* (Waltham, Mass.), April 1978, pp. 19–31.

28. This was the formulation in Mengistu's speech on the "national democratic revolution," *The Ethiopian Herald,* Apr. 21, 1976.

29. The position of the opposition was expressed above all in a clandestine

publication called *Democracia,* which circulated in Addis Ababa during this period.

30. In the spring of 1978, according to diplomatic sources, the Cuban ambassador to Ethiopia tried to convince Mengistu to undertake discussions with a prominent member of the discredited MEISON, Negedde Gobeze, who had escaped from the country. Without Mengistu's clear permission, Negedde was brought back into the country during one of Mengistu's trips abroad. Upon his return, Mengistu reacted sharply to this attempt to force his hand. Negedde was sent out of the country again, and the Cuban ambassador was recalled.

31. See Ottaway and Ottaway, *op. cit.,* pp. 147 ff.

32. For details, see Collins, *loc. cit.,* p. 15.

33. *Le processus de la révolution démocratique populaire au Mozambique,* pp. 89–91.

34. *Ibid.,* p. 93.

35. FRELIMO Program in *Bulletin,* No. 9–10, p. 21.

36. The text of the law was reprinted in *Tempo,* No. 439, Mar. 4, 1979, pp. 25–33.

6. Cuba, the Soviet Union, and Africa

1. The surrogate thesis is elaborated in monographs published by the Institute for the Study of Conflict (London). See David Rees, *Soviet Strategic Penetration of Africa,* Conflict Studies, No. 77 (November 1977), pp. 1–21; and especially Brian Crozier, *The Surrogate Forces of the Soviet Union,* Conflict Studies, No. 92 (February 1978), pp. 1–20. The same thesis is implicit in an earlier analysis by Peter Vanneman and Martin James, "The Soviet Intervention in Angola: Intentions and Implications," *Strategic Review* (Cambridge, Mass.), Summer 1976, pp. 92–103.

2. See, in particular, the testimony by Lourdes Casal, in *Hearings before the Subcommittee on Inter-American Affairs of the Committee on International Relations, House of Representatives* (hereafter cited as *Hearings*), 95th Cong., 2nd sess., March 14 and 15; April 5 and 12, 1978, pp. 80–85. See also Nelson Valdes, "Revolutionary Solidarity in Angola," in Cole Blasier and Carmelo Mesa-Lago, eds., *Cuba in the World* (Pittsburgh: University of Pittsburgh Press, 1979), pp. 87–117. For Havana's view on Cuban internationalism, see the articles, statements, and speeches published in *Granma,* the official organ of the Communist Party of Cuba.

3. For a comprehensive examination of Cuba's overseas military missions and combat operations prior to Angola, see William J. Durch, *The Cuban Military in Africa and the Middle East: From Algeria to Angola,* Professional Paper No. 201 (Arlington, Va.: Center for Naval Analyses, September 1977), pp. 25–33. For a more up-to-date analysis, see Jorge I. Domínguez, "The Armed Forces and Foreign Relations," in Blasier and Mesa-Lago, *op. cit.,* pp. 53–86.

4. See Edward Gonzalez, "Complexities of Cuban Foreign Policy," *Problems of Communism* (Washington, D.C.), November–December 1977, pp. 1–15; and *idem,* "Institutionalization, Political Elites, and Foreign Policies,"

in Blasier and Mesa-Lago, *op.cit.,* pp. 3–36. A modified version of the paladin thesis is presented by Roger W. Fontaine in his "Cuban Strategy in Africa: The Long Road to Ambition," *Strategic Review,* Summer 1978, pp. 18–27.

5. According to Rees, for example, the USSR by the 1970s had acquired sufficient mobility to actively promote its strategic interests in Africa, as evidenced by the massive Soviet intervention in Angola. The objective of this Soviet "strategic penetration" of Southern Africa, he argues, is to "create a cluster of Marxist client States fully responsive to Moscow's strategic dictates for further struggle against the West." The stakes in this struggle over Africa are not just political but involve Soviet denial of strategic resources and sea routes to the West. Rees, *op. cit.,* pp. 2–5.

6. Casal thus suggests that in its backing of Cuba, "the Soviet Union has become much more 'ideological,' much more willing to commit itself in practice to . . . proletarian internationalist adventures, if you want to call them that. . . ." *Hearings,* p. 102.

7. See, in particular, Gonzalez, "Institutionalization, Political Elites, and Foreign Policies," *loc. cit.,* pp. 23–26.

8. This position is plainly stated, although rather baldly, by Crozier. According to him, Moscow "relies increasingly on surrogates to achieve its objectives. For instance, by sending a Cuban expeditionary force to Angola instead of a Soviet one the USSR avoided a confrontation with the West and minimized any risk that independent African countries would feel threatened." In short, it was a "Soviet decision to send Cuban troops to Angola" in the furtherance of Soviet objectives, with Castro becoming "an enthusiastic accomplice in Soviet designs." Crozier, *op. cit.,* p. 1.

9. During his visit to Somalia in March 1977, for example, Castro insisted that the USSR remains the stalwart champion of the liberation movement: "The Soviet people is the firmest and most loyal ally of those of us who struggle for independence and revolution, the firmest and most loyal ally of Somalia and Cuba and of other independent countries." *Granma Weekly Review,* Mar. 27, 1977, p. 2. Henceforth, all references to *Granma* are to the Weekly Review Edition.

10. See Gonzalez, "Complexities of Cuban Foreign Policy," *loc. cit.,* pp. 10–12; and "Institutionalization, Political Elites, and Foreign Policies," *loc. cit.,* pp. 23–26, and 29–33.

11. See Durch, *op. cit.,* pp. 14–30, for a detailed discussion of Cuba's military activities in these countries prior to Angola.

12. Colin Legum has noted the contrast in African receptivity to Soviet and Cuban military missions. See his "The USSR and Africa: The African Environment," *Problems of Communism,* January–February 1978, p. 10.

13. Durch, *op. cit.,* pp. 22–23; and Valdés, *loc. cit.,* p. 93.

14. With respect to the last point, the relatively high regard that Cuba's foreign aid programs in Africa enjoyed prior to Angola was due in large measure to the fact that Havana dispatched personnel rather than money or materials to the continent. See for example, Jorge I. Domínguez, "Cuban Foreign Policy," *Foreign Affairs* Fall 1978, p. 95.

15. See, in particular, Rees, *op.cit.*, pp. 1–13; and Crozier, *op.cit.*, pp. 1–18. Both of these studies detail the subversive techniques and the political, economic, and military linkages employed by the Soviets to extend their influence in Africa.

16. In recognizing Southern Africa's abundance of raw materials, Soviet writers usually stress their importance for the Western economies but remain mute as to their potential significance for the USSR and Eastern Europe. See V. Baryshnikov, "Raw Material Resources of Africa," *International Affairs* (Moscow), December 1974, pp. 135–36. On the other hand, Moscow's post-1970 emphasis upon a new international division of labor between the more advanced socialist bloc and the developing countries does indicate that a number of African countries would in fact become important suppliers of raw materials to the USSR. See S. Skachkov, "Economic Cooperation of the Soviet Union and the Developing Countries," *Kommunist* (Moscow), No. 12, December 1973.

17. During the early 1970s, the Soviets obtained virtually exclusive use of seven airfields as well as servicing facilities in four harbors in Egypt, and they also gained landing privileges for their reconnaissance planes and permission to construct a naval complex at Berbera, on the Gulf of Aden, in Somalia. However, they found these major strategic gains erased in 1976 and 1977, respectively, as a result of their disputes with Egypt and Somalia. The USSR did, nonetheless, retain access to at least some air facilities in Guinea; moreover, in recent years it has signed treaties with Angola (1976), Mozambique (1977), and Ethiopia (1978) calling for unspecified cooperation in the military sphere. On Soviet strategic aims and capabilities, see Vanneman and James, *loc. cit.;* and U.S. House of Representatives, Committee on International Relations, *The Soviet Union and the Third World: A Watershed in Great Power Policy?* (Washington, D.C.: U.S. Government Printing Office, 1977), Supplement.

18. Richard Lowenthal, "Soviet 'Counterimperialism,'" *Problems of Communism,* November–December 1976, pp. 52–63.

19. For the contextual background as well as elaboration of this thesis, see Legum, *loc. cit.*, pp. 1–19; and especially David E. Albright, "The USSR and Africa: Soviet Policy," in *ibid.*, pp. 20–39. The latter provides a useful summary-analysis of past and present Soviet policy. For earlier studies that analyze pre-1973 Soviet policy in greater detail but which support the above thesis, see Morton Schwartz, "The USSR and Leftist Regimes in Less-Developed Countries," *Survey* (London), Spring 1973, pp. 207–44; Roger E. Kanet, "Soviet Attitudes toward Developing Nations Since Stalin," in Roger E. Kanet, ed., *The Soviet Union and the Developing Nations* (Baltimore: Johns Hopkins University Press, 1974), pp. 27–50; and Arthur Jay Klinghoffer, "The Soviet Union and Africa," in *ibid.*, pp. 51–77.

20. For the changes in Soviet policy after the mid-1960s, see Kanet, *loc. cit.*, pp. 35–44; and Klinghoffer, *loc. cit.*, pp. 58–64.

21. See Colin Legum, "Africa's Contending Revolutionaries," *Problems of Communism,* March–April 1972, pp. 2–15.

22. The structural constraints imposed by Africa's underdevelopment were

recognized by Soviet observers in both the pre- and post-Angolan periods. See, for example, Vladimir Lee, "The National Liberation Movement Today," *International Affairs* (Moscow), December 1969, pp. 42–46; and V. Solodovnikov, "Elimination of the Colonial System, An Expression of the General Crisis of Capitalism," *ibid.*, August 1976, p. 24. In Communist eyes, the "socialist orientation" of the "revolutionary democrats" is further restrained by "objective" and "subjective" factors at work domestically: these are the petty-bourgeois constituency of the radical leaders, which prevents them from altering production relations along more socialistic lines, and the distrust these leaders have toward the masses, which prevents them from mobilizing the populace for revolutionary change. See the discussion held by Soviet and Afro-Asian representatives on "Revolutionary Democrats and the Socialist Orientation," *World Marxist Review* (Toronto), November 1975, pp. 32–48, but esp. pp. 41–42.

23. Gerald J. Bender, "Kissinger in Angola: Anatomy of Failure," in René Lemarchand, ed., *American Policy in Southern Africa: The Stakes and the Stance* (Washington, D.C.: University Press of America, 1978), pp. 69 and 76; and esp. Charles K. Ebinger, "External Intervention in Internal War: The Politics and Diplomacy of the Angolan Civil War," *Orbis* (Philadelphia), Fall 1976, pp. 687–89. For the definitive study of the Angolan situation, see John A. Marcum, *The Angolan Revolution, Vol. 2: Exile Politics and Guerrilla Warfare* (Cambridge, Mass.: MIT Press, 1978).

24. See Bender, *loc. cit.*, pp. 71–87; and Ebinger, *loc. cit.*, pp. 669–71, and 686–91, for the impact of these developments within Angola itself. For an analysis of Soviet perspectives and activities, see Jiri Valenta, "The Soviet-Cuban Intervention in Angola, 1975," *Studies in Comparative Communism* (Los Angeles), Spring/Summer 1978, pp. 3–33.

25. For a detailed analysis of the impact of the Sino–Soviet rivalry on the Angolan liberation movements, see Ebinger, *loc. cit.*, pp. 687–92.

26. This view is elaborated in Colin Legum, "The Soviet Union, China and the West in Southern Africa," *Foreign Affairs*, July 1976, pp. 746–62.

27. On the changing military mission and capabilities of the FAR as they affected the Angolan intervention, see my "Complexities of Cuban Foreign Policy," pp. 9–10; and Jorge I. Domínguez, *Cuba: Order and Revolution* (Cambridge, Mass.: Harvard University Press, Belknap Press, 1978), pp. 345–61.

28. See Ebinger, *loc. cit.*, pp. 689–92; and Legum, "The Soviet Union, China and the West in Southern Africa," pp. 750–53.

29. On the Cuban military buildup in Angola, see Gonzalez, "Complexities of Cuban Foreign Policy," pp. 10–11; Bender, *loc. cit.*, pp. 89–96; and Durch, *op. cit.*, pp. 39–51. On the motivating factors for and supporting role of the Soviets during the 1975 intervention, see the detailed analysis by Valenta, *loc. cit.*, pp. 7–33.

30. See *ibid.*, p. 30. For an opposing argument, see Bender, *loc. cit.*, pp. 96–108.

31. See Albright, *loc. cit.*, pp. 33–34.

32. See Legum, "The Soviet Union, China and the West in Southern Af-

rica," pp. 753–59. For additional information, see also Rees, *op. cit.*, pp. 9–14.

33. For a detailed analysis of the Soviet-Cuban involvement in Ethiopia, see David E. Albright, "The Horn of Africa and the Arab–Israeli Conflict," in Robert O. Freedman, ed., *World Politics and the Arab–Israeli Conflict* (Elmsford, N.Y.: Pergamon Press, 1979), pp. 147–91.

34. On the dilemma facing Moscow in choosing between Somalia and Ethiopia, see *ibid.*, pp. 160–63, 165–67; and the special reports by F. Stephen Larrabee, "Somalia and Moscow's Problems on the Horn of Africa," *Radio Liberty Research* (Munich), RL 158/77, July 5, 1977, pp. 1–12; and "Somali-Soviet Relations in the Light of Siad Barre's Visit to Moscow," *Radio Liberty Research*, RL 209/66, Sept. 2, 1977, pp. 1–14.

35. Albright, "The USSR and Africa: Soviet Policy," p. 28.

36. This active form of leverage is distinct from the *passive* leverage that Cuba enjoys owing to its "special relationship" with the USSR. Cuba derived passive leverage, for instance, once Moscow found that it had to commit itself to Fidel Castro's regime after 1960 because of the increasing Soviet political, ideological, strategic, and economic stake in Cuba. In contrast, since the mid-1970s the Castro regime exercises *active* leverage, whereby it obtains new, favorable treatment from the USSR because of Cuba's growing importance in Africa and in the Third World in general.

37. On the economic front, for instance, Moscow concluded a five-year economic and technical agreement with Havana covering the 1976–80 period. Signed on April 14, 1976, the agreement provides for a 250 percent rise in total Soviet-Cuban trade from the level of the previous five years; it also calls for Soviet construction of a nuclear power plant and steel mill in Cuba, and for the indexing of Soviet crude oil prices to Cuban sugar prices (*Granma*, Apr. 25. 1976, p. 2). The reequipment of the FAR with new weaponry will be discussed later in another context.

38. On Castro's 1977 journey to Algeria, Libya, South Yemen, Somalia, Ethiopia, Tanzania, Mozambique, and Angola, see the report in *Africa* (London), No. 69, May 1977, pp. 84–85. For details of the visits made by African delegations, consult the weekly editions of *Granma;* a convenient listing is contained in U.S. Central Intelligence Agency, National Foreign Assessment Center, *Cuban Chronology—A Reference Aid*, RP 78–10073 (Washington, D.C., March 1978). On the expanded role of Cuban military advisers in the post-1975 period and the new buildup of Cuban combat forces in Angola and Ethiopia, see the testimony of Lt. Col. John A. Fesmire, Cuban analyst, Defense Intelligence Agency, in *Hearings*, p. 11; Domínguez, *op. cit.*, pp. 93–100, *passim;* and especially the semimonthly issues of *African Confidential* (London).

39. For further details on the joint Cuban and Soviet involvement in Ethiopia, consult *ibid.*, March 3, 1978, pp. 1–4, and March 31, 1978, pp. 5–6; and Albright, "The Horn of Africa and the Arab–Israeli Conflict," pp. 166–

40. According to U.S. government sources, Soviet trade subsidies for the Cuban economy—composed principally of preferential prices for Soviet purchases of Cuban sugar and nickel and for Soviet petroleum sold to Cuba—are

expected to rise to three-and-a-half times their 1975 level by the end of 1978. It is estimated that the Soviets are now underwriting the Cuban economy at a rate of more than $2.5 billion a year, as compared to an average annual rate of around $550 million in the early 1970s. In 1978, moreover, the Soviets committed themselves to buy Cuban sugar at a preferential price of around 40 cents a pound, as against their earlier preferential price of 31 cents and the current world market price of 8–11 cents. The increased price that the Soviets will pay for Cuban sugar will be partially offset by the higher price that they will charge the Cubans for Soviet petroleum—$8.50 a barrel, rather than $7.25—but the new preferential price on petroleum is no greater than the price charged Eastern Europe. For additional data and analysis, see the quite comprehensive and informed staff paper prepared by Lawrence H. Theriot, *Cuban Foreign Trade: A Current Assessment* (Washington, D.C.: U.S. Department of Commerce, Office of East-West Policy and Planning, Industry and Trade Administration, 1978).

41. For an account of the conspiracy, based in part on conversations with Angolan leaders, see Gerald J. Bender, "Angola, The Cubans, and American Anxieties," *Foreign Policy* (New York), Summer 1978, pp. 23–26.

42. See Bender, "Kissinger in Angola: Anatomy of Failure," pp. 69 and 78, and Ebinger, *loc. cit.*, pp. 687–89, on the anti-Neto actions of the Soviets in the pre-1975 period.

43. See Albright, "The Horn of Africa and the Arab–Israeli Conflict," pp. 168, 187.

44. See *The Observer* (London), Feb. 26, 1978.

45. Castro declared that Ethiopia "needs internal peace," and that Cuba therefore supported a "peaceful and just solution" to the Eritrean problem. *Granma*, May 7, 1978, p. 2. The moderate tone of the Cuban president's speech was in marked contrast to Mengistu's harsh statements on the same podium. See *ibid.*, pp. 3–5.

46. On the shifts in the Soviet stance, and the various factors influencing Soviet policy, see Albright, "The Horn of Africa and the Arab–Israeli Conflict," pp. 168, 187.

47. Between January 1975 and December 1977, Rodríguez was the most frequent Cuban visitor to Moscow, making a total of 12 trips. But most of his visits were for economic consultations, and he met with Brezhnev only once and then in the company of Raúl Castro, Minister of the Revolutionary Armed Forces. During the same period, Raúl was the second most frequent visitor, with four trips. Moreover, during his stays he met with Brezhnev three times and consulted with Soviet military leaders. Fidel paid two visits to Moscow and met with Brezhnev on both occasions. Data compiled from U.S. Central Intelligence Agency, National Foreign Assessment Center, *Cuban Chronology—A Reference Aid*, pp. 79–87.

48. At the conclusion of his visit to Tanzania on Mar. 21, 1977, for example, he declared that "we will not make any concessions on matters of principles in order to improve relations with the United States." (*Granma*, Mar. 27, 1977, p.1.) In a lengthy press interview with exile-Cuban and U.S. journalists a year and a half later, he reaffirmed this position with specific regard to Cuban military activities in Africa. (*Ibid.*, Sept. 17, 1978, p. 6.)

49. At the same time, Castro cannot overplay his hand if he is to minimize or deflect charges from conservative and anti-Communist governments within the Third World that Cuba is acting as a surrogate of the Soviet Union in Africa. Although the Belgrade meeting of nonaligned countries in the mid-summer of 1978 produced criticism that Cuba's expanding presence in Africa—as an external power in its own right—posed a threat to African states, such criticism did not upset the plans to hold the Sixth Conference of Nonaligned States in Havana the following autumn. For Cuba's rebuttal, see the speech by Foreign Minister Isidoro Malmierca, *Granma,* Aug. 13, 1978, p. 9.

50. *Los Angeles Times,* Apr. 5, 1977, p. 5.

51. For the new nomenclature of ranks, see *Granma,* Dec. 5, 1976, p. 12. See also Domínguez, *Cuba: Order and Revolution,* pp. 350–53, for a more extensive analysis.

52. On recent Soviet military assistance to Cuba, see the testimony of Fesmire, in *Hearings,* pp. 4–9, 14. See also Domínguez, "The Armed Forces and Foreign Policy," pp. 54–58.

53. According to information supplied to the author by Wayne S. Smith, Director of Cuban Affairs, Department of State, the MIG-23s arrived in Cuba at least as early as the spring of 1978, with assembly beginning in the late spring. The exact number of MIG-23s that were on the island as of February 1979 was unknown, but U.S. intelligence reports indicated that the MIG-23s then in Cuba were not designed for nuclear missions.

54. See Fesmire, *loc. cit.,* p. 14.

55. The Angolan figure is taken from Domínguez, "Cuban Foreign Policy," p. 94; and the overall African figure from Fesmire, *loc. cit.,* p. 11.

56. The PCC had less than 50,000 members and aspirant members at its founding in 1965 and remained a weak, ineffectual apparatus throughout the remainder of the 1960s. In fact, it was the FAR, rather than the party, that most resembled a "sovereign institution" at the time. The FAR could claim exclusive title to revolutionary legitimacy as the descendent of the original Rebel Army that overthrew Batista; it provided much of the leadership within the upper echelons of the government and party during the 1960s; and it assumed a pivotol socioeconomic role, including a managerial one in the crucial 1970 harvest. Only in the 1970s did the PCC begin to gather strength, with its membership (including aspirants) rising to 202,802 by fall of 1975 and with its First Party Congress finally taking place in December 1975—more than a decade after the party's establishment. For a more detailed analysis, see Edward Gonzalez, "Castro and Cuba's New Orthodoxy," *Problems of Communism,* January–February 1976, pp. 1–19.

57. On various aspects of the Cuban-Soviet military relationship, see Domínguez, "The Armed Forces and Foreign Relations," pp. 54–58 and 73–77. For a listing of the various visits by Cuban and Soviet military delegations, and other related visits, during the three-year period commencing January 1975 and ending December 1977, see U.S. Central Intelligence Agency, National Foreign Assessment Center, *Cuban Chronology—A Reference Aid,* pp. 79–87.

58. It should be mentioned here, however, that the Soviet press has given only passing mention to Cuba's military and political impact in Africa. This

state of affairs may reflect big-power chauvinism as well as sensitivity about the Soviet Union's more limited role. See, for example, Valenta, *loc. cit.*, p. 32.

59. Joan Barth Urban, "Contemporary Soviet Perspectives on Revolution in the West," *Orbis*, Winter 1976, pp. 1359–402. Zarodov gained sudden notoriety when he was received by Brezhnev on Sept. 17, 1975, after publication of one of his articles by *Pravda* on Aug. 6. For Zarodov's militant viewpoint, see his report on a theoretical conference, "Alliance of World Socialism and the National-Liberation Movement," *World Marxist Review*, October 1974, pp. 61–73.

60. Suggestive of heightened Soviet interest in Africa as a theater for renewed revolutionary advances are the articles on recent African developments published by the Soviet journal *International Affairs*. In particular, see V. Solodovnikov and N. Gavrilov, "African Tendencies of Non-Capitalist Development," *International Affairs*, March 1976, pp. 31–40; K. Uralov, "Angola: The Triumph of the Right Cause," *ibid.*, May 1976, pp. 51–57; Anatoly Gromyko, "The October Revolution and Africa's Destiny," *ibid.*, September 1977, pp. 95–104; Anatoly Gromyko, "Neo-Colonialism's Manoeuvres in Southern Africa," *ibid.*, December 1977, pp. 96–103; and V. Kudryavtsev, "Africa Fights for Its Future," *ibid.*, May 1978, pp. 31–39. In the aftermath of Angola, *International Affairs* devoted a greater number of articles to Africa: 12 in 1975, 14 in 1976, 19 in 1977, and 16 in 1978.

61. For an analysis of the treaty and its various ramifications, see F. Stephen Larrabee, "Moscow Signs Friendship Treaty with Angola," *Radio Liberty Research*, RL 436/76, Oct. 13, 1976, pp. 1–2.

62. This observation is made by John R. Thomas, "Soviet Foreign Policy and the Military," *Survey*, Summer 1971, p. 151.

63. There is a growing sense among Soviet observers, for instance, that external assistance or intervention by the USSR, Cuba, and other socialist countries—usually listed in that order—can have a decisive impact on both the orientation and stability of the new African regimes. See Solodovnikov and Gavrilov, *loc. cit.*, pp. 34–38; Uralov, *loc. cit.*, p. 53; Gromyko, "The October Revolution and Africa's Destiny," pp. 98–101; Kudryavtsev, *loc. cit.*, p. 31; and G. Kim, "World Socialism and Present-Day National Liberation Revolutions," *International Affairs*, August 1977, pp. 67–77. See also the emphasis upon the need for joint actions by socialist countries for the effective promotion of "internationalism," in Boris Ponomaryov, "International Significance of the 25th CPSU Congress," *World Marxist Review*, May 1976, pp. 12–16.

64. For a Soviet assessment of these factors, see Victor Tyagunenko, "Trends, Motive Forces of National-Liberation Revolution," *ibid.*, June 1976, pp. 119–26. See also the discussion by Soviet and Afro-Asian representatives, "Revolutionary Democrats and the Socialist Orientation," *loc. cit.*, pp. 32–48.

65. The suddenness and magnitude of the massive Soviet airlift to Ethiopia that began in late 1977 are in themselves evidence of both the Soviet Union's new global capabilities *and* its willingness to commit itself in Third World

arenas. Still, the Soviet leadership is likely to move with some caution, and to weigh a number of factors, before undertaking major overseas commitments. See Thomas Hammond, "Moscow and Communist Takeovers," *Problems of Communism,* January–February 1976, pp. 48–67.

66. Solodovnikov and Gavrilov, *loc. cit.,* p. 33.

67. *Ibid.,* pp. 33–34.

68. Soviet commentators are understandably cautious regarding the transition of revolutionary democracies to socialist status, but some seem to hint at the possibility on grounds of the new correlation of forces in the world. Asserting that the world balance of forces favors socialism, for instance, Solodovnikov and Gavrilov assert that revolutionary democrats can adopt policies that go beyond reforms and that instead promote "the growth of socialist elements in the economy and society." Moreover, increased contacts and joint actions with the socialist states, they maintain, can heighten the influence of "scientific socialism" on these leaders, who have yet to adopt it as a "coherent doctrine." *Ibid.* Another Soviet writer stresses that the world socialist system is "a key economic, military and political factor" in assuring not only the success of national-liberation revolutions but also the consolidation of power by the new regimes and their deepening of the revolutionary process. See Kim, *loc. cit.,* p. 71.

69. Bender, for example, has described the highly favorable impact that Cuban technicians have made on the Angolans because of close social relations. The Soviets, by contrast, are unpopular, for they have been unable to assimilate and remain patronizing and impatient toward Angolans. See Bender, "Angola, the Cubans, and American Anxieties," pp. 9–11.

70. See Valenta, *loc. cit.,* pp. 21–22; and F. Stephen Larrabee, "Fresh Nuances in Soviet Policy towards Angola," *Radio Liberty Broadcast,* RL 70/76, Feb. 6, 1976, pp. 1–2.

71. On the Cuban economy and Cuba's trade dependency, see Carmelo Mesa-Lago, "The Economy and International Economic Relations," in Blasier and Mesa-Lago, *op. cit.,* pp. 169–98; and Theriot, *loc. cit.* The 1976 GNP figure is calculated on the basis of data presented in Table I of Theriot's study.

72. According to an extensive report by David Lamb, President Neto has become "keenly disappointed with the efficiency and expertise of his civilian Cuban advisers." Senior Cuban advisers have been removed from government ministries, Cuban medical personnel have been roundly criticized for their limited knowledge, and Cuban technicians have proved incapable of managing either the oil fields or the sugar refineries. As a result, the Neto regime has been turning to the West for technical help, even while it continues to rely on the Cuban military for its security. See "Angola Moving to End Isolation from West and Dependency on Cubans," *Los Angeles Times,* Dec. 3, 1978, pp. 6–7.

73. See Fesmire, *loc. cit.,* pp. 4, 11; and Domínguez, "Cuban Foreign Policy," p. 94.

74. See Domínguez, *Cuba: Order and Revolution,* pp. 354–56, for an analysis of these problems.

75. At the end of 1977, for example, Castro spoke of a "new field for exports" for Cuba which would entail sending brigades of construction workers, doctors, engineers, technicians, and other trained personnel on "internationalist missions." See *Granma,* Jan. 15, 1978, p. 2. This speech, along with a previous one in *ibid.,* Jan. 1, 1978, pp. 2–4, contains valuable demographic data.

76. Regarding the new commitment of civilian personnel to Angola, Cuban Vice-President Ramiro Valdés disclosed at the end of 1978 that Cuba would raise the number of Cuban technicians, specialists, and political advisers working in Angola to 10,700 in 1979. *Latin American Political Report* (London), Jan. 5, 1979, p. 3.

77. Conceivably, Cuba could station perhaps 50,000 or more combat personnel in Africa and the Middle East without jeopardizing the island's security or over-taxing the economy. In any case, as of mid-March 1979, Western reports estimated that there were 300 to 500 Cuban advisers working with their Soviet and East European counterparts in Marxist-ruled South Yemen. On Feb. 23, 1979, the latter became engaged in a border war with Yemen, which is backed by Saudi Arabia and the United States. (*Los Angeles Times,* Mar. 13, 1979, pp. 1, 16.) Although the two sides have held talks to try to resolve their disagreements, sporadic fighting still continues as of mid-1979. Meanwhile, it appears that Cuban combat troops may have to remain in considerable number in both Angola and Ethiopia for some time to come. In Angola, the continuation of anti-MPLA guerrilla operations by UNITA, coupled with recent incursions by both Rhodesian and South African forces, have prevented Luanda from consolidating its hold on southern Angola in particular. Moreover, the MPLA forces still lack the military proficiency to guarantee the survival of the Neto regime, which thus remains dependent on the presence of Cuban troops. (On the Rhodesian and South African raids into Angola, see *ibid.,* Mar. 7, 1979, p. 4.) In Ethiopia, the Mengistu forces by late 1978 were successfully prosecuting the war against the Eritrean rebels without direct Cuban involvement save for advisers and logistical support (see *ibid.,* Nov. 29, 1978, p. 14). But in the Ogaden, Somali guerrillas were again carrying on a fierce war against the Ethiopians; by March 1979, they reportedly controlled the bulk of the territory, pinning down the Ethiopian troops and their Cuban support detachments in eight major towns in the Ogaden. See *ibid.,* Mar. 7, 1979, p. 16.

7. *Sino–Soviet Rivalry in Africa*

1. U.S. Central Intelligence Agency, *Communist Aid to the Less Developed Countries of the Free World, 1977,* ER 78–10478U (Washington, D.C., November 1978).

2. A loan of $401 million was extended to Tanzania and Zambia in 1970. In 1976, the Chinese announced that they were providing an additional $55 million or so as an outright grant to cover cost overruns. U.S. Central Intelligence Agency, *Communist Aid to the Less Developed Countries of the Free World, 1976,* ER 77–10296 (Washington, D.C., August 1978).

3. The following discussion is based on data derived from *The International Transfer of Conventional Arms, A Report to the Congress from the U.S. Arms Control and Disarmament Agency, April 12, 1974* (Washington, D.C.: U.S. Government Printing Office, 1974), and the annual reports of the U.S. Arms Control and Disarmament Agency on world military expenditures and arms transfers, published since 1975. It should be noted that there are a couple of problems with these data which make it quite difficult to draw meaningful conclusions from them. First, the Agency provides only aggregate figures. For example, it gives the dollar value of total Soviet or Chinese arms transfers to a particular African country during a given period (say 1967–76), but it does not present breakdowns by year. Second, the Agency does not supply information with a constant base year from report to report, so one cannot readily assess changes in arms transfers. The documents issued through 1978, for instance, cover the following periods: 1961–71, 1963–73, 1965–74, 1966–75, and 1967–76. Nonetheless, it is possible to arrive at some judgments about general patterns and trends by putting information from the various reports together.

4. African Institute, USSR Academy of Sciences, *Russia and Africa* (Moscow: Nauka, 1966), pp. 7–15.

5. See O. B. Borisov and B. T. Koloskov, *Sino-Soviet Relations, 1945–1973: A Brief History* (Moscow: Progress Publishers, 1975), esp. p. 12.

6. For a Soviet account of China's policy toward Africa, see G. U. Astafyev and A. M. Dubinsky, eds., *From Anti-Imperialism to Anti-Socialism: The Evolution of Peking's Foreign Policy* (Moscow: Progress Publishers, 1974), pp. 112–24. Unless otherwise noted, the following discussion of China's African policy as seen through Soviet eyes is taken from this source.

7. O. B. Borisov and B. T. Koloskov, "Peking's Foreign Policy After the 10th Congress of the CPC," *International Affairs* (Moscow), July 1974, pp. 32–44.

8. New China News Agency (Peking), "Soviet Claws Stretching to African Continent," July 3, 1977.

9. *Ibid.*, "Soviet Expansion to Africa Doomed to Failure," May 1, 1977.

10. *Ibid.*, "Soviet Revisionists Stir Up Civil War in Angola," July 26, 1975.

11. *Ibid.*, "Intensified Soviet–U.S. Rivalry over Southern Africa," Sept. 23, 1976.

12. "Exposure of the Soviet Revisionists' Colonial Expansionism," *Jenmin Jih-pao* (Peking), Feb. 2, 1976.

13. New China News Agency, "Tempestuous Storm Sweeps African Continent," Dec. 27, 1976.

14. "Exposure of the Soviet Revisionists' Colonial Expansionism," *loc. cit.*

15. New China News Agency, "Chinese Representative Denounces Soviet South African Intervention in Angola at U.N.," Mar. 26, 1976.

16. *Ibid.*, "Varied Theme for Invariable Objective," Oct. 28, 1976.

17. *Ibid.*

18. *Ibid.*, "Look at Its Past, and You Can Tell Its Present," Dec. 9, 1975.

19. "Varied Theme for Invariable Objective," *loc. cit.*

20. "A Chapter on African People's Anti-Imperialism," *Jen-min Jih-pao,* Dec. 18, 1965.

21. "Varied Theme for Invariable Objective," *loc. cit.*

22. "Look at Its Past, and You Can Tell Its Present," *loc. cit.*

23. "Tempestuous Storm Sweeps African Continent," *loc. cit.*

24. "Soviet Claws Stretching to African Continent," *loc. cit.*

25. New China News Agency, "Brezhnev's 'Revolutionary Conscience' Is Ambition for Aggression and Expansion," Mar. 21, 1976.

26. *Ibid.*

27. "What Are the Criminal Objectives of the Soviet Revisionists' Intervention in Angola?" *Jen-min Jih-pao,* Dec. 7, 1975.

28. "Exposure of Soviet Revisionists' Colonial Expansionism," *loc. cit.*

29. "Soviet Expansion to Africa Doomed to Failure," *loc. cit.*

30. "Look At Its Past, and You Can Tell Its Present," *loc. cit.* The Chinese, interestingly, did not always refer to the three Angolan liberation organizations by name. They were the MPLA, the National Front for the Liberation of Angola (*Frente Nacional de Libertação de Angola*—FNLA), and the National Union for the Total Independence of Angola (*União Nacional pro Independencia Total de Angola*—UNITA). The Soviet Union backed the MPLA, while the Chinese supported the FNLA.

31. New China News Agency, "Africa Will Never Allow the Soviet Union's Outrageous Interference," Nov. 7, 1975.

32. *Ibid.,* "Clumsy Soviet Tactics in Angola," Dec. 31, 1975.

33. "Exposure of Soviet Revisionists' Colonial Expansionism," *loc. cit.*

34. "Brezhnev's 'Revolutionary Conscience' Is Ambition for Aggression and Expansion," *loc. cit.*

35. "Chinese Representative Denounces Soviet South African Intervention in Angola at U.N.," *loc. cit.*

36. New China News Agency, "New Noose around Neck of New Tsars," Feb. 27, 1976.

37. *Ibid.,* "New Tsars' Major Step in Expansion—A Commentary on the Zairian Situation," Mar. 20, 1977.

38. *Ibid.,* "New Soviet-Cuban Attack on Zaire," May 18, 1978.

39. *Ibid.*

40. "Strongly Condemn the Invasion of Zaire by the Soviet-Cuban Hired Mercenaries," *Jen-min Jih-pao,* May 19, 1978.

41. Tai Shan-hung, "The Arsonist in the Horn of Africa," *ibid.,* Feb. 13, 1978.

42. *Ibid.*

43. "Speech by Vice-Premier Teng Hsiao-ping," New China News Agency, June 8, 1978.

44. See David E. Albright, "The USSR and Africa: Soviet Policy," *Problems of Communism,* January–February 1978, p. 34.

45. This was again demonstrated in the 1978 Zaire incident. China voiced strong support for Zaire against the "Soviet-Cuban mercenaries' invasion," dispatched Foreign Minister Huang Hua to Zaire to dramatize that backing, and later even sent military instructors to help train Zaire's navy. But the

burden of repelling the invasion fell on Belgium, France, and the United States.

8. The African–American Nexus in Soviet Strategy

1. See Robert Legvold, "The Nature of Soviet Power," *Foreign Affairs* (New York), October 1977.

2. Edward Wilson, *Russia and Black Africa Before World War II* (New York: Holmes and Meier, 1974).

3. Patrick McGowan, "Africa and Non-Alignment: A Comparative Study of Foreign Policy," *International Studies Quarterly* (Detroit), September 1968.

4. Robert Legvold, "Moscow's Changing View of Africa's Revolutionary Regimes," *Africa Report* (Washington, D.C.), March–April 1969, p. 57.

5. See W. Scott Thompson, *Power Projection: A Net Assessment of Soviet and American Capabilities,* Agenda Paper (New York: National Strategy Information Center, 1978).

6. Catherine Hoskyns, *The Congo Since Independence* (London: Oxford University Press, 1965), pp. 214, 217.

7. References to this in the Soviet press are frequent. See, for instance, Foreign Broadcast Information Service, *Daily Report—Soviet Union* (Washington, D.C.—hereafter *FBIS-SOV*), Dec. 27, 1977, pp. B6–7, where what was officially a humanitarian rescue is called an "intervention to save Tshombe's reactionary regime."

8. Personal observations of the author—then an assistant to the U.S. Secretary of Defense.

9. Michael MccGwire, "Changing Naval Operations and Military Intervention," *Naval War College Review* (Newport, R.I.), Spring 1977.

10. *Daily Times* (Lagos), July 13, 1967.

11. Interviews, U.S. Department of State, December 1969.

12. On this point, see W. Scott Thompson, "Africa for the Africans?" *Commentary* (New York), September 1978.

13. For a different view, stressing the autonomy of Cuban decision-making in this period, see William J. Durch, *The Cuban Military in Africa and the Middle East, from Algeria to Angola,* Professional Paper No. 201 (Washington, D.C.: Center for Naval Analyses, September 1977).

14. See Colin Legum and Bill Lee, *Conflict in the Horn of Africa* (New York: Africana Publishing Co., 1977), pp. 1–13.

15. *The New York Times,* Dec. 14, 1969.

16. Interviews, U.S. Department of State and U.S. Department of Defense, December 1969.

17. John Spencer, "Ethiopia: A Friend the U.S. Abandoned," *The New York Times,* Dec. 5, 1975, p. 46.

18. In this section, I draw on personal interviews with officials of the U.S. Department of State, U.S. Department of Defense, and several intelligence agencies of the U.S. government, all conducted during April 1978. See also Donald R. Katz, "Children's Revolution: A Bloodbath in Ethiopia," *Horn of Africa* (Summit, N.J.), July–September 1978.

19. In fairness to the Soviets, the similarity of the Ethiopian regime's actions and their own in 1917 must be stressed, for it seems to have had an enormous impact on their policy toward Mengistu. Specifically, it made them overlook the opportunistic side to his actions. For example, a Radio Moscow broadcast in December 1977 remarked, with a slight sense of outrage, that "the American press is spreading lies about the Soviet Union's policy in Ethiopia, where democratic revolutionary forces are in government." Moscow in English to North America, Dec. 24, 1977, in *FBIS-SOV*, Dec. 27, 1977. Other Communist parties also appear to have been impressed with the truly revolutionary nature of Mengistu's government. Thus, a senior official of the Italian Communist Party who visited the United States in the spring of 1978 accounted for his party's switch from support of Somalia to support of Ethiopia at the same time Moscow did by noting how struck he and his colleagues had been with the "revolutionary character" of what was occurring in Ethiopia.

20. See U.S. Central Intelligence Agency, *Communist Aid to Less Developed Countries of the Free World, 1977*, ER 78–10478U (Washington, D.C., November 1978); *The Washington Post*, Mar. 5, 1978. During Mengistu's state visit to Moscow in May 1977, Leonid Brezhnev hailed the Ethiopian leader's "achievement in the reconstruction of the old, historically outlived order, the consolidation of [Ethiopia's] independence and the creation of necessary conditions for building a new society." Moscow TASS in English, May 6, 1977, in *FBIS-SOV*, May 9, 1977.

21. Interview conducted at the Department of State during June 1977.

22. I am grateful to Dr. Hussein Adam for enlightening me on Somali perceptions.

23. MccGuire, *loc. cit.*, p. 19.

24. See International Institute of Strategic Studies, *Strategic Survey 1976*, (London, 1977), p. 60.

25. Iran offered to serve as a conduit in October 1975, when this writer was at the Department of Defense.

26. The author was at the time an official in the U.S. Department of Defense.

27. See *The New York Times*, May 25 and 26, 1977, for Fahd's visit. Also interview, U.S. Department of State, June 1977.

28. "Crossed Wires," *Newsweek* (New York), Sept. 26, 1977.

29. Moscow Domestic Service in Russian, Apr. 1, 1978, in *FBIS-SOV*, Apr. 3, 1978.

30. Interviews conducted in Iran, Thailand, and India during July–August 1977.

31. "U.S. Avoiding Big Involvement in Africa's Horn," *The New York Times*, Oct. 3, 1977.

32. Moscow TASS in English, Nov. 19, 1977, in *FBIS-SOV*, Nov. 21, 1977.

33. "U.S. Aides Frustrated over Soviet Gains in Ethiopia," *The New York Times*, Dec. 29, 1977.

34. See my *Power Projection*, Part V. The details come from personal interviews, Department of Defense, March 1978.

35. See P. Janka, "Kremlin's Buildup in the Horn," *Soviet Analyst* (London), Jan. 26, 1978, p. 6.

36. See "The Ogaden Debacle," *Newsweek,* Mar. 20, 1978.

37. Interview, U.S. Department of State, April 1978.

38. Interview with senior White House official, Mar. 7, 1978. For Soviet reactions, see Radio Moscow in English to North America, Mar. 30, 1978, in *FBIS-SOV,* Apr. 3, 1978.

39. Compare Arthur Schlesinger, Jr., "Russians and Cubans in Africa," *Wall Street Journal* (New York), May 2, 1978, and Radio Moscow in English to North America, Mar. 30, 1978, in *FBIS-SOV,* Apr. 3, 1978. The essence of each argument was that strategic arms agreements are no favor to the *Soviet* side. Threats to cancel the talks would be, in Schlesinger's words, "cutting off our nose to spite our face." According to Moscow, "the United States has just as much a stake in these talks. . . ." The assymetry of the prospective agreement which both sides had in view at that time—with Soviet preponderance in almost every single critical variable—was not considered pertinent.

40. See *The New York Times,* Mar. 10, 1978.

41. See Richard Burt, "New Opportunity in Africa," *ibid.,* Mar. 13, 1978.

42. *The New York Times,* Feb. 19, 1978.

43. See Gerard Chaliand, "The Horn of Africa's Dilemma," *Foreign Policy* (New York), Spring 1978.

44. *Al Ayam* (Khartoum), May 23, 1978, as reported in Foreign Broadcast Information Service, *Daily Report: Middle East and North Africa* (Washington, D.C.—hereafter *FBIS-MEA*), May 24, 1978; Damascus Domestic Service, June 6, 1978, in *FBIS-MEA,* June 6, 1978; Addis Ababa Domestic Service in Amharic, Nov. 28, 1978, in Foreign Broadcast Information Service, *Daily Report: Sub-Saharan Africa* (Washington, DC—hereafter *FBIS-SSA*), Nov. 29, 1978; Rome ANSA in English, Nov. 29, 1978, in *FBIS-SSA,* Nov. 30, 1978; Paris AFP in English, Dec. 7, 1978, in *FBIS-SSA,* Dec. 8, 1978.

45. James Wasserstrom, "Another International Division of Labor: The East Germans in Africa," pp. 4–6. Unpublished manuscript available at the Fletcher School of Law and Diplomacy.

46. For both quotes, see *FBIS-SOV,* Apr. 26, 1977.

47. French officials in particular were irritated by the lack of American interest or concern with respect to Shaba I. European chancelleries avoided public criticism of the U.S. president on this matter only in order to take further measure of the new Carter administration. The effect of American disdain, however, should not be underestimated. Interviews in Paris, May 1978.

48. Crawford Young, "The Unending Crisis," *Foreign Affairs,* Fall 1978, p. 169.

49. The most interesting aspect of the ensuing debate in the United States over the credibility of the president's claim of Cuban-Soviet involvement was the use of the counterclaim of President Fidel Castro of Cuba to cast doubt on Carter's opinion.

50. See Thompson, *Power Projection.*

51. See *The New York Times,* Dec. 18, 1975, and Jan. 4 and 5, 1976.

52. "Cuba Called Stabilizer in Angola: President Concurs with Statement by Ambassador Young," *The Washington Post,* Apr. 17, 1977.

53. See W. Scott Thompson, "Cuba and the Soviet Union in Southern Africa: A Pessimistic Prognosis," Hudson Research Service, Aug. 18, 1977.

54. Interview, New York, April 1978, and interviews, U.S. Department of State, 1978.

55. Interview, New York, April 1978.

56. See the Soviet-Cuban communiqué of Apr. 24, 1978, reprinted in *Survival* (London), July–August 1978, pp. 170–71.

57. Interview, Washington, D.C., April 1977.

58. "Southern Africa: Testing the Ground Rules of Détente," Academy of Political Science, forthcoming.

59. Radio Moscow Domestic Service, July 2, 1977, in *FBIS-SOV,* July 5, 1977.

60. TASS International Service in Russian, May 20, 1977, in *FBIS-SOV,* May 23, 1977.

61. *The New York Times,* Oct. 19 and Nov. 4, 1977; July 13 and 14, 1978.

62. Radio Moscow in English to North America, Apr. 18, 1977, in *FBIS-SOV,* Apr. 20, 1977.

63. Vladimir Petrov, TASS, June 6, 1977, in *FBIS-SOV,* June 7, 1977.

64. B. Pilyatskin, "The South African Knot and U.S. Strategy," *Izvestiya* (Moscow), Aug. 11, 1977, in *FBIS-SOV,* Aug. 17, 1977.

65. A frequent theme in conference discussions in which this writer has participated is that Young has made American policy, previously unpalatable owing to the Vietnamese war, the role of multinationals, etc., much more acceptable. This theme figures more in the arguments of "realists" than in those of "idealists," who see no need to justify Young's positions.

66. Radio Moscow Domestic Service in Russian, Mar. 28, 1978, in *FBIS-SOV,* Mar. 29, 1978.

67. See *The New York Times,* Dec. 18, 1975, and Jan. 4 and 5, 1976.

68. *E.g.,* TASS, July 12, 1977, in *FBIS-SOV,* July 13, 1977.

69. "U.S. Policy toward Third World Analysed," *Novoye Vremya* (Moscow), June 3, 1977, as translated in *FBIS-SOV,* June 14, 1977.

70. *Izvestiya,* Mar. 19, 1978, in *FBIS-SOV,* Mar. 22, 1978.

71. Interviews, U.S. Department of State, 1977–78, and Quai d'Orsay, June 1978.

72. See U.S. Defense Nuclear Agency, "Measures and Trends, U.S. and USSR: Strategic Force Effectiveness," draft interim report, February 1978.

73. T. K. Jones and W. Scott Thompson, "Central War and Civil Defense," *Orbis* (Philadelphia), Autumn 1978.

74. See W. Scott Thompson and Brett Silvers, "South Africa in Soviet Strategy," in Chester Crocker and Richard Bissell, eds., *South Africa into the 1980s* (Boulder, Colo.: Westview Press, 1979).

75. *Ibid.*

76. See W.C.T. van Rensburg, "Africa and Western Lifelines," *Strategic Review* (Cambridge, Mass.), Spring 1978.

77. The argument is frequently made by administration spokesmen that the

Soviet Union already has the power to sever the U.S. oil supply, with or without bases along the sea lanes around Africa, if it wishes to risk war. This point is true but trivial, for it ignores the growth in options that a proliferation of basing privileges would afford the Soviets. It is the parallel in the realm of power projection of the now wholly discredited argument of "overkill" at the central strategic nuclear level.

78. A. Bovin, "Contours of the 'Policy of Balance,'" *Izvestiya*, Mar. 24, 1978, as translated in *FBIS-SOV*, Mar. 24, 1978.

79. Vladimir Yermakov (of Novosti), "Bitter Consequences of American Policy in Northeastern Africa," *Rude Pravo* (Prague), Aug. 30, 1977, in *FBIS-SOV*, Sept. 9, 1977.

80. V. Yermakov (guest writer from Novosti), *Le Monde* (Paris), Aug. 18, 1977.

Conclusion

1. For a concurring view with supporting technical data, see International Institute of Strategic Studies, *Strategic Survey 1978* (London, 1979), especially p. 12.

2. This linkage is implicit in the chapter discussions but not dealt with specifically. For detailed analysis, see D. Bruce Jackson, *Castro, the Kremlin, and Communism in Latin America* (Baltimore: Johns Hopkins University Press, 1969).

3. For such a prediction by the outgoing U.S. Army Chief of Staff, General Bernard W. Rogers, see *The Washington Post*, June 16, 1979.

Contributors

DAVID E. ALBRIGHT is senior text editor of the journal *Problems of Communism*. Previously, he worked as research associate and editor at the project on The United States and China in World Affairs at the Council on Foreign Relations in New York. He is the editor of *Communism and Political Systems in Western Europe*, the coeditor of the forthcoming *The Communist States and Africa*, and author of numerous articles.

EDWARD GONZALEZ is professor of political science at the University of California, Los Angeles, and a consultant at The Rand Corporation. His many writings on Cuba include *Cuba Under Castro: The Limits of Charisma*, *Post-Revolutionary Cuba in a Changing World* (coauthored with David Ronfeldt), and numerous articles. He is currently engaged in a long-term comparative study of international leverage exercised by smaller powers.

COLIN LEGUM is an associate editor of *The Observer* (London), editor of the *Africa Contemporary Record* and *Africa Currents*, and coeditor of the *Middle East Contemporary Survey*. His many books include *Pan-Africanism: A Short Political Guide*, *South Africa at the Crossroads*, *Southern Africa: The Secret Diplomacy of Détente*, *Conflict in the Horn of Africa* (coauthored with Bill Lee), and *Western Crisis in Southern Africa*.

MARINA OTTAWAY has taught at the University of Addis Ababa and at the University of Zambia. A fellow at the Woodrow Wilson International Center for Scholars, she is working on a comparative study of Marxist and non-Marxist socialist regimes in Africa. Her previous works include two coauthored volumes (with David Ottaway), *Algeria: The Politics of a Socialist Revolution* and *Ethiopia: Empire in Revolution*.

W. SCOTT THOMPSON is associate professor of international politics at the Fletcher School of Law and Diplomacy, Tufts University. He is author of *Ghana's Foreign Policy* and *Unequal Partners: Philippine and Thai Relations with the United States, 1965–75*; editor of *The Third World: Premises of U.S. Policy*; and coeditor of *Lessons of Vietnam and Strategic Options for the Early Eighties*.

JIRI VALENTA is assistant professor and coordinator of Soviet and East European affairs at the Naval Postgraduate School, Monterey, California. He is coeditor of *Eurocommunism between East and West* and author of *Anatomy of a Decision: Soviet Intervention in Czechoslovakia, 1968*, and numerous articles on Soviet and East European affairs.

EDWARD T. WILSON is a vice-president of the Riggs National Bank, Washington, D.C., where he serves in the International Division. He formerly worked in the U.S. Department of Commerce and, later, as Director for East–West Trade for the U.S. Chamber of Commerce. He is the author of *Russia and Black Africa before World War II*.

GEORGE T. YU is professor of political science at the University of Illinois at Urbana-Champaign. His works on Chinese policies and activities with respect to Africa include *China and Tanzania: A Study in Cooperative Interaction* and *China's African Policy: A Study of Tanzania*. He is also the editor of *Intra-Asian International Relations*.